Peasant Rebellion and Communist Revolution in Asia

John Wilson Lewis, Editor. In ten essays, the revolutionary experience of Vietnam, Thailand, Korea, Malaya, Indonesia, Burma, India, and China is examined theoretically and from the point of view of three main questions. In what social settings did Communist revolutions take root or fail? How did Communist organizations arise and respond to the social pressures for rebellion or order? To what extent did the structure of revolt correspond to society-wide structures? $12.95

Latin America and the United States
The Changing Political Realities

Julio Cotler and Richard R. Fagen, Editors. It is clear today that the realities of Latin America are changing more rapidly than knowledge about those realities, that Latin America can no longer be understood as merely the shadow cast by the Colossus of the North. In an effort to explore the nature of these political relations, a group of distinguished social scientists present twenty-two papers covering such topics as the politics of the multinational corporation, military elites and military thinking, and the sources of U.S. foreign policy. Paper, $4.95ˣ; cloth, $18.75

VOLUME 415   SEPTEMBER 1974

THE ANNALS

of The American Academy *of* Political
and Social Science

RICHARD D. LAMBERT, *Editor*

ALAN W. HESTON, *Assistant Editor*

POLITICAL CONSEQUENCES

OF AGING

Special Editor of This Volume

FREDERICK R. EISELE

Assistant Professor of Social Policy
Pennsylvania State University
University Park, Pennsylvania

PHILADELPHIA

The articles appearing in THE ANNALS are indexed in the *Reader's Guide to Periodical Literature,* the *Book Review Index,* the *Public Affairs Information Service Bulletin,* and *Current Contents: Behavioral, Social, and Management Sciences.* They are also abstracted and indexed in *ABC Pol Sci, Historical Abstracts, International Political Science Abstracts* and/or *America: History and Life.*

International Standard Book Numbers (ISBN)

ISBN 0-87761-181-5, vol. 415, 1974; paper—$3.00
ISBN 0-87761-180-7, vol. 415, 1974; cloth—$4.00

Issued bimonthly by The American Academy of Political and Social Science at Prince and Lemon Sts., Lancaster, Pennsylvania 17604. Cost per year: $15.00 paperbound; $20.00 clothbound. Add $1.00 to above rates for membership outside U.S.A. Second-class postage paid at Lancaster and at additional mailing offices.

Editorial and Business Offices, 3937 Chestnut Street, Philadelphia, Pennsylvania 19104.

CONTENTS

EUROPE

UNITED STATES

POLITICAL THOUGHT

CONTENTS

ECONOMICS

PREFACE

America is aging. The proportion of its population now over 65 years of age—11 percent—has almost tripled since 1900 and could grow to almost 20 percent in the next century. The emergence of this stratum of elderly is historically unprecedented. Demographically, falling birth rates and rising life expectancy rates have produced societal aging only in a handful of countries in the most advanced stages of industrialization. Simultaneously, the social meanings of growing old—once an ambivalent mix of neglect and resignation—are changing; retiree and senior citizen are becoming new stages in the life cycle.

The political consequences of these dramatic shifts have been neither widely noticed nor clearly analyzed. Societal aging has been, in fact, an iceberg issue in the history of social policy. The tip has been known for decades, but its deeper outlines and implications are only beginning to be fathomed. Private citizens tend to think of aging as a personal fate rather than as a public issue. Scholars originally concerned with aging—mostly biologists and psychologists—have focused chiefly on microanalytic factors. Politicians and others seeking legislation favorable to the elderly present their case as nonpartisan and, therefore, "nonpolitical." All who are involved labor under a double burden of public disinterest: (1) the generally negative value placed on any kind of obsolescence in a culture obsessed with newness; (2) the often dry and technical nature of the critical issues, such as income maintenance and health care organization.

As a result, analyses of macrolevel consequences of aging have been sparse, scattered and usually written for specialists. This has been true particularly in the area of public policy—where available information becomes quickly outdated—and in political behavior—where uninformed generalization has flourished without empirical evidence. Educated lay people interested in the latter, for example, have had to rely on often highly speculative popular predictions of the "coming political power of a senior citizenry."

The present volume of THE ANNALS is designed to make available to the generalist the best and most current thinking on the topic. The contributors—academicians with long experience in fields related to aging and public policy, and practitioners conversant with the technicalities of law and administration—represent a cross-section of ideologies and viewpoints. For the most part, their perspectives are long range, attempting to situate and to analyze the issues in their broader, historical context. Hopefully, the volume will stimulate wider public awareness of, and informed debate over, the political consequences of aging.

FREDERICK R. EISELE

The Aging of Populations and Societies

By Donald O. Cowgill

ABSTRACT: Modernization of societies is accompanied by a demographic transition which results in the aging of populations. Yet, modernization also results in a lowered status for older people. The salient aspects of modernization which produce this effect are held to be: (1) the application of modern technology in the fields of health and economics, (2) urbanization and (3) education. Each of these factors sets in motion a chain reaction which tends to undermine the status of the aged. However, there are some signs that this trend is being reversed in the most modernized societies.

Donald O. Cowgill, who received his Ph.D. in Sociology from the University of Pennsylvania, has been Professor of Sociology at the University of Missouri, Columbia, since 1967. He has also taught at Drury College, Drake University and Wichita State University; as Visiting Professor, at Mindolo Ecumenical Center in Zambia, University of Wisconsin, University of Rhode Island and Mahidol University in Thailand; and, as Fulbright Lecturer, at the University of Chiengmai. He has served as President of the Midwest Sociological Society, the Midwest Council for Social Research in Aging and the Kansas Citizen's Council on Aging. He is a member of the American Sociological Association, the Population Association of America and the Gerontological Society. Professor Cowgill has published extensively in the demography and ecology of aging and in the cross-cultural study of aging; he is co-editor of Aging and Modernization.

ONE of the dilemmas of modern societies is that, while sociological processes have fostered a devaluation of old people, demographic processes have led to increasing numbers and proportions of aged in their populations. Thus, such societies have larger proportions of older people than ever before, while at the same time older people have less value and utility to those societies. These countertrends give rise to the further anomaly that societies whose relative affluence permits them to provide the greatest comfort and security to their aged members instead deprive them of useful roles and consign high proportions of them to relative poverty.[1]

The purpose of this article is to examine the two horns of this dilemma. First, I shall attempt to explicate the demographic processes which result in the aging of populations; then, I shall seek to unravel the more subtle and complicated sociological processes which currently appear to contribute to the relative degradation of older people.

THE DEMOGRAPHY OF AGING

A population is said to be aging when the elderly segment of that population is increasing faster than the rest of the population. There are several ways in which this change can be measured. However, the most common index—and one of the most useful—is the change in the percent of the total population which is 65 years of age and over.

Selected cases of aging populations

Utilizing this index, table 1 shows that several populations have experienced a remarkable degree of

aging in the last 120 years.[2] France had already aged appreciably by 1851, when 6.5 percent of her population was 65 and over; the process has continued with only slight variations since then. The latest figures show more than double that percentage—13.4 percent. England is slightly behind France in this aging trend, but the general trend is the same. In 1851 only 4.6 percent of the British population was 65 and over. The percentage increased decade by decade with only slight interruptions; the most recent figures indicate that 12.4 percent of the British population is 65 and over. Sweden shows the same trend: in 1850 only 4.8 percent of the Swedish population was 65 and over; by 1970 the percentage had increased to 12.8. The Netherlands manifests the same pattern, with only a slight interruption at the time of the First World War: from 4.7 percent 65 and over in 1849, the aged population has increased to 10.1 percent. A younger population—resulting from the effects of continued immigration—but one which shows the same trend, is that of Australia: from 1.7 percent 65 and over in 1871, this population has matured to the point that 8.3 percent of the population is now aged by this index. In the United States of America the trend has been from 2.9 percent in 1870 to 4.1 percent in 1900 to 9.9 percent in 1970.

Cross-national comparisons of the extent of aging

It is obvious from the review of these cases (1) that aging is a

2. Earlier figures for France, England, Sweden and Australia taken from Edward Rosset, *Aging Process of Population* (New York: MacMillan, 1964), chap. 9; latest figures in each case calculated from *Demographic Yearbook 1971* (New York: United Nations, 1972), table 7.

1. John Kenneth Galbraith, *The Affluent Society* (Boston, Mass.: Houghton Mifflin, 1958), p. 338.

TABLE 1

PERCENT OF POPULATION 65 AND OVER, SELECTED COUNTRIES, 1850–1970

DATE*	FRANCE	ENGLAND	SWEDEN	NETHERLANDS	AUSTRALIA	UNITED STATES
1850	6.5	4.6	4.8	4.7	NA	NA
1860	6.7	4.7	5.2	4.9	NA	NA
1870	7.4	4.8	5.4	5.5	1.7	2.9
1880	8.1	4.6	5.9	5.5	NA	3.4
1890	8.3	4.8	7.7	6.0	NA	3.8
1900	8.2	4.7	8.4	6.0	NA	4.1
1910	8.4	5.2	8.4	6.1	4.3	4.3
1920	9.1	6.0	8.4	5.9	4.4	4.7
1930	9.3	7.4	9.2	6.2	6.5	5.4
1940	NA	9.0	9.4	7.0	7.3	6.8
1950	11.8	10.9	10.3	7.7	8.0	8.1
1960	11.5	11.8	11.2	8.7	8.4	9.2
1970	13.4	12.4	13.7	10.1	8.3	9.9

SOURCES: Except for the United States, data for years prior to 1970 are from Edward Rosset, *Aging Process of Population* (New York: MacMillan, 1964), chap. 9. For the United States, data from 1870 to 1960 are from U.S., Department of Health, Education and Welfare, Special Staff on Aging, "Population Trends, National, 1790–1960," *Facts on Aging*, no. 1 (Jan. 1963). Data for 1970 are from United Nations, *Demographic Yearbook 1971* (New York: United Nations, 1973), table 7.

* Since the date of census-taking varies in different countries, the date used in the table is merely approximate. For actual date in each case, see original sources.

developmental process and (2) that the process has not proceeded as far in Australia as it has in the other countries used to illustrate the process. We must then infer that at any given time different areas of the world will be in different stages of such a developmental process. Therefore, it may be instructive to compare the percentages of population 65 and over in various countries at the present time (shown in table 2).

It will be noted that these percentages range from 1 to more than 22 percent—that is, from only 1 person who is 65 and over out of a hundred persons in the total population to more than 1 out of 5. Of course, Monaco is an abnormal case in which immigration of elderly retired persons has resulted in a high proportion of aged in the population. However, if one disregards such extreme cases, there is probably a fair

indication of the normal range of aging in contemporary populations in table 2—that is, a range from about 1 percent in an extremely young population to about 15 percent in an old, but normally aging, population.

Elsewhere I have proposed a classification of populations according to their degree of agedness, and I continue to use that classification here.[3] Populations with less than 4 percent 65 and over are called young; those with 4 to 6.9 percent are described as youthful; those with 7 to 9.9 percent are denominated mature; and those with 10 percent or more 65 and over are called aged. Examination of table 2 indicates that, with the exception of Green-

3. Donald O. Cowgill, "The Demography of Aging," in *The Daily Needs and Interests of Older People*, ed. Adeline M. Hoffman (Springfield, Ill.: Charles C. Thomas, 1970), pp. 35–38.

TABLE 2

PERCENT OF THE POPULATION 65 AND OVER IN VARIOUS COUNTRIES

COUNTRY	PERCENT 65 AND OVER	COUNTRY	PERCENT 65 AND OVER
YOUNG POPULATIONS		MATURE POPULATIONS	
New Guinea	1.1	Japan	7.0
Kuwait	1.6	Uruguay	7.5
Nigeria	2.0	Yugoslavia	7.5
Zambia	2.1	Canada	7.9
Greenland	2.3	Australia	8.3
W. Samoa	2.7	New Zealand	8.4
Guatemala	2.7	Poland	8.4
Nicaragua	2.9	Romania	8.5
Colombia	2.9	Finland	8.6
Haiti	3.0	Gibraltar	8.6
Costa Rica	3.1	Iceland	8.8
Ecuador	3.2	Bulgaria	9.5
Korea	3.2	United States	9.9
Bahamas	3.4		
Kenya	3.5	AGED POPULATIONS	
Afghanistan	3.5		
Sri Lanka	3.5	Netherlands	10.1
Tunisia	3.5	Italy	10.4
Mexico	3.7	N. Ireland	10.5
Paraguay	3.8	Czechoslovakia	10.6
Uganda	3.8	Ireland	11.1
Iran	3.8	Switzerland	11.3
Liberia	3.9	Hungary	11.5
Turkey	3.9	Denmark	12.0
		Scotland	12.1
YOUTHFUL POPULATIONS		England & Wales	12.4
		Luxembourg	12.6
Swaziland	4.1	W. Germany	12.6
Algeria	4.4	Norway	12.9
Botswana	4.6	France	13.4
Surinam	4.6	Sweden	13.7
Guadaloupe	4.7	Austria	14.1
Iraq	5.1	E. Germany	15.5
Martinique	5.1	Monaco	22.1
French Guiana	5.3		
Tanzania	5.5		
Lesotho	6.4		

SOURCES: Data computed from *Demographic Yearbook 1971* (New York: United Nations, 1972), table 7. Effective dates vary from country to country ranging from 1962 to 1971. See original source for actual dates.

land, all of the young populations are in Africa, Asia, Latin America and Oceania. They range from New Guinea with just over 1 percent to Liberia and Turkey with just under 4 percent. They include: Nigeria, Zambia, Korea, Sri Lanka—formerly Ceylon—Colombia, Afghanistan and Mexico. The youthful populations, while somewhat older, are also found in Africa, Asia and Latin America. They range from Swaziland to Lesotho and obviously include areas which are in more advanced stages of modernization than those with young populations. The mature populations include the more recently modernized parts of eastern Europe, Japan and the modernized parts of the New World, which have until recently been kept young by immigration—that is, Iceland, Australia, New Zealand and Canada. The aged populations are found entirely in Europe, mainly western and northern Europe—that is, those parts first affected by industrialization and modernization.

Aging and the demographic transition

It should be evident from the above discussion that the aging of populations is a modern phenomenon, something which has never occurred to human populations before. It began first in the populations of western Europe and has progressed to the greatest degree in those same populations. This aging of populations is a by-product of a demographic revolution which is usually called the demographic transition. It has commonly been viewed as a consequence of the Industrial Revolution, but it is much more closely related to changes in public health and education than to changes in modes of production.

In its major outlines the demographic transition is a long term and presumably permanent change in the level of the vital rates of population change, a drastic and permanent reduction of both death rates and birth rates.[4] The time required to complete the transition may vary from several centuries to only a few decades.

4. Transition theory was first stated by Warren S. Thompson in "Population," *American Journal of Sociology* 31 (May 1929), pp. 959–975. It was reformulated by Frank W. Notestein in "Population—the Long View," in *Food for the World*, ed. T. W. Schultz, (Chicago, Ill.: University of Chicago Press, 1945). Other statements of it

Mortality rates decline first, followed—with a lag of a generation or so—by fertility rates. Since death rates decline first, an early effect of the transition is an increase in the rate of population growth. Since World War II this process has been set in motion with such rapidity and on such a scale in the newly developing areas of the world that it has been dubbed a population explosion.

The scale of the change is dramatic: death rates fall from a range of 25 to 35 deaths per 1,000 persons in the total population per year to a new range of 5 to 15 deaths per 1,000; births drop from a range of 35 to 55 per 1,000 in the population to a low range of 10 to 20 per 1,000. Such major changes in vital rates certainly mark a major transition in human demography; indeed, they probably warrant the application of the more dramatic term, revolution.[5] These revolutionary changes in vital rates result not only in changes in rates of population growth; they also effect drastic changes in the structure of the population in which they are occurring. One of those changes is the age composition.[6]

Declining mortality in the initial stages of the transition permits more babies to stay alive and more

include: Kingsley Davis, "The World Demographic Transition," THE ANNALS 237 (January 1945), pp. 1–11; Donald O. Cowgill, "Transition Theory as General Population Theory," *Social Forces* 41, no. 3 (March 1963), pp. 270–274.

5. Ronald Freedman, ed., *Population: The Vital Revolution* (Chicago, Ill.: Aldine, 1964).

6. For a discussion of other changes accompanying the transition, see, Donald O. Cowgill, "Transition Theory as General Population Theory," *Social Forces* 41, no. 3 (March 1963), pp. 270–274, reprinted in *Social Demography*, ed. Thomas R. Ford and Gordon F. DeJong (Englewood Cliffs, N.J.: Prentice-Hall, 1970), pp. 627–633.

children to reach maturity. Thus, since the major reductions in deaths occur with reference to infant and child mortality, the effect of changing mortality alone is more likely to be a younger, rather than an older, population.[7] It is only in the latter part of the transition—when the birth rate begins to decline, reducing the child population—that the population as a whole begins to age. However, the total range of the change which then takes place is highly significant, as we have seen: from as little as 1 percent of the population 65 and over to as much as 15 percent.

Aging of the electorate

It may be assumed that if a population is aging, the segment of it which is of voting age will be aging also. However, this is not a perfect relationship. As we have seen, the proportionate aging of the total population does not begin until the birth rate starts to fall. Similarly, the electorate does not begin to age until about twenty years later, when the constricted cohorts of births begin to come of age. If there are fluctuations in the birth rate, it is possible for the electorate to be aging at the same time that the population as a whole is "younging," as happened in the United States during the baby boom following World War II.

Nevertheless, if we disregard the

recent lowering of the voting age, there has been a continuous aging of the electorate of the United States during this century (shown in table 3). If we take the population 20 years of age and over as representative of the electorate, we can see that while the proportion in the younger ages has steadily declined, the proportion in the upper ages has increased. In fact, more than two-thirds of this adult population were under 45 in 1900, while in 1970 only slightly more than half were that young. On the other hand, the proportion of this adult population which was 65 and over more than doubled during the same period, increasing from 7.9 percent in 1900 to 15.9 percent in 1970. The potential political significance of this shift is emphasized if we remember that larger proportions of older people actually exercise their franchise than people in their early twenties.[8]

Characteristics of the older generation

In societies with aged populations the older generation differs from the younger in many ways other than simply age. The older generation has a higher ratio of females and of widows. The elderly have less formal education; they have lower incomes; and they are less mobile.

Older populations usually have higher proportions of females. This is caused by the higher death rate among males, a progressive attrition which occurs throughout the age span. The surplus of males at birth is dissipated by middle age; from that point on, males are a progressively smaller minority in each older age group. Consequently, in

7. For detailed discussions of the relative effects of declining mortality and fertility upon age structure, see, Albert I. Hermalin, "The Effects of Changes in Mortality Rates on Population Growth and Age Distribution in the United States," *Milbank Memorial Fund Quarterly* 44, no. 4, pt. 1 (October 1966), pp. 451–469; and Ansley J. Coale, "The Effects of Changes in Mortality and Fertility on Age Composition," *Milbank Memorial Fund Quarterly* 34, no. 1 (January 1956), pp. 79–114.

8. U.S., Bureau of the Census, *Current Population Reports*, series P-20, no. 143, p. 9.

TABLE 3

COMPOSITION OF POPULATION 20 AND OVER BY BROAD AGE GROUPS,
UNITED STATES 1900–1970

AGE GROUP	1900	1910	1920	1930	1940	1950	1960	1970
20–44	67.6	67.1	64.6	62.4	59.4	56.9	52.4	51.0
45–64	24.5	25.1	27.3	28.5	30.2	30.7	32.7	33.1
65 and over	7.9	7.8	8.1	9.1	10.4	12.4	14.9	15.9

SOURCE: Computed from U.S., Bureau of the Census, *1970 Census of Population: U.S. Summary* (Washington, D.C.: Government Printing Office, 1972), table 48.

the United States in 1970 there were only 72 males per 100 females 65 years of age and over.[9] Furthermore, this sex ratio has been declining steadily since 1930, when it was approximately balanced thanks to the carry-over effect of earlier immigration streams which brought greater numbers of males into the United States population. With the curtailment of immigration in the 1920s, the carry-over effect on the sex ratio of the total population has been diminishing. Moreover, since most immigrants are young adults at the time of migration, the effects of immigration do not show up in the aged population until several decades later. Thus, the impact of immigration upon the aged population of the United States was still quite evident at the time of the 1950 census: 26.2 percent of the white population 65 and over was foreign-born.[10] By 1970 this percentage had decreased to 16.3. It will continue to decline for the remainder of this century.

However, this decreasing effect of immigration is less important for the

declining sex ratio among the aged than the increasing difference between the mortality rates. During this century female mortality rates have declined much more than male mortality rates. Of course, this results in a much greater increase in female life expectancy and, thus, in a higher survival rate of females into older ages.

Older populations also differ from younger ones in marital status. Since death inexorably takes its toll and since remarriage of widowed persons is not universal, an older population generally includes a higher proportion of widowed persons. Given the sex ratios and differential mortality rates noted above, one should expect more widows than widowers in the older population. For example, in the United States in 1970 52 percent of the females 65 and over were widows and 17 percent of the males of the same age were widowers.[11]

These sex differentials are widened by two further factors: (1) most husbands are several years older than their wives; (2) widowers have a much greater probability of remarriage than widows. In the United States in 1970 37 percent of all women 65 to 69 years of age were widows, and the percentage

9. U.S., Bureau of the Census, "We the American Elderly," Special Report no. 10 on the 1970 Census (Washington, D.C.: Government Printing Office, 1973), p. 6.

10. Henry D. Sheldon, *The Older Population of the United States* (New York: John Wiley and Sons, 1958), p. 13.

11. "We the American Elderly," p. 10.

increased rapidly with increasing age: more than three-fourths—77 percent—of the women 85 and over were widows. The comparable percentages for males were 9 percent in the 65 to 69 age group and 43 percent among those 85 and over.

In all modernizing nations the oldest generation has less formal education than younger generations. For example, whereas more than half of all adults in the United States have completed high school, most of the population 65 and over have no more than eight years of formal education.[12] It should be noted, however, that this is clearly a generational difference; it is not a function of the process of aging. As will be noted later, this generational gap emerges as an aspect of the modernization process, and it is probable that the difference will diminish in postindustrial society.

In modern societies retirement from the labor force has become increasingly prevalent among older people in the population during the last century. In the United States in 1890 about two-thirds of the males 65 and over were still in the labor force.[13] By 1940 the proportion had dropped to 42 percent, and by 1970 it had decreased still further to less than 25 percent.[14] During the same period the proportion of older women who were in the labor force had increased slightly, but still amounted to only 10 percent.[15] There appears to be no doubt that retirement from remunerated employment is becoming the pre-

dominant mode for older people in modernized societies.

The societies which have evolved this pattern of retirement are also societies which have become wage economies; hence, the livelihood of most people, including the aged, is determined by how much money they receive. For most of those who have retired, this income comes in the form of old age insurance benefits—administered by the government—and/or private pensions. Unfortunately, such income is only a fraction of the income paid to those who are still active in the labor force. Thus, retirement usually entails a considerable curtailment of income. In the United States in 1969 the median income of families headed by persons 65 and over was only half the median of that for all families: $4,895 as compared to $9,596.[16] There is therefore a financial penalty attached to aging in modern societies.

Recent news of the growth of retirement communities in Florida and California have fostered the illusion of high mobility of aged people in the United States; yet, the fact is that the people who are moving to these communities are the exceptions. In general, older people are much less mobile than those in their younger years. For example, whereas 40 percent of the total population 5 years of age and over changed residence between 1965 and 1970, only 23 percent of the population 65 and over made such a move.[17] The older populations tend to be more stable in residence.

The limits of aging

Theoretically, the upper limit to which a population can age in terms

12. Ibid., p. 11.
13. Margaret S. Gordon, "Work and Patterns of Retirement," in *Aging and Leisure*, ed. Robert W. Kleemeier (New York: Oxford University Press, 1961), p. 18.
14. U.S., Bureau of the Census, *1970 Census of Population: United States Summary* (Washington, D.C.: Government Printing Office, 1972), table 78.
15. Ibid.

16. "We the American Elderly," p. 12.
17. Calculated from *1970 Census of Population*, table 196.

of the percent 65 and over is 100 percent, but any society which aged to this degree—or even approximated it—would be facing imminent extinction. With no children in the population and all of the adult population past the potentially reproductive ages, it would be merely a matter of time until the population would die off. It is also correct to presume that inordinately high proportions of aged persons in a population are a signal of slow growth, stability or even decline. The question thus becomes: in terms of aging, when do we reach a point of stability?

There is no single answer to this question, but perhaps we may gain perspective on it from noting three types of calculations. In the first place, we may note the degree of aging of those populations which appear to be nearing the end of the transition. Inspection of table 2 suggests that post-transitional populations may expect to have from 14 to 16 percent of their populations 65 and over. This figure varies not only with the current levels of mortality and fertility, but also in relation to their prior histories. A second type of figure is afforded by stable population theory. As an example, Keyfitz and Flieger have calculated the percent of the population which would be 65 and over in a stable population characterized by the age-specific birth and death rates extant in England and Wales in 1968; such a population would have 13.3 percent of its population 65 and over—only about 1 percent above the actual level in contemporary England.[18] However, this is the level of aging calculated upon actual fertility levels in 1968—fertility levels

which were well above mortality levels and still provided a margin of increase in the population. What would the ratio be in a stationary population with post-transitional mortality rates? One such figure is provided in projections based on the United States. Assuming slightly declining mortality rates to the year 2000, no immigration and replacement level fertility—that is, 2.11 births per woman—the population would become stationary in the year 2037, and in that year 16 percent of the population would be 65 and over.[19]

Is aging of population, then, a predictable trend? Can we anticipate that those populations which are now young will inevitably age as the populations of western Europe have already done? Of course, the answer to these questions is negative. There is nothing inevitable about the process. There are many developments which could prevent or reverse the process, but most of these are in the nature of disasters—such as nuclear warfare, widespread famine, widespread lethal pollution or a new virulent epidemic disease—which would reverse the worldwide downward trend in mortality rates.

Indeed, some pessimists believe that such an outcome is more probable than the completion of the transition.[20] Certainly, the assump-

18. Nathan Keyfitz and Wilhelm Flieger, *Population* (San Francisco, Cal.: W. H. Freeman, 1971), p. 34.

19. Jacob Siegel and William E. O'Leary, "Some Demographic Aspects of Aging in the United States," *Current Population Reports: Special Reports*, series P-23, no. 43 (February 1973), p. 6.

20. Donella H. Meadows, Dennis L. Meadows, Jørgen Randers and William W. Behrens, III, *The Limits of Growth* (New York: Universe Books, 1972); Paul R. Ehrlich, *The Population Bomb* (New York: Ballantine Books, 1968); Harrison Brown and Edward Hutchings, Jr., *Are Our Descendants Doomed?* (New York: Viking, 1970).

tion that fertility decline is a reflex effect of economic development and will occur automatically in time to avoid such disasters is not warranted.[21] One does not have to be a pessimist to predict that unless fertility rates are drastically reduced in the Third World, some form of lethal disaster is probable. However, if we avoid such disasters and if fertility rates are reduced, this will amount to the completion of the transition, and it will inevitably result in the aging of population.

SOCIETAL AGING

The social consequences of demographic aging are exceedingly complex. Since such demographic aging is an entirely new phenomenon—most of it having occurred within the last century—it should not be surprising that traditional cultures provided no ready-made modes of adjustment to the presence of such a high proportion of older people in the population. Nor should it surprise us that there have been some strains and problems involved in the adjustment.

At times the problems loom so large that some people get the impression that demographic aging is undesirable, something to be avoided. This is unfortunate, since it tends to dim the luster of one of man's crowning achievements. Surely, throughout history the prolongation of life has been a perennial preoccupation of individuals and societies.[22] That this objective has

been achieved to such a degree in modern societies must rank as one of the greatest boons of modern progress. Indeed, it may be argued that average life expectancy is a more valid and meaningful measure of progress or modernization than the more common indices of gross national product per capita or consumption of electricity per capita.

The demographic transition is a necessary accompaniment of the modernization process. Reduction of mortality is one of the early goals of modernization, and experience has taught that unless fertility is also curtailed, many of the hoped-for economic gains become impossible. However, if fertility is reduced, the population begins to age. We must therefore conclude that the aging of populations is also a necessary accompaniment of modernization. Nevertheless, modernization has thus far tended to devalue old people and to reduce their status.[23]

The meaning of modernization

Modernization is such a multifaceted phenomenon that writings about it remind one of the blind men's descriptions of the elephant: such writings usually reflect the disciplinary contexts or the theoretical orientations of the writers. Some see the process primarily in terms of changes in the sources of power—that is, the shift from primary reliance on animate power to extensive use of inanimate sources of power.[24] Closely similar are those

21. See, Donald O. Cowgill, "The Use of the Logistic Curve and the Transition Model in Developing Nations," in *Studies in Demography,* ed. Ashish Bose, P. B. Desai and S. P. Jain (Chapel Hill, N.C.: University of North Carolina Press, 1970), pp. 157–165.

22. Gerald J. Gruman, *A History of Ideas about the Prolongation of Life* (Philadelphia, Pa.: American Philosophical Society, 1966).

23. Donald O. Cowgill and Lowell D. Holmes, eds., *Aging and Modernization* (New York: Appleton-Century-Crofts, 1972), pp. 322–323; also, Erdman Palmore and F. Whittington, "Trends in the Relative Status of the Aged," *Social Forces* 50 (1971), pp. 84–91.

24. Marion J. Levy, *Modernization and the Structure of Societies* (Princeton, N.J.:

who tend to identify modernization with industrialization or with economic development.[25] Without specifying the particular aspects of society which are transformed, some see it as a transformation in imitation of more advanced societies.[26] Social psychologists are likely to stress changes of attitudes and values.[27] Some place the emphasis upon transformation of political institutions, the emergence of nationalism and the growth of political consciousness, including the demand for citizen participation.[28] The functionalists tend to stress institutional differentiation.[29]

Just as all of the blind men were correct, so all of these views of modernization are correct; each writer is merely emphasizing a different aspect of the same process. In an effort to incorporate all of these facets in one statement, I have defined the process as follows:

Modernization is the transformation of a total society from a relatively rural way of life based on animate power, limited technology, relatively undifferentiated institutions, parochial and traditional outlook and values, toward a predominantly urban way of life based on in-

animate sources of power, highly developed scientific technology, highly differentiated institutions matched by segmented individual roles, and a cosmopolitan outlook which emphasizes efficiency and progress.[30]

Comprehensive as it is, even this definition merely samples the range of the societal transformation involved. Its main thesis is contained in the phrase "transformation of a total society"; there is no aspect of the society which is not drastically changed in the process. A second major point to be emphasized about this formulation is that the process is unidirectional; the change is always away from a rural, traditional form of society in the direction of an urbanized, high-energy, highly differentiated type of society. This is not to assert that the process is uniform; it is merely to emphasize that modernization always produces changes in the same direction, regardless of the unique qualities of each traditional society.[31]

Salient aspects of modernization

One limitation of the assumption of such a holistic view of the process of modernization is that it is difficult to discuss it without permitting such discussion to develop into a treatise of excessive length and complexity. In order to avoid this pitfall it is necessary to abstract those aspects of the total process which

Princeton University Press, 1966); Fred Cottrell, *Energy and Society* (New York: McGraw-Hill, 1955).

25. Walt W. Rostow, *The Economics of Take-Off into Sustained Growth* (New York: St. Martin's Press, 1963).

26. Reinhard Bendix, "Proba Definicji Modernizacji" (Towards a Definition of Modernization), *Studia Socjolgiczno Polityczne* 25 (1968) pp. 31–43.

27. Alex Inkeles and David H. Smith, "The Fate of Personal Adjustment in the Process of Modernization," *International Journal of Comparative Sociology* 11 (June 1970), pp. 81–114.

28. Daniel Lerner, *The Passing of Traditional Society: Modernizing the Middle East* (New York: Free Press, 1958).

29. S. N. Eisenstadt, *Modernization: Protest and Change* (Englewood Cliffs, N.J.: Prentice-Hall, 1966).

30. Donald O. Cowgill, "Aging and Modernization: A Revision of the Theory," in *Late Life*, ed. Jaber Gubrium (forthcoming).

31. Nettl makes a convincing case that each society is unique in origin, will be uniquely selective as modernization occurs and may be expected to retain its individuality in its modernized form. See, J. P. Nettl, *International Systems and the Modernization of Societies* (New York: Basic Books, 1968), pp. 42–57.

are especially relevant to the problem at hand.

In the present context the problem at hand is the societal response to the aging of population, and this amounts to the analysis of the interaction of modernization and demographic aging. For this type of analysis it appears that the most salient aspects of modernization include: (1) the application of modern health technology within a society; (2) the application of scientific technology to economic production and distribution; (3) urbanization; and (4) the extension of literacy and mass education. The question to be examined is: how do each of these aspects of modernization contribute to the generally observed downgrading and reduction of status of the aged in modern societies?

Aging and health technology

Modern health technology is one of the most obvious exports from modernized societies to contemporary developing—that is, modernizing—societies. Yet, there is scant mention of this aspect of modernization in the massive literature about the process.

Since World War II the introduction of modern forms of sanitation and control of communicable disease into erstwhile traditional societies has produced dramatic demographic effects. Initially, these are seen in terms of lower mortality rates, especially lower infant and child mortality. Without commensurate reduction in fertility—and, so far, no developing society has reduced fertility as early and rapidly as they have reduced mortality— this touches off a population explosion. Not only is there a rapid increase in the total population: because birth rates remain high while larger proportions of the babies are kept alive, the early effect of these measures upon the age composition of the population is a "younging" effect—that is, a disproportionate increase in the number of children in the population. In the long run, however, the application of modern health technology not only prevents death in infancy and childhood but also prolongs life at all stages. Moreover, if this development is coupled with the introduction of contraception—another aspect of such technology—it may produce a reduction of fertility and with it the progressive aging of the population.

As the lives of workers are prolonged, death no longer creates openings in the labor force as rapidly as it once did. Thus, competitive pressures are generated between the generations in the labor force. Eventually, a social substitute for death as the means of exit from the labor force is instituted in the form of the practice of retirement.

At the same time, at least until the present, modernized societies have been characterized by the work ethic—in its earlier, European form known as the Protestant ethic— which makes the work role the chief role in life and allocates rewards, both material and nonmaterial, accordingly. Consequently, retirement from this most valued and status-giving role is accompanied by a reduction in rewards, including monetary income and psychologically satisfying status.

In sum, then: in the long run the introduction of modern health technology contributes to the aging of population and its work force. This in turn creates pressures toward retirement, forces people out of the most valued and highly rewarded roles, deprives them of utility, curtails their income and lowers their status in the society. This chain of events is depicted in the top line of figure 1.

Economic technology and aging

A second salient aspect of modernization is the introduction of modern economic technology. This creates many new occupations and transforms most of the old ones. It is only natural that the people coming forward to fill these new jobs should be those not yet established in careers—namely, the young. They become the pioneers in a developing society, and they are rewarded both financially and psychologically for filling roles which are highly valued in the society. Older workers carry on in the more traditional work roles, some of which become obsolete and most of which are less highly valued and, therefore, less well remunerated. Both obsolescence and youthful competition eventually create pressure for retirement and with it the loss of income and status, as previously noted. Thus, health technology and economic technology separately and in interaction conduce to the restriction of the roles of the aged in society and toward their relative financial and psychological deprivation. The role of economic technology in this process is depicted on line 2 in figure 1.

Aging and urbanization

The third salient factor in modernization is urbanization. The excess rural population created by the population explosion flocks to the cities to take over the new jobs created by economic development. Of course, it is the young who migrate. Their migration produces physical separation from the parental family and tends to foster the establishment of permanently separate residence, thus breaking down the extended family in favor of the nuclear conjugal unit. Neolocal marriage becomes the norm in a modernizing society. Residential separation fosters social and intellectual separation of the generations.

Paralleling the physical migration of the young away from the rural parental home to the cities is a subtler, but no less real, social mobility: the young move into the new, more glamorous, better-paying urban jobs, leaving behind—both physically and psychologically— the grubby, archaic, rural way of life. The young are in the stream of progress; the old are left behind. The young have improved their station; the old stand still and suffer by comparison.

This is a new and revolutionary pattern emerging out of a traditional society in which the elderly had high status, important roles and positions of power. Now the status relationships are reversed; it is the young who have the higher status and who are doing things which are held to be more important. In the process of migration and entry into the urban economy they have, to a large degree, escaped from the control of their elders.

Thus, urbanization also provides advantages to the young and handicaps to the aged. It tends to invert the statuses of the generations and leave the elderly in relative deprivation. The dual process stemming from urbanization is shown in figure 1.

Aging and education

A fourth salient aspect of modernization with respect to aging is education. In traditional societies most of the population is illiterate. An early effort in all modernizing

FIGURE 1

AGING AND MODERNIZATION

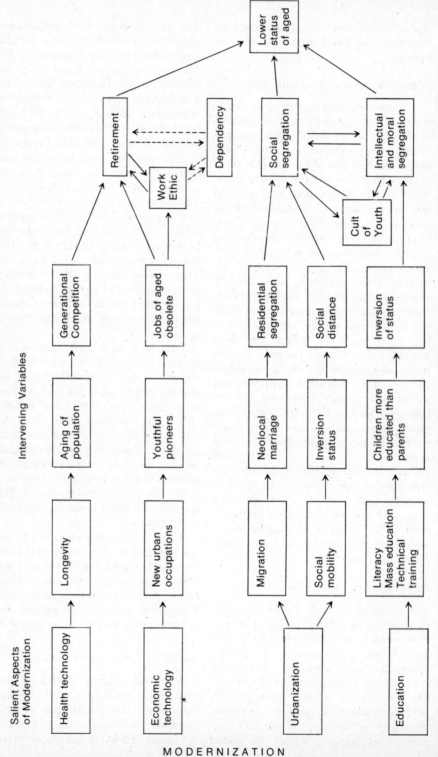

SOURCE: From Donald O. Cowgill, "Aging and Modernization: A Revision of the Theory," in *Late Life*, ed. Jaber Gubrium (forthcoming).

societies is the drive to promote literacy. Following close upon the heels of this effort is the movement to provide progressively higher levels of education for all the youth of the society. Paralleling this movement, in turn, is the effort to provide vocational education for the workers in the newly developing industries.

Be it noted that the main targets of all such educational efforts are the young. Therefore, in a modernizing society the young always have an opportunity to acquire more education than their elders. In some societies this is an avowed objective.

This also constitutes an inversion of status, and the consequences are no doubt most dramatic in the early stage of the process—when the children are literate and the parents illiterate. In this stage the parents must rely upon the children to translate for them many communications from the outside world. This elevates the status of the children and subordinates the elderly to the young, at least for this function.

This dramatic contrast only illustrates the long range consequences which occur in a society in which the young are always more knowledgeable, more skilled, more attuned to the times than their elders. Certainly, in these circumstances there can be no mystique of age; there can be no reverence for the aged deriving from their superior knowledge. In such a society the aged will have lost most of their power over the young within their family and kin group. So, one can see that education, too, contributes to the down-grading of the elderly in modern societies. The process is diagrammed on the bottom line of figure 1.

Aging and the work ethic

In this analysis the work ethic is treated as a factor which has thus far conditioned and modified the effects of modernization on the status of the aged, but not as an essential ingredient of the modernization process itself. This is, of course, a moot point. The Weberian point of view would ascribe to it the central role of prime motivator.[32] I do not dispute the key role played by the work ethic, whether derived from Protestantism or from other sources, in the most modernized societies.

However, there appears to be room for reasonable doubt that it is as essential to the process as is generally believed by those whose perspective is derived from Western capitalist countries. Some developing nations, modernizing by selective imitation, may succeed without so great an emphasis upon this cultural value. It also appears that some of the most modernized societies are in the process of softening and modifying the value in the necessity of coming to terms with extensive and increasing amounts of leisure.

Aging and the cult of youth

Another persistent, but perhaps extraneous, factor in fostering the devaluation of the aged in the most modernized societies is what is termed here the cult of youth—that is, the prevalent value system which glorifies youth as a symbol of beauty, vigor and progress and discriminates in favor of youth in employment and in the allocation of community re-

32. Max Weber, *The Protestant Ethic and the Spirit of Capitalism* (New York: Charles Scribner's Sons, 1958).

sources. I have already noted that an overwhelming proportion of educational effort and resources is directed to youth. The same point can be made with reference to recreation and, to a lesser degree, to health resources.

In view of the strong tendency toward status inversion during the modernization process—particularly in relation to the creation of new jobs, the migration of the young to the cities, the social mobility of the younger generations and the superior education of the young—it may appear that the cult of youth is an inevitable accompaniment and conditioner of the modernization process. However, this also is a moot point. It may be that in the later stages of the process—as the center of gravity shifts with the aging of populations—the cult of youth may be partially neutralized, if not by the emergence of a self-conscious subculture of the aging,[33] at least by the sheer weight of the needs and demands of increasing numbers and proportions of the aged.

Aging and the future

As we have seen, then, modernized societies have large numbers and proportions of the aged. Yet, these aged are forced to be nonproductive; then, they are penalized for their nonproductiveness with reduced incomes and relatively low status. Barring catastrophic reversals, populations which have completed the transition will continue to be aged—that is, they will continue to have much higher proportions of

older people than any populations in prior history.

Is the temporal correlation between modernization and the reduction in status of the aged a necessary and predictable one? That the correlation is real has been confirmed by Palmore and Whittington.[34] That the relationship is functional—that is, causal—has been one of the main theses of this article. If it has been established that a reduction of the status of the aged has resulted from modernization, it should be possible to predict that the same thing will happen wherever modernization occurs.

Indeed, it is probable that this will happen in other parts of the world as they modernize. However, the relationship does not appear either inevitable or necessarily permanent. Any change in the factors and relationships diagrammed in figure 1 would change the outcome and, as noted previously, two factors are included which do not appear to be inherent and necessary to the modernization process: the work ethic and the cult of youth. Both of these factors appear to have been present and influential during the development of the presently highly modernized societies, but they do not appear to be essential elements in the process. If either or both of them should be absent or should appear with less strength, the outcome could be significantly modified.

Furthermore, Palmore and Manton find evidence that the relation-

33. Arnold M. Rose, "The Subculture of the Aging: A Framework for Research in Social Gerontology," in *Older People and Their Social World*, ed. Arnold M. Rose and Warren M. Peterson (Philadelphia, Pa.: F. A. Davis, 1965), pp. 3–16.

34. Palmore and Whittington, "Trends in the Relative Status of the Aged"; see, also, Irwin Press and Mike McKool, Jr., "Social Structure and Status of the Aged: Toward Some Valid Cross-Cultural Generalizations," *Aging and Human Development* 3 (1972), pp. 297–306.

ship is curvilinear, that while the margin of difference between the educational level and occupational pursuits of the aged as compared with the younger adult population is greater in the more modernized societies, there is a point beyond which this is no longer true.[35] In other words, the aged in the most advanced countries suffer from less educational and occupational disadvantage than the aged in countries which are slightly less advanced on the modernization scale. This suggests a possible bottoming-out of the trend and a tendency toward convergence in the most advanced stages of modernization.

This is an encouraging hint, and there are corroborating indicators to give it credence. The late stages of the demographic transition entail convergence of vital rates and a tendency toward stability. As a country becomes highly modernized it is probable that the benefits of medical technology become more widely accessible and, therefore, that the differential effects by social class, area of residence and age tend to decrease. There certainly is strong indication that the differences between the life styles and standards of living of rural and urban residents diminish in the late stages of the transition. It is also probable that there is an upper limit to the amount of time and resources which a society will devote to mass public education and that as most of the population achieves the general functional level, the differential level of achievement between the generations will begin to decrease. In-

deed, this appears to be indicated in the data analyzed by Palmore and Manton.[36] In a more general vein, it is reasonable to suppose that if one out of seven, or even more, persons in a population is 65 and over, societies will continue to invent and institutionalize social and cultural means of coping with this condition.

Retirement and Social Security are two early responses to this phenomenon. However, retirement is largely negative in its impact on the older people themselves in that it deprives them of a key role in life. It is probable that over time new roles for the aged will evolve, roles which have value to the society and provide purpose and status to those performing them. The early forms of Social Security were intended to provide a minimum income to the retired and some inducement for the elderly to leave the labor market. However, Social Security benefits have universally been inadequate to provide a satisfying life style. There will be continued efforts to find forms of income maintenance for the elderly which are both socially feasible and individually sufficient. Experimentation will also continue in the effort to provide opportunities for adequate medical care, suitable housing, healthful diet, meaningful leisure and cultural pursuits, appropriate educational experiences and vital religious life.

SUMMARY

Modern society has made great strides in the application of sophisticated technology to the control of mortality and fertility. Yet, while the application of both forms of

35. Erdman Palmore and Kenneth Manton, "Modernization and the Status of the Aged: International Comparisons," *Journal of Gerontology* 29, no. 2 (March 1974), pp. 205–210.

36. Ibid.

technology eventually results in relatively aged populations, these societies have been slow and faltering in adapting their institutions to this new demographic phenomenon. The early, fumbling attempts have been compromises between the interests of youth-oriented society and the needs of the old people themselves. The results have been injurious to the dignity and status of the elderly. Recently, however, there have been some encouraging signs that the more advanced societies may have begun to close the gap, that they are beginning to catch up with their demographic trends, that their institutions and cultures are beginning to reflect more attention to the needs and interests of this increasing segment of their populations. It is predictable that this should happen, particularly in societies in which the political institutions are responsive to an electorate, since the electorate itself is aging. Many of the institutional adaptations which are needed must perforce be proposed, debated, compromised and adopted within the political arena.

Social Mythology and Reform: Income Maintenance for the Aged

By ROBINSON HOLLISTER

ABSTRACT: Debate over the need for reform of Social Security is reviewed in this article. Even prior to recent developments, reformers have attacked the myth that Social Security is closely analogous to private insurance, and they have argued that payroll tax financing—adopted and sustained in order to foster the illusion of a contributory system—is highly, and unnecessarily, regressive in its impact. Supporters of the system as originally conceived point to its success in terms of size, broad political acceptance and effectiveness in reducing poverty among the aged. The recent major changes in the system, culminating in the 1972 Social Security Amendments, are reviewed. It is argued that these changes sharpened the debate. Higher benefits required higher payroll taxes—thereby raising, in the reformers' eyes, the price of the insurance myth—paid primarily by low income workers. The creation of the Supplementary Security Income program appears to make income redistribution features of Social Security redundant. Defenders of the system resist the reformers' suggestions for tidying up the structure. Suggested reforms will, they argue, strip the system of the mystique of contributory social insurance and saddle Social Security with the stigma of a welfare-like, means-tested system; in such a case, they argue, the system will become vulnerable to political conflict. They maintain that social myth is necessary cement in the construction of durable social institutions.

Robinson Hollister is Associate Professor of Economics at Swarthmore College and Lecturer at the Fels Center for Government, University of Pennsylvania. He participated in the design and analysis of the New Jersey Negative Income Tax Experiment. He is co-editor of Income Maintenance: Interdisciplinary Approaches to Research *and author of a forthcoming book entitled* Poor People, Poor Theories, Poor Programs.

HERMAN Melville's little read, and even less appreciated, novel *The Confidence Man*[1] begins:

At sunrise on a first of April, there appeared suddenly . . . a man in cream-colours, at the waterside in the city of St. Louis.

His cheek was fair, his chin downy, his hair flaxen, his hat a white fur one, with a long fleecy nap. He had neither trunk, valise, carpetbag, nor parcel . . . he stepped aboard the favourite steamer *Fidele*, on the point of starting for New Orleans.

The man works his way through the crowd on the boat and comes next to a placard announcing a reward for the capture of a mysterious imposter.

Pausing at this spot, the stranger so far succeeded in threading his way, as at last to plant himself just beside the placard, producing a small slate and tracing some words upon it, he held it up before him on a level with the placard, so that they who read the one might read the other. The words were these:

"Charity thinketh no evil"

The crowd around the placard jostles him aside.

. . . the stranger quietly turned, and writing anew upon the slate, again held it up:

"Charity suffereth long, and is kind."

illy pleased with his pertinacity, as they thought it, the crowd a second time thrust him aside, and not without epithets and some buffets, all of which were unresented.

The lamb-like man is a mute.

The stranger now moved slowly away, yet not before altering his writing to this:

1. Herman Melville, *The Confidence Man* (Indianapolis, Ind.: Bobbs Merrill, 1971).

"Charity endureth all things."

Shield-like bearing his slate before him, amid stares and jeers he moved slowly up and down, at his turning points again changing his inscription to—

"Charity believeth all things."

and then

"Charity never faileth"

The word charity, as originally traced, remained throughout uneffaced, not unlike the left-hand numeral of a printed date, otherwise left for convenience in blank.

At this point, nearby, the ship's barber opens his shop:

. . . . jumping on a stool, he hung over his door, on the customary nail, a gaudy sort of illuminated pasteboard sign, skilfully executed by himself, gilt with the likeness of a razor elbowed in readiness to shave, and also, for the public benefit, with the two words not unfrequently seen ashore gracing other shops besides barbers':

"No Trust"

The mute is, perhaps, the first guise, or masque, of the confidence man. As the novel progresses other figures appear who inspire confidence or distrust among the crowd. We are never sure who is the impostor, who the victim, which the confidence man and which the exposer of confidence men. This, according to some Melville critics, is his comic commentary on the role of religion in society. Is religion an ultimate form and source of trust among men or is it a confidence game?

TRUST AND CONFIDENCE

I would like to use these images in discussing the debate over the reform of the Social Security system in the United States. Is the Social Security system a form and source of trust among men or is it a confidence game? Are the supporters of the Social Security system as currently structured—persons I shall refer to as the priests of Social Security—confidence men or are they the purveyors of trust and charity? There are those—whom I will call Johnny-come-lately-reformers—who, like the barber, would post the sign "No Trust" over the Social Security system. Are they unveilers of confidence men or destroyers of social trust?

Schema

The issues I wish to raise are really quite simple, but the Social Security system to which I wish to apply them is quite complex, as are most social institutions of trust or most confidence games. Thus, I must spend a good deal of time on technical details in order to make some simple points. Therefore, in order to motivate—or obviate—the reader's task of working through technical details, I will make my simple basic points at the outset in the abstract:

(1) there are dangers in building a social institution around a consciously conceived myth;

(2) in recent years, as the program matures, the inherent contradictions in the Social Security myth have been coming into sharper relief;

(3) thus, the price paid for the social myth is rising;

(4) in spite of points (1) through (3), one must seriously consider whether—as the priests of Social Security warn us—social myth is not the necessary cement with which to hold together social institutions.

In the section which follow I will first sketch out the features of the system as it existed prior to the major Social Security Amendments of 1972 and will provide the standard positive and negative critique of the system at that stage. Then, I will describe the developments in the system embodied in the 1972 amendments and indicate their great importance. This consideration of the system will facilitate the analysis of both the technical and the philosophical arguments between the priests of Social Security and the Johnny-come-lately-reformers which is presented in the final section of the paper.

In what follows I will focus on the debate about the aspects of the Social Security system which relate to retirement benefits. The system also includes elements involving benefits for survivors of covered workers, for disability and blindness and for medical care. There are equally important issues to be discussed concerning these features, but the limits of space preclude taking them up here.

FEATURES OF THE SOCIAL SECURITY SYSTEM PRIOR TO THE 1972 AMENDMENTS

In order to discuss the debate over reform it is necessary for me to sketch out a few of the details of the system which existed—and which persist in the present — prior to the 1972 amendments to the Social Security Act. Since I wish to discuss primarily the retirement system, I will omit most details relating to survivors, disability and medical care provisions of the system.

Description

From the outset the system has been financed through a payroll tax. In 1937 the tax was paid on the first $3,000 of each covered worker's earnings, and the amount was 1 percent taken from the employee and 1 percent paid by the employer. As the coverage of persons and the type and level of benefits have risen, this tax has been increased slowly, but steadily, so that at present the first $13,200 of earnings are taxed and the employee pays 5.85 percent and the employer 5.85 percent. The funds from the payroll tax are paid into a trust fund. However, the trust fund is just large enough to cover current benefits; it does not represent the sum of accumulated assets for workers who have been paying over the years.

In order to receive retirement benefits a worker now entering the system will have to have forty quarters of covered employment by the time he or she retires. Naturally, those who were older when the system started have different eligibility limits, and the provisions for covering survivors and disabled are different.

Another feature of eligibility for benefits for those between 65 and 72 deals with earnings; it is often called the retirement test. Individuals between 65 and 72 may earn up to $2,400 per year without penalty; if they earn more, their benefits are reduced by fifty cents for each dollar earned. "This provision . . . is included in the law to assure that monthly benefits will be paid to a worker only when he has substantially retired."[2] Those over 72 receive their full benefits regardless of their annual earnings. Property—or unearned—income does not affect benefits.

The amount of benefits a retiree receives is related to the average of his covered earnings, with the average determined after subtracting the five years of lowest earnings. Covered earnings are earnings which have been subject to the payroll tax—for example, the first $13,200 are currently taxed, so earnings over $13,200 are not covered. Some jobs are not covered by Social Security—at the outset about four out of ten workers were not covered, now the figure is one out of ten—so that earnings in such jobs are neither taxed nor included in the average of covered earnings used in determining benefits.

The relationship of monthly benefits received after 65 to the average monthly covered earnings prior to 65 varies with the level of earnings. Table 1 gives some examples for benefits under the 1971 law. Those with lower monthly average earnings receive benefits which are a higher percentage of their past average earnings than those with high monthly past earnings; benefits are skewed so as to redistribute benefits toward lower earners. Also, workers are now allowed to retire at the age of 62 rather than 65 as required in the past. If they elect to do so, their benefits are permanently reduced on an actuarial basis to reflect the fact that they will be paid benefits over a longer period than if they had retired at 65.

Evaluation of pre-1972 features

With these bare outlines of the system in mind, we can turn to the evaluation of the system's features as they existed prior to the 1972

2. U.S., Department of Health, Education and Welfare, *Social Security Programs in the United States*, DHEW no. (SSA)73-11915 (1973), p. 30.

TABLE 1

THE RELATIONSHIP OF RETIREMENT
BENEFITS TO AVERAGE COVERED
EARNINGS UNDER SOCIAL
SECURITY, 1971

| AVERAGE MONTHLY EARNINGS | MONTHLY BENEFITS | |
	SINGLE	COUPLE
$250	$145	$218
$750*	$293	$443

* In 1971 no retired worker could have average covered earnings any greater than $432. This was so because the income limit to the payroll tax was substantially lower than at present.

amendments. I will deal first with the positive aspects and, then, turn to the shortcomings.

The designers and supporters of the system as it stands have emphasized several interrelated virtues of the program. First, it is a contributory system—many like to call it social insurance. The contributory essence is highlighted by the clearly identifiable Social Security tax which allows the worker to have the feeling that he is paying something now which will in some sense determine what he will receive in the future. Second, the sense of the system as being contributory is reinforced by the fact that the benefits are graduated so that, in general, those who have had higher earnings and paid more in the past will get higher benefits than their lower-earning cohorts who paid less in Social Security tax. Third, the system is compulsory in the sense that all—in covered industries—must pay the payroll tax; however, as a result of compulsory participation, it yields "benefits as a right." Fourth, the retirement test is an important part of the system in that it emphasizes that the system is meant to replace earnings.

Fifth, many of the above-mentioned features are similar to those of private insurance or pensions, but Social Security is to be differentiated from private insurance in that it is shaped by considerations of public needs, as well —indeed, for this reason it is referred to as social insurance. These public needs are reflected in the fact that people with lower past earnings have greater unmet needs and, therefore, that they receive benefits at a higher percentage of their average past earnings than do those with high past earnings. In addition, unlike private insurance, retirement benefits under Social Security are periodically increased across the board as average needs rise with the rise in average living standards.

A sixth key feature is the effect of Social Security on the extent of poverty among the aged. For example, in 1966—a date chosen because of the availability of detailed data—60 percent of the Social Security benefits went to people whose income without Social Security would have been below the poverty line and, of this group, 90 percent were lifted from poverty by virtue of the Social Security payments. Finally, it is important to point out that Social Security is the largest income maintenance program. In the fiscal year 1973 it paid out $42 billion dollars to 25 million recipients.

Yet, while the Social Security system is generally recognized as the most successful social program in the history of the country, a number of shortcomings—even as it stood prior to the 1972 amendments—are widely noted. The most fundamental criticism is that two incompatible functions have been bound into one system, with the result that neither function is adequately performed. One function is to provide a social transfer mechanism so that individuals may have income in their older years which exceeds any earnings they may have for those years.[3] The second function is to redistribute income within cohorts of the aged so that some sort of income floor is provided for the poorest. Putting these two functions in a single program means that each is compromised by the constraints imposed by the other.

The income redistribution—or poverty reduction—function is compromised by the necessity of tying benefits to past earnings. If a person was poor before the age of 65 and if his benefits are less than 100 percent of his average past earnings, he will, of necessity, be poor after 65. At best, the system as it stands yields about 80 percent of earnings averaged over the working lifetime. Moreover, since earnings in the early working years are lower due to youth and to a lower economywide wage level, benefits are usually less than 50 percent of earnings just prior to retirement. The ineffectiveness of Social Security as a poverty support is illustrated by the fact that, whereas 12 percent of all persons are poor, 19 percent of those over 65 are poor. Alternatively, one can note that 16 percent of the aged who receive Social Security benefits are poor in spite of their Social Security income—that is, their income including Social Security falls below the poverty line.

3. See, Paul Samuelson, "An Exact Consumption-Loan Model of Interest," *Journal of Political Economy* 66 (December 1958), pp. 467–482; or "Social Security," *Newsweek*, 13 February 1967, for the theoretical justification for such a social mechanism.

The functioning of the system as a social mechanism for transferring income toward older age is impaired by the redistributive features of the system. It is not a federalized annuity-type system, since the amount one receives relative to one's age cohort is only roughly related to the amount one has paid in Social Security taxes.[4] The ratio of benefits to past payroll tax paid is generally higher for low wage earners.[5]

A second major shortcoming of the system which has been pointed out is that it discourages work among the aged. The retirement test feature of benefits amounts to placing a 50 percent tax on earnings within a certain range for workers 65 to 72. For example, in 1970 the law stated that a beneficiary could earn up to $1,680 without having benefits reduced. From $1,680 to $2,880 benefits would be reduced by 50 cents for each additional dollar earned—that is, the recip-

4. For example, if an individual works for three quarters of each year in the public sector which is not covered and for one quarter in a covered job, he still qualifies for Social Security benefits. Moreover, he will get the same retirement benefits as someone his age who worked at an equal wage for all four quarters in the covered sector. The first individual will have paid one-fourth the amount of Social Security taxes as the second.

5. This should not obscure the fact that, under the law—both as currently conceived and as it stood in 1971—all workers will receive more in benefits than they pay in Social Security tax. John Brittain estimates that an average worker will get about 4 percent real rate of return on the payroll taxes he has paid. Any such estimates require a number of assumptions, but Brittain's seem broadly reasonable. See, John Brittain, "Statement," in *Future Directions in Social Security*, U.S., Congress, Senate, Special Committee on Aging (Washington, D.C.: Government Printing Office, 1973), part 3, p. 176.

ient's net income would go up by only 50 cents for each additional dollar earned, resulting in a reduction equivalent to a 50 percent tax rate. Any earnings over $2,880 caused benefits to be reduced by one dollar for each dollar earned, up to the point where benefits were reduced to zero[6]—that is, the equivalent of a 100 percent tax rate on earnings.

To some it may seem a relatively trivial point that there may be some discouragement of work effort among those 65 to 72. In fact, the retirement test was originally included in the system when it was designed during the 1930s in order to encourage older workers to retire to make more jobs available for the many unemployed nonaged workers. This rationale makes little sense today.

In any case, earnings are not a trivial matter as a source of income for the aged. This is illustrated in table 2. In 1972 the poverty line was approximately $2,500 for a couple aged 65 and over and $2,000 for a single individual aged 65 and over. Thus, the divisions according to these income cut-offs in table 2 provide an approximate, but not exact, separation according to poor and nonpoor within families with aged heads and within aged unrelated individuals. For families with aged heads it is evident that the difference in earnings between those below $2,500 total income and those above is by far the largest difference in income by source. If those in poor families had, in fact,

6. The law was subsequently changed in several steps. The current law allows $2,400 of earnings before benefits are reduced; after that, benefits are reduced 50 cents for each additional dollar earned. This means that while the 100 percent tax range no longer exists, the 50 percent tax range still does.

earnings anywhere near those of nonpoor families, they would clearly escape poverty. For unrelated individuals the differences in earnings between the low income and high income groups is not as substantial. Even so, if individuals with incomes below $2,000 had earning opportunities as great as those available to individuals with incomes above $2,000, they would have had average income sufficient to lift themselves from poverty.

The potential effect of the retirement test built into Social Security may well go beyond its direct effect of discouraging work effort in the range where benefits are reduced because of earnings. This is so due to the possible influence of social legislation in setting standards for retirement which the private sector quickly adopts. The labor force participation rate of males 65 and over has fallen from 45.8 percent in 1950 to 24.4 percent in 1972. Many attribute this decline to older persons' increasing income which allows them to enjoy the luxury of retirement. However, there is an important question about the proportion of retirements which are involuntary, forced by increasingly severe private sector retirement rules. It is noteworthy, for example, that the sharpest declines in aged male labor force participation occur when the unemployment rate is high. In fact, for the period 1966 to 1969 when unemployment rates were at their lowest point since 1953, the labor force participation of males over 65 actually increased. After 1969, as unemployment began to rise again, the aged male labor force participation rate resumed its long term decline.

Other evidence suggestive of

TABLE 2

SOURCES OF INCOME FOR FAMILIES WITH HEAD OF HOUSEHOLD 65 AND OVER AND
FOR UNRELATED INDIVIDUALS 65 AND OVER, 1972

INCOME	ERN ($)	SS ($)	DIV ($)	PA ($)	UI ($)	PRV ($)	ATI ($)
FAMILIES							
Below $2,500 (N = 1,132,000)	131	1,569	131	218		131*	2,179
Above $2,500 (N = 6,458,000)	4,461	2,468	1,329	95	475	664	9,492
All families (N = 7,590,000)	3,759	2,340	1,170	84	418	585	8,356
INDIVIDUALS							
Below $2,000 (N = 2,238,000)	28	1,050	70	154	70	28	1,400
Above $2,000 (N = 3,943,000)	892	1,688	1,313	94	328	375	4,690
All individuals (N = 6,181,000)	586	1,447	827	103	241	241	3,445

SOURCE: Unpublished tabulations from Current Population; survey conducted by the United States Bureau of the Census.

DEFINITIONS: ERN: average income from earnings; SS: average Social Security and railroad retirement income; DIV: average income from dividends, interest, net rental, estates, trusts, net royalties; PA: average income from public assistance or welfare payments; UI: average income from unemployment compensation, workmen's compensation, veteran's benefits, government employee pensions; PRV: average income from private income from private pensions, annuities, alimony and so on; ATI: average total income.

NOTE: Of those 65 and over, 69 percent were in families, while 31 percent were unrelated individuals.

* Since the number of families receiving PRV income in this income class is less than 75,000, total UI + PRV is given.

considerable involuntary retirement among the aged is provided by the data on the characteristics of those persons taking advantage of the early retirement provisions under Social Security—that is, retirement at 62 rather than 65, with permanently lowered benefits. In general, these early retirees have had considerably more spells of unemployment and lower wages than those who retire with full benefits at 65.[7] The early retirees hardly conform to the picture of persons with higher income taking the opportunity to indulge in the leisure of early retirement. The opportunity for the aged to work is important not only for its pure economic return, but also because work is the most important force for social integration in the society. If the example of social legislation encourages the private sector to lower retirement age, to stiffen retirement standards and, thereby, to

7. See, Julian Abbott, "Covered Employment and the Age Men Claim Retirement Benefits," *Social Security Bulletin* 37, no. 4 (April 1974), pp. 3–16; and the works cited therein.

increase the extent of involuntary unemployment, then it has indirectly contributed to the increased social isolation of the aged.[8]

A third major shortcoming of Social Security created prior to 1972 is that its method of financing is regressive. A worker subject to the payroll tax with earnings just at the maximum level—the maximum of $12,000 in 1972 and of $13,200 at present—pays the same absolute amount of Social Security tax as a man with earnings ten or twenty times that amount. Thus, the Social Security tax is a higher proportion of income for those with low incomes than for those with very high incomes.

In addition, it is argued by many that the tax which is nominally paid by the employer is, in fact, shifted to the worker.[9] The employer tax raises the price of a manhour of labor. Therefore, the employer will hire the same amount of labor as he would if there were no tax only if the workers will accept a wage lower by the amount of the tax. Whether the employers' portion of the tax is fully or only partially shifted to the employee is a matter of some dispute. However, the myth that the employer pays the tax disguises the full extent of the true tax on low incomes.

Finally, the most broadly stated complaint is that the originators and supporters of the system have misused the analogy with insurance in order to disguise many of the above-listed shortcomings. The critics argue that, unlike private insurance or annuities, benefits do not reflect the accumulated value of payments in a fund—in addition to accrued interest—but rather are set by the changes in legislation over time. The benefits, in fact, reflect a transfer from the younger generation to the older generation in each period. The benefits of each individual bear only a very rough relationship to the value of Social Security taxes paid over the past lifetime (see, for example, footnote 3). One analyst concludes:

The insurance analogy constitutes a "pre-emptive strike" against potential taxpayer and legislative resistance to payroll tax increases; the budget minded legislator in particular may be soothed by the conception that each prospective recipient will pay his own way under the system instead of living off the taxpayers in general.[10]

THE 1972 AMENDMENTS AND RELATED DEVELOPMENTS

Major increases in Social Security benefit levels and shifts in its structure began to take place with legislative action in the fall of 1969. Moreover, they were more or less continuously under debate in the process of enactment or under revision until the culminating action of the 1972 Social Security Amendments. Some minor adjustments have been made since the 1972 amendments, but they stand as the major landmark in a period of extraordinary activity in the area of Social Security legislation.[11] These legislative changes covered a wide variety of provisions; however, I

8. For a fuller discussion of this issue, see, U.S., Congress, Senate Special Committee on Aging, *Future Directions in Social Security* (Washington, D.C.: Government Printing Office, 1973), part 5, pp. 375–393.

9. See, John Brittain, *The Payroll Tax for Social Security* (Washington, D.C.: Brookings Institution, 1972), chaps. 2 and 3.

10. Ibid., pp. 10–11.

11. A convenient summary and overview of this period can be found in Robert Ball, "Social Security Amendments of 1972: A Summary and Legislative History," *Social Security Bulletin* 32, no. 3 (March 1973), pp. 3–25.

will sketch out just a few of the most important ones in order to set the background to the new debate between the priests of Social Security and the Johnny-come-lately-reformers.

Benefits

The statutory benefit levels were sharply increased: from December 1970 to December 1973 the minimum benefit was increased by 54 percent and the maximum, by 66 percent. During the same period the consumer price index went up by 23 percent. The increase in benefits was clearly more than enough to offset inflation during this period. These changes were sufficient to improve the real income of those over 65 relative to the real income of the rest of the population. A further increase in benefits of 11 percent across the board, signed into law at the end of 1973, was to be accomplished in two steps: 7 percent in March 1974 and the remainder in July 1974. By July of 1974 the minimum benefit for a worker 65 and over will be $93.80 per month and the maximum $295.37.

Indexing

Starting in 1975 benefits will be automatically increased by the same percentage amount as the increase in the consumer price index. In addition, the threshold at which the retirement test takes effect—the level of annual earnings permissible before benefits are reduced—will be increased automatically at the rate of increase in the average wage level for all employees in the economy.[12]

12. The annual exempt amount of earnings—the retirement test threshold—was legislatively increased from $1,680 to $2,100 in the 1972 amendments and then to $2,400 in 1973.

Financing

In order to finance the increase in benefits and some extensions in coverage, the payroll tax was increased substantially both by extending the base of taxable earnings—from $7,800 in 1969 to the current $13,200—and by increasing the tax rate for both employees and employers. These changes were only the last and most dramatic stage of a long history of increases in the payroll tax.

The payroll tax has risen much faster than other federal taxes. As a percentage of all federal tax receipts it has risen from 4 percent in 1949 to 30 percent in 1973. Now, the revenue from the payroll tax is equal to about 50 percent of the revenue from the federal income tax. Moreover, if one includes both the employer and employee portion of the payroll tax—on the grounds, argued above, that the employer portion is in fact shifted to the employee—over half the population pays more in payroll taxes than it does in federal income taxes.

Finally, given the regressivity of the payroll tax, the effects of the increases since 1969 have worked to shift the combined burden of the payroll—again assuming the worker pays both employer and employee tax—and federal income tax toward lower income families. For example, for families with incomes below $3,500 and for those with incomes between $9,000 and $13,000, the combined effect of changes in the payroll tax and reductions in the income tax have actually been to increase the total federal tax burden.[13] For the poorest—that is, those with in-

13. For details, see, Charles Schultze et al., *Setting National Priorities: the 1974 Budget* (Washington, D.C.: Brookings Institution, 1973), pp. 45–63.

comes below $3,500, who pay no federal income tax—the increases in the payroll tax have amounted to a 22 percent increase in their federal tax burden since 1969.

It should also be noted that the base earnings limit for the payroll tax will also be increased automatically with increases in the average wage level for all employees. In addition, the law has scheduled increases in the payroll tax rate for both employer and employee to 6.05 percent in 1978, to 6.30 percent in 1981 and to somewhat higher levels further in the future.

Supplemental Security Income

The most revolutionary shift in the Social Security structure was the creation of a new national program, starting in 1974, of financial assistance to low income persons 65 and over, the blind and the disabled. The program is called Supplemental Security Income (SSI). This program replaces federal and state programs of aid to the aged, blind and permanently and totally disabled. For an eligible person with no other income it will pay, as of July 1974, $146 a month—$1,752 annually—and $219—$2,628 annually—for a couple. The structure of benefits approximates that of a negative income tax in that, after a certain amount of excluded income, benefits are reduced by 50 cents for each additional dollar of income (see table 3 for an example). The provisions for determining eligibility are related to financial need, but are somewhat complex. The definition of what shall be counted as income is also complex.

The program will be fully federally administered by the Social Security administration and will be federally financed from general revenues. States will be allowed to add supplementary payments to the SSI benefits; furthermore, those state supplements will not be counted as income in determining the SSI benefits. Those who received SSI benefits may not participate in the federal food stamps program.

The SSI program represents a major step forward in income maintenance for the aged. Its major strong points are:

(1) In general, SSI will yield an increase in cash income for the aged poor.
(2) A national minimum income standard will be set for aged, blind and disabled. Under the previous federal and state programs minimum cash assistance levels were set by the states and varied considerably from state to state.
(3) Eligibility conditions for the program will be uniform across the nation. In the federal and state programs these conditions also varied across state lines.
(4) Administration of welfare programs for the aged will be simplified by consolidation in the single, national administrative structure. States may also opt to have the Social Security administration administer their state supplement programs.

The SSI program does have a number of features to which critics have pointed as potentially troublesome. I will deviate here, briefly, from the main line of development of this essay to sketch out these troublesome features.

Problems with the SSI structure can for the most part be traced to the fact that SSI is really a legacy of

TABLE 3

INCOME POSSIBILITIES FOR HYPOTHETICAL AGED COUPLE*

MTR	ERN($)	SS($)	SSI($)	SSET($)	FPIT($)	NI($)
	0	1700	1168	0	0	2868
.0585						
	780	1700	1168	46	0	3602
.5585						
	2400	1700	358	140	0	4318
.5585						
	4300	750	358	252	0	5156
.6985						
	5300	250	358	310	140	5458
.7085						
	5320	240	358	311	143	5464
.9585						
	5800	0	238	339	215	5484
.7085						
	6276	0	0	367	286	5623
.2085						
	6300	0	0	368	290	5642

SOURCE: Formulas used for the table are adapted from Michael Taussig, "The Social Security Retirement Program and Welfare Reform," in Studies in Public Welfare, U.S., Congress, Joint Economic Committee (Washington, D.C.: Government Printing Office, 1973), paper no. 7, p. 26, table 1.

DEFINITIONS: MTR: marginal tax rate on earnings; ERN: husband's annual earnings; SS: annual Social Security benefits; SSI: annual Supplementary Security Income benefits; SSET: annual employee payroll tax for Social Security; FPIT: annual federal personal income tax; NI: net income after transfer and taxes = ERN + SS + SSI − SSET − FPIT.

* Couple aged 65 to 71; no asset income; Social Security benefit entitlement $1,700 per year; only husband has earnings opportunity.

the Nixon administration's broader proposal for welfare reform—the Family Assistance Plan. When Congress finally rejected the proposals in that plan pertaining to the nonaged population, it decided to retain and pass into law the provisions designed to reform the welfare programs for the aged, blind and disabled; these provisions became the SSI program. Most of the shortcomings of SSI are ones which had been pointed out by critics of the more general Family Assistance Plan.[14] If reform of the aged,

14. Compare, for example, the extensive critique of SSI provided in, U.S., Congress, Joint Economic Committee, Studies in Public Welfare, paper no. 10, October 1973; and D. Lee Bawden et al., "The Family Assistance Plan: Analysis and Evaluation," Public Policy 19 (Spring 1971), pp. 323–354.

blind and disabled programs had been undertaken independently of the Family Assistance Plan, the resultant program would undoubtedly have been rather different in many details.

The basic problem in any welfare reform proposal lies in the potential conflicts between the goals of equity and those of appropriate incentives. In order to assure equity, one would like to have the program treat people who are in like circumstances in a similar fashion. The problem arises when one begins to define explicitly what are to be considered like circumstances. For example, when one begins to define what shall be considered income one must decide: should income in the form of Social

Security benefits be treated the same as, or different from, earnings; how should one take into account the potential or actual income from assets? As soon as rules are set regarding these questions, incentives are created for people to change the form of their income or assets in order to maximize their benefits or to minimize their penalties.

Examples of possible inequities or adverse incentives due to the rules adopted in SSI are numerous. For example, the rules allow $20 per month of income of any sort before reduction of benefits. Any unearned income above this amount results in one dollar reduction for each dollar of unearned income. For earned income, however, an additional $65 a month can be accrued without reduction of benefits, and after that benefits are reduced by 50 cents for each additional dollar earned. Thus, a single individual with only unearned income of $155 a month would receive an SSI payment of $11, whereas an individual with only $155 of earnings would receive $111 in SSI benefits. This will surely strike some people as inequitable.

At first glance, this sort of differentiation would appear to give strong incentives to work effort, since earned income is treated more generously than unearned income. However, the fact that SSI will be superimposed on a system which already includes payroll taxes, income taxes and reductions in benefits under the Social Security retirement test, means that for some the work incentives are quite adverse. This possibility is illustrated in table 3.

The case illustrated in table 3 is for a worker 65 and over and his wife with no income from assets and with Social Security benefits close to the minimum. The first column of table 3 gives the marginal tax rate at each level of income. This rate is the combined effect of the federal personal income tax, the employee's part of the Social Security tax, the implicit tax on SSI due to the reduction of benefits as income increases and the implicit tax due to the reduction of Social Security benefits under the retirement test. One can see, for example, that as earnings increase by $480 from $5,320 to $5,800, the actual net income of the couple would increase by only $20 from $5,464 to $5,484. This particularly high marginal tax rate, 96 percent, occurs because the retirement test and the SSI benefit reduction are both working in this range, as well as federal payroll and income taxes. Obviously, the financial incentive for work effort over this range is virtually nil.

One should note further that in this example the marginal tax on earnings is about 70 percent or more in the range of earnings from about $4,300 to $6,300. It is true that the structure of SSI was designed to improve on the work incentive features of the programs it replaced—for example, Old Age Assistance—but the population covered by SSI will be considerably larger; thus, the work disincentive features, though somewhat ameliorated, cover a far larger group. It is estimated that about 3.7 million aged persons will receive both SSI and Social Security benefits. This amounts to about 71 percent of the potential SSI eligibles, 25 percent of over-65 Social Security recipients and 18 percent of all persons over 65. Therefore, the example illustrated in table 3,

32 THE ANNALS OF THE AMERICAN ACADEMY

while it cannot be considered typical, does have some relevance for a substantial group of the aged.

Other problems of equity and incentive involving the treatment of assets for the purposes of eligibility, and the relationship of SSI to food stamps and Medicaid eligibility and the character of state supplementation have been pointed out, but there is not space here to go into the details.[15]

THE IMPORTANCE OF THE 1972 DEVELOPMENTS

The revisions in the Social Security program from 1969 through 1972 have had a profound effect on the character of the debate about the future of income maintenance for the aged. Several features of the changed context stand out.

The explosive burden of welfare

The conjuncture of rapid expansion of Social Security in the last few years and increased sensitivity to demographic trends has caused alarm in some quarters about the future costs of the Social Security system and the burden it will place on future workers. One analyst estimated: " . . . [if inflation continued at 2.75 percent and average wage levels grew at 5 percent per annum] and if Congress never again sweetens the program the maximum retirement benefit will rise to $7,236 in 1980 and will top $30,000 by the year 2010. Meanwhile the maximum contribution per worker will reach $8,288 with income up to $66,300 then subject to Social Security tax." The analyst does not, however, mention that if

those projections are correct, the average income level will also have risen over five times by the year 2010. She goes on to conclude:

The practice of providing retirees with far larger benefits than they contributed cannot continue indefinitely. At some point, the growing burden on the labor force will become both an economic and political time bomb. . . . The whole history of Social Security is a good example of how Government adopts policies that encourage consumers to spend while disregarding their effect on production and investment.[16]

Clearly, part of what motivates this sort of concern is the sharp increases in benefit levels in the last few years and the awareness that declining birth rates will have effects on the age structure of the population such that the ratio of persons over 65 to those in the working ages will increase. Some estimates of the age structure and labor force are presented in table 4. The aged dependency ratio is the ratio of those over 65 not in the labor force to the total labor force. The figures give a rough indication of the likely burden of the costs of the Social Security system on the working population in those years. The projections[17] do indicate a slowly increasing ratio up to the year 2000 and, subsequently, sharper rates of increase.

16. Mary J. Wilson, "Social Security: An Inflation Hedge?" *New York Times*, 13 January 1974.
17. It must be remembered that such projections are quite sensitive to assumptions made about how the labor force participation of the aged will change in the future. Since, as noted above, the decline in the aged male labor force participation rate has been particularly precipitous over the last two decades, assumptions about future aged labor force participation rates are particularly difficult to make with any confidence.

15. For detailed discussions of these points, see, Joint Economic Committee, paper no. 10.

TABLE 4

DEPENDENCY RATIOS

	1972	1980	2000	2020
Aged dependency*	.18	.19	.20	.25
Total dependency*	1.36	1.19	1.10	1.12

SOURCE: The underlying population projection for the dependency ratios are from Census Series E, which is the lowest population growth projection. The labor force participation projections and dependency ratios are from Dennis Johnston, "Illustrative Projections of the Labor Force in the U.S. to 2040" in *Economic Aspects of Population Change*, Commission on Population Growth and the American Future, research reports vol. II, p. 172, table 5.

* Aged dependency: persons 65 and over not in the labor force/total labor force; total dependency: all persons not in the labor force/total labor force.

When assessing the potential burden of future workers, however, one should also take into account the magnitude of other claims. The shifting age structure does mean a higher portion of aged, but it also means a lower portion of the population in the youngest—0 to 18—age groups, which also make dependency claims on the working population. The total dependency ratio gives a crude indication of the overall dependency burden on future workers. The projections show that this ratio will decline sharply to the year 2000, and that even in 2020 it will still be considerably below the dependency ratios of the present and the recent past. While the relative burden of Social Security costs will rise, it is likely that the social costs of programs associated with the younger dependency groups will fall relatively. I know of no study which attempts to assess future costs of Social Security in the context of likely costs of other social programs, but the above crude indicators suggest that

alarm about explosive Social Security costs needs to be balanced by more realistic assessments of overall social costs.

The relative income position of the aged

While concern about the future costs of Social Security appears to have been growing as a result of recent developments, relatively little attention has been focused on the fact that the recent increases in benefits reflect a fundamental shift in the implicit social judgment about what the relative income position of the aged portion of the population should be. Since 1968 the relationship between average covered earnings before 65 and benefits has been increased by over 50 percent.

In 1968 it was estimated that a single retiree who had worked in manufacturing would qualify for Social Security benefits equal to about 0.29 of his earnings in manufacturing the year before retirement—this sort of figure is referred to as the replacement ratio. By January of 1972 it was estimated that a single retiree who had been working in manufacturing would have a replacement ratio of 0.34.[18] My rough calculation is that by July 1974 a single manufacturing retiree would have a Social Security benefit equal to 0.38 of his wage in

18. The 1968 and 1972 replacement ratios are cited as they were reported by the National Retired Teachers Association and the American Association of Retired Persons in *Future Directions*, part 5, pp. 334–342. The replacement ratio is lower than the ratio of benefits to average covered earnings because, in general, the earnings of a worker in the year prior to retirement will be greater than the average over the period of his covered earnings. Thus, the denominator for the replacement ratio is larger than for the ratio of benefits to average covered earnings.

the year prior to retirement. This, then, amounts to a rise of 30 percent in the replacement ratio for such workers. While some feel that a replacement ratio of 0.38 is still too low, the 30 percent rise in this ratio over six years represents a substantial improvement in the relative income position of such over-65 workers.

SSI absorbs one of the basic Social Security functions

In reviewing the shortcomings of the system as constructed before 1972, it was noted that one of the two basic functions of the system was to redistribute income within cohorts of the aged so that some sort of income floor would be provided for the poorest. This, however, is exactly the function of the SSI program. With the creation of SSI—a uniform national low income support program for the aged—we now have two separate policy instruments with which to perform the two functions that the single Social Security program had previously sought to perform. SSI makes a good part of the income redistribution functions of the Social Security system redundant. Rather than having to live with a system compromised in its ability to perform either of its functions fully because of the constraints imposed by the other function, it is now conceptually possible not only to fashion each program to perform a single function effectively, but also to integrate the programs rationally.

The cost of Social Security myths has risen

The price which society pays for maintaining the myth of Social Security as an insurance program has risen substantially as a result

of the changes initiated around 1972. In order to finance the rise in benefits and extension in coverage, it has been necessary to raise sharply the level of the payroll tax. The burden of the payroll tax on the lower income groups has, as noted above, been substantially increased. The Congress could have financed all or some of these changes through general revenues, thus placing less of the burden on lower income workers. In choosing to stick with a Social Security tax as the basic financing instrument, Congress has forced the low income worker to shoulder a heavy burden in order to maintain the appearance of a social insurance program.

While the level of earnings at which the retirement test begins to reduce earnings has been increased considerably and the 100 percent marginal tax on earnings caused by the retirement test over a segment of the earnings range has been removed, the fact that benefits have increased means that the range of earnings over which the retirement test will be reducing earnings—and thereby operating as a marginal tax rate—has also been increased.[19] Therefore, the cost—in

19. With the earnings test in effect in 1970 and the single worker minimum benefit at that time, the retirement test would have operated to reduce benefits for anyone with earnings between $140 and $250 per month. For someone with the maximum equivalent of the current maximum—that is, the current maximum discounted by the percentage legislative increase since 1970—the retirement test operated for monthly earnings between $140 and $350. With the current retirement test, at the minimum single worker benefit the retirement test on earnings operates between $200 and $388 per month in earnings and at the maximum benefit it operates between $200 and $591 per month in earnings. Thus, the range over which the implicit marginal tax rate in the retirement test operates has been expanded.

terms of adverse work incentives —of "proving" by means of the retirement test that the system is an earnings replacement system has increased.

PRIESTS AND REFORMERS

The 1972 amendments and related developments are viewed rather differently by the priests of Social Security and the Johnny-come-lately-reformers.

The priests' view

The originators of the Social Security system and the supporters of the concepts as originally conceived—many of whom have done yeoman labor in the administration of the program, in congressional lobbying for it and in academic analysis of it—are those I will characterize as the priests of Social Security, in part because their rhetoric takes on priestly tones and often involves many appeals to the original scriptures of the founding fathers of the system. In general, the priests see aspects of the 1972 amendments as realizations of their fondest hopes; in their eyes the system has matured and reached its finest flowering. They feel this is so primarily because: (1) the 1972 developments have broadened the coverage of the system to include nearly all workers and classes of dependents; (2) benefit levels have been substantially increased and brought near to a level which might be deemed adequate relative to general living standards; and (3) indexing of the benefit levels—that is, increases coming automatically with price level rises—provides systematic protection against inflation.

The priests appear somewhat uneasy about the creation of the Supplementary Security Income program. They recognized the need to do something about the patchwork of federal and state programs of old age assistance and aid to the blind and disabled. However, they fear that SSI may perhaps be a mistake, particularly because it is to be administered by the Social Security administration. Since it is a means-tested program—that is, in order to determine eligibility and benefits, income and assets, or means, must be determined—it may contaminate the image of the Social Security administration. As long as those programs were largely run by the states, Social Security was not touched by the stigma of welfare; now, with SSI, the carefully preserved distinction between Social Security as social insurance and the other programs as welfare is perhaps blurred in the public mind. The priests could not very well fight hard against the passage of SSI, since it clearly meant a rise in cash income for many aged persons, so they have accepted it with what I perceive to be less than great enthusiasm.

The reformers' view

The Johnny-come-lately reformers are social analysts, primarily economists, whose interest in the problems of Social Security has increased considerably in recent years—thus, the priests call them Johnny-come-latelys. They tend to look at the program as one form of income redistribution, both within generations and across generations, and to put considerable weight on technical concepts of efficiency and equity. In their view the changes in the system related to the 1972 amendments have heightened the contradictions already inherent in the pre-1972 structure and have brought into sharper relief the high costs of the social myths upon which the system is said to be constructed, as well as the fact that those costs are borne in particular by lower income persons. The raising of the payroll tax in order to finance higher benefits has, in their view, broadened the scope of regressive federal taxation and, combined with the reductions in the federal income tax—which is more progressive in its impact—has made the overall structure of federal taxation more regressive.

The rise in benefits has, as noted above, spread the negative work disincentives caused by the implicit tax over a broader range of older persons. The retirement test is repugnant to reformers not only because of its negative work disincentives, but also because of its inequitable impact. For example, those over 65 who must rely on earnings as a major additional source of income receive reduced Social Security benefits; yet, other income—of the same, or greater, amounts—from nonearnings sources leaves Social Security benefits unaffected.[20]

Finally, the introduction of SSI, in the view of the reformers, makes

the redistributive features of the Social Security benefit structure redundant. Now, they argue, the myth that the single, unitary system can adequately serve both the income maintenance and intergenerational transfer functions is dispensable, and each element—SSI and Social Security—can be reformed to serve its single function more effectively.

Point and counter-point on reform

The Johnny-come-lately reformers argue that, first and foremost, it should be explicitly recognized that Social Security is not insurance. Once this fact is recognized, the system can be financed through a more progressive system of taxation. There are a number of proposals for achieving a more progressive form of financing,[21] but I will not attempt to spell them out here, especially since the main argument can be simply stated:

It is misleading to think of payroll taxes as individual contributions destined to be returned to the contributor at a later date; it is far more accurate to think of the social security system as a national pension scheme, whose benefit levels are determined by the national priority accorded to the needs of the retired, the disabled and survivors and whose costs are paid for by a tax on current earners. Once this point of view is accepted, there is no logical reason why the tax used to support the pension system should impose hardship on the poor. The arguments for financing pensions out of a progressive tax that exempts the poor are just as strong as those for

20. The estimated cost of removing the retirement test is about $4 billion annually which, if financed by the payroll tax, would require adding about one-fourth of a percentage point to both the employee and employer contributions. To the extent that removal of the retirement test did result in increased earnings among the aged, some of these tax costs would be recovered through the federal payroll and income taxes. Proposals have also been put forward to make all income, regardless of source, subject to the retirement test. This has been rejected by the priests because, among other reasons, "the idea that Social Security benefits are intended as a partial replacement of earnings from work would be diluted or lost." See, National Retired Teachers report in *Future Directions*, part 5, p. 379.

21. See, Michael Taussig, "The Social Security Retirement Program and Welfare Reform," in *Studies in Public Welfare*, U.S., Congress, Joint Economic Committee (Washington, D.C.: Government Printing Office, 1973), paper no. 7, pp. 37–38; Schultze et al., *Setting National Priorities*, pp. 57–64; Brittain, *Payroll Tax*, chap. 5.

financing other government expenditures in this way.[22]

The reply of the priests of Social Security to this argument deserves quotation at length, both because it is not easily summarized and because it is important to have a sense of the quality of the rhetoric. Professor J. Douglas Brown of Princeton University, one of the founding fathers of Social Security, comments:

To understand the effectiveness of contributory social insurance in meeting human risks, it is necessary to treat it as an integrated mechanism. Wage earners are willing to contribute because they will receive benefits as a matter of right when they or their families need them most. For centuries, working people have learned that one cannot get something for nothing; at least, you cannot count on it . . .

Contributions and benefits in social insurance are not separable entities, artificially stuck together, but are, rather, inseparable, interlocking elements in a single concept. Without this interlock, you end up with a program of doles financed by general taxation. It was such a scheme, under the name of the Townsend Plan, which we were desperately seeking to avoid in 1934-35 . . . This close integration of contributions and benefits in the concept of contributory social insurance, paying benefits as a matter of right, is the reason why those of us who have worked longest in the development of the OASDI [Social Security] program oppose altering the rate of contribution for lower income participants according to some ancillary test of need.

That is, Brown is saying, to finance more progressively would be to introduce a means test, undercutting the contributory insurance feeling workers have:

You see where our differences lie. I am also convinced that the feeling of self-respect is vital to social insurance to make it work. People are willing to pay these payroll taxes because it gives them a feeling of self-reliance . . . The association of the benefit with the payment or a contribution which makes it a matter of right, is a powerful mystique. It is an integral part of the concept of Social Security.[23]

The Johnny-come-lately-reformers, in turn, put forward another proposal. All right, they say, if the contributory principle is central to the viability of the Social Security system, let us explicitly recognize it and, then, follow it correctly by splitting the two functions of the system. SSI can be improved and take the place of the income maintenance function of Social Security. The Social Security benefits can be closely related to payroll taxes actually paid over the working lifetime prior to 65. There would be no skewing of the benefits toward the low income workers: their special needs would be met through SSI. After the age of 65 all workers would receive benefits which would be the same proportion of their paid payroll tax. The system would operate as a federalized pension insurance program. There would be no retirement test, since the federal pension would simply reflect past payroll tax payments. This dual system of Social Security for pensions and SSI for low income needs determined by the worker's current income from all sources would perform the two functions of the current system with greater efficiency and equity; moreover, neither function would be compromised by the constraints of the other. The issue

22. Schultze et al., *Setting National Priorities*, p. 60.

23. J. Douglas Brown, "Statement," in *Future Directions*, part 3, pp. 188–202.

of the regressivity of the payroll tax would evaporate, since benefits would be strictly tied to the tax.[24]

The priests of Social Security respond in horror to such a proposal. With respect to the aspect of an improved, separate SSI, Wilbur Cohen—former secretary of health, education and welfare—stated:

I . . . oppose any wholesale substitute for the social security system, whatever its name (such as a negative income tax, a guaranteed income or what have you) that makes payments only to the poor. A program for the poor will most likely be a poor program.[25]

J. Douglas Brown conjures more vivid imagery to counter the reformers' proposals to tinker with the time-tested system:

It is said that a panel of aerodynamicists, after careful research, found that the wings of the bumblebee provided insufficient lift to support the bumblebee in flight. It is fortunate that the bumblebee, in its million years of evolution, did not know about this scientifically determined shortcoming.

The aerodynamicists made two mistakes.

One, they intensively examined the bumblebee's wings without taking the time to understand the way a whole, live bumblebee functions.

Two, they failed to realize that living things, through long response and adjustment to conditions, develop the capacity to do what is necessary for effective survival . . .

As with bumblebees, so with many social institutions, if they are dissected into their separate parts, those parts appear to a specialist to be ill-designed and unworkable. But through long evolution as integrated entities, the institutions have gained a mysterious capacity to survive and function effectively.

Among such social institutions are the Government of the United States, the U.S. Constitution, the U.S. Senate, the Roman Catholic Church, Harvard University, and contributory social insurance. Of these, only the Catholic Church is older than the early beginnings of the contributory mutual benefit associations for the protection of workers out of which social insurance systems developed.[26]

This brings us to the central tenet of the priests of Social Security. A system which explicitly recognizes the separate functions of the current system—shifting funds from earnings to later life on the one hand and income maintenance on the other—will be socially divisive. The system must be shrouded in the social myth of contributory social insurance in order to operate. If one makes explicit the system's functions, the system will become a political football. The social myth exacts a price—that is, it is a regressive system in which the poor bear a disproportionate burden to support that myth; however, they argue, if one removes the myth, the social contract will dissolve.

George Rohrlich comments: "In a nutshell, what one finds lagging, if not altogether missing, in our current notion of distributive justice is a sense of social solidarity."[27] The priests seem to be saying: the

24. Taussig, "Social Security Reform," pp. 29–35, spells out the details of this dual system quite clearly, drawing on earlier work by James Buchanan, "Social Insurance in a Growing Economy: A Proposal for Radical Reform," National Tax Journal 21, no. 4 (December 1968), pp. 386–395.
25. Wilbur Cohen, as cited in Wilbur Cohen and Milton Friedman, Social Security: Universal or Selective? (Washington, D.C.: National Debate Seminars, American Enterprise Institute for Public Policy Research, 1972), p. 12.

26. Brown, "Statement," p. 189.
27. George Rohrlich, "The Place of Social Insurance in the Pursuit of the General Welfare," Journal of Risk and Insurance 36, no. 4 (September 1969), p. 348.

whole ingenious structure of Social Security is fragile; thus, do not tamper with, do not be excessively tidy about the details of, the system. If it were made clear to the general public either that the system is an intergenerational transfer mechanism—the young supporting the old in each period, which is the essence of the reformers' first proposal—or that the system redistributes income within the aged cohort from high earners to low earners—which is essential to the reformers' second, dual system proposal—social conflict will emerge, and the system will disintegrate. It is working, they argue, so leave it alone.

CONFIDENCE MEN AND SOCIAL INSTITUTIONS

Is the social myth a necessity? This is the deep issue in the debate over Social Security, the possible kernel of truth to be found in the warnings of the priests of Social Security not to ignore the original scriptures. What is the cement which holds together a social system? What is necessary to avoid conflict between the young and the old or the rich and the poor? Must we have the confidence man in order to build social institutions? While I would like to think not, I cannot argue the point with much persuasion.

Melville, whose whole book plays with the ambiguities of confidence—both private and public—concludes his work:

The cosmopolitan [talking to an old man] said sadly: "Though this is a theme on which travellers seldom talk to each other, yet, to you, sir, I will say, that I share something of your sense of security. I have moved much about the world, and still keep at it; nevertheless, though in this land, and especially in

these parts of it, some stories are told . . . to make one a little apprehensive, yet I may say that, neither by land nor by water am I ever seriously disquieted, however, at times, transiently uneasy, since, with you, sir, I believe in a Committee of Safety, holding silent sessions over all, in an invisible patrol, most alert when we soundest sleep, . . . In short, I never forget that passage of Scripture which says "Jehovah shall be thy confidence." The traveller who has not this trust, what miserable misgivings must be his; or, what vain, short-sighted care must he take of himself."

"Even so," said the old man lowly . . . "let me see;—is there anything I have forgot? Something I . . . remember. Something, my son . . . told me this morning . . . something before I got into my berth . . . Something for safety . . ."

"Let me give a little guess, sir. Life-preserver?"

"So it was . . . said the boat supplied them, too. But where are they? I don't see any. What are they like?"

"They are something like this sir, I believe," lifting a brown stool with a curved tin compartment underneath; "yes, this, I think, is a life-preserver, sir; and a very good one, I should say, though I don't pretend to know much about such things, never using them myself."

"Why, indeed now! who would have thought it? *that* a life-preserver? That's the very stool I was sitting on, ain't it?"

"It is. And that shows that one's life is looked out for, when he ain't looking out for it himself. In fact any of these stools here will float you, sir, should the boat . . . go down . . . But since you want one in your room, pray take this one!" handing it to him. "I think I can recommend this one; the tin part," rapping it with his knuckles, "seems so perfect—sounds very hollow."

"Sure it's *quite* perfect though?" Then, anxiously putting on his spectacles . . . "well soldered? quite tight?"

"I should say so, sir; though indeed, as I said, I never use this sort of thing myself. Still, I think that in case of a wreck . . . you could have confidence in that stool for a special providence."

"Then, good-night, good-night; and Providence have both of us in its good keeping."

"Be sure it will," eyeing the old man with sympathy, as for the moment he stood, money-belt in hand, and life preserver under arm, "be sure it will, sir, since in Providence, as in man, you and I equally put trust. But, bless me, we are being left in the dark here" . . .

"Ah, my way now," cried the old man, peering before him . . .

"I have indifferent eyes, and will show you" . . .

The next moment, the waning light expired . . . while in the darkness which ensued, the cosmopolitan kindly led the old man away. Something further may follow of this Masquerade.

Rational Planning and Organizational Imperatives: Prospects for Area Planning in Aging

By ROBERT B. HUDSON

ABSTRACT: The federal grant strategy found in the Older Americans Comprehensive Services Amendments of 1973 represents a marked departure from earlier strategies of the Older Americans Act. While the national goal of the legislation is more clearly specified and funding has significantly increased, the introduction of new substate planning bodies—Area Agencies on Aging—is seen here as the most important change. The new national strategy is geared toward the development of these new agencies, and its success will depend very much on their discharging the functions assigned to them. This paper argues that, because the new legislative strategy is based on a rational goal model and conceptualizes the area agencies accordingly, it neglects certain requisites of organizational life. Using, instead, a social system perspective of the area agencies and their environment, the paper suggests that these agencies will, of necessity, concern themselves with matters other than those mandated in the legislation. These other concerns will affect both the national objectives which the area agencies choose to emphasize and the intensity of their effort. Specifically, the area agencies may view the mandate to draw-in and mobilize resources at the area level as not in their organizational interests. The paper concludes that: their engaging in this role in tentative fashion will result in either incremental or goal-displaced activities; their embarking in this role wholeheartedly may prove dangerous to them organizationally and may result in substantial modifications in the national strategy and their role in it.

Robert B. Hudson is Assistant Professor of Politics and Social Welfare at the Florence Heller Graduate School for Advanced Studies in Social Welfare of Brandeis University. He is also Project Director of a five-year nationwide study of the state aging agencies. Professor Hudson received his Ph.D. in political science from the University of North Carolina at Chapel Hill.

A S explicitly goal-oriented statements, laws are conventionally evaluated in terms of their real or potential effectiveness in attaining stated goals. The needs which goals are designed to meet are transformed into objectives, and procedural steps are spelled out to insure that activities and resources are allocated in ways functional for goal attainment. To the extent that procedures and allocations are not closely tied to goals, there is a presumption that effectiveness is impaired. Exclusive attention to the question of goal attainment may contain its own costs, however. These lie principally in the goal model's basing the prescriptive dictum that activities not tied to goal attainment are dysfunctional on the empirical assumption that relevant actors will totally preoccupy themselves with attainment of the goal.

The new Title III strategy of the Older Americans Act is premised largely on such a goal model. Its being successfully implemented rests in large part on the validity of the assumptions which the goal model makes about individual and organizational behavior. This paper examines implications of the new aging legislation in these terms and offers another perspective from which to view and anticipate agency activity. This second perspective calls into question some of the assumptions on which the new legislation is based, focusing particular attention on a major ambiguity in the mandate to the new agencies being brought into existence to plan for aging services.

THE NEW SERVICE STRATEGY

The Older Americans Comprehensive Services Amendments are the latest federal attempt to devise a system which will insure the delivery of coordinated services to the aging population. The new amendments differ from earlier versions of the Older Americans Act in that they set national priorities for service delivery, authorize the expenditure of significant new funds and call for the establishment of a new level of planning agencies within the states. Each of these changes—in mandate, funding and structure—represents marked departures from earlier legislation. Here, the establishment of the Area Agencies on Aging is seen as the most critical development. Responsibility for service planning falls to these new State Agencies on Aging, with the existing state agencies on aging now to be one step removed and to be charged with monitoring the area agencies and serving in a more general advocacy role at the state level.

Under previous authorizations— those of 1965, 1967 and 1969 —the federal Administration on Aging was not empowered to set specific national objectives. Furthermore, the listing of older Americans' needs was so general and encompassing that it could scarcely begin to serve as an operational guide to those charged with working under the act. Additionally, the state agencies were required to pass down to the community level very much the larger portion of the formula grant funds which they received. As appropriations grew, the state agencies found themselves under increasing political pressure to distribute these funds on a roughly proportional basis in their states. These factors combined to produce a fragmented program in which resources were badly diluted.[1]

The 1973 Title III program is more tightly integrated administratively, and there is greater congruence between goals and resources. A two-part national goal is established through which federal, state and area agencies will be working to: (1) "secure and maintain maximum independence and dignity in a home environment for older persons capable of self-care with appropriate supportive services"; and (2) "remove individual and social barriers to economic and personal independence for older persons" (sec. 301). The law specifies target populations—poor and minority group older persons—who are to receive priority attention, and the concentration of these target populations is to be used in determining which of a state's planning and service areas are to receive priority designation. Those parts of the states designated as priority areas are to receive special planning grants for development of a comprehensive and coordinated network of services. In addition, these areas will receive a disproportionate percentage of the formula grant funds which come to the states for services, and they will receive these funds on a generous 90-10 matching basis.

1. For discussions of earlier experiences under earlier versions of the Title III grant program, see, Robert H. Binstock, *Planning* (Washington, D.C.: White House Conference on Aging, 1971); Bernard Greenblatt and Theodore Ernst, "The Title III Program: Field Impressions and Policy Options," *Gerontologist* 12 (1972) pp. 191-196; and Robert B. Hudson, "Client Politics and Federalism: The Case of the Older Americans Act" (Paper presented at the Annual Meeting of the American Political Science Association, New Orleans, Louisiana, 4 September 1973).

Recognizing that even this substantially increased funding alone is not sufficient to provide for the full range of services older persons will need to remain in a home environment, the law and regulations also place heavy emphasis on pooling "untapped resources of public and private agencies."[2] In this regard the area agencies are to serve variously as catalysts, organizers and advocates in order "to make existing service systems more effective and accessible to the elderly, and to marshall and expand existing resources on behalf of the elderly to the maximum extent possible."[3] The intended cumulative effect of resources which are drawn in and those made available through Title III appropriations is to reorient existing service systems, to tap additional resources for the purposes of improving and inaugurating new services and to insure access for older persons to all of these.

DEVELOPMENT OF THE AREA AGENCIES

Procedurally, development of the area agencies will follow through several steps. To bring the area agencies into existence, the state agencies are charged with: (1) seeing that the state establishes planning and service areas—which may or may not correspond to other substate planning jurisdictions— for purposes of aging planning;

2. *Federal Register* 8, no. 196 (11 October 1973), p. 28049.

3. Administration on Aging, "Proposed Strategy for Implementing the State and Area Programs of the Administration of Aging under The Older Americans Act in FY 1973 and Beyond," mimeographed, (March 1972), p. 21.

(2) determining which of these areas should be designated as high priority—that is, eligible for special funding for both planning and services; (3) determining what type of agency or organization is to be designated as an area agency—either public or private nonprofit; and (4) making the initial planning grant to such an agency for purposes of comprehensive aging planning.

The staff of the new agency is to develop an area plan designed to develop comprehensive and coordinated programs and to carry out the following major functions, among others:

—provide leadership,
—determine needs,
—inventory resources,
—establish "measurable" program objectives,
—plan with existing planning agencies,
—through contract or grant, (a) coordinate delivery of existing services and (b) pool untapped resources of public and private agencies.[4]

In order for the plan which the area agency submits to be approved by the state agency, it must provide for a "continuous process of planning," the coordination of existing resources and the pooling of untapped resources.

There are, however, restrictions on the uses to which these funds can be put. The area agency is not to use these funds to provide services itself, but is to plan for, and oversee the implementation of, services by other providers. As to what services:

[A] State agency may award funds to include as part of the area plan, support for those service programs

4. *Federal Register*, p. 28050.

found necessary to assist older persons to become aware of the social services available in the area (information and referral and outreach services), and to assist them in having access to these services (transportation and escort services), and support for other social services needed by older persons, but which no public and private agencies of the area can or will provide.[5]

The intent of these restrictions is to insure that the funds available under the Title III authorization are used expressly for services seen as requisite for older persons' being able to maintain themselves in a home environment.

Information about services which are available and the means of gaining access to them are deemed essential for this purpose. Only when these are assured can funds be used for other purposes. The additional services the area agency can fund are limited to "gap-filling"—namely, those which will more fully integrate the existing service system.

Beyond these service areas, remaining funds are to be used for coordinating the service system and pooling untapped resources. How this is to be done is left quite open, apart from the "special emphasis" which is to be given to social service funds under the Social Security Act, revenue sharing, other titles of the Older Americans Act—VI and VII[6]—and the infor-

5. Ibid., p. 28050.
6. The Title VII Nutrition for the Elderly program is the other major grant program to the states under the Older Americans Act. While nutrition grants are made by the state agencies directly to the providers, the state agencies are to fold-in these grants with area plans, where the latter are in effect. Title VII is, nonetheless, much more of a traditional categorical grant program than the new Title III and is not analyzed in this paper.

mation and referral services of the Social Security district offices.[7] The charge here, however, is to go beyond what the funds available under Title III will provide. The central purpose of these nonservice stipulations is to bring greater resources—in the form of both funds and services—to bear on the needs of the noninstitutionalized aging. By improving existing services and generating resources for new ones, this mobilizing or drawing-in charge will allow expansion of the service network and will help to assure the continuation of programs at such time as federal support is withdrawn.[8]

The mandate to the new area agencies thus consists of several components. While they are all geared to the self-support goal for older persons, they involve overseeing development of specific support services, improving upon and coordinating the existing service network and locating additional resources for purposes of inaugurating new programs. Having briefly outlined the purposes of the legislation and this charge to the area agencies, examination of how the area agencies will go about implementing their multifaceted charge remains. In spite of the detailed fashion with which certain of the agencies' functions are spelled out, choices—involving which tasks to emphasize, what strategies to use and how to interrelate work on the different components—will have to be made.

THE EMPHASIS ON RATIONAL PLANNING

By carefully laying out objectives, concentrating resources and suggesting procedures as to how they can most effectively be related to one another, the new strategy improves markedly on its predecessors. Funds are no longer to be dispensed on a nearly proportional basis, but rather are to be applied in a concentrated and goal-directed manner. Critics, both in and outside government, of earlier activity sponsored by Older Americans Act funds, called for greater rationalization in the program; the latest version sets out explicitly to accomplish this. Great care is taken in linking Title III appropriations and resources presumably available in the substate planning areas to program objectives which, taken together, will further the overall legislative goal. The task is laid out, and the area agencies are being established expressly to implement it.[9]

The strength of a rational planning model lies in its emphasis on goal attainment. Goals are first established, and particular procedural steps which will lead toward the accomplishment of the goal are then settled. Because goal attainment remains the paramount concern, resource application can be undertaken efficiently: the criterion for determining the utility of particular resources is their functionality for the goal. The alternatives may be numerous, but constant recognition of the goal allows for the employment of a reasonably unambiguous decisional guide.

7. For this and other specific tasks set out for the area agencies, see, Administration on Aging, *Area Plan Application Format* (October 1973).

8. Only under exceptional circumstances are Title III funds to be forthcoming beyond a three year period for any given service in a priority area. *Federal Register*, p. 28051.

9. For a brief discussion of how models formulated for purposes of scientific investigation have been employed in the applied field, see, Roland L. Warren, *Truth, Love, and Social Change* (Chicago, Ill.: Rand McNally, 1971), pp. 56–58.

As in the case of any model, the validity of the rational planning model lies in the assumptions on which it is predicated. Critical to the rational planning model are the assumptions which it makes about the motivations underlying the actions of relevant actors. There is a presumption that maximization of the stated goals will be the principal factor guiding the behavior of those involved. If other concerns are acknowledged, they are not explicitly recognized. Behavior and resource allocations which are premised on values other than maximizing goal attainment cannot be readily accommodated or justified. As Etzioni remarks: "The fact that an organization can become more effective by allocating less means to goal activities is a paradox."[10]

A goal model is essentially non-behavioral. It takes a very particular view of the individual actors and organizations which are called on to bring about the desired goal. Actors are conceived as tools or instruments to be used in the realization of the goal. This metaphorical depiction raises the critical, but unanswered, question of the goal model: used by whom? That, within the goal model, actors are not used by each other represents the model's major shortcoming. The question asked by the goal model is not by whom, but rather for what. These two queries are not simply different ways of asking essentially the same question. Etzioni isolates the distance between them in observing that: "Goals, as norms, as sets of meanings depicting target states, are cultural entities. Organi-

zations, as systems of coordinated activities of more than one actor, are social systems."[11]

By eliminating other behavioral determinants, the goal model risks inability to account for a wide variety of activity—much of which may take place in the name of planning. Goals may frequently be cited as measures of organizational effectiveness, but concerns other than goal attainment must be acknowledged if valid assessments are to be made of organizational potential. The rational goal model's shortcomings rest in its inability to account for these additional motivations. Roland Warren states its limitations concisely:

In the abstract-rational model for planning, the substantive aspects are abstracted from the total situation; the political aspects are considered extraneous; rational calculation is confined to the substantive aspects, tends to be organized into discrete units, and is final-state oriented; the action system and the planning system do not coincide, and the tendency is toward monastic decision-making."[12]

GOALS AS ADAPTIVE MECHANISMS

In order for the behavior of organizations to be more adequately anticipated, a second approach is required. This approach would allow accommodation of organizational activity, predicated on a basis other than that of pursuing a goal conceived as bringing about change in a situation external to that organization. Most basically, such an approach would view an organization as in some sense greater than the goals it is pursuing. It would call for recognizing the variety of different agendas the actors in-

10. Amitai Etzioni, "Two Approaches to Organizational Analysis: A Critique and a Suggestion," *Administrative Science Quarterly* 5 (September 1960), p. 269.

11. Ibid., p. 258.
12. Warren, *Truth*, p. 59.

volved may have and, toward that end, understanding what motivates actors to behave in particular ways.

This can be done by approaching organizations as sets of actors existing and interacting in particular environments. From this perspective organizational activity is conditioned by the position the organization wishes to occupy vis-à-vis different elements in that environment and, conversely, by the way in which those elements wish to position themselves toward it. The environment imposes on any organization various constraints, both positive and negative, with which it must deal.[13] All organizations—whether they service, sell or plan—must have external support to exist. To get support, organizations must be perceived as functional by those on whose support they depend; to maintain it, they must demonstrate that they perform the sanctioned roles in a more desirable fashion than any would-be competitor.

Treating the organization in system terms need not necessarily imply that an organization's only concern is survival. A second subtype of the systems approach speaks to the effectiveness of an organization in carrying out its activities. "[An effectiveness model] defines a pattern of interrelations among the elements of the system which would make it most effective in the service of a given goal."[14] Using the survival model, activities are either functional or nonfunctional; with the effectiveness model, activities are evaluated in terms of their furthering a particular goal.[15]

What is common to both of these subtypes is that activities or goals are a primary means organizations employ to establish themselves in their environments. They are critical to both existence and role definition. "The goal-setting problem . . . is essentially determining a relationship of the organization to the larger society, which in turn becomes a question of what the society (or elements within it) wants done or can be persuaded to support."[16] To the extent that organizations must demonstrate that their activities are functional for the ends of those who are supporting them, the two models will converge.

An organization, however, is by no means totally confined by the demands placed on it by others. It may initiate certain activities on its own which will serve to generate support from other sources. Its ability "to carve out policy space"[17] in this manner may, in fact, give it rather wide latitude in dealing with others. Setting goals independent of particular pressures or inducements from the environment is a major component of organizational

13. For a discussion of organizations as social systems, see, S. N. Eisenstadt, "Bureaucracy, Bureaucratization, and De-bureaucratization," *Administrative Science Quarterly* 1 (December 1959), pp. 302–320. Environmental factors are addressed in William R. Dill, "The Impact of Environment on Organizational Development," in *Concepts and Issues in Administrative Behavior*, ed. Sidney Mailick and Edward H. Van Ness (Englewood Cliffs, N.J.: Prentice-Hall, 1962), pp. 94–109.

14. Etzioni, "Two Approaches," pp. 271–272.

15. Ibid.

16. James D. Thompson and William J. McEwen, "Organizational Goals and Environment: Goal-Setting as an Interaction Process," *American Sociological Review* 23 (February 1958), p. 23.

17. For a discussion of policy space and its meaning to organizations, see, Arnold J. Meltsner, "Political Feasibility and Policy Analysis," *Public Administration Review* 32 (November/December 1972), pp. 859–867.

strength. In the instance of strength, as well as weakness, the determination is still relational. In the former case, it happens that the one organization possesses certain resources—information, expertise, legitimacy, funds, clients—which other actors value. If they wish to gain access to such resources, they will have to modify their activities to suit the stronger party.

The overall point in viewing organizations in system terms is that: (1) organizations must take cognizance of their setting if they wish to survive and prosper; and (2) their choice of goal—here conceived as particular ways of altering elements of their environment—is at once a consequence of that environment and a means of shaping it. "An organization can survive so long as it adjusts to its situation; whether the process of adjustment is awkward or nimble becomes important in determining the organization's degree of prosperity."[18]

Viewing the Area Agencies on Aging in this manner puts the new Older Americans Act strategy in a different perspective than that outlined earlier. In that configuration the area agencies were conceptualized as organizations established for the express purpose of implementing a national goal strategy through a series of developmental procedural steps. Funds would be made available to the new agencies for purposes of initiating selected services, and they would also be encouraged to mobilize other resources which might be available in their more immediate setting.

In the social system model the area agencies become organizations established by superordinate actors on whose support they are totally dependent. This being the sole source of their support, they must conform to the demands which these actors make upon them. Should the area agencies wish to free themselves from these constraints, it would be incumbent upon them to develop support from other sources. Only in this way would they be able to pursue activities not mandated by federal or state aging officials.

ANTICIPATING AREA AGENCY BEHAVIOR

This situation raises a variety of questions about how the area agencies can be expected to develop and what effect different courses they may take will have on the new national goal. For the area agencies a first concern must be the manner in which they wish to internalize the programmatic demands which have been developed for purposes of carrying out the new aging strategy. The legislation and guidelines detail a series of tasks, all of which are presumably required. Yet, there are choices, at least of emphasis, which must be made.

For the area agencies the most important of these will be deciding what priority to give to establishing the linkage services[19] spelled out in the legislation relative to the more general, but highly valued, role of mobilizer of area resources. The national strategy depicts these as interrelated tasks to be carried out concurrently and in support of each other, but they represent more dis-

18. Thompson and McEwen, "Organizational Goals," p. 25.

19. I use the term linkage services to refer to the support and gap-filling services mandated in the 1973 amendments.

tinct alternatives to the area agencies.

Development of the linkage network is marked by three notable characteristics. First of all, the manner in which it is to be set up is spelled out in considerable detail. Information and referral, transportation and support services are isolated as specific services which must be provided in all priority areas. Only if it can be clearly established that such services already exist and are being effectively utilized by the target populations enumerated in the legislation can federal funds be used for other purposes. Because area agencies are to be set up in areas with high concentrations of minority and poor older persons, it is unlikely that adequate linkage services will be in existence. Second, establishment of these services is a distinct and measurable task. It can be readily documented what services are available and which subgroupings of the older population are using them. Third, devoting primary attention to development of these services is an activity which the area agencies can undertake on their own terms at the area level. Apart from contracting for specific services, it will not be necessary for the area agencies to involve themselves actively with other actors who might make demands or inroads on the agencies with which they do not wish to deal.

These central aspects of the linkage network portion of the national strategy are well suited to the area agencies' situation. In the first instance they are provided with explicit instructions for allocating the funds which federal legislation provides. As organizations with no other means of support, they must be responsive to such demands, and specific priorities have been set for the use of federal monies. Since these requirements are also subject to quantitative measurement, however meaningful in larger terms that may be, the area agency is in the position of knowing that its success will be subject to evaluation in those areas where performance can be assessed. Were it determined that the agency's performance was less than adequate, sanctions might be imposed which could threaten its existence.

Finally, the ability of area agencies to undertake the linkage service task at the area level without the need of involving other actors—excepting contracted service providers—serves to establish the role as unique to them. It becomes their policy space or, in system terms, the goal which distinguishes them from other actors in their environment. It is absolutely essential that an organization be able to demonstrate its uniqueness, because without it there is no rationale sufficient to justify its existence. That the linkage role which federal legislation sets for the area agencies is also funded, divisible, and measurable, enhances the ability of the agency to demonstrate that it has established an identifiable role for itself.

For the area agency as a recently conceived organization, the mobilizing or drawing-in role is marked by rather different characteristics. It possesses few of the advantages of the linkage service network mandate and, in fact, is notable for the risks it brings to a fledgling organization. There are no dollars attached to specific draw-in activities for the area agencies, as was true with linkage services. It is possible—that is to say, the regulations do not forbid it—that the agencies might combine the linkage network and draw-in roles, but there seems little reason on the face of it for the area agencies to want to do this.

The principal advantage of establishing the linkage network independently of other organizations was the definitive role it provided for the area agencies. For this to be combined with the draw-in role would negate this uniqueness and visibility, thereby cancelling out this singularly important function. Should it choose to minimize the draw-in role, for these or other reasons, the area agency would not leave itself as open to criticism as would be the case were it to downplay the linkage service network mandate.

An organization's success in mobilizing other resources and bringing about meaningful change for its clients is extremely difficult to determine. The types of organizations with which one would be engaged, the purpose of such joint activity and the tangible benefits which would result from it—as differentiated from the benefits which would have resulted without engaging in such activities—are not subject to the same precision in measurement as is a more finite and divisible undertaking, such as developing a linkage service network. Moreover, in the instance of the national aging strategy, there is no statement of what the end product of such activity should be other than serving the goal of independent living for older persons.

Even should an area agency choose to undertake the mobilizing role, it runs certain organizational risks. These risks vary from minor alteration in organizational goals all the way to cooptation by the other parties with whom it might be dealing.[20] In the case of the area agencies, draw-in would result from entering into some type of cooperative undertaking with other agencies or public bodies. At the very least, a cooperative venture —as opposed to either contention[21] or competition[22]—requires that the participating parties at some point agree among themselves on the end toward which they are working. The unstated part of such a cooperative arrangement is that it makes no necessary assumptions about the terms to which the parties might agree. While each party must see a reasonable likelihood that there will be a positive outcome for itself, this still leaves open a wide range of possibilities.

The danger lies in the dynamics of deciding upon the goal toward which they will jointly work. The agreement will be a function of the relative strengths of the parties involved: the party possessing fewer resources desired by the other —funds, expertise, clients and legitimacy, for example—will have

20. See, Eisenstadt, "Bureaucracy," pp. 311–314, for a discussion of three possible outcomes of interactions among organizations.
21. This being the alternative option posited by Meyerson and Banfield, wherein the parties actively seek to have their own ends prevail over those of other parties as terms of the arrangement; in Martin Meyerson and Edward C. Banfield, *Politics, Planning, and the Public Interest* (New York: Free Press, 1964), pp. 305 ff.
22. This being the alternative posed by Thompson and McEwen wherein differences in goal-setting decisions between two parties are mediated by a third. The authors also divide cooperation into three subtypes—bargaining, co-optation and coalition—which are distinguished by the degree of environmental control over an organization's decisions as reflected in the timing involved in reaching mutual accord. Thompson and McEwen, "Organizational Goals," pp. 25–28.

to modify its demands or goals more than will the more established partner. When these resources are conceived as elements constituting organizational strength, the agreement the two work out regarding what—actually, whose —goal they will jointly pursue becomes a formal statement of the power relations between them.

No organization can realistically contemplate entering into joint ventures with others independent of these considerations. The risks an organization runs by embarking on cooperative undertakings are proportional to the disparity between its strength and that of its partner and to the percentage of resources which it would contribute. Area agencies are weak organizations in these terms; therefore, any joint undertaking into which they might enter could not but involve a rather substantial portion of whatever organizational resources they possess.

No one is more aware of these realities and the risks entailed than the area agencies themselves. Their resources are central to establishing organizational integrity, and they would not willingly jeopardize them simply to entice another organization to join with them in pursuit of an external goal which can only serve some lesser organizational purpose. There remains, however, the national aging mandate which specifies that they undertake the mobilizing and drawing-in role. Thus, the area agencies are put in the position of having to demonstrate that they are willing to work at drawing in additional resources for the aging, but knowing at the same time that they run clear risks in doing so. This may serve to set limits on the types of mobilizing activities in which they are likely to engage. The histories of social grant-in-aid programs—aging among them—indicate that the larger goals which cooperative efforts are designed to realize frequently fall short. The underlying factor is the priority given to organizational concerns other than attainment of such goals.

Organizations can minimize their involvement and vulnerability when taking part in cooperative efforts, both in the choice of goal activities and the manner of participation. First, they may embark on very limited ventures. These would be activities designed to tap only marginal resources of their partners.[23] Cooperative efforts may also be highly goal-displaced. Here, "in the course of adopting means to attain organizational goals the means may become ends in themselves that displace the original goals."[24] This may manifest itself as "planning for planning"[25]; occupying oneself with the minutia rather than the important issues[26]; or defining the effort in procedural, rather than goal, terms.[27]

23. Roland L. Warren, "The Model Cities Program: Assumptions, Experience, Implications" (Paper presented at the Annual Forum Program, National Conference on Social Welfare, Dallas, Texas, 17 May 1971), pp. 17–18.

24. Peter M. Blau and W. Richard Scott, *Formal Organizations* (San Francisco, Cal.: Chandler Publishing, 1962), p. 229.

25. Cyril Roseman, "Problems and Prospects for Comprehensive Health Planning," *American Journal of Public Health* 62 (January 1972), p. 17.

26. Roland L. Warren, "Comprehensive Planning and Coordination: Some Functional Aspects," *Social Problems* 20 (Winter 1973), p. 358.

27. C. L. Estes, "Barriers to Effective Community Planning for the Elderly," *Gerontologist* 13 (Summer 1973), p. 180. For a discussion of goal displacement as manifested in local aging planning, see, C. L. Estes, "Community Planning for the El-

A third alternative is for organizations to participate in cooperative ventures which are nonthreatening and positive-sum. The goals selected are what Theodore Lowi has termed distributive ones—that is, the largess of some party external to those involved is simply taken in, or passed on, as a form of bounty to groups the participating agencies may wish to indulge.[28] A further advantage of distributive goals or policies for these organizations is that they are subject to almost infinite disaggregation. Whatever commodities are involved —money, clients or functions—are divided among the participants, creating the positive result that all parties get something.

While Lowi discusses this primarily as a trait among legislators, the same phenomenon can be discerned in the work of interagency coordinating and advisory councils. In the name of comprehensive or coordinated planning, the parties will undertake to write particular portions of the plan. Their dividing up the task in this manner can be readily justified as an appropriate division of labor in terms of their particular areas of expertise, but in so doing they also further their organizational interests. Each organization can define the task in a manner most conducive to its concerns and can do so under the legitimizing rubric of serving some sanctioned external goal. Warren reports that comprehensive planning in the Model Cities program was undertaken by

different task forces with little relation to each other, either within the task forces or among them.[29] Estes found aging planning agencies in Dallas devoting much time to defining and redefining goals which would differentiate one planning group from another and would do so in a manner which would be functional for "organizational survival, maintenance, and enhancement."[30]

Finally, organizations may enter into joint ventures with each other or participate in order to preserve their individual autonomy from one another. If the parties are cooperating only to demonstrate that they are concerned with making services more comprehensive or with delivering them more effectively, their position vis-à-vis each other will be essentially defensive. Sundquist and Davis, studying community action agencies, found that local agencies served on boards "not to coordinate, but to preserve their vested interests";[31] Roseman makes the same critique regarding Comprehensive Health Planning.[32] On this point, Warren argues that "The coordination strategy has functioned for at least a century, mostly latently, to reduce for the agencies the threat of competition, in the name of 'avoiding duplication of services.' "[33]

29. Warren, "Model Cities Program," p. 11.
30. Estes, "Barriers to Effective Community Planning," p. 180.
31. James Sundquist with David W. Davis, *Making Federalism Work* (Washington, D.C.: Brookings Institution, 1969), p. 75.
32. Roseman, "Comprehensive Health Planning," p. 17.
33. Warren, "Comprehensive Planning and Coordination," p. 360. The coordination mandate to state and substate planning bodies generally is made more difficult by the fact of many of them being given the same charge. For listing of recent social legislation calling for coordinative activities, see, Sundquist with Davis, *Making Federalism Work*, pp. 19–27.

derly: A Study in Goal Displacement" (Paper presented at the Annual Meeting of the Gerontological Society, Miami, Florida, 9 November 1973).
28. Theodore Lowi, "American Business, Public Policy, Case-Studies, and Political Theory," *World Politics* 16 (July 1964), pp. 677–715.

There is nothing about the area agencies which gives one reason to think that they will be any less subject to these pressures toward goal minimization than other agencies similarly charged. In view of the advantages open to them in concentrating on funding a linkage service network, they will not be inclined to involve themselves heavily with other actors, and even then it may only be to demonstrate their compliance with federal regulations. Efforts made in this direction will likely be incremental, goal-displaced and positive-sum, such as those outlined above.

AN AMBIGUOUS STRATEGY

This discussion serves to point up a critical ambiguity in the federal legislation. The amended Older Americans Act calls on the area agencies to perform one role which is essentially administrative: overseeing the development of support and gap-filling services. At the same time it charges them with tasks which are, in fact, quite different: drawing in outside resources and making other planners and providers more responsive to the service needs of older persons. To the area agencies, conceptualized in system terms, these may appear not only as separate, but largely incompatible, alternatives. The first of these mandated roles not only allows reliance on federal resources, but in certain respects very nearly requires it. In order to have their plans approved and to receive federal funds, the area agencies must adhere with great care to guidelines and instructions which the federal Administration on Aging has devised. Thus, the area agencies not only are required to see to the establishment of the linkage network, but are to develop specific services toward this end.

As argued here, the consequence of these requirements is to make the second task of mobilizing resources and redirecting other service structures not an attractive alternative. It asks the agencies, in effect, to engage actively with other actors in the area environment when they have not yet been able to set the terms for their own existence in that environment. The area agencies cannot reasonably be expected to undertake the mobilizing role until this minimum requirement of organizational self-definition has been met. Required to do it, their efforts will probably be marginal. The linkage service network mandate does represent such a definable role for the area agencies, but the numerous restrictions regarding its implementation will impede the development of the area agencies as autonomous organizations. The purpose of these restrictive guidelines is presumably to insure that the area agencies develop their service networks in line with the national strategy, but they serve at the same time to make the mobilizing role both difficult and, if undertaken ambitiously, organizationally dangerous.

The principal conclusion to be drawn from this analysis is simply that both aspects of the national goal strategy cannot be maximized simultaneously. The detailed instructions regarding development of the linkage network fosters reliance on the federal aging structure, while mobilizing resources requires that attention be concentrated at the area level. Furthermore, for the area agencies to undertake the mobilizing role seriously would necessitate their being willing and able to modify goals set a priori in order to meet whatever demands the parties with whom they would be negotiating for these resources might make. The notion that there are untapped resources lying around out there to be taken merely for the asking is untenable. That such an assumption could find its way into regulations and guidelines bespeaks of the importance of utilizing a conceptual model which can account for the dynamics of interorganizational activity.

It is also quite clear that, having to choose which of these two mandates to emphasize, the area agencies will devote themselves primarily to developing the linkage service network. That is the course dictated by both their internal organizational needs and by the manner in which their sole source of external support has structured its demands. Were the conditions placed on the area agencies less stringent and detailed, it might be more feasible for them to bring additional resources to bear on their client population. As things

currently stand, however, it is not really in their interests to do so.

While the original rationale for the area strategy was based on the need to develop an infrastructure of support for aging services at the substate level, the way in which the Older Americans Act Amendments are being implemented will serve instead to reinforce the vertical aging structure. Maintenance of such vertical ties has been a common characteristic of federal grant programs—regulations about draw-in, coordination or their equivalent notwithstanding. While many of the reasons for this are similar to those raised in this paper regarding the area agencies, the more immediate point to make in conclusion is simply that no amount of central direction from federal and state aging agencies can generate resources which are controlled by different actors at different levels.

The Role of the Federal Government in the Provision of Social Services to Older Persons

By Byron D. Gold

ABSTRACT: Financing the provision of social services is one of six roles played by the federal government in its effort to improve the circumstances of the elderly. Support for meeting the needs of older persons and the forms in which this support is rendered by society leave substantial numbers of the elderly with unmet needs. Whether the market system can respond to such needs is unclear; until such a response occurs, however, society will depend on social services to fill the gap. Social services for older persons can be grouped into four categories; one of the four consists of services which assure access to the other three. Nowhere in the nation is a complete range of services available even to a small number of older persons, which is a reflection of how recent a phenomenon is the commitment of public resources for this purpose. Most of the resources committed have come from the federal government. They have been made available under three distinct approaches: the first, through the public welfare system; the second and third, through different titles of the Older Americans Act. Because public awareness of the unmet needs of the elderly is likely to increase with participation in the newly implemented federal program of cash assistance— Supplemental Security Income (SSI)—further evolution of the federal role can be anticipated. Furthermore, the approaches through which federal financing is made available will probably remain eclectic.

Byron D. Gold, Special Assistant to the United States Commissioner on Aging, is currently on loan to the Center for the Study of Welfare Policy, School of Social Service Administration, University of Chicago, to conduct a study of the evolution of federal policy on provision of services to the elderly. Mr. Gold was principal Program Advisor to Arthur S. Flemming, Special Consultant on Aging to the President of the United States, and was Director, Division of Program and Legislative Analysis, United States Administration on Aging. In 1969 to 1970 he served as Staff Director, President's Task Force on Aging; in 1971 he was Staff Director, Section on Planning, White House Conference on Aging. Mr. Gold also held several other positions in the United States Department of Health, Education and Welfare.

BEYOND engaging in measures which benefit all citizens, the federal government plays at least six roles directly focused on improving the circumstances of the elderly. The first and most important of these roles is assuring an adequate income —for example, through the Social Security program. A second role is providing certain noncash benefits which, nevertheless, have a measurable economic value; one example is federal financing of health care for the elderly. A third role involves the protection of rights; the law which prohibits discrimination against older workers—defined as persons between the ages of 40 and 64—illustrates one way in which this role is performed. Conducting intramural, and supporting extramural, research into both the causes and manifestations of human aging is a fourth role; the activities of the newly-created National Institute of Aging—one of the National Institutes of Health—is an illustration. In order to meet the costs of providing a variety of social services to subsets of the older population, the federal government, in its fifth role, tenders financial support to public and private organizations at the state and local levels. An example is the financing of the program, recently implemented under the Older Americans Act, which provides meals to ambulatory older persons in group settings and to shut-ins in their homes. A final role involves attempts under terms of the Older Americans Act to assure that governmental actions aimed at furthering the other five roles occur with some orchestration not only at the federal level, but also at the state and substate levels.

Analysis of the legislation on which these six roles are based discloses that: (1) the circumstances of the elderly are a major policy concern of the federal government;[1] (2) the government's concern is, for the most part, of fairly recent origin; (3) since its inception that concern has undergone substantial evolution, which to some degree can be seen as a reflection of the growth and elaboration of public awareness about, and interest in, changes in the way old age is experienced within American society; (4) further evolution, probably of an even greater magnitude, can be anticipated; and (5) such evolution may well result, in addition to substantive changes in one or more of the roles, in the strengthening of their interrelationships. The detailed examination which follows affords a complex illustration of these conclusions. This examination will include consideration of the circumstances of old age to which social services are addressed; the nature of such services; the components of the federal role in the provision of such services; and prospects for further evolution of that role.

SOCIAL SERVICES AND THE CIRCUMSTANCES OF OLD AGE

For the relatively few individuals who, before this century, survived into old age, that period of life meant loss of health, income, spouse and companions. For the relatively large

1. For explanations of how and why this concern has developed, see, Robert H. Binstock, "Interest-Group Liberalism and the Politics of Aging," *Gerontologist* 12 (Autumn 1972), pp. 265–280; Henry J. Pratt, "Organizing the Aging in National Politics: A Study of Three Mass Membership Organizations" (Paper presented at the Midwest Political Science Association Convention, Chicago, Illinois, April 1972); and Dale Vinyard, "The Senate Special Committee on the Aging," *Gerontologist* 12 (Autumn 1972), pp. 298–303. Henry J. Pratt is currently preparing a book on this subject.

number of individuals who now survive into old age, the losses are, at some point, still the same. What has changed, however, is the support for meeting needs of the elderly and the ways in which such support is rendered by society. While these differences in the forms of support involve both income and nonincome needs, the scope of this paper precludes treating income needs. Hence, the focus is exclusively on nonincome needs in the following discussion of differences in supports concerning the family, the long term care institution, the ecology of daily life and social agencies.

The diminishing centrality of the family in meeting the needs of its older members means that most older persons, if they live long enough, have no assurance of tender care in the event of incapacitation; nor can they even be sure that death will occur in the presence of persons who are concerned about them. For some of the elderly the family role has thus been replaced by the long term care facility. Increased reliance on the long term care facility as the site where some of the very old must spend their last days is coupled with society's inability to find an effective means of standardizing the quality of care in such facilities. Many older persons abhor the prospect of being ultimately institutionalized and resent the absence of alternative arrangements to that form of care. For those elderly who are finally placed in an institution for want of such alternatives, placement may result in damage to their sense of psychological well-being; for some it may threaten their very existence.

Even if incapacitation does not occur, a narrowed concept of family responsibility for older members causes some older persons to have fewer social contacts, a diminished sense of serving as a link between the past and the future, less of a sense that one's accumulated knowledge is worthy of respect and fewer opportunities to perform tasks useful to other members of the family. It also may mean more difficulty in negotiating the tasks of daily living. This latter consequence of changed family behavior is exacerbated by the disappearance of a multitude of community amenities —such as well-patronized mass transportation and the so-called mom-and-pop grocery store—the fear of victimization from crimes against person and the widespread use of the computer as an aid to commercial transactions. Finally, the well-meaning response of public and voluntary social agencies more often than not confronts those older persons who require some form of social intervention with a confusing maze of unclear responsibilities, opaque policies and unpredictable bureaucratic behavior.

Since these problems are so pervasive, it is impressive that a majority of older persons seem to meet their own needs effectively—sometimes under the most adverse conditions —with no, or only minimal, intervention from social agencies. It is not surprising, however, that a minority take advantage of such interventions; furthermore, it seems reasonable to assume that more would utilize them were they available. While at present it is not possible to say precisely how many older persons are unable to satisfy their needs[2]—and which of these

2. Attempting to do so is a current concern of the Department of Health, Education and Welfare. Recent support for extramural research by the Administration on Aging reflects this concern. See, "Administration on Aging Research and Development Strategy: Fiscal Year 1974–1975" (Washington, D.C.: Administration on Aging, 1974).

needs they cannot meet—the number is probably substantial. Whatever the number, it is to the unmet needs of these individuals that social services are addressed.

Social scientists who specialize in social welfare policy disagree on the definition of social services and on the manner in which they are to be distinguished from other forms of social intervention.[3] The experts do agree, however, that social services have something to do with meeting human needs which cannot be satisfied through the market system.

An obvious reason for the unresponsiveness of the market system to the needs of older persons in that their income is disproportionately low. Recent data show that 19 percent of persons over the age of 65 had incomes at or below the so-called poverty threshold; these individuals constituted 15 percent of Americans with incomes at or below that threshold.[4] Grim as these figures are, they probably understate the extent of economic deprivation among the elderly. Other measures of income adequacy suggest that a large number of older persons cannot maintain a standard of living which most middle-class Americans would consider decent.[5] Therefore,

one means of improving the responsiveness of the market system would be to improve the income status of older persons.

The extent to which more adequate income would assure the elderly the capacity to satisfy needs in the marketplace is not, however, all that clear. Whether entrepreneurs would ever be able to perceive the aggregate of a demand which is widely diffused in the larger society is uncertain. Whether the aggregate could ever be large enough to make services addressed to the special needs of the elderly widely available —low cost delivery of groceries, for example—is uncertain. Even if the diffused aggregate of demand among the elderly were substantial enough to be perceived and to provoke a response, it is also uncertain whether that response would be adequate in terms of quality and accessibility.

Although the income status of the elderly has improved considerably in recent years,[6] a response from the market has not been forthcoming. Perhaps the improvement has not been significant enough; perhaps not enough time has yet elapsed to detect a response. Unless and until

3. For a discussion of various definitions and the implications of selecting one over another, see, Alfred J. Kahn, *Social Policy and Social Services* (New York: Random House, 1973); Martin Rein, *Social Policy: Issues of Choice and Change* (New York: Random House, 1970); and Hagith R. Shlonsky, "Toward a Framework for Analysis of Social Welfare Institutions," in *Social Service Delivery Project* (Chicago: University of Chicago School of Social Service Administration, Center for the Study of Welfare Policy, 1972).

4. U.S., Department of Commerce, Bureau of the Census, unpublished estimates for 1972.

5. The United States Department of Labor computes budgets for retired couples which

reflect a lower, intermediate and higher standard of living. In 1972 the lower budget required an income of $3,400; the intermediate budget, an income of $5,000; and the higher budget, an income of $7,700. Using those computations as a standard, in 1972: 1.1 million couples had incomes below the lower level; 2.2 million couples had incomes below the intermediate level; and 3.5 million couples had incomes below the higher level. U.S., Department of Labor, Bureau of Labor Statistics, unpublished statistics for 1972.

6. One factor has been the increase in Social Security benefits which, since the end of 1969, have risen almost 70 percent—much faster than the rate of inflation. Another is the gradual emergence of a group which Professor James Schulz of Brandeis University has described as a pension elite.

such a response occurs, society will depend to an increasing degree on social services to fill the gap.

DESCRIPTION OF SOCIAL SERVICES FOR THE ELDERLY

What, then, are the social services which aim to ameliorate the situation of the elderly? Before cataloging the variety of forms which such interventions can take, I should like to point out that, while some of the elderly require a number of these services, no one older person will require all of them; indeed, many of them are mutually exclusive. Also, although each service addresses a pocket of need in the older population, the dimensions of each pocket are not to be construed as equal.

While the lists are intended to be suggestive and not encyclopaedic, they are essentially similar to other such lists.[7] However, opinions of compilers differ. Medical care and legal representation, for example, are not included here because the needs addressed by these services can be satisfied through the market; they frequently appear in other compilations. The order in which services are presented has no special significance.

Social services for more incapacitated older persons include:

—preparation of meals at a central site and delivery of them to an older person's residence;
—daily conversations by telephone which serve to reassure

older persons that their welfare is a matter of concern;
—assistance with homemaking tasks which, depending on how incapacitated the older person is, ranges all the way from occasional assistance with household chores, such as shopping, to continuing performance of all the major work associated with maintaining a home;
—if home repair services of a suitable quality and quantity are not available in the market, provision of workmen and, when necessary, materials for home repairs;
—provision of escorts to facilitate difficult trips;
—para-nursing care provided at home;
—care during the day in a long term care setting.

Social services for older persons with more capacity include:

—opportunities for increased social contact, such as meals in a group setting;
—opportunities to be useful, such as recreation and participation in programs through which service to others can be rendered;[8]
—various kinds of adult education tailored to the interests of older persons, including assistance with preparation for retirement, consumer education and education for the creative use of time;
—various kinds of assistance with finding employment, including counseling, job training and, if private employment is unavailable, the provision

7. Examples are contained in the regulations implementing Title III of the Older Americans Act [45 C.F.R. 903 (1973)] and in Carole J. L. Collins, "Social Service Needs of the Aged," in *Social Service Delivery Project* (Chicago: University of Chicago School of Social Service Administration, Center for the Study of Welfare Policy, 1972).

8. Two examples are the Foster Grandparents Program and the Retired Senior Volunteer Program.

of a job in a public employment setting, such as a park beautification project or a day care center for children.

Social services for older persons with special needs include:

—various kinds of assistance addressed to the needs of physically disabled older persons, such as training public housing staff in sign language or purchasing braille equipment for recreation centers;
—protection of the vital interests of that small group of older persons unable to look after their own interests because of mental deterioration;
—various kinds of counseling, including legal, psychological, economic, medical and housing.

In addition to the three kinds of social services listed, there is a fourth kind: services which assure the access of older persons to other social services, to goods and services available through the market and to public benefits to which they might be entitled, such as veteran's benefits. These access-assuring services include the provision of transportation—in some instances in the form of low cost point-to-point transportation which more closely resembles service by taxi than service by bus. They also include locating those older persons who have unmet needs, determining what those needs are, linking such persons with the appropriate agency—whether public or private—for meeting those needs, following through to ascertain whether the needs have been met and, if necessary, serving as an advocate for the older person with the agency.[9]

Referring once again to the supports formerly provided by family and community, the effect of social services becomes more apprehensible. Services can: (1) offer substitutes for family care; (2) make available alternatives to the social roles provided by family and community; (3) function as a surrogate for society in assuming the responsibility for older persons with special needs; (4) facilitate access to community resources.

COMPONENTS OF THE FEDERAL ROLE

The complete range of services just described is not available even to a small number of older persons in any community in the nation. In a small number of communities some of these services are available to all older persons who require them. This unevenness reflects just how recently the public sector has taken on a major role with regard to providing social services to the elderly.

While the role has included elements of planning, mobilizing society, developing knowledge and skilled manpower, setting standards and determining objectives, the critical element has been the willingness of the public sector to share

9. This form of service is commonly known as information and referral. For several years InterStudy—a Minneapolis-based research organization—has conducted an in-depth study of the information and referral concept as it applies to the needs of older persons. The study, supported by the Administration on Aging and directed by Dr. Nicholas Long, has generated an extensive set of publications.

the cost of providing social services to the elderly. Historically, the social agencies which initially attempted to perform this function were located in the voluntary sector. Even in the heyday of private charity, however, the resources of the voluntary sector were never equal to the extraordinary costs necessary to make these services more universally accessible. That objective became possible only in the late 1960s, when public policy began to evolve toward the use of substantial public resources for its accomplishment.

The bulk of the public resources used for this purpose has been federal, although all levels of government have contributed to some extent. For example, because federal resources have been tendered primarily through grants-in-aid to states, state management of resources has constituted an important contribution. Notwithstanding the importance of such contributions, the decision of the federal government to commit significant amounts of resources for this purpose has been critical.

The commitment of federal resources has encompassed familiar questions of federal policy concerning the appropriate extent of federal responsibility, eligibility for services, distinctions between more important and less important services and the most effective organizational arrangements for the provision of services. In the late 1960s one possible set of answers began to emerge through the mechanism of the nation's public welfare program; for reasons not involving the elderly, that approach has been, at least temporarily, shut off. Two different sets of recent amendments

to the Older Americans Act suggest different answers; these approaches are just getting underway. In the material which follows the three approaches are treated more fully.

SOCIAL SERVICES FINANCED UNDER TERMS OF THE WELFARE TITLES OF THE SOCIAL SECURITY ACT

From the enactment in 1935 of Title I of the Social Security Act—the Old Age Assistance program (OAA)—the federal government has been sharing with states part of the cost of providing a limited number of caseworker-oriented social services to a small number—primarily OAA cash recipients—of older persons.[10] For the most part these services have been forms of intervention rendered by state or county employees. Providing a broader range of services to a larger number of older persons, many of whom would not have been cash recipients, potentially developed in 1967 in the wake of changes in statutory authority. For reasons which will become clear below, the potentiality

10. For an account of the historical evolution of the provision of services under the welfare titles of the Social Security Act, see, Bruce Jansson, *Brief Chronology of Development of Federal Policy Pertaining to Social Services* (Chicago: University of Chicago School of Social Service Administration, Center for the Study of Welfare Policy, 1972).

In fiscal year 1972, slightly more than 275,000 older persons received at least one service; the majority received only one service. The cost to the federal government of providing those services was $200 million. Almost 95 percent of the older persons to whom services were provided were OAA recipients, of whom there were approximately 2.1 million. "Effect of Cutbacks in Social Service Funds on Delivery of Services to Aging" (Unpublished Administration on Aging memorandum, 10 May 1973).

has not yet been realized. The potentiality depended on two features of the welfare titles[11] which preexisted the 1967 changes. One feature was that eligibility for services was not limited to recipients of cash assistance, but could also include former and potential cash recipients. Potential had always been defined generously. In view of the extent of economic deprivation among the elderly, a large number of older persons could easily be construed as potential recipients of cash assistance.

A second feature was that federal financing for the provision of social services under terms of the welfare titles was open-ended—that is, under the law the federal government pledged to meet 75 percent of the costs incurred by state governments for the provision of social services to persons eligible for such services, no matter how large those costs were, so long as they were incurred in accordance with the terms of the law. The only practical limit on federal expenditures was that the federal outlay of three dollars did not occur unless a state government was willing to expend one dollar of its own resources.

In 1967 Congress for the first time

authorized federal participation in the cost of social services purchased from nonpublic sources.[12] In implementing this change the Department of Health, Education and Welfare (HEW) also permitted states to use resources donated by the voluntary sector as the nonfederal share with which to earn federal funds. The purpose of this policy was to make the provision of social services more attractive to those state governments which, despite the incentive of 75 percent federal cost sharing, remained unwilling to come up with the 25 percent nonfederal share from their own resources.

The combined effect of these two changes on state programs for the elderly could have been profound. For example, a United Fund, instead of paying $10,000 of its resources to a voluntary agency for the provision of homemaker services to the elderly, could donate its funds to a state welfare agency. The agency, in turn, could purchase $40,000 of homemaker services from the voluntary agency by using the $10,000 donation to earn the federal share of the contract costs. Despite being given these new authorities, during the next five years state welfare agencies showed extreme reluctance to finance the development, expansion or improvement of social services for the elderly, the administration of which was not under their immediate control.[13]

11. In addition to Title I—OAA, in 1967 these were Title IV-A—Aid to Families of Dependent Children (AFDC), Title X, Aid to the Blind and Title XIV, Aid to the Permanently and Totally Disabled. The Social Security Amendments of 1972 (86 Stat. 1462) replaced the cash assistance portions of Titles I, X and XIV with a new Title XVI—the Supplementary Security Income Program (SSI) for the Aged, Blind and Disabled (42 U. S. C. 1381)—and the service aspects of each of the three titles with a new Title VI—Grants to States for Services to the Aged, Blind or Disabled (42 U. S. C. 1305). The terms of Title VI are in no way different from the terms of the titles it replaces. The implications of SSI for the provision of services are discussed at a later point.

12. Social Security Amendments of 1967, 81 Stat. 877.
13. An estimated $196 million was expended in fiscal year 1971 by federal, state and local governments for the provision of services under the welfare titles to the aged, blind and disabled. Of this amount, only 11.1 percent was used to purchase services from private sources. Although estimated total expenditures increased to $477 million during fiscal year 1972, the share of serv-

Yet, there is evidence to suggest that the provision of services might have expanded considerably during the last two years. By 1972 voluntary agencies concerned with the elderly began to recognize the potential inherent in the purchase of service and donated resources techniques. Since several state welfare agencies had already applied these techniques liberally in the Aid to Families with Dependent Children (AFDC) program in connection with day care services and many others were about to do so, it is reasonable to assume that, in time, they would have also been willing to use the techniques in the OAA program. Moreover—since one intended effect of the proposed Older Americans Act Amendments of 1973 was the aggregation of unmet needs throughout the nation—Title I, with its open-ended appropriation, was a likely source for financing services to satisfy such needs.[14]

However, beginning in 1972 Congress and HEW imposed limitations on the provision of services under all four welfare titles. These limitations resulted from the search of states for fiscal relief early in the 1970s. As the state fiscal crunch had worsened and proposals for sharing federal revenues with no strings attached remained stalled, several bigger states fastened upon the possibility

of financing as many human resource programs as possible under the welfare titles. The shift was to be accomplished through purchase of service agreements between the state welfare agency and the other state agencies administering the programs. Candidates for this method of financing were programs being financed by exclusively nonfederal funds or by federal funds requiring a larger state share than 25 percent.

The impact of this strategy was immediate. Federal expenditures for services provided under all four welfare titles increased from $750 million in fiscal year 1971 to $1.7 billion in fiscal year 1972 and were projected to increase to $4.7 billion in fiscal year 1973.[15] Faced with this prospect, Congress enacted general revenue sharing, but in the same measure imposed a $2.5 billion annual ceiling, beginning with fiscal year 1972, on federal expenditures for social services financed under the welfare titles.[16] The open-end on appropriations was closed. While expenditures in connection with the OAA program do not appear to have been rising substantially, services for the elderly were not exempted from this policy decision.

Early in 1973—for reasons which are open to varying interpretation— HEW proposed new regulations governing the provision of social services.[17] Had the proposed regula-

ices purchased from private sources increased to only 11.3 percent. U.S., Department of Health, Education and Welfare, "Cost Analysis of Social Services, Fiscal Year 1972," prepared by Touche Ross and Co.; excerpts of the report constitute Appendix C of *Staff Data and Materials on Social Services Regulations*, U.S., Senate, Committee on Finance, 93rd. Cong., 1st. sess., 4 May 1973.

14. For one illustration of the expectations associated with this strategy, see, U.S., Senate, Special Committee on Aging, *The Rise and Threatened Fall of Service Programs for the Elderly*, 93rd. Cong., 1st. sess., March 1973.

15. U.S., Senate, Committee on Finance, *Social Service Regulations*, p. 2.

16. Fiscal Assistance to State and Local Governments, 86 Stat. 919. The provision of social services to the elderly is one of eight categories for which local governments can use general revenue sharing funds.

17. Proposed regulations for Service Programs for Families and Children and for Aged, Blind, or Disabled Individuals: Title I, IV (Parts A and B), X, XIV and XVI of the Social Security Act; 38 Fed. Reg. 4608 (1973).

tions been allowed to go into effect, they would have markedly changed the nature of public welfare service provision, for example: eligibility would have been made much more restrictive; purchases of services would have been placed under strict controls; the use of donated resources for matching federal funds would have been prohibited; and—explicitly creating a priority—mandated services would have continued in connection with the AFDC program, but would have been eliminated for the other programs. Under the proposed regulations a state welfare agency wishing to do so —and only if it had a portion of its allotted funds still available after providing the services for which it was mandated—could provide services to the aged, blind and disabled. However, its obligation would be limited to providing each eligible person with only one of a long list of services.

As a result of the storm of protest which developed, HEW somewhat modified the final version of the revised social service regulations. This version was published early in May 1973 and was to have been effective on July 1, 1973.[18] In the final version the distinction concerning mandated services was not eliminated.

Congress had purposely kept the language in the Social Security Act governing the provision of services flexible. To this day, for example, Congress has never specified the services to be provided, the definitions of eligibility or the rules concerning the purchase of services. Matters such as these were left to the discretion of the executive branch. In this instance, however, so

much concern had been aroused in Congress that later in May the Senate Finance Committee—which has jurisdiction over the public welfare portions of the Social Security Act—took the rare step of convening a hearing to determine how HEW, in devising the revised regulations, had used the discretion which historically Congress had granted it concerning public welfare service provision.

Apparently, the department's justification of its stewardship was not fully satisfactory to the Congress. Twice since the hearing Congress has delayed the effective date of the final version.[19] Thus, the previous regulations remain in effect.[20] A consequence of this unusual congressional intervention into the regulatory process has been the unwillingness of state welfare agencies to expand the provision of social services, at least until the future direction of federal policy becomes clearer.

SOCIAL SERVICES FINANCED UNDER TERMS OF THE OLDER AMERICANS ACT

Even if the expanded provision of social services in a public welfare context had not been stalled, not all older persons with unmet needs would have been eligible for such services. No matter how generously potential-recipient-of-cash-assistance was defined, a large number of older persons who required services

18. 38 Fed. Reg. 10782 (1973), further clarified in 38 Fed. Reg. 14375 (1973).

19. Renegotiation Amendments of 1973, 87 Stat. 152; Social Security Benefits-Increase, 87 Stat. 947. Before the second delay was enacted, the department again modified the final version. This modification, which will be effective when and if the congressionally imposed suspension is removed, appears in 38 Fed. Reg. 30072 (1973).
20. 45 C.F.R. 222 (1973), as modified in 39 Fed. Reg. 1443 (1974).

would have been excluded by virtue of their income and/or assets, even if such services were unavailable from other sources. Moreover, the low income elderly were only one of several groups within the larger population of persons eligible for public welfare services and, clearly, not the group claiming the greatest attention from state welfare agencies. The development, expansion and improvement of services to older persons was not a priority.

These considerations were not new in 1967. The argument that unmet needs were distributed widely throughout the older population— that they were not exclusive to older persons with low income—had figured prominently in the deliberations of Congress leading to the passage of the Older Americans Act in 1965.[21] Also, it was argued that the elderly would receive the attention they deserved only if their unmet needs were separated from the problems of other groups and action to deal with them was taken independently.

In theory, the enactment of the Older Americans Act signified an alternative approach to the provision of social services to the elderly; the act was based on the approach of treating all the elderly as potential recipients of services. In fact, negligible appropriations before fiscal year 1973 precluded the possibility of a viable alternative. Those services which were provided are best described as community demonstra-

tions on the possible effects of services. Noteworthy, however, is that from the inception of these demonstrations—which were financed under Title III of the act—the outlines of two distinct, alternative approaches can be seen, both of which were age-based instead of income-based.

One of these approaches is reflected in the financing of a series of activities which Robert Binstock has characterized as advocacy-planning.[22] Embraced by this term were such activities as assessment of needs, inventory of resources and joint planning of solutions. Frequently, some form of access-assuring services was also included. The theory which animated this approach was that through such activities public and voluntary social agencies could be persuaded to devote resources under their control to the provision of new, additional or better services to older persons.

The other approach is reflected in services directly financed through Title III. The theory which animated this approach was that the only certain means of assuring the provision of services to the elderly was paying for them.

As a result of two recent pieces of legislation, both approaches are now contained in separate portions of the Older Americans Act. In 1973 Title III was totally restructured, and the funds appropriated to carry it out were markedly increased.[23] Service provision in conjunction with Title III takes place in accordance with an embellished version of the theory embodied in advocacy-planning. Earlier—in 1972—a new

21. Older Americans Act, 79 Stat. 219. For an example of congressional deliberations prior to the enactment of the statute, see U.S., Congress, Committee on Education and Labor, Subcommittee on Education, *Hearings on H.R. 7957 and Similar Bills Before the Select Subcommittee on Education of the House Committee on Education and Labor*, 88th. Cong., 1st. sess., 1963.

22. Robert Binstock, *Planning—Background and Issues* (Washington, D.C.: White House Conference on Aging, 1971).

23. Older Americans Act Amendments, 87 Stat. 30.

Title VII focusing on the provision of nutrition services to older persons was enacted.[24] Service provision in conjunction with Title VII takes place in accordance with the theory embodied in the second approach.

The considerations which led to these enactments are beyond the scope of this paper. They have been, and continue to be, treated at length elsewhere.[25] Something more, however, should be said about the expectations associated with each approach.

TITLE III APPROACH

Under Title III the entire nation is divided into substate regions. Ultimately, in each of those regions a plan for addressing the unmet needs of the older persons residing in that region will be developed by a substate agency on aging. State Agencies on Aging will use Title III resources to fund portions of the plan.[26] Other portions will be funded through: state resources; resources of county and local governments, recently augmented through general revenue sharing; user fees; resources of voluntary social agencies;

24. Nutrition Services Amendments to the Older Americans Act, 79 Stat. 219.

25. Robert B. Hudson, "Client Politics and Federalism: The Case of the Older Americans Act," rev. ed. (Paper presented at the American Political Science Association Meeting, September 1973), is an excellent treatment of the considerations leading to the enactment of the Older Americans Act Amendments of 1973 which restructured Title III. The enactment of Title VII is the subject of a work in progress by Byron D. Gold.

26. In fiscal year 1974 $96 million were made available under Title III. Of that amount, $12 million were allocated to state agency operations; $16 million, to demonstrations; and $10 million, to substate agency operations. The remaining $58 million were used to initiate, to expand or to improve services.

and other federal resources, such as those available under Title VI of the Social Security Act or Title VII of the Older Americans Act.

In the 1973 statute access-assuring services are the only services for which provision is mandated. This singular requirement, which originated in the Congress, reflects the concern for facilitating full utilization of available services. As this article is being completed, there are indications that Congress will shortly underscore this concern by reserving certain Title III funds exclusively for the implementation of those portions of substate plans which deal with the provision of transportation.

While the objective is to respond to all of the unmet needs of all of the older persons residing within the region, the response will be incremental. Needs perceived as more important by older persons will be met before needs perceived as less important. The needs of older persons who have less income or who are members of minority groups will receive priority consideration.

Underlying the approach represented by Title III are several assumptions: that the order of priority in which unmet needs are addressed is a matter for substate determination; that substate agencies will be able to use Title III resources as catalysts for new, additional or better services; that, as such services are provided to small numbers of older persons, the benefits which accrue from doing so will become manifest; and that, consequently, political pressure will develop for allocating more public resources to meeting the needs of more persons, as well as a wider range of needs.

TITLE VII APPROACH

Under Title VII meals are provided to older persons by public and voluntary social agencies. Most meals are furnished in group settings, but some are delivered at home. Older persons who receive meals under such auspices also may receive other social services, such as nutrition education, transportation to and from the site where the meals are served, opportunities for recreation, various forms of counseling and linkage with the providers of other required services not available from the agency providing the meals. Perhaps the most important additional service provided is the opportunity for social contact.

To obtain Title VII funds with which to defray the costs of providing meals and ancillary social services, social agencies apply to state agencies on aging. In fiscal year 1974 $100 million were appropriated;[27] the funds permitted the provision of nutrition services to a far more limited number of older persons than the federal government believed could benefit. When an appropriation is not open-ended—as it is not in Title VII—an unfortunate consequence is that services cannot be made available to all persons with equal needs. Stiff eligibility criteria are one means of rationing the supply of scarce services. While the eligibility criteria for Title VII are specific, they are not stiff. Presumably, at some point demand will therefore outstrip supply, and inequities will multiply.

27. Although Title VII was enacted during fiscal year 1972 and the appropriation of funds was authorized for fiscal year 1973, a series of conflicts between the executive and legislative branches unrelated to Title VII delayed implementation until fiscal year 1974.

Underlying the approach represented by Title VII are three related assumptions: that the provision of certain services must be assured; that the setting of priority services is a matter to be determined by the national government; and that the only certain way of assuring the provision of these services is to make federal funds available for a specific purpose.

PROSPECTS FOR FURTHER EVOLUTION OF THE FEDERAL ROLE

At the outset of reviewing the prospects for further evolution of the federal role, it is useful to recognize that, while recent increases in federal financing have been relatively large, the amount of federal resources devoted to the provision of services to the elderly and the number of older recipients remain small. While this fact is problematic now in light of unmet needs about which national awareness already exists, it will be even more troublesome as participation in the SSI program rises and the unmet needs come increasingly to public attention.

For a variety of reasons, a large shortfall always existed between the number of older persons living in, or at the brink of, poverty and the number of persons receiving Old Age Assistance. Due to this shortfall, the unmet needs of persons not receiving OAA were largely invisible. SSI—perhaps because of the federal administration, the intention of the federal government to locate and to offer every possible recipient the option of participation, the connotation that it is not a welfare program—which, of course, it is—and the single national standard for determining eligibility—may be able to eliminate the shortfall. To the extent that the program does so, it will simultaneously cause many unmet needs—heretofore artificially concealed from national consciousness—to surface. The surfacing of these needs, in turn, will probably foster further evolution in the federal role.

Most probably, evolution in the federal role will not yield a single federal approach. Undoubtedly, such a result would be tidier for administrators and more comprehensible to the concerned public. Conflicting interests and viewpoints in Congress, however, virtually mandate a federal role based on multiple approaches.

Congressional reaction to earlier Department of Health, Education and Welfare proposals concerning the Title VII approach is illuminating in this regard. During the deliberations leading up to the passage of Title VII, HEW proposed that nutrition services for the elderly be provided through the public welfare system.[28] After enactment, the department proposed that Title VII be merged with Title III.[29] Both proposals were rejected; yet, significantly, Congress legislated the Title III approach shortly after rejecting the latter proposal. The prospect, then, is for continued eclecticism

involving the attenuation of the three existing approaches and, perhaps, the addition and/or substitution of other approaches.

The question of whether broadened provision of services can be achieved through the public welfare approach depends on the legislative and administrative branches resolving their conflict concerning regulations. As of this writing, the suspension of the latest version is scheduled to remain in effect until December 31, 1974. There are some indications that, before the suspension expires, Congress will either concretize in law some variant of the previous regulations or, at the least, continue the suspension.[30]

The fate of the Title III approach will probably depend on the extent to which the assumptions underlying the approach prove to be correct as implementation proceeds. The nature of the assumptions underlying the Title VII approach suggest that future reliance on that approach will probably be independent of developments which transpire as Title VII is implemented. From time to time, Congress will probably use this approach to assure that additional needs are addressed. To some extent this has already taken place. Under other statutory authorities the federal government has made funds available to assure older persons opportunities for both employment and volunteer service in socially useful community roles.

Two other possibilities deserve mention. Under legislation proposed by Senator Edward Kennedy and Congressman Wilbur Mills,[31]

28. See, for example, the testimony of John B. Martin, commissioner on aging, in *Hearings on H.R. 17763 Before the Select Subcommittee on Education of the House Committee on Education and Labor*, 91st. Cong., 2nd sess., 1970.

29. See, for example, the testimony of Elliot Richardson, Secretary of Health, Education and Welfare, in *Hearings on Bills to Strengthen and Improve the Older Americans Act of 1965 Before the Select Subcommittee on Education of the House Committee on Education and Labor*, 92nd. Cong., 2nd. sess., 1972.

30. *APWA Washington Report* 9, no. 2 (22 April 1974), p. 3.

31. H.R. 13870, 93rd. Cong., 2nd sess., 1974.

a Medicare approach would be developed. Medicare—which does not cover the expenses associated with long term institutional care—would be amended to cover the costs of providing a continuum of care, including social services which allow individuals to avoid institutionalization as long as possible and care within institutions should such care become necessary. A nonprofit corporation which would purchase care for all beneficiaries residing within the substate regional boundaries encompassing the corporation's jurisdiction would serve as the mechanism through which this continuum would be provided. Should some variation of this proposal be enacted, the effects could only be extraordinary for a number of reasons—not the least of which would be the enormous increase in available federal resources for the provision of services and the impetus which would be given to the formation of a personal care industry.[32]

Finally, yet another approach would emerge if legislation were enacted to make social services universally available—in lieu of perpetuating the provision of services as an activity of the public welfare system—to persons of all ages without regard to considerations of income. An analogue to this concept is the provision of public education. While a number of proposals to effect this concept have been put forth in recent years,[33] it is somewhat doubtful whether public policy is yet ready for a reform of this magnitude.

---

32. For some years the Levinson Institute at Brandeis—of which Robert Morris, an advocate of the proposal, is director—has been studying aspects of this concept. Morris and his colleagues have produced a number of publications. For example, see, U.S., Senate, Special Committee on Aging, *Alternatives to Nursing Home Care: A Proposal Prepared . . . by Staff Specialists at The Levinson Gerontological Policy Institute*, 92nd Cong., 1st. sess., 1971.

33. For an interesting example, see, Robert Morris, "Welfare Reform 1973: The Social Services Dimension," *Science* 10 (August 1973), pp. 515–522.

Political Factors in the Emerging Legal Age Status of the Elderly

By Leonard D Cain

ABSTRACT: Political pressures to enact laws which provide distinctive status to the elderly are much in evidence. The premises regarding equality and equity which provide the rationale for the plethora of old-age-related laws are less clear, and the consequences of these laws on the status of older people are poorly understood. Early legal efforts to distinguish between the infant and the adult provide an antecedent for current efforts to distinguish between the adult and the elderly. The shift from functional age to formal age criteria also provides a context for consideration of current age-related issues. The politics of aging today, for the most part, accepts the inequality of the elderly and uses formal—chronological—age as a basis for eligibility for services which alleviate the negative consequences of inequality. The courts are likely to be called upon shortly to consider the Constitutionality of use of chronological age to determine legal status and of current strategies to promote equity.

Leonard D Cain is Professor of Sociology and Urban Studies and Associate Director for Training of the Institute on Aging at Portland State University. A member of the American Sociological Association, he received his Ph.D. in Sociology from the University of Texas. Professor Cain's research has been conducted in the fields of age statuses, social change and urbanization; in addition to scholarly articles, his publications include Growth and Government in Sacramento.

"Injustice arises when equals are treated unequally, and also when unequals are treated equally."[1]

ARISTOTLE'S cryptic observation identifies the contemporary dilemma which surrounds the efforts to provide both equality and equity for the elderly through law. If the elderly are indeed equal to adults, but are treated unequally, injustice prevails. Arguments to abolish compulsory retirement laws would appear to provide a means for the promotion of justice. If the elderly are both equal and treated equally, there appears to be no basis for the establishment of any separate age status in law for the elderly at all, except possibly to protect the maintenance of equal treatment.

If the elderly are unequal to

1. This phrase—quoted in M. Ginsburg, *On Justice in Society* (Ithaca, N.Y.: Cornell University Press, 1965)—is attributed to Aristotle, as recorded in Plato's *Laws, Book VI*. From *Laws*, itself, Plato records "the Athenian" as saying: "When equality is given to unequal things, the resultant will be unequal, unless due measure is applied. . . . There are two kinds of equality . . . the one of these any State or law-giver is competent to apply in the assignment of honours—namely, the equality determined by measure, weight, and number . . . but the truest and best form of equality . . . dispenses more to the greater and less to the smaller . . . Justice . . . consists in . . . the natural equality given on each occasion to things unequal"; Plato, *Laws, Book VI*, trans. by R. G. Bury (Cambridge, Mass.: Harvard University Press, 1926), pp. 413, 415.

Plato proposed a use of chronological age to designate an old age status: "A Law-warden shall hold office for no more than twenty years, and he shall be voted into office when he is not under fifty years of age. . . . The more he exceeds the minimum age, the shorter shall be his term of office; so that if he lives beyond the age of seventy, he must no longer fancy that he can remain among those officials holding an office of such high importance"; ibid., pp. 405, 407.

adults, but are treated equally, injustice may also prevail. Support of legislation which provides social services or economic support differentially to the elderly also provides a means for the promotion of justice. Current national policy centers upon the providing of justice by accepting the elderly as unequals and by enacting laws which are designed to overcome the negative consequences of that inequality. Thus, a separate legal status for the elderly takes form.

ANTECEDENTS: LEGAL DISTINCTIONS BETWEEN INFANT AND ADULT

Until recent decades legal age issues focused upon efforts to distinguish between the status of infant and that of adult. Law was called upon to provide a distinction between those who were presumed to be nonresponsible and those who were presumed to be responsible for their acts, between those who were in need of special protection by the state and those who were granted full citizenship rights.[2]

A traditional illustration of the ambiguity associated with this issue is the question of whether "old enough to fight" properly translates into "old enough to vote." The effort to distinguish between the violation of the law by an infant—a juvenile delinquent act—and by an adult—a criminal act—is another. The rationale for the establishment of the juvenile court system in America in the early twentieth century was to provide justice to the youthful offender

2. L. D Cain, "The Growing Importance of Legal Age in Determining the Status of the Elderly," *Gerontologist* 14, no. 2 (April 1974), p. 167.

by treating those designated as un-equals, because of immaturity, to be treated as unequals.

The *Application of Gault* case,[3] rendered by the United States Supreme Court in 1967, is instructive at this point, because it illustrates the difficulty in determining the distinction between infant and adult and especially because it portends some future Court decision which will surely confront the issue of distinguishing between the adult and the elderly. Justice Fortas wrote:

From the inception of the juvenile court system, wide differences have been tolerated—indeed insisted upon—between the procedural rights accorded to adults and those of juveniles. In practically all jurisdictions, there are rights granted to adults which are withheld from juveniles. . . . It has been held that the juvenile is not entitled to bail, to indictment by grand jury, to a public trial or to trial by jury.

Justice Fortas, for the majority, continued:

The early reformers [in the Juvenile Court Movement] were appalled by adult procedures and penalties, and by the fact that children could be given long prison sentences and mixed in jails with hardened criminals. They were profoundly convinced that society's duty to the child could not be confined by the concept of justice alone. . . . The child was to be "treated" and "rehabilitated."

Accordingly, the highest motives and most enlightened impulses led to a peculiar system for juveniles, unknown to our law in any comparable context. The constitutional and theoretical basis for this peculiar system is—to say the least—debatable.

3. *Application of Gault*, 87 S. Ct. 1428 (1967); majority opinion of Justice Fortas.

Finally, the justice reminds us:

If Gerald [Gault] had been over 18, he would not have been subject to Juvenile Court proceedings. For the particular offense immediately involved, the maximum punishment would have been a fine of $5 to $50, or imprisonment in jail for not more than two months. Instead, he was committed to custody for a maximum of six years. If he had been over 18 and had committed an offense to which such sentence might apply, he would have been entitled to substantial rights under the Constitution. . .

Will some future justice label some law which utilizes a certain older chronological age or age span to provide distinctive privileges or denials to the elderly as "peculiar?" Can we imagine some future Court decision which declares: "If Elderly Citizen X had been under 65 he would not have been subject to compulsory retirement; he would have been entitled to substantial rights to equal employment opportunities as defined in federal and state fair employment practices legislation." Or, a future Court may rule: "If Adult Citizen Y had been over 65 he would not have been subject to the so-called full fare on publicly owned rapid transit; therefore, he acted quite properly in refusing to pay a fare larger than the 65-year-old who preceded him onto the train." Gerontologists have much to learn from legal decisions which seek to clarify the rights of the young.

ANTECEDENTS: THE TRANSITION FROM FUNCTIONAL AGE TO FORMAL AGE

Clark and Anderson have stated well the context in which legal definitions have become increasingly important:

In societies where old age is defined in *functional* terms, it is onset of biological deterioration (as this affects mobility, strength, or other abilities required in adult work) that signals the end of active adult status. That is, old age is defined by observed changes in physical condition—and its onset corresponds with the individual's need to restrict his activities substantially. However, in human groups which define old age in *formal* terms, change of status is linked to other factors—usually to some external event which is arbitrarily invested with symbolic significance.

Clark and Anderson emphasize that in the contemporary Western world formal definitions, based on chronological age, continue to replace functional definitions. They illustrate:

It is nearly impossible in American society today to live one's life without having the exact date of one's birth . . . made a matter of public record. . . . In most American commercial and industrial enterprises, a worker is defined as "old" at the age of sixty-five, and at that time he is retired from gainful employment. The Federal Government, through its Social Security Act, has given official sanction to this [formal-temporal definition of old age]. . . . adult responsibilities are now relinquished relatively so early that there yet remains for most older people a long span of years devoid of social meaning.[4]

In our society it has been chronological age which has been "arbitrarily invested with symbolic significance." However, not just one chronological age: one law may specify 65, another 62, another 60 or even 55 or younger; the age 72 has been given special meaning in

at least one law, the Social Security Act.[5]

Clark and Anderson have isolated two distinctive old age statuses: one begins with a formal application of an older chronological age, still typically 65, and ostensibly ends when functional old age becomes a reality; the second corresponds to the functional old age of a previous epoch. There is a major problem for the complex, commercial-industrial society. Some citizens are functionally old by, or before, age 65. When careers are bureaucratized and pension schemes are computerized, how is justice to be achieved in the realms of work, retirement and pensions? How does such a society protect the rights of younger workers as they anticipate occupying the positions held by older workers?

There remain some age status determinants which have not been preempted by chronological criteria—that is, they remain functional. For example, eligibility to occupy public housing may depend on one's ability to maintain oneself without assistance. Inexorably, some tenants will experience functional decline. Public housing administrators have no resort to a legally specified chronological age to initiate eviction proceedings. Neither are concise definitions of functional old age sufficient to justify eviction available to them. What are the Constitutional rights of a citizen under such circumstances? What laws are needed to protect both the resident and the administrator?

Another issue, to be elaborated upon later, is that of maintaining the right to drive an automobile in

4. M. Clark and B. G. Anderson, *Culture and Aging: An Anthropological Study of Older Americans* (Springfield, Ill.: Charles G. Thomas, 1967), pp. 6–10.

5. Cain, "Importance of Legal Age," pp. 170–171.

later years. Again, inexorably, older drivers suffer loss of functions vital to the safe operation of an automobile. Yet, who has the right to deny a person—because of old age, including functional old age—the means of maintaining mobility? Controversies surrounding formal versus functional criteria for determining old age statuses are likely to remain for the indefinite future.

BUILDING THE CASE FOR INEQUALITY OF THE ELDERLY

A vital component of the advocacy for legislation which gives distinctive service-oriented status or economic relief to the elderly is the amassing of evidence, usually generated by social and biological scientists, which indicates either the inferior competitive prowess of the elderly in obtaining goods and services or their greater need for medical or other services. The gerontological movement has concentrated on developing and utilizing such data. Hearings before congressional committees abound in this type of evidence.

The proposed Older Americans Tax Counseling Assistance Act[6] presumes a need for special services. Senator Frank Church—Democrat, Idaho—testified:

Upon reaching 65 the aged taxpayer is oftentimes confronted with an entirely new set of rules, usually far more complex than the tax provisions during his preretirement years. He may find it necessary, for example, to complete the retirement income credit schedule, determine the taxable portion of his an-

6. U.S., Senate, Special Committee on Aging, *Protecting Older Americans Against Overpayment of Income Taxes* (Washington, D.C.: U. S. Government Printing Office, 1974), pp. 13–14.

nuity, or compute the taxable gain on the sale of his personal residence. . . . For the untrained . . . elderly taxpayer, these complex tax relief measures can prove to be mind boggling.

Perhaps the most troubled individual is the aged widow, who typically has low or moderate income and very little experience in tax matters. For her, the tax law is usually a jumble of gobbledygook with numerous pitfalls.

However, with appropriate counseling many of these obstacles can be overcome for the elderly taxpayer.

There is a peculiar irony in this defense of the proposed act. Supposedly, a worker is retired at 65 or so because of reduced competency; however, it is specified that a person in the newly retired state is likely to be confronted with a new set of tax rules which are much more complicated than those he was called upon to apply during his younger years.

Senator Church, who introduced the bill to approve the act, continued:

Briefly stated, this proposal would permit the Internal Revenue Service to strengthen the tax counseling program for older Americans by expanding the training and technical assistance available for volunteer tax consultants—most of whom would be elderly persons. . . . Additionally, our proposal would authorize the Internal Revenue Service to conduct a retirement income credit alert to help assure that all persons eligible for this provision take advantage of this tax relief measure. . . . Leading organizations in the field of aging have estimated that perhaps one-half of all elderly persons eligible to use the retirement income credit do not claim the credit on their tax return.

Such arguments identify differential conditions, differential capacities and differential pressures;

from them comes a distinctive legal age status for the elderly.

What is especially intriguing about this particular argument is that it is the admitted complexity and, supposedly, dysfunction of previous attempts to provide special assistance to the elderly—in this case, tax relief measures—which necessitates the passage of still another law. Is there not a message here: namely, that there is a need for Congress and for gerontologists to pause, to disengage from old age politics and to reconsider how best to serve the needs and to protect the rights of older citizens?

Hopefully, in this process a clearer understanding of the distinctive legal status of the elderly may emerge. To what extent do the elderly experience functional decline, and at what age? To what extent do they suffer from socially imposed restraints and deprivations—from so-called ageism? Are these restraints based solely on unfounded biases; or do they seek, for example, to treat all older people equally; or to provide for efficiency in administering pension funds; or to protect the morale of younger workers? To what extent do the existing laws, designed to improve the status of the elderly, actually produce new dependencies —as they apparently do in the case of income tax relief measures?

A quite different way of building the case for inequality is to argue that administering a policy based on functional, rather than formal, criteria for old age is too complicated to bear fruitful results. Thus, a recognized inequality in treatment is a supportable position. Justice Rehnquist, in a case in which the Court majority invalidated a

policy which required pregnant public school teachers to take a leave without pay, observed in a dissenting opinion:

Since this right to pursue an occupation is presumably on the same lofty footing as the right of choice in matters of family life, the Court will have to strain valiantly in order to avoid having today's opinion lead to the invalidation of mandatory retirement statutes for governmental employees. In that event federal, state, and local governmental bodies will be remitted to the task, thankless both for them and for the employees involved, of individual determinations of physical impairment and senility.[7]

Should the challenge to develop functional age criteria for retirement be seen as a "thankless task" or as an opportunity to promote freedom of choice for older citizens?

The point to be made here is that the politics of aging—whether it is exhibited in gerontological efforts to provide special benefits to the elderly or in attempts to extend adult benefits or rights until the onset of functional old age—has yet to encounter thoroughgoing assessment by the Court. That time is likely to come soon.

SOME EXAMPLES OF COUNTER-
SYSTEM MODEL BUILDING[8]

One means of activating the politics of aging has been to promote

7. Cleveland Board of Education v. La Fleur, 94 S. Ct. 791 (1974); dissent of Justice Rehnquist.

8. Advocacy of "countersystem model building" has been presented in G. Sjoberg and L. D Cain, "Negative Values, Countersystem Models, and the Analysis of Social Systems," in Institutions and Social Exchange: The Sociologies of Talcott Parsons and George C. Homans, ed. H. Turk and R. L. Simpson (Indianapolis: Bobbs-Merrill, 1971), pp. 213–229. "The countersystem

model statutes. Among the foremost examples of countersystem models designed to alter the status of the elderly are the forty proposals to be found in *A Handbook of Model State Statutes.*[9] A close examination of the model statutes, however, reveals that a general confrontation of the equality-equity issue has been avoided: in fact, legislative adoption of some of the proposals would probably compound the issue.

For example, the proposal which seeks to remove age-based discrimination in automobile insurance rates states:

No insurance company authorized to transact business in [state X] . . . shall cancel, refuse to issue or renew, reduce liability limits of, or increase the premium of any motor vehicle insurance policy issued to a resident of this State for the sole reason that the policy holder is a certain age. This Section does not apply to policy holders or applicants below the age of [twenty-six] years.

The rationale for such a statute is that, since automobile insurance coverage is a practical necessity for a driver and since an increased rate for the elderly may result in immobilization, age alone is not a legal basis for, in effect, denying the right to drive. It is puzzling that precisely the same argument was

not insisted upon to protect the rights of the driver under twenty-six.

Another proposed statute deals with fair employment practices legislation. It suggests:

It is an unlawful discriminatory practice for an employer or licensing agency 1) to refuse to hire . . . or 2) to discriminate in promotion or compensation . . . any individual between the ages of [forty and sixty-five] solely because of his age.

Tacitly, discrimination against, say, a sixty-six year old is condoned. If a sixty-six year old driver is to be protected, why not a worker of the same age?

Another complication reflected in this series of model statutes is that, although age sixty-two is suggested as the onset of old age, in most of the proposals—with the exception of fair employment practices—no rationale for any particular chronological age is provided. Would it not be wise to consider age status synchronization[10] as an appropriate policy goal for the determination of old age, at least if formal, chronological criteria are to be insisted upon?

Bernstein has argued persuasively that lawyers "must try to design new legal arrangements, possibly whole institutions, to ease the burdens of aging and to maximize the opportunities of the

---

model invites social scientists to cope rationally and systematically with alternatives in the future. . . . Countersystem analysis beckons sociologists to consider the implications of the persistence, redirection, or dissolution of existing values or structures"; ibid., pp. 224–225.

9. National Council of Senior Citizens, Inc., Legal Research and Services for the Elderly, *A Handbook of Model State Statutes: Legislative Approaches to the Problems of the Elderly* (Washington, D.C.: National Council of Senior Citizens, 1971), pp. 99–104.

10. L. D Cain, "Life Course and Social Structure," in *Handbook of Modern Sociology*, ed. R.E.L. Faris, (Chicago: Rand McNally, 1964), pp. 272–309: "separate institutions have been assigned responsibility for establishing age status sequences, frequently with the result that individuals experience asynchronization in moving through the life course. The use of age for defining legal status, for example, may not result in a status pattern synchronous with career patterns, and family responsibilities do not synchronize with earning capacity" (p. 288).

elderly."[11] Kraus, after excoriating defense attorneys for delaying cases of elderly plaintiffs as a means of increasing the likelihood that death will come before settlement is reached, has proposed that trial preference be given to older litigants.[12]

One of the most thorough examinations of the legal status—both extant and preferred—of the elderly is that of Alexander and Lewin, *The Aged and the Need for Surrogate Management*.[13] Their report concludes with a comprehensive model statute, Model Estate Advisors and Managers Act. Until recently the elderly under American law in most states have been subjected to denial of the right of self-management under provisions of law applicable to lunatics. Many states have recently adopted procedures for separate incompetency proceedings exclusively for the elderly. Alexander and Lewin observe:

There is a deeply held belief that older people require special legal protection. A number of jurisdictions by express language in their statutes and probably the rest by judicial interpretation provide special provisions for property management to persons who are unable to manage their affairs but who are not technically "insane." There ought to be a corresponding concern that older people are treated by the law in the same manner as the young.

11. M. C. Bernstein, "Aging and the Law," in *Aging and Society*, ed. M. W. Riley, J. W. Riley, Jr., and M. E. Johnson (New York: Russell Sage Foundation, 1969), vol. II, *Aging and the Professions*.

12. J. Kraus, "The Legal Problems of the Elderly Poor," *New York Law Journal* 165 (1971), pp. 1ff.

13. G. J. Alexander and H. D. Lewin, *The Aged and the Need for Surrogate Management* (Syracuse, N.Y.: Syracuse University, 1972).

Two distinguishing features of incompetency in old age are identified by Alexander and Lewin: (1) that there is often a period of "not-quite-incompetency," in which intervention of some sort may be needed; and (2) that there is an inevitability to the state of incompetency if one lives long enough. The fine line between competency and incompetency—and, therefore, the difficulty in providing satisfactory legal age provisions—is exemplified in a statement by McAvinchey, quoted by Alexander and Lewin:

These [old people who may be called not-quite-competent incompetents] know what they are doing, they want to do just what they are doing, and want to live the way they are living. Still, from our present sociological way of thinking they need care, some of them their estates, most of them their persons.[14]

In their model statute Alexander and Lewin offer a bold attempt to protect the right of the elderly to self-management as long as possible, to encourage the competent to plan effectively for a future incompetency and to support and protect the individual as incompetency unfolds.

An unusual proposal—and a fascinating use of chronological age—is found in the president's response to proposals regarding private pensions which were generated at the 1971 White House Conference on Aging. In offering means of protecting pension rights of workers from losses which often result from changing employment

14. Frank L. McAvinchey, "The Not-Quite-Incompetent Incompetent," *Trusts and Estates* 95 (1956), pp. 872–873; as quoted in Alexander and Lewin, *Surrogate Management*, p. 60.

or from mismanagement of pension funds, the president proposed:

Older workers need pension vesting protection because they lack the opportunities of younger people to start new careers and build new sources of retirement income. If the older worker loses his job or wants to move to a new job, he can't afford to lose his accumulated pension rights; but that is what happens unless those pension rights are vested. To change this situation, the President's proposal would establish the Rule of 50 as a Federal standard under which all pensions would become 50 percent vested when an employee's age plus years of participation in a plan total 50, increasing 10 percent for each year of service thereafter until fully vested.[15]

The model statutes reviewed here, the many more similar to them, the ideas and pressures continuing to come from the gerontological movement and the many unheralded and unreviewed ordinances being introduced by local governments suggest that the legal status of the elderly will surely remain in a state of flux for the foreseeable future.

LEGISLATIVE VERSUS EXECUTIVE DETERMINANTS OF THE STATUS OF THE ELDERLY: THE NUTRITION PROGRAM FOR THE ELDERLY

Lessons in civics inform us that legislative bodies pass laws, and that executives sign and administer those laws. However, it is increasingly apparent that the administrative branch of federal and state government has become involved in making policy decisions which

15. U.S., Senate, Committee on Labor and Public Welfare and the Special Committee on Aging, *Post-White House Conference on Aging Reports—April, 1973: Towards A New Attitude on Aging* (Washington, D.C.: U.S. Government Printing Office, 1973), p. 28.

have the effect of making law itself. The legal status of the elderly, for example, has been directly affected by such policy decisions.

Congressman Claude Pepper—Democrat, Florida—recently registered a complaint against this administrative role in testimony before the Senate Select Committee on Nutrition and Human Needs; he raised reservations about the nutrition program for the elderly only three months after the president had signed it into law:

The proposed rulemaking for Title VII for the nutrition programs for the elderly . . . raises several concerns regarding the administration's intent to carry out the nutrition program as provided in the law . . . The law clearly states that the Administration on Aging was intended to administer the program. The proposed rulemaking places the administration of the nutrition program in the Social and Rehabilitation services.

Second, the proposed rulemaking imposes an areawide bureaucracy between the State agencies and the community level nonprofit private and governmental sponsors of the nutrition programs.

My third comment concerns the income standard proposed in the rulemaking . . . [Although the legislation prevents a means test] for all practical purposes these guidelines provide a means test by using the definitions that relate to the general objectives of the legislation as the criteria of eligibility.

My [fourth] comment . . . concerns the limit of 20 percent imposed on any State for expenditures of a State's allotment to carry out the provisions for required supporting social services to the nutrition program . . . In the guidelines . . . transportation is referred to rather incidentally.

One other provision in the proposed rules [which] raises serious policy issues . . . is . . . that the State plan shall provide that each [nutrition] project shall have a council which . . . will be responsible for "the establishment of suggested fee guidelines" . . . It is certainly clear that the intent of the Congress was that no means test should be utilized in any manner whatsoever, and that in appropriate cases individuals would participate in the program even when they are not able to pay anything.[16]

Corker has placed the contest illustrated by Congressman Pepper's remarks into a broader, partisan struggle for the allegiance of elderly voters. According to Corker, the current Republican administration is trying to cultivate the support of, and to protect the economic security of, older citizens who have worked hard during long careers. In contrast, the Democratic Congress is following more closely the objectives of pressure groups seeking not only to augment the incomes of older citizens— regardless of degree of previous accomplishments—through governmental assistance, but also to increase governmental contributions for direct social services to the elderly who need them. "The stakes in this political contest are high; if either side can build a substantial bloc of support among older citizens, the effect on the

national political balance would be significant."[17]

CONCLUSIONS

The few examples cited and the few issues raised herein hardly begin to introduce either the extent to which formal, chronological definitions of old age have been introduced into law or the attendant consequences for the status of the elderly. Much more historical research needs to be done, and new and probing questions about current developments need to be asked. Perhaps the most important aspect of the problem is the recognition of the fact that no concerted efforts have been made to ascertain the links among social and biological research of the attributes of the elderly, the political activism which builds upon research discoveries to promote new laws regarding the elderly and the actual consequences of these new laws upon the status of the elderly. It appears to be inevitable, however, that within a short period the courts will be called upon to determine the extent to which formal, and the extent to which functional, definitions of old age are compatible with the protection of equality and the promotion of equity among the elderly under the Constitution.

16. C. Pepper, in U.S., Senate, Select Committee on Nutrition and Human Needs, Hearing of 14 June 1972, *Part 2: Nutritional Needs of Nation's Older Americans* (Washington, D.C.: U.S. Government Printing Office, 1972), pp. 244–249.

17. Bruce D. Corker, "Nutrition Program for the Elderly: Amendments to the Older Americans Act of 1965," *Harvard Journal on Legislation* 10, no. 2 (February 1973), pp. 198–216.

Reforming Private Pensions

By FRANK CUMMINGS

ABSTRACT: As the recent report of the Senate Labor Subcommittee indicates, some new, comprehensive and humane rethinking of our overall approach to private pensions is clearly needed. Controversy over the reform of pension plans has focused on vesting, funding, fiduciary standards and the prohibition of unethical conduct and conflicts of interest in the handling of pension funds. In the first section of this paper these issues are discussed in terms of the current situation: the dimensions of the pension industry, the current legal framework within which the industry operates and the techniques of the professionals in the field are analyzed. The issues are then discussed in terms of the proposed pension reform bill, which is pending before a Senate-House conference committee. A legislative assessment of the bill concludes the paper.

Frank Cummings is a Partner in the Washington, D.C. law firm Gall, Lane and Powell and Lecturer at Columbia Law School of Columbia University. He is also a Public Member of the United States Labor Department's Advisory Council on Employee Welfare and Pension Benefit Plans. Formerly, Mr. Cummings was Minority General Counsel of the Senate Labor and Public Welfare Committee.

TOO few participants who work under private pension plans actually get a pension, and too many who work long—ten, twenty, twenty-five or more—years get nothing. They get nothing not as the result of the machinations of evil men with bad motives, but rather as a result of badly designed plans. Many such plans either fail to provide reasonably attainable, vested, non-forfeitable interests or provide no vesting at all, even after long years of work, unless the employee actually reaches retirement age under the same employer. However, long term employment is no longer typical, because most Americans are, instead, mobile. Thus, as they move from job to job they forfeit pension after pension along the way. This constitutes the vesting side of the private pension controversy. There is also a funding side: there are too many plans within which the pension promise—even if vested—is so woefully underfunded that, if the employing enterprise should terminate, there might as well be no promise at all.

WHO LOSES AND WHY

Listed below are some of the cases which keep turning up with increasing frequency; the case histories are quoted verbatim from a recent report of the Senate Labor Subcommittee:

Case Number 1—Underfunding

A large steel mill engaged in the production of iron and steel materials maintains a pension plan with total assets of $19½ million. However, its accrued vested liabilities are in excess of $66 million. In the event of plan termination, under its current financial structure, less than ⅓ of accrued vested benefits could be paid through available pension assets. This plan started in 1950, and the employer is funding only current benefits costs.

Case Number 2—Vesting

This employer is a nation-wide department store whose pension plan contains no vesting provisions prior to qualifying for early retirement. Early retirement requirements consist of age 55 and 15 years of continuous service, or age 50 and 20 years of continuous service. Under the terms of plan eligibility, any worker of the thousands employed who would terminate employment prior to attaining age 50 will forfeit all benefits, not withstanding the number of years of employment.

Case Number 3—Portability

Mr. X began employment for a Midwest meat-packing company in 1927, at one of the employer's two plants in the same city. During World War II, he was sent to work in the other plant in the city because of the need to fulfill government contracts. He remained there until 1965 when the plant closed. The employer would not permit him to transfer back to the former plant as a regular employee, but only as a casual and intermittent laborer at the former plant. When the plant was closed, Mr. X was paid a total of $231.55 for his accrued pension benefits, despite 38 years of continuous employment with the same employer. Since he was reemployed in his old plant as a casual laborer, he was not eligible for any pension benefits after 1965. In 1970, he was dismissed because he was overage at 65. He did not receive any pension benefits. In sum, this employee was dismissed at age 66 after 43 years of continuous employment with the same employer and with no benefits to him except $231.55, paid to him in 1965.

Had he been permitted to carry his pension benefits and credits from both plants with the same employer, which were located a few streets apart, Mr. X would have been eligible for a pension.

Case Number 4—Overfunding

This pension plan belongs to one of the largest retail food chains in the United States. As of December 31, 1969, the pension plan assets' value totaled $118 million, and total accrued vested benefits were $60 million. The plan's vesting requirement is age 50 and 20 years of service.[1]

These cases deal primarily with vesting and funding—and I include the subject of reinsurance as an aspect of any realistic solution to the funding problem.

The other side of the pension controversy focuses on fiduciary standards and the prohibition of unethical conduct and conflicts of interest in the handling of pension funds. The most notable recent case history involved the deposit of vast pension reserves of the United Mine Workers Welfare and Retirement Fund into a noninterest-bearing account with a bank owned by the United Mine Workers of America.[2]

Faced with these and other difficulties in obtaining real security from the private pension plan system, many employees have sought solutions on an individual basis. On occasion, devices have been found which are of some help. However, in this case the strictures of the *Internal Revenue Code* are sometimes less of a help than a hindrance.

A pension on an individual basis poses these alternatives: (1) if an employee contributes his own money, he loses the tax advantages of sections 401-404 of the code; (2) if the employer pays, it will most often be discriminatory—in violation of section 401—and thus those advantages will also be lost; (3) as of this year, the Internal Revenue Service (IRS) is taking one more step to demolish an individual's option to plan his own pension by charging the individual with immediate constructive receipt of any compensation he elects to defer through use of a "salary reduction agreement" which provides for employer contributions to a pension plan in the same amount as the salary reduction;[3] (4) the final option open to the employee is a simple, deferred compensation agreement without tax deferral for the employee, unless the plan is either unvested—which risks forfeiture—or unfunded —which risks nonpayment.[4]

Clearly, some new, comprehensive and humane rethinking of our overall approach to private pensions is needed. There will doubtless be some cost in any new approach. However, we already pay a substantial cost whenever we let a worker retire without adequate resources—that is, the cost of welfare and related programs, of reduced purchasing power in a significant segment of our economy, and of lower morale and productivity. Therefore, the price of pension reform needs to be evaluated against these other costs and in terms of the benefits it will yield.

Before getting into details of legislation, however, one ought to examine the current situation first.

1. U.S., Senate, Report no. 92-634, 92nd Cong., 2nd sess., 1972, pp. 87–88.

2. *Blankenship* v *Boyle*, 329 F. Supp. 1089 (D.D.C. 1971), 337 F. Supp. 296 (D.D.C. 1972).

3. U.S., Department of the Treasury, proposed regulation, 37 Fed. Reg. 25938 (6 December 1972).

4. Rev. Rul. 60-31, 1960-1, Cum. Bull. 174.

Where are we now with regard to the dimensions of the pension industry, the current legal framework within which the industry operates and the techniques of the professionals in the field?

THE CURRENT SITUATION

General background

The aggregate size of private pension reserves is now in excess of $166 billion,[5] with another $148 billion in public pension funds. The growth of the private total has been approximately 10 percent per year. As far as I can tell, this represents the largest aggregate of essentially unregulated capital in the nation.

Two years ago the Senate Labor Subcommittee completed its *Statistical Analysis of Major Characteristics of Private Pension Plans*.[6] The study itself was based on answers to a thirty-two-page questionnaire sent out to a carefully designed cross-section of the industry; a total of 1,500 plans were surveyed. The major conclusions were these:

1. Approximately one-third of the pension plans studied had both a minimum age and service requirement for participation in a pension plan. An additional 25 percent had a minimum service requirement only, and approximately 35 percent of the plans had no age or service requirements for eligibility to participate.

2. The most common normal retirement age was 65 (occurring in almost 90 percent of the plans). In over half of these plans, a service requirement also

5. Securities and Exchange Commission, *Statistical Bulletin* 32, no. 8 (4 April 1973).
6. Republished in U.S., Senate, Report no. 92-1150, 92nd Cong., 2nd sess., 1972, pp. 73–148.

existed, in a few cases as much as 30 years. In the case of over one-fourth of all participants, attainment of age 65 and at least 15 years of service was required for a normal retirement benefit.

3. About 13 percent of the plans studied did not provide for any vesting at all. For those plans which had vesting provisions expressed as a combination of age and service, the combinations most frequently encountered were in the range of from 40 to 44 years of age with from 15 to 19 years of service. However, more stringent vesting formulas were also encountered; 8 percent of the plans had both an age and a service vesting qualification which required at least age 50 and 20 years of service for a vesting right. In the plans where only a service requirement was established for vesting, over one-fourth of these plans required more than 15 years of service to qualify. Among pension plans containing vesting provisions, over 55 percent had only a service requirement.

4. Over 30 percent of private pension plans were utilizing a deferred graded form of vesting, by which a certain percentage of a participant's accrued retirement benefit is vested initially, and the percentage increases periodically as the employee completes additional service. Profit-sharing plans utilize this type of vesting more frequently (over three fourths of all such plans).

5. Information regarding the assets and liabilities of pension plans was reported inconsistently and incompletely by a sizable number of pension plans. However, of those plans which did report appropriately, over 45 percent had a ratio of assets (valued at market) to total liabilities of over 75 percent, and three-fourths of the plans had a ratio of market assets (valued at market) to vested liabilites of over 75 percent. While this finding established that a majority of pension funds are generally well-funded, the responses also revealed a significant minority of plans

which were substantially underfunded. Over 10 percent of the plans reporting disclosed a ratio of assets (valued at market) to vested liabilities of 50 percent or less.

6. Only 40 percent of private pension plans had formal restrictions pertaining to investment of pension plans assets, and less than one-half of all plans required annual audits by an independent licensed or certified public accountant.

7. Over 35 percent of the pension plans studied, covering a similar number of participants, did not provide an opportunity for participants to request a hearing on claims; less than 30 percent of all plans provided for a written denial of such claims; and only 30 per cent of all plans provided for review procedures with respect to denial of claims.

From the answers to the questionnaires, the Senate Labor Subcommittee also extracted benefit level data; this information was published in its 1971–1972 interim report.[7] The key result was the disclosure that the median normal retirement benefit level under private plans in 1971 was $99 per month.

What becomes of individual participants, working—and moving—within this system? No comprehensive study has yet been conducted—and perhaps never will be—because of the difficulty inherent in tracing individuals as they move from plan to plan. The Senate Labor Subcommittee did do a limited study of eighty-seven plans—fifty-one with no vesting or late vesting and thirty-six with vesting after ten years of service or less. The report contains the following summary:

7. U.S., Senate, Report no. 92-634, 92nd Cong., 2nd Sess., 1972, p. 26.

1. Four percent of all participants since 1950 in the 51 no vesting or later vesting plans have received normal, early or deferred retirement benefits; eight percent of all participants in the 36 earlier vesting plans have received such benefits.

2. Five percent of all active participants since 1950 who left the plans have received normal early or deferred retirement benefits; 16 percent of all active participants since 1950 who left the 36 plans have received such benefits.

3. Seventy percent of all participants since 1950 in the 51 plans have forfeited without qualifying for benefits; 38 percent in the 36 plans have forfeited without qualifying for benefits.

4. Ninety-two percent of all active participants since 1950 who left the 51 plans forfeited without qualifying for benefits; 73 percent of all active participants since 1950 who left the 36 plans forfeited without qualifying for benefits.

5. Of the total forfeitures in the 51 plans since 1950, 85 percent were participants with five years service or less; of total forfeitures in the 36 plans since 1950, 80 percent were participants with five years service or less.

6. In the 51 plans, for every two participants who has received a normal, early or deferred retirement benefit since 1950, one participant forfeited with more than 15 years service, for every one participant who received a benefit, one participant with more than ten years service forfeited, three participants with more than five years service forfeited, and 16 participants with more than five years service or less forfeited.

7. In the 36 plans, for every one participant with more than 15 years service who forfeited since 1950, 24 participants received normal, early or deferred retirement benefits; for every participant with more than 10 years service

who forfeited, seven participants received such benefits; for every participant with more than five years service who forfeited, one participant received such a benefit; for every participant who received such a benefit, four employees with five years service or less forfeited.[8]

One cannot say, of course, whether the employees who forfeited under these plans eventually earned a pension under other plans in other jobs with other employers. There is no doubt, however, that they worked a long time for nothing under these particular plans.

Legal requirements before the 1974 Reform Bill

Three significant tax advantages to a "qualified" pension plan have been granted under the *Internal Revenue Code;* together, they constitute a gigantic bonus from our tax laws. The employer gets a tax deduction for his contributions to the plan.[9] The employee, for whose benefit the contributions are made, gets a tax deferral—that is, the money contributed on his behalf is not taxed until he retires, a time when his tax bracket is much lower.[10] The trust fund itself may accrue income, dividends and capital gains without any tax whatever on its income or growth.[11] The government has granted these concessions to private pension plans because these plans have served a socially useful purpose.

However, have they? Some have, but many have not. Moreover, they need not have done so in order to remain qualified under the code.

For, the code has required—except under special circumstances—no vesting at all until the employee actually retired and no funding beyond payment of current service costs, in addition to an amount equal to interest on unfunded past service liabilities—which the plan need never fund at all.[12]

So, for example, the Studebaker plan could pay employees but 15 percent of vested benefits when its South Bend plant shut down in 1964.[13] Studebaker's plan provided vesting and funding, but it had no obligation to do so under the code as it existed at that time. A plan, even though it was one hundred years old, was not required to fund past service costs; nor did it have to provide vesting at all. In either event—or in both—the plan remained qualified under the code.

The code did touch upon fiduciary standards, in the sense that it contained a list—section 503—of prohibited transactions. However, this did not prohibit the trust, for example, from investing in the securities of the employer; consequently, the plan was subjected to the same risks it would have been if it were unfunded: if the employer collapsed, so did the plan. Even if the code had effectively prohibited all self-dealing, what would the measure have remedied? If a beneficiary complained, the plan was disqualified, the *fund* lost its tax exemption, and the employee lost even more of his retirement security.

The Welfare and Pension Plans Disclosure Act created a set of

---

8. Ibid., p. 129.
9. *Internal Revenue Code,* §404.
10. Ibid., §§402, 403.
11. Ibid., §§401, 501 (a).

12. Rev. Rul. 69-421, part 6 (d).
13. U.S., Senate, Committee on Finance, *Federal Reinsurance of Private Pension Plans, Hearings on S. 1575,* 89th Cong., 2nd sess., 1966, p. 50.

disclosure requirements and an agency full of files. Yet, the trustees of a plan could still do just about anything, so long as their actions were disclosed. Congressional investigations have turned up all sorts of misappropriations of pension funds which were, in fact, disclosed—that is, duly filed under the act. Even if the Labor Department discovered inadequate disclosure, it simply asked the plan to amend its disclosure forms to add additional information. The department's action rarely did the individual pension participant any good.[14]

Some time ago there was a developing interest in pension plans—particularly profit-sharing retirement plans—insofar as they created securities under various securities acts.[15] Later amendments somewhat diminished the interest in pension plans, with two exceptions.[16] Outside the area of registration requirements as set forth in the securities acts, there has been some litigation concerning the application of fiduciary standards in these laws; that controversy continues.[17]

The National Labor Relations Act affords, again, only peripheral regulation which does not really affect the central issue of who-gets-what. Pensions are a mandatory bargaining issue,[18] although recently the benefit levels of those already retired turned out to be only a permissive bargaining subject[19]—a distinction which I suspect will turn out to be more technical than real. We also know that a plan cannot, on its face, limit participation on the basis of union membership.[20] Such a restriction is, again, more apparent than real, since eligibility can generally be limited on other grounds, such as hourly salary rates, with the same result. The real discrimination—against all employees but those who manage to stay with one employer until retirement age—is not covered by this act.

Ordinary trust law—although it applies only to trustees in the classic sense—is another problem for current regulation. Key decisions in pension administration are often made by persons not holding the legal status of trustee. Pension administrators need not be trustees. Investment discretion may be vested in labor-management committees, who are not trustees in the legal sense. In effect, all sorts of other persons—investment counselors, actuaries, accountants, employers and unions—may be making fiduciary decisions while

14. See, U.S., Senate, Committee on Government Operations, Permanent Investigations Subcommittee, *Hearings on Diversion of Union Welfare-Pension Funds of Allied Trades Council and Teamsters Local 815*, 89th Cong., 1st sess., 1965, p. 482; U.S., Senate, Report no. 1348, 89th Cong., 2nd sess., 1965, p. 27.

15. *SEC* v *Variable Annuity Life Ins. Co.*, 79 Sup. Ct. 618, 359 U.S. 65 (1959), *reversing* 257 F. 2d 383 (3d Cir. 1964), *cert. denied*, 377, U.S. 953 (1964).

16. See, *Institutional Investor Study, Report of the Securities and Exchange Commission, Summary Volume*, H. Doc. No. 92-64, Part 8, at 69-70 (1971).

17. See, *Local 734 Bakery Drivers Pension Fund Trust* v *Continental Illinois National Bank*, Dkt. No. 72 Civ 2551 (N.D. Ill. 1972); and the general discussion in Panel Discussion, "Conflicts of Interest and the Regulation of Securities," *Business Lawyer* 28 (1973), p. 545.

18. *Inland Steel Co.* v *NLRB*, 170 F.2d 247 (7th Cir. 1948), *cert. denied on this issue*, 336 U.S. 960 (1949), *affirmed on other grounds sub nom. Communications Assn.* v *Douds*, 339 U.S. 382 (1950)

19. *Chemical Workers* v *Pittsburgh Plate Glass Co.*, 30 L. Ed. 2d 341, 78 L.R.R.M. 2974 (1971).

20. *Kroger Co.*, 164 N.L.R.B. 362 (1967), *enforced in part*, 401 F2d. 682 (6th Cir. 1968), *cert. denied*, 395 U.S. 904 (1969).

not occupying the legal position of a fiduciary.

The lack of comprehensiveness in ordinary trust law once led a Senate subcommittee to conclude that: "The application of well-established doctrines of trust law to the field of employee benefit trust funds is a most difficult task."[21] The American Bar Association observed: "Under the typical employee benefit trust agreement the beneficiaries [the employee participants] have very insubstantial enforceable rights."[22] Thus, it has been possible for courts to hold that the exercise of rights reserved by the employer with respect to a pension plan is "conclusive in the absence of fraud or such gross mistakes as imply bad faith or a failure to exercise an honest judgment," and evidence to sustain the burden of showing such fraud, bad faith or mistake "must be more than a mere preponderance, it must be overwhelming."[23] Furthermore, even those rights which a pension participant does have often prove to be illusory when he tries to use the legal processes which, at a first glance, might seem to be available to him.[24]

Consider the average problem faced by a lawyer when a potential client walks through his door and says either "they owe me a pension" or "they are misusing the money in the pension fund." If the lawyer aks "Who are they?" how many employees would know the corporate name of the employer; the exact name and location of the trust and trustees; the location of the bank holding the money; the name of the insurance company through which the plan is funded, if it is funded that way; the identity and addresses of the unions involved, including the international and local unions, their officers and the names of those officers who have been designated as trustees? How many employees know even the real name of the plan or trust and its technical terms?

Assume—even though one rarely has the right to do so—that the employee knows the answers to all the questions. Then, the legal problems have just begun. Which state law applies? The bank is in one state; the corporation is in another state; the employees are in several other states; the union is in another state; and the contract may not specify a choice of law. Should this matter be decided—probably after costly litigation—how would one find both a court with jurisdiction to serve process in all the states (a federal court, of course, can serve process only within the state in which it sits)[25] and the legal means to bring in all the necessary parties?

Assume further—though, in most cases, one has no right to assume —that a court able to serve process on all the necessary parties could be found. What would one sue for? If one is suing to stop misuse of the money by the trustees —rather than for a pension—the recovery goes not to the plaintiff employee, but back into the fund. It is essentially a derivative ac-

21. U.S., Senate, Report no. 1734, 84th Cong., 1st Sess., 1956.

22. American Bar Association, "Report of the Committee on Trust Administration and Accounting, Exculpatory Clauses/Their Legal Significance," *Real Property, Probate and Trust Journal* 1, no. 4. (Winter 1966), p. 530.

23. *Menke v Thompson*, 140 F.2d 786, 791 (8th Cir. 1944).

24. See, generally, Warren Elliott, *Federal Fiduciary Standards for Welfare and Pension Plans* (New York: Association of Life Insurance Counsel, 1968 p. 366.

25. Fed. R. Civ. P. 4 (f).

tion from which the plaintiff recovers nothing more than increased security for his pension expectancy. If, on the other hand, the employee is suing for a pension, the recovery is the discounted value of one pension—unless the plaintiff can put together a rare class action, or a union finances the lawsuit at substantial expense to itself.

Now, consider the cost of litigating the very complex questions of law which I have just discussed. How much is the lawyer going to charge for this lawsuit? Even if the lawyer takes only a minimal fee for this elaborate lawsuit, in most cases his fee will necessarily far exceed the amount of recovery—the discounted value of one pension. Moreover, compounding the problem is the fact that most misdeeds by pension administrators are brought to light in lawsuits by employees who have yet to vest. Thus, even if the case is won, the client does not receive the recovery; he may not even get a pension. Of course, there are class actions—which work on occasion. There are lawsuits financed by persons other than individual pension participants—for example, unions, by resort to their treasuries.

Nevertheless, most pension claims for benefits are unpromising. If the action is simply to rectify a breach of fiduciary standards not involving an actual denial of benefits, the recovery goes back into the fund, not to the individual participant. The plaintiff is therefore financing a lawsuit, somewhat in the public interest, at considerable—usually prohibitive—expense to himself. If the plaintiff is already retired, he may not live long enough to enjoy the benefits of his recovery. In short, private lawsuits under previously existing law did not provide a meaningful remedy for the employee in most pension cases. A national law with a national agency to enforce it was needed to remove this whole matter from the area of ordinary garden-variety litigation, since it simply did not work.

The pension professionals

A wide variety of professionals are at work in the private pension system. The key men are lawyers, accountants, actuaries, union leaders, corporate financial executives and professional pension planners and consultants—who are often actuaries or lawyers, although they need not be.

First, a few words about the lawyers. What I have to say here is not absolute and leaves room for many notable exceptions—hopefully, including myself. Most lawyers working regularly in this field are tax lawyers, because the principal rules of the game are tax rules. The client is the contributing corporation; the object is to secure tax qualification. This is certainly a legitimate and necessary objective; however, as noted above, it has had little to do with the beneficiary's income security. The rest of the legal profession—including labor lawyers—seems to have abdicated in favor of the tax lawyers. In my view, this is a tragedy, because too often—although not always—no one is representing the interests of the beneficiaries at the planning stage.

Second, within our system of collective bargaining, the underlying assumption is that the union protects the employee's interests, that the employer protects corporate financial interests and that bargaining eventually leads to some viable compromise. Only rarely do we look behind the union's demands to see if individual concerns are being properly represented. Moreover, all issues are not arbitrated in this way; for example, bargaining is not even required in the case of pension rights for those already retired.[26]

One must keep in mind, however, that a union, after all, is supposed to be a democratic organization. It is therefore usually dominated by its younger members, who have little concern with pensions. Thus, many pension plans have developed with benefit levels which increase year after year, but with vesting so deferred that only a few members ever actually receive those benefits. There are notable exceptions, of course—for example, the steel workers and auto workers. Exceptions tend to occur in industries where strong seniority systems protect the older workers from layoff and permit the median age of the work force to rise. Too often, however, unions—particularly those representing low-wage workers—are either unable or unwilling to press for earlier vesting.[27]

Employers, on the other hand, cannot reasonably be expected to fight hard for a reallocation of dollars already spent. That is, during the bargaining process the employer and the union decide upon a dollar figure—total increased labor cost—to reach a settlement; the union specifices that X percent of this amount is to be paid in wages and Y percent in pensions. Since the total increased labor cost is not affected by the wage-pension breakdown, no employer in his right mind would risk a strike to force an increase in Y with a corresponding decrease in X. In short, the dynamics of collective bargaining simply break down—not always, but often—when it comes to pensions.

Accountants, who audit, and actuaries, who project, are the final group of professionals involved. An accountant can tell what assets and liabilities are now; however, if a pension plan is being considered, one needs to know whether it will be solvent in twenty years. Projecting such variables as interest rates, contribution rates, employee turnover, life expectancy, and other factors over that period of time thus makes up the lexicon of actuarial assumptions.

The irony is that while accountants are licensed, the actuaries—who are the key men—are not licensed in any state. Most actuaries are highly skilled professionals, but they need not be. At least a significant number of them are nothing more than salesmen who package and sell pension plans tailored to suit the needs of buyers who want a decent benefit level at minimum cost—an easily obtainable objective if the plan is set up so that almost everyone forfeits his credits. Again, not all of the salesmen function this way, but a substantial number do. In sum, the professionals at work in this system give no real assurance that the legitimate pension expectations of long-service workers will be

26. Compare, *Allied Chemical Workers* v *Pittsburgh Plate Glass Co.*, 404 U.S. 157 (1971), with *Inland Steel Co.* v *NLRB*, 1970 F.2d 247 (7th Cir. 1948), *cert. denied on this issue*, 336 U.S. 960 (1949), *affirmed on other grounds sub. nom. Communications Assn.* v *Douds*, 339 U.S. 382 (1950).

27. See, U.S., Senate, Committee on Labor and Public Welfare, Subcommittee on Labor, *Hearings on S.3598*, Testimony of Andrew Biemiller for the AFL-CIO, 92d Cong. 2nd sess., part 3, 1974, p. 1114.

realized. The need for a new law is clear.

THE REFORM BILL

As this analysis is written—May 1974—a pension reform bill is pending before a Senate-House conference committee. Bills were passed by the House—H.R.2—and by the Senate—S.4, repassed as H.R.4200 and, then, repassed as an amendment to H.R.2. Thus, it is impossible to predict with precision the exact content of the bill which will emerge from the conference. Hardly a paragraph in more than six hundred pages of text is identical in the two versions.

Nevertheless, there are striking similarities in the substance of both versions of the bill. It therefore seems safe to predict that a pension reform bill will become law and that at least a certain core of substance will survive the conference. The general headings of the bill seem clear: vesting, funding, plan termination insurance, fiduciary standards and certain tax benefit limitations, as well as general procedural reform. Without getting into the highly technical aspects of the legislation—which are likely to be revised, in any event—one can say that several major reform elements—which are discussed below—will almost certainly be included in the conference report and will become law this year.

Vesting

As indicated above, current law requires no vesting at all. An employee, working for any number of years and reaching any age, can leave an employer without taking any pension interest with him. The only exception is that after an employee retires, his pension interest must vest and become nonforfeitable.

The reform bill will require that after participation in the plan for a given number of years, an employee must earn a vested —nonforfeitable—pension interest. That is, he will earn a nonforfeitable right to a deferred life annuity contingent only upon his survival until retirement age. He cannot lose that interest by changing jobs; by being discharged, laid-off or disabled; or by discontinuing his participation in the plan in any other way.

The number of years provided in the bill for vesting is a point of disagreement between the two houses. However, it seems likely that the conference report will provide alternative schedules. The first alternative will be 100 percent vesting after ten years of participation; the second schedule will be "graded vesting"—that is, 25 percent vesting after five years, increasing gradually to 100 percent after fifteen years.

This schedule has been severely criticized for failing to vest the rights of relatively short-service employees who work less than five years. There are certain employees—for example, secretaries and aerospace engineers—who tend to move from job to job with such frequency that they may continue to forfeit pension after pension even after the new bill becomes law. On the other hand, the horror stories which generated the ground swell of political support for the reform bill will be cured by the vesting standard.

The more highly mobile occupations, moreover, can still find a solution to their problems by implementing plan-design opportunities which are not mandated by the bill, but which are always possible through employee organization. The most obvious solution is the formulation of multiemployer plans. The professional engineering societies, for example, have stated their intention to develop a multiemployer plan covering all professional engineers; all credits would funnel into a single plan. Thus, the members will be able to move from job to job without forfeitures.

On the other hand, categories of employees—such as secretaries—without well-developed professional organization are unlikely to accomplish anything in this direction. By and large, they are left out by the reform. Complaints will doubtless continue to be made, and the bill will need tightening in future years.

Supplementing the vesting standards are other provisions in the bill dealing with eligibility and participation. These stipulations are designed to prevent the exclusion from participation of workers under a stated age. The most likely provision to emerge from the conference committee will be a rule that employees over the age of 25 must be included. Again, one can argue that there is no excuse for excluding anyone, whatever his age. However, the bill is a compromise.

Funding

The provision covering funding is perhaps the most complex of the standards in the bill. As indicated above, the pension promise is one of the few undertakings which a twentieth century corporation may make without really being forced to keep it. It is essentially a nonrecourse undertaking. The employer sets up the plan; the plan makes a promise of benefits which must be kept to the extent that the plan has the money to pay those benefits. The limit of the employer's undertaking is to make contributions "as actuarily determined." If for any reason the plan should terminate before it is fully funded, the employer himself has no liability for benefits. Furthermore, there are practically no enforceable rules governing the actuarial practices which determine the rate of contributions.

To understand how contributions may lag behind benefit liabilities, one must examine the notion of past service credit. An employer normally sets up a plan because he has some older employees who are about to retire and he wants to provide them with pensions. However, most of their service occurred before there was a plan—before any contributions were made. Accordingly, the employer grants credit for past service; past service credit is always initially unfunded.

In addition, the employer grants credit for future service which, presumably, will be funded currently as the plan goes along. Even if the future service is funded currently, the past service remains a liability. How much time does the employer have to catch up? Under present law, he need never catch up, so long as he does not fall further behind. Thus—unless the plans last until infinity—whenever a plan terminates, there will be a deficit; someone will necessarily lose benefits.

The reform bill requires a catchup in no more than thirty years. Yet, even that rule, standing alone, would be inadequate to provide real security. Taken together with the "reinsurance provisions," the bill does guarantee adequate funding.

Plan termination–reinsurance

The bill establishes a federal plan termination insurance program, analogous to the Federal Deposit Insurance Corporation (FDIC). If the fund is insufficient to pay benefits, the plan termination fund pays off. However, this does not end the matter. Once the plan termination insurance pays off, the employer is liable to refund the payments to the reinsurance fund up to a stated percentage of his net worth. Thus, for the first time the law pierces the nonrecourse feature of most pension plans and makes the employer directly liable, at least to some extent.

Fiduciary standards

For the first time the bill establishes federal standards of conduct for pension fund managers as a matter of federal law. Such standards can be found in many state laws already, but enforcement has been weak or nonexistent and has depended primarily upon private law suits.

If one lesson has been learned from examining the history of pension litigation, it has been that such law suits are inadequate to regulate the conduct of pension trustees. The amount of recovery rarely exceeds the lawyer's fee. So, the key to federal enforcement is not so much that the law becomes federal, but that a federal agency is empowered to enforce the law. Employees need not depend upon private lawyers, who must be paid privately.

The fiduciary standards themselves are uncertain. The Senate standards are strong; the House standards are weak. One cannot predict at this point which will survive the conference.

Tax features

In addition to the many substantive rules governing private pension plans, a number of features are included in the bill which relate almost exclusively to tax law— maximum deductions for contributions and the like. An upper limit is placed upon benefits and contributions which may receive favorable tax treatment. Certain changes are made in the formulae governing rules against discrimination in favor of highly compensated employees.

However, the most critical tax amendments are those which relate to the right of the individual to do his own pension planning. For the first time the tax law will permit an individual who is not covered by any pension plan to contribute up to $1500 per year to his own individual retirement account (IRA) and to get a tax deduction for retirement saving. In addition, the allowable limit on contributions to Keogh plans for the self-employed and for partners in uncorporated businesses has been raised from $2,500 per year to $7,500 per year. The latter features were included in the bill in an attempt to encourage retirement savings and pension coverage for workers—some 50 percent of the work force—who presently do not participate in the private pension system at all.

Again, the bill is a compromise. Why limit the IRA to employees who have no coverage? Why not make it available to employees who have coverage under pension plans whose benefits are so low as to be trivial? Why limit the Keogh plan to $7,500 and impose no such limit on corporations—especially since any partnership can avoid the Keogh limits by converting to corporate form? These political compromises can only be explained in terms of vote counts and lobbying pressure.

A LEGISLATIVE ASSESSMENT

No legislation is perfect, and pension bills are no exception to the rule. No bill eliminates every possible forfeiture. Each bill makes a judgment. When—that is, after how many years of employment— does forfeiture of benefits caused by a change of jobs become unfair or unjust?

Of course, it is always possible to go further. It is possible to set up an immediate vesting standard as a matter of law. However, the legislator must balance the interests of the employees with those of the employers, who need to keep a string on the plan as an inducement to retain their best employees. Then, there is the argument that a legislative straitjacket would kill the goose that laid the golden egg.

I cannot judge issues such as these on an absolute basis. Yet, certain things are clear:

—the bill could have gone much further without killing any geese—except those which have been laying rotten eggs all along;

—the bill will mandate a formidable array of standards which will generate a great many improvements in the private system;

—the new law sets the nation on the right track.

The last point is, perhaps, the most important. Standards legislation is always a foot-in-the-door proposition: the basic framework is laid out; then, year after year, Congress improves on the standards within that framework.

Congress has made a cost judgment. The judgment is that industry can afford the limited improvements in this legislation and that the private pension system will expand despite federal controls. The cost of this legislation—as limited as it is—will be substantial; no one can estimate exactly what that cost will be.

Yet, we are already paying the cost of widespread destitution in old age. We pay it in welfare cost and in all sorts of public assistance to older people who worked hard during their earlier years, who had pride in themselves and in their abilities, but who nevertheless are unable to provide for themselves any longer. Why not give them the dignity of being able to live in their retirement years on money they have earned?

To a very limited extent, we do so already under Social Security. But Social Security, at best, will never provide more than a bare, subsistence income level. Why, at the age of 65, should the typical middle class American—who has lived his whole working life on a middle class income—be suddenly thrown to the very bottom of the economic barrel? Moreover, whose resources are being discussed anyway? This reform is not welfare, not reallocation of money from the rich to the poor. The reform will simply give a worker the use of the money he earned when he needs it most and will let him pay tax on it at that time.

One can argue over whether the judgment Congress has reached should have required more money for more people with more vesting and more funding. Yet, it ought to be obvious that the direction of the legislation is proper and that the steps taken were long overdue. Henceforth, the question will not be whether there should be federal standards, but simply what improvements and changes in the law should come next.

The Political Economy of Nursing Homes

By MARY ADELAIDE MENDELSON AND DAVID HAPGOOD

ABSTRACT: The nursing home industry receives three-quarters of its income from government. The industry earns high profits while providing poor patient care. Considerable swindling of government funds occurs. One category is nickel and diming, which consists of clipping every possible dollar from government money as it passes through nursing home accounts. Another method—large scale and often within the law—involves the manipulation of ownership and mortgages. There are several causes for the failure of government to control nursing home swindles. While there is no lack of regulations, the will to enforce them is lacking. Industry lobbyists are especially influential at the state level, where the Medicaid rate is set. The federal government has failed to collect basic information about the industry and denies the public ready access to the reports on nursing home inspections. The industry's immunity from regulation, in large part, results from the lack of countervailing pressure from the public.

Mary Adelaide Mendelson is the author of Tender Loving Greed, *a study of the nursing home industry, published this year by Alfred A. Knopf. Mrs. Mendelson graduated from Radcliffe and received her Masters Degree in Political Science from the University of Michigan. She has been a consultant to the Federation for Community Planning of Cleveland since 1964.*

David Hapgood is a journalist. His most recent book is the forthcoming The Screwing of the Average Man, *to be published by Doubleday.*

THE nursing home industry is highly profitable, having expanded greatly in response to government financing of health care for the elderly and the indigent. Yet, as has been widely documented, most nursing homes fail to provide a decent environment for their charges in spite of government financing. The chronic inability of government at all levels to make increased spending on nursing homes result in better patient care rather than in higher profits for the industry constitutes a dramatic case of the failure of government regulation.

INTRODUCTION

In the past—a past which seems very distant now—families took care of older people. They lived out their last years in the homes of their grown children. That, too, has changed: older people now live alone as long as they can. However, for many, that time ends long before the end of their lives. Thus, for those who are sick or who are alive but cannot manage alone, the only answer is the nursing home.

Usually, these people cannot pay for the nursing homes they need, because the old are generally poor, as well as sick. People over sixty-five have less income than younger people; at the same time, they need more health care. Health insurance never covers long term nursing home costs; moreover, for a variety of reasons, the children of old people frequently cannot pay these bills either. This leaves only the government.

Americans have turned over the responsibility for older people—at least for those who are sick and poor—to the state. What happens to old people is decided not by families, but by bureaucracies. The nursing home industry, although privately owned, is a government industry much like the Lockheed Aircraft Corporation. By 1971 two-thirds of the million people in nursing homes were supported by government, and more than three-quarters of the $3.5 billion income of nursing homes was public money.

Public money began flooding the health-care system, including nursing homes, after the 1965 adoption of Medicare and Medicaid. Medicare—title XVIII of the Social Security Act—provided federal financing for up to one hundred days, following hospitalization, in a nursing home. Medicaid—title XIX—which is financed jointly by the federal and respective state governments, pays for an unlimited nursing home stay.

These two acts set off a series of profound changes in nursing homes. In the years after Medicare and Medicaid, health-care prices, including those for nursing homes, went up much faster than the general price level. The mode of operation of the new health-care programs guaranteed excess profits but no benefit to the patient—especially in the case of the nursing home industry. Having taken on the responsibility for sick and poor older Americans, the government has nevertheless failed to exercise the will to ensure the proper carrying out of this responsibility by the institutions to which the old have been entrusted, although there is theoretically an elaborate regulation network to cover both Medicaid and Medicare.

HOW MEDICAID WORKS

Medicaid—by far the biggest source of money for nursing homes, because it has no time limit—is regulated mainly by the states. Each state, usually through its health department, licenses and inspects nursing homes which accept Medicaid patients. The state inspector decides whether the home is meeting state and federal standards. Also, while Medicaid was intended for the medically indigent—that is, those who cannot afford the care they need—each state decides who is eligible for Medicaid. The income limit varies from state to state and can be somewhat higher than the income limit for welfare. In this system the local welfare caseworker plays an essential part. The caseworker decides whether an applicant is eligible for Medicaid and, if the applicant has some resources—Social Security, in most cases—how much more Medicaid should pay the nursing home for his care. Most importantly, it is the caseworker who usually chooses the nursing home for the Medicaid patient. Thus, the nursing home operator is dependent on the inspector—who could close his home for violations—and on the caseworker—who can either guarantee or close off his supply of patients. It is in these relationships that the corruption and indifference of nursing home regulators are most painfully evident.

The states also decide the rates which nursing homes are to be paid for Medicaid patients. Generally, there are two ways of paying the Medicaid bill: (1) flat rate, whereby the nursing home directly receives a set fee per patient per day and (2) cost plus, whereby the nursing home is reimbursed for its costs, plus a "reasonable" profit. Washington's role is mainly confined to paying the federal share of the cost, which ranges from 50 to 80 percent depending on the state. Medicare, which pays for about 4 percent of the nursing home population, operates entirely on federal money and the cost-plus approach.

These, however, are not the only ways in which federal money reaches the nursing home. If a patient gets Social Security, his Medicaid bill is reduced by that amount. The Veterans Administration (VA) also pays nursing homes for the care of some patients coming from VA hospitals.

The advent of Medicaid and Medicare was a clear signal to those seeking a fast way to make money. Those businessmen and hustlers already in the industry saw the new money as a way to expand their operations and their profits. The industry expanded, and prices went up. The patients suffered, not so much because anyone set out to make them suffer—although that happens, too—but because lack of effective controls resulted in lack of incentives for improving patient care. If anything, the operators of nursing homes were motivated to do exactly the opposite: much of the increased profits could come out of the hide of the patient.

Flat rate Medicaid money is the most profitable to the operator and the hardest on the patient. If the government will pay, say, $14 a day per patient, the way to make money is obviously to cut daily costs as far below $14 as one can. Some costs, such as real estate taxes and interest, cannot be cut. Thus, costs which can be lowered are those incurred by patient care, and that is where the operators cut corners.

First of all, one can buy cheap food in the smallest possible amounts. In the 1970s operators were found who fed patients on less than $1.00 a day; one, in Chicago in 1970, managed to feed his patients on $.78 a day. Not surprisingly, many nursing home patients are emaciated.

One can also cut corners on staff: hire a cheaper practical nurse rather than a registered nurse. One can pay the lowest rate for aides by hiring people who cannot hold a job anywhere else. The patients will suffer—for example, incompetent aides, who seem to be taking out their own inadequacies on the people in their charge, are responsible for much of the brutality in nursing homes—but the profits will go up.

These variable costs are that part of the nursing home operation which is the most subject to governmental regulation—at least on paper. Thus, if the operator can cut these costs, it is because the regulators let him get away with it. From the point of view of the operator, it is cheaper to buy off an inspector or caseworker than to pay the cost of decent patient care.

The game of profit is played differently if the nursing home is not paid a flat rate per patient per day, but is reimbursed for its costs. This is the method used by Medicare and also by Medicaid in some states. In this situation there is no incentive to cut costs, since the costs are passed on to the government; the operator's opportunity to increase profits lies in padding his bills. This swindle is made easy by the fact that the government rarely conducts any effective audit of nursing home bills.

ANCILLARY FRAUD

The extra—or ancillary—services which the government purchases for nursing home patients provide a rich field for exploitation. Here, the opportunity for profit lies in the operator's rela-

tionship with people for whose goods and services the government pays. Although the operator does not collect the money himself—it is paid directly to the supplier—he has the power to determine who will collect, since he chooses the suppliers and decides how much they are to deliver. Thus, the operator decides which pharmacist will get the considerable drug business his home provides. Since he has no motive to demand a lower price—the government is paying—it is common practice for him to demand a kickback from the pharmacist he chose. If the operator is at all unscrupulous, he has other opportunities to make extra money. He can order expensive brand-name drugs and let the pharmacist fill the prescription with much cheaper generic drugs which are identical to the brand-name drugs; the government pays the higher price and the operator and pharmacist split the difference. Or, he can order drugs in unnecessarily large quantities. Or—most simply and with the greatest profit—they can bill the government for the drugs which are never delivered at all.

The operator also chooses the physicians who will be paid for attending those patients who do not have their own doctors. If both are unscrupulous, the result is the gang visit, as it is known in the trade —that is, the physician whips through the nursing home in a couple of hours, glancing at only the most urgent cases, and later bills the government as if he had given individual attention to each patient. In its investigation of Ohio nursing homes the General Accounting Office (GAO) found not a few examples of such gang visits. One doctor billed the government for 487 visits within a sixteen-day period, including 90 on one day and 86 on another. A podiatrist put in for 750 visits, including 32 on one Sunday. All these doctors were also handling their usual load of non-Medicaid patients. Physicians and other health professionals can also order, at government expense, goods and services which the patients clearly do not need.

Such swindles may seem petty when viewed individually. However, in sum, all those nickels and dimes add up to many millions, if not billions, of dollars a year. Nursing home operators and their collaborators can engage in these deals safely, because there is little risk of being caught and, even if caught, virtually no risk of being punished. Neither the GAO nor any other investigating agency has looked at more than a small fraction of the records. Yet, if the pattern found so far is typical of the industry—and there is every reason to believe it is—then there are literally millions of frauds waiting to be uncovered.

The nursing home operator and his partners are not punished, except in rare and extreme cases. Typically, if a government auditor catches the operator and, say, the doctor cutting a little extra on the side, all the auditor does is force them to give back the money. The case is not sent over to the district attorney for criminal prosecution, nor is any move made to revoke the operator's license. The operator's explanation—usually "clerical error"—is allowed to stand. This happens even when the same operators are caught time and time again in the same types of fraud. While the explanations begin to wear thin, no attempt is made to deter the operators from trying

again. There is, indeed, no reason for them not to try again.

HIGH LEVEL SWINDLES

Beyond these types of swindles—which are known to those who follow the Medicaid scandals—is a quite different kind of fraud, cloaked in secrecy and complexity, unknown to the public and even to many nursing home critics. Frauds at this level are the most sophisticated method for hustling the government for nursing home money. The opportunity, once perceived, has drawn into the nursing home field con men and manipulators whose skills and imagination put them in a class apart from those operators whose stealing is limited to kickbacks from pharmacies and doctors. Few of these newcomers have any experience in nursing homes or in any other aspect of the health field. All they know is how to make money, and they sense that the nursing home is a good place to use their talent.

The basic strategy of these speculators is to manipulate the ownership and mortgaging of those nursing homes which receive guaranteed government income in order to extract the most revenue and to pay back the least amount in the form of income taxes. Among the costs of operating a nursing home are the costs of ownership—that is, the amount paid out in either rent or mortgage interest payments—costs which are reimbursed by the government when it pays for its Medicaid and Medicare patients. The higher the cost of ownership, the more the government pays. Of course, the government payment does not stay with the operator; it goes on to the owner—if the operator pays rent—or to the mortgage holder—if the operator is also the owner. Thus, higher ownership costs seem to benefit someone other than the operator.

The solution is to make the owner appear to be someone other than the operator, while in fact the same people are collecting at both ends. If, for example, a man owns a nursing home, he may "sell" it to someone who turns out to be a friend or a relative, then "rent" it back at a rental which requires the government to increase its payments. He splits the profit between himself as operator and himself, in different guise, as owner. Or, alternatively, he may build a nursing home and rent it, at a very high figure, to a "nonprofit" corporation he or his friends have created. The government will pay more to that corporation, because of the high rental, than the amount—which would have been based on the cost of building the home—it would have paid to him directly. The extra payment, of course, comes back to the owner in the form of the extra high rent. He may sell the home at an inflated price to some associates, who use the price as a basis for getting higher payments from the government. In each of these maneuvers the amount being received has been increased by increasing the apparent cost of ownership. The same principle can be applied to other costs. One can drive up the costs of supplies by paying more than market price to suppliers, who turn out to be either one's associates or oneself under another corporate name.

The method varies somewhat according to the way the government pays off. In a straight cost-reimbursement situation—all Medicare patients and in some states

Medicaid patients, also—the payoff is immediate, for the government pays exactly the apparent cost, plus a percentage of profit. If the cost is raised, the payment goes up automatically. In the case of homes paid on flat rate system, the payoff is not so quick. Here, the nursing home industry must use the higher costs of ownership as a basis for lobbying the state for an increase in the flat rate. In the almost annual bouts of lobbying over the rates, the nursing home representatives use those costs as apparent hard evidence that they need more money. Unless the state looks behind the figures, they will appear to be convincing evidence; since, in fact, the states usually take the industry's figures and simply shave them a little, the contrived cost increases eventually produce the desired effect.

A universal reason for such complex transactions is to hide the incredibly high profits made by the nursing home industry. For one thing, too visible profits might undercut the poormouthing which accompanies the industry's pleas for higher rates. In practice, these profits do not seem to matter. For example, in the late sixties nursing homes were successfully lobbying for higher rates at the same time that stock speculators were pronouncing the industry to be the hottest thing on Wall Street.

In a broader sense, this industry —as does any other—spends much of its inventive skill in trying to minimize the amount of income tax it has to pay. When one makes as much money as most nursing homes do, that can be a problem. Shifts of ownership can help. If, for example, one sells the home at an inflated figure and then rents it back, the profit can be taken as capital gains instead of regular income, and the tax will be lower.

Shifting costs to the nursing home is a way of shifting profits out, into another corporation set up for that purpose. Such an arrangement may permit one to diffuse the profits—perhaps by putting family on the payroll—before Internal Revenue can get at them. The nursing home chains, which have the best accountants, have pioneered this territory. One chain has at least five subsidiaries from which it buys goods and services.

It should be emphasized that many of these tax-avoidance ploys are legal. Legal or not, however, the taxpayer bears the cost of the nursing homes' excessive profits.

Manipulating mortgages is another aspect of profit making in the nursing home industry. Despite the many protestations to the contrary, there is no safer risk than the nursing home. With guaranteed government revenue, with a growing elderly population and with high occupancy rate, there is, as one Wall Street expert said, "no way" not to make money in this business. What could be a better bet than to lend—or borrow—money against guaranteed government revenue? In this manner many shoestring operators have gotten their start. If they can scrape together enough in loans—often from the original owner—for the down payment to buy a home, they can get a first mortgage on the home at the normal interest rate of 6 to 8 percent. That home can subsequently be used as collateral for second and third mortgages at much higher rates of interest. Although these interest payments can then be used as the basis for higher reimbursement, there is, in fact, no requirement that the money from

such second and third mortgages be used for the nursing home itself.

Government revenue, in effect, endorses pyramiding and other dubious business practices. The sure supply of government-supported patients allows nursing home owners to take risks which other kinds of businesses cannot afford. Not only that: by underwriting manipulations that artificially increase nursing home costs, the government also guarantees unnecessary increases in the rates it pays for patient care. That, too, has a double effect, for each increase in rates drives onto Medicaid people who were able to pay their own way when the rates were lower. Higher rates thus increase the number of patients supported by government, as well as the rate paid for each patient. In these many ways government policy—or lack of policy—has served to enrich nursing home owners at the expense of both taxpayers and patients.

TOLERANT REGULATORS

This situation—in which ever larger amounts of government money disappear, ever higher profits are made and patient care is not at all improved—is tolerated by governmental regulators at all levels. The problem is not a lack of regulations; the industry is festooned with rules which theoretically determine its conduct. However, the regulations are not enforced.

Year after year the rules laid down by government are disobeyed. Thus, reformers who demand better regulations miss the point, and in a way that is dangerously deceptive. It is relatively easy for reformers to achieve a change in the regulations and then to go home believing that they have made a lasting change in the way the nursing home industry actually operates.

The nursing home industry has won for itself a large degree of immunity from accountability to those who finance it. How this has been done is not entirely clear, for there is no comprehensive information on nursing home lobbying——or, for that matter, on its profits or on its ownership. Enough is known, however, to suggest why the industry finds government such an easy target.

The state is the crucial level of government. The Medicaid reimbursement rate, by far the most important source of revenue in the industry, is set by the state legislatures. Moreover, nursing home inspection is generally a state function.

The industry seems to be influential in the state legislatures. Since nursing homes are widely dispersed, most legislators have at least one in their district. Owners and operators show up regularly as campaign contributors. Although the amounts one hears about——$500 or $1,000—are paltry when compared to the amounts which change hands in presidential elections, that kind of money can buy considerable influence in a state legislature, especially in the absence of countervailing pressure.

The absence of such pressures largely results from the way Medicaid is financed. Although the state legislature sets the Medicaid rate, the federal government pays from 50 to 80 percent of the bill. So, a state legislator considering competing demands for money knows that half, or more than half, of what he votes for nursing homes will not have to be paid by state taxes: a dollar for the nursing homes only costs the state from 20 to 50 cents. Thus, nursing home lobbying can pay high returns.

In a recent speech John Timothy McCormack, an Ohio state representative from Cleveland, set forth his view of the relative pressures on state legislators:

The nursing home industry is very well organized, is well represented in terms of lobbyists in the Legislature . . . There is not a high degree of interest relative to nursing homes in the Legislature. There is not a high degree of knowledge and there is very little public attention focussed on the problem. . . . The only voice that has come through clearly is that of the nursing home industry. . . . The industry, in fact, plays the dominant role in the establishment of rates that are set by the Legislature. Now that undoubtedly means that the best way to determine what the rates will be for the nursing homes [is] to look at the most recent edition of the nursing home industry magazine, [see] which Senator is featured on the cover with his biographical statement and given credit for saving the industry. Determine how much power that Senator has and you can probably determine just how those rates might be established in the Legislature.

In Washington the federal agency most concerned with nursing homes is the Department of Health, Education and Welfare (HEW). It has shown little effective interest in the industry, and its consistent policy of secrecy has kept the public and Congress in the dark about nursing home realities. It is mainly because of HEW that the basic facts about nursing home ownership and profits remain unknown. When Congress mandated HEW to find out who owns nursing homes, the agency evaded the legislative intent by permitting empty replies, such as the statement that a given nursing home's owner was a corporation. As for profits, HEW has simply never tried to find out, although it would seem impossible to evaluate nursing home reimbursement rates without knowing what profits the industry is making.

The most blatant form of secrecy practiced by HEW involves the reports of nursing home inspections. If there is any single piece of information to which the public should be entitled, it is the inspector's current report on a nursing home. Any member of the public—not to mention the taxpayers, who may be interested in what the home is doing with their money—should have the right to see the reports before choosing a nursing home. The only effect of hiding that information is to protect both the operator who runs a bad home and the inspector who lets him get away with it.

That fig leaf was at last ripped—or so it seemed—from the industry in 1972 by the courts: a successful suit by a newsman, Mal Schechter, of the magazine *Hospital Practice*, forced HEW to grant access to Medicare inspection reports. The bureaucracy resisted stubbornly. HEW interpreted its defeat in the courts to mean only that Schechter himself could have access to the eight reports on which he had brought his suit, not that the public at large had any right to see Medicare inspection reports.

In 1972 the Congress adopted legislation requiring HEW to make public both Medicare and Medicaid reports. This law did not, however, settle the issue because, as always, the agency—not Congress—is to implement the law. HEW was far from giving up

the struggle to keep the public in the dark. As of this writing, the regulations proposed by HEW would only make public an extract from the inspector's report, not the full report. Furthermore, that extract in the case of Medicare could only be seen—not ordered by mail or phone—at a Social Security office. In the case of Medicaid one can inspect the extract at the local welfare office. Thus, a member of the public can see those extracts, if he is willing to find his way to the proper office, no matter how far, and if—the biggest if of all—he happens to find out that he is entitled to the information. No one is broadcasting the news.

The distance between HEW's policy of secrecy and a policy of protecting the public interest can be most clearly measured by contrasting what the agency did with what it has not done. At no time did HEW take the simple, effective step of ordering operators of all nursing homes receiving federal money to post the latest inspection report prominently in the home, with copies available to potential applicants. Such a procedure would make available to those most concerned the inspector's judgment on the home and would also enable someone reading the posted report to contrast it with the reality around him.

Much of government's role in overseeing the spending of its money has been, in effect, abdicated to the health industry. This has happened in the choice of what are called fiscal intermediaries. When Medicaid and Medicare were created, it was obvious that they would cause a flood of paper work in the form of millions of individual bills being presented to government for payment. Medicare and, in some states, Medicaid retained existing organizations to process the papers—that is, to audit and to pay the individual bills for the government. This lightened the government work load, but it also removed from government much of the responsibility of the newly created programs.

The organizations selected as fiscal intermediaries in most parts of the country are Blue Cross and its sister organization, Blue Shield. Blue Cross is itself part of the health industry. Controlled by hospitals and doctors, it was founded to help hospitals collect their bills. It has always defended the interests of the health industry in conflicts with those—whether consumers or government—who pay the bills. Nursing homes are first cousins to hospitals; their financial practices are similar, and so are the ways in which their costs are unnecessarily inflated and passed on to government. Therefore, when government chose Blue Cross as a fiscal intermediary, to a large extent it was allowing the health industry to regulate itself.

Some of those who made nursing home policy for HEW have had direct ties to the industry. For some years the chairman of HEW's National Advisory Council on Nursing Home Administration was Harold Baumgarten. Baumgarten was president of one corporation operating a nursing home and director of another—facts never mentioned in the extensive biographical material about him which HEW published. The HEW staff man for that Council was Charles A. Cubbler; he was a director of the nursing home corporation of which Baumgarten was president. When HEW was instructed by Congress to draft standards nursing homes would have to meet to qualify for Medicaid—a question of crucial importance to the industry—the agency hired Harold Smith as a consultant to write the standards. Smith was not only a former official of the Louisiana Nursing Home Association, but was also serving as chairman of the Legislative Committee of the American Nursing Home Association at the time he was hired by HEW.

WHY REGULATION FAILS

Such examples should not be read to mean that personal connections between the industry and its regulators, nor the occasional instances of outright corruption, are the only explanation for the failure of government regulators. There are other, less dramatic, factors involved. One is the familiar phenomenon of bureaucratic lassitude. If the typical nursing home regulator is to do his job well, he must work hard and suffer recurring conflicts with those whom he regulates. He must do so, moreover, with little support; in fact, he is under constant pressure to go easy on the nursing homes and under little or no pressure to do the opposite. Being human, inspectors usually succumb to the strongest pressures.

The difficult, small-scale nature of nursing home regulation is another important factor. In the regulation of this industry there are no great decisive moments on which public attention can focus, no equivalents of the congressional votes on the ABM or the Lockheed loan. Instead, the action takes place in 23,000 nursing homes across the country, and the failure of the regulators is not found in dramatic actions, but in numberless small duties left undone. Those lobbying for nursing home reform cannot mobilize themselves for a single pitched battle; they must be prepared to exert continuing pressure over many years and in many places.

The Nixon administration's nursing home reform program provides an illustration. In August, 1971, the president announced an eight-point program to deal with the problems of nursing homes. Of the eight points, the most important was the promise to cut off Medicare and Medicaid funds to nursing homes which did not meet "reasonable standards." By mid-1973 it became obvious that little had improved, in spite of the president's announced intent: only one of every two hundred patients in a Medicaid-eligible home was actually moved to another—presumably better—home. Furthermore, for two years demands for reform could be warded off with a reference to the decisive actions which were in the making.

Lack of effective public pressure is, of course, the most basic reason for the failure of nursing home regulation. The primary victims— the patients—are unable to make effective protest against their lot. Most patients do not have concerned relatives; relatives who are concerned have not constituted an effective lobby. The financial victims of the nursing homes—the taxpayers—are no more effectively organized to combat this form of waste than they are any other. Older people—strong lobbyists on some issues—have not had much impact on nursing home policy. One possible reason is that older people have more reason than most to fear an institution in which they may soon find themselves. Most of all, the lack of public pressure for nursing home reform may simply be another expression of our turning away from the realities of old age.

Old Age Associations in National Politics

By HENRY J. PRATT

ABSTRACT: The past decade has seen an unprecedented outpouring of federal laws, executive orders and new appropriations intended to benefit the elderly. A frequently overlooked, but quite significant, factor in this development has been the increased organized activity on the part of senior citizens themselves. In marked contrast to the old age groups of an earlier period, the elderly in recent years have coalesced behind groups with a high level of political rationality and internal organizational discipline. While aging groups are of various types and seek to fill a variety of functions, there is reason to focus on one category—the mass-membership organization—as especially important in helping to give shape and focus to widespread latent sentiments in the old age population. The rather striking success of three such groups—the American Association of Retired Persons-National Retired Teachers Association, the National Council of Senior Citizens and the National Association of Retired Federal Employees—can be analyzed in terms of their having found sources of income outside member dues, having created bureaucracies recruited on the basis of performance criteria rather than charisma and having capitalized effectively on the emergence in recent years of a more benign climate for old age activity. By combining these criteria the groups considered appear capable both of insuring their own organizational survival and of continuing to exert an influence on federal policy makers.

Henry J. Pratt is Associate Professor of Political Science at Wayne State University. Educated at Dartmouth College, University of Michigan and Columbia University, he is author of a study of the National Council of Churches entitled The Liberalization of American Protestantism: A Case Study in Complex Organizations. *He is also editor of a volume of readings,* Ethno-Religious Politics. *He has contributed articles to various journals in political science and is currently on leave of absence to write a book dealing with the emergence of an old age policy system in the federal government.*

IN AN era when political scientists and other social analysts have come to recognize the importance of interest groups in shaping national policy—an importance that some have maintained has reached excessive proportions[1]—the tendency to minimize interest group influence in the increasingly salient matter of federal policy toward the aging is remarkable. Some recent accounts purporting to treat the politics of age have disregarded voluntary associations entirely;[2] others, although alluding to the existence of pressure groups in this field of action, maintain that their influence is marginal.[3] Commentaries of a slightly earlier period, still often cited, shared this opinion regarding associations of the aging.[4]

The empirical data used to support these conclusions have been mainly of two types: (1) psychological findings indicating that many aged persons do not naturally seek to maintain a high status and an active role in society, but rather tend to withdraw from society and politics as a natural consequence of their waning physical and mental energies—the theory of disengagement;[5] (2) data on the actual behavior of aging interest groups in the 1930s, '40s and '50s, pointing toward the conclusion that such groups tended to be highly ephemeral, politically unrealistic, internally strife-ridden and inept at lobbying. Abraham Holtzman's 1963 study of the Townsend Movement of the 1930s, for example, traced the lack of political success of this once-large mass movement to the overbearing and inflexible character of its founder and leader, Dr. Francis E. Townsend; the weakness in the corporate structure of the organization; and the incessant revolts and schisms among movement activists.[6] Similar findings were reported in a study of the Ham and Eggs Movement in California, where organizational problems again proved insurmountable in the long run.[7]

Even articles reporting on apparent interest group successes during these years—for example, Walter Polner's study of the Railroad Retirees National Pension Association's efforts to gain enactment of a

1. Theodore Lowi, *The End of Liberalism* (New York: W. W. Norton, 1969).

2. John Schmidhauser, "The Political Influence of the Aged," *Gerontologist* 8, no. 2, part II (Spring 1968), pp. 44–49; also, see his "The Political Behavior of Older Persons," *Western Political Quarterly* 11 (1958), pp. 113–124.

3. Ronald W. Geason, "Politics of Age: Attitudes and Trends" (Paper delivered before the Gerontological Society, Houston, Texas, 1971). Geason observes: "It appears that the aged will not only continue to be ineffective in their attempts to influence policy formulation, but the power they do have relative to other groups will even decrease" (p. 6).

4. Fred A. Cottrell, "Governmental Functions and the Politics of Age," in *Handbook of Social Gerontology*, ed. Clark Tibbetts (Chicago, Ill.: University of Chicago Press, 1960), p. 656. Cottrell reiterated this general theme in interpreting the passage of Medicare: "The Aging and the Political System," in *Aging and Social Policy*, ed. John C. McKinney (New York: Appleton, Century and Croft, 1966), pp. 98–99 and *passim*.

5. For elaboration of this theory see, Jackson K. Putnam, *Old Age Politics in California: From Richardson to Reagan* (Stanford, Cal.: Stanford University Press, 1970), p. 13; Angus Campbell, "Politics Through the Life Cycle," *Gerontologist* 12, no. 2, part I (Summer 1971), p. 113 table I and p. 117.

6. Abraham Holtzman, *The Townsend Movement: A Political Study* (New York: Basic Books, 1963); pp. 199–207.

7. Frank A. Pinner, Paul Jacobs and Philip Selznick, *Old Age and Political Behavior, A Case Study* (Berkeley, Cal.: University of California Press, 1959).

national railroad retirement system in the mid-1930s—on close reading reveal evidence of group incapacity either to resolve internal differences or to concert action over more than a brief span of time.[8] In a 1969 essay summarizing the findings in the extant literature on aging interest groups Michael Kay Carlie discounted the suggestion that the aging themselves may at times campaign effectively in their own behalf and concluded instead that in the 1960s, just as in the '30s, "there are reasons to believe that an interest group approach still will not work."[9] Effective pressure for enacting legislation beneficial to the aging, he maintained, has emanated primarily from non age-based organizations.

In view of this substantial unanimity of informed opinion on the above matter, one should be cautious in advancing contrary lines of reasoning. It is apparent, nevertheless, that events since 1965 have not entirely squared with what the above analyses would have led one to predict. In a recent paper Robert Binstock notes several instances in which groups representing the aging have succeeded in exerting effective pressure on the federal bureaucracy.[10] Press dispatches dealing with the 1971 White House Conference on the Aging similarly suggest that age-based groups were instrumental in altering initial Nixon administration plans for the conference, even to the point of persuading the White House to ease aside the intended conference chairman, John Martin, in favor of a man believed to have greater interest group backing, Arthur S. Flemming.[11] The threat of an interest group boycott of the conference was a major weapon in wringing concessions from a reluctant administration.

Dale Vinyard has noted in a recent essay that interest groups acting as spokesmen for the aging have, from time to time, joined hands with the Senate Special Committee on the Aging to urge particular policies or interpretations on a certain agency.[12] In interviews conducted in 1973 the present author found widespread evidence of old age group activity on Capitol Hill and in the executive branch of government. How were these senior citizen organizations able to get started? Once organized, where did they derive the resources, material and other resources necessary to their survival? How did they go about developing the talent and skill necessary to exert tangible political leverage?

NATIONAL GROUPS PRESENTLY ACTIVE

While many groups interest themselves in aging matters from time to time, only a handful—ten at the present time—are both engaged in

8. Walter Polner, "The Aged in Politics, A Successful Example: The NPA and the Passage of the Railroad Retirement Act of 1934," *Gerontologist* 2 (1962), pp. 207–215.

9. Michael Kaye Carlie, "The Politics of Age: Interest Group or Social Movement," *Gerontologist*, 9 no. 4 (Winter 1969), pp. 259–263.

10. Robert H. Binstock, "Interest Group Liberalism and the Politics of Aging," *Gerontologist* 12, no. 3, part I (Autumn 1972), pp. 271–277.

11. Judith A. Turner, "White House Report/Conference on the Aging Seeks Changes in Attitude Toward the Elderly," *National Journal*, 25 September 1971, pp. 1666–1672; *New York Times*, 2 December 1971, p. 22.

12. Dale Vinyard, "The Senate Special Committee on the Aging," *Gerontologist* 12 no. 3, part I, (Autumn 1972), pp. 298–303.

politics at the national level and preoccupied, more or less exclusively, with old age problems. Four of these are trade associations: the American Association of Homes for the Aging, the American Nursing Home Association, the National Council of Health Care Services and the National Association of State Units on Aging. One, the American Gerontological Society —with about 2,000 individual members and several affiliates—is a professional association. Another organization, the National Council on the Aging, is a loose confederation of some 1,400 public and private social welfare agencies. A very recent group, the National Caucus on the Black Aged, is a coalition of about 150 professionals attempting to bring to light the particular plight of the black elderly. Finally, and not least in importance, are the three mass-membership organizations: the National Council of Senior Citizens (NCSC), initially constituted in the early 1960s to campaign for Medicare, but later broadened to include the whole gamut of senior citizen concerns; the National Retired Teachers Association (NRTA) and the American Association of Retired Persons (AARP), which function as one organization (NRTA-AARP) in national politics; and the National Association of Retired Federal Employees (NARFE).

Rather than attempting the unwieldy task of treating each of the ten organizations individually, it seems appropriate to select for detailed analysis three of them, known to manifest a particularly acute and sustained interest in national legislative issues. The three mass-membership organizations mentioned—NCSC, NRTA-AARP and NARFE—lend themselves

well to this purpose, since their interventions in the national policy arena are backed by at least the apparent support of hundreds of thousands of voters in all walks of life, whereas the interventions of others are more easily dismissed as the expressions of special interests. There is an obvious risk of oversimplification in this restriction of focus, but the advantages accruing from greater depth of analysis would seem to outweigh the risk.

ORIGINS, GOALS, BASES OF SUPPORT

In order that the analytical material in a later section may be fully comprehended, it is first necessary to present certain basic data about the three groups, in particular their goals, resources and organizational growth. Each organization will be considered separately.

National Council of Senior Citizens

The NCSC originated in the early 1960s as an agency intended to generate pressure for enactment of Medicare. It was built around the remnants of the Senior Citizens for Kennedy, organized for the 1960 presidential campaign. The earlier group was headed by Representative Aime Forand—Democrat, Rhode Island—who in 1957 had introduced the first widely publicized bill to provide health insurance for the elderly. Richard Harris has pinpointed the moment when the NCSC concept was first conceived:

At the [1961] White House Conference on the Aging, Forand had got into a discussion with several union leaders who were considering whether it was desirable to organize older people to work for Medicare. Some of the men he talked to opposed the idea on the grounds it would inevitably lead to a kind of Townsend Movement. Among those who held this position was Nelson Cruikshank, head of the AFL-CIO's Department of Social Security.

Then, in the summer of 1961, the two men who ran programs for retired workers in the AFL-CIO—Charles Odell of the United Auto Workers and James Cuff O'Brien of the United Steel Workers—decided to go ahead with the project on a part-time basis, despite the opposition of Cruikshank and other labor leaders. They persuaded their unions to put up small amounts of money and prevailed on Forand to lend his name as Chairman.[13]

Though vocal and energetic in its support of the Medicare crusade, the NCSC was handicapped in these years by limited funds and staff resources. "When I came down here," Executive Director William R. Hutton remarked to an interviewer in 1965, "the office was a dilapidated flat, the one secretary worked at the kitchen table and kept the press releases in the bathtub, and there was precious little in the way of funds. The AMA had all the money, and we had all the old people."[14] Typewriters were borrowed from the industrial union department of the AFL-CIO, and a part-time staff man was loaned by the UAW. Despite its meager resources, however, the consensus among observers is that the NCSC and other organizations did manage to play a significant role in the passage of Medicare.[15]

From a small, highly specialized organization whose early efforts were focused largely on a single legislative issue, the NCSC has grown both in membership and in diversity of goals since 1965. There are currently over 3,000 affiliated senior citizens clubs throughout the country, with a combined membership of over 3,000,000. The national office estimates that the local clubs are distributed about equally into three categories: trade union retiree groups, religious and ethnic groups and social welfare retirees. The three million membership figure includes many persons who identify with NCSC only in a very general sense, and for this reason it bears mentioning that the number of directly-contributing, dues-paying members—Gold Card Members—is currently 250,000—an increase of more than 250% since 1971.

Although the national leaders have worked to expand their membership base beyond that of labor union retirees—with the result that the rolls now include a number of middle class and nonunion-related persons—the leadership of NCSC is nevertheless securely in labor-union hands, particularly in the hands of the more politically aggressive and socially involved industrial unions. Of the fifty persons in a recent year—1972—serving on the organization's national board, only sixteen did not come from the union movement; among the four national vice-presidents, three were former union officials.[16] The current president, Cruikshank, and the executive director, Hutton, both have many years of union involvement. As a visitor to the NCSC's 1971 national convention, the author was impressed by the degree

13. Richard Harris, "Annals of Legislation," *New Yorker*, 16 July 1966, p. 51.
14. Ibid.
15. James L. Sundquist, *Politics and Policy: The Eisenhower, Kennedy and Johnson Years* (Washington, D.C.: Brookings Institutes, 1968), pp. 310–311, 314.

16. Interview with William R. Hutton, NCSC Executive Director, January 1972.

to which these social background characteristics were reflected in the style and rhetoric of the leaders: they frequently addressed one another as brother, and there were resolutions memorializing deceased labor officials. This union predominance in NCSC affairs has important implications for the organization's political behavior, as subsequent discussion will suggest.

The National Retired Teachers Association-American Association of Retired Persons

If the origins of the National Council of Senior Citizens were in the first instance political, one should note that the goals of the NRTA-AARP, while always including a political dimension, have tended to subordinate political goals to those of individual uplift and social betterment. The National Retired Teachers Association was founded in 1947 by Dr. Ethel Percy Andrus, a prominent California educator and Los Angeles high school principal with close ties to the National Education Association. The initial goals did include legislative objectives, such as improved state teacher pensions and federal tax benefits for retired teachers. However, Dr. Andrus was more directly concerned with efforts to improve the image and raise the relative status of retirees generally and to provide, through private enterprise, for their material needs. By 1955, eight years after its founding, the organization had attained a national membership of 20,000—a significant, but by national standards not especially impressive, number.

In that year Dr. Andrus was introduced to a Poughkeepsie New York insurance agent, Leonard Davis, a man forty years her junior. Prior to their meeting Davis, in consultation with Robert Decormier —then president of the New York State Retired Teachers Association —had persuaded a leading insurance underwriter, Continental Casualty Company, to write life insurance policies for 800 New York State retired teachers on an experimental basis, despite the then prevalent view in the industry that retirees constituted poor actuarial risks. Dr. Andrus had long been convinced that the frustrations experienced by elderly persons across the country in obtaining life insurance constituted a major element in their frequent financial distress. In the course of a series of meetings Dr. Andrus and Davis drew up an arrangement under which NRTA members nationwide would become eligible for the New York State type of benefits; as his part of the bargain, Davis agreed to invest $50,000 of his own capital —an investment, incidentally, which has paid off handsomely for him: the value of his NRTA-AARP related insurance holdings by 1972 being valued at about $184 million.[17]

Once implemented, the Davis-Andrus plan proved immensely popular, with 5,000 NRTA members signing up to participate in the first few months. So great was the interest that retirees outside the teaching profession began to ask for such policies. Rather than turn these persons away as ineligible, Andrus and Davis took steps to found a new organization, the American Association of Retired Persons, which was to have a far broader constituency than its parent body.

17. *Washington Post,* 13 February 1972, p. 1.

Chartered in 1958, the new group shared the staff and headquarters of NRTA, but had its own board of directors and regional affiliates. The AARP has prospered not only through its ever-expanding membership, but also by virtue of the fact that the insurance operation— later expanded to include travel, pharmacy, and training services— returned a fixed percentage of premiums and fees. This revenue was to help meet NRTA-AARP operating expenses,[18] a matter for more extended consideration later in this discussion.

In view of its auspicious beginnings, it is scarcely surprising that combined dues-paying membership of NRTA-AARP easily makes it the largest organization of its kind in the country. It grew in size from a modest 150,000 in 1959 to about 1 million in 1969 and to a remarkable 6.02 million in late 1973. This current figure makes the association one of the largest voluntary bodies in Washington.

The organization's underlying perspective and social outlook has generally been closely linked to that of business enterprise, especially the insurance industry, with which the group has evolved a symbiotic relationship. Illustrative of its underlying predispositions was the health care proposal introduced by Dr. Andrus in the course of the July 1959 Forand bill hearings before the House Ways and Means Committee. The Andrus plan, while not identical to that being offered by the American Medical Association, was not inconsistent with it. Dr. Andrus proposed the formation of a trustee-ship to initiate and administer the health insurance plan for the elderly which she espoused. The trustees would include equal numbers of representatives of health care—"such as AMA and AHA"— of business—"such as the United States Chamber of Commerce"— representatives of the aged—"such as NRTA and AARP"—and representatives of labor—no illustrations given. In administering the program the trusteeship was to begin by submitting specifications "to the insurance industry and/or Blue Cross and Blue Shield for competition." After accepting the best bid or bids and arranging for the collection of premiums, the trusteeship would then transfer all premiums paid to the respective insurance company or companies.[19]

NRTA-AARP was not on record as opposing the Medicare measure passed by Congress in 1965, but neither was it among the bill's active promoters. A bias toward the industry-management viewpoint on current issues is also implicit in the fact that not a single former labor union official currently sits on the AARP board of directors, whereas a number of former businessmen do. However, since the early 1970s, when the office of executive director was filled by Bernard Nash, the organization has worked to gain acceptance in official Washington as a strictly nonpartisan body. The fact that its voice is now heeded by leading Democrats, as well as by Republicans, suggests that these ef-

18. Margaret Adams, "The Story of AARP," *Modern Maturity*, October-November 1971, pp. 72–74.

19. U.S., House of Representatives, Committee on Ways and Means, *Hearings on Hospital, Nursing Home and Surgical Benefits for OASI Beneficiaries*, H.R. 4700, 86th Cong., 1st sess., 13–17 July 1959, pp. 510–511.

forts have met with a large measure of success.

National Association of Retired Federal Employees

Just as the specialized needs of retired educators have been an important factor in the decision to maintain the National Retired Teachers Association as an autonomous group within the NRTA-AARP structure, so the special situation of the federal government retiree has made possible the survival of NARFE in the face of newer and more expansive mass-membership organizations. The NARFE was founded in February 1921, around the time of the passage of the Federal Employees Pension Act, and has served both as a vehicle for case work arising from this act and as a means of pressing for subsequent enlargement of benefits to federal retirees. The organization had a hand in the passage of the 1959 Federal Employees Health Benefits Law and the 1962 amendments to the pension act providing for cost-of-living annuity increases.

While the existence of federal legislation affecting government retirees has been fundamental to the survival of NARFE, it has by no means guaranteed success, even on issues where a narrowly focused group such as this might be assumed to have an advantage over larger and more amorphous retiree organizations. In recent years NARFE income, discounting the factor of inflation, has grown comparatively little, increasing from $259,000 in 1956 to $329,000 in 1960 and $543,000 in 1971. In 1969 and 1970 the group ran a net operating deficit.[20] During a period

of unprecedented membership growth in the other two mass-membership groups, NARFE's rolls have increased only modestly: a 15 percent increase from 1968 to 1972 and a further 17 percent growth— to 182,000—in the past two years.

NARFE's lack of substantial growth is at least partially responsible for the organization's tendency to concentrate on bread-and-butter issues of direct substantive concern to members, while relating only marginally to more broadly defined social, economic and legislative questions. Whereas NCSC and AARP produced a veritable flood of position papers, policy statements and political propaganda in connection with the 1971 White House Conference on the Aging, NARFE leaders did not do a great deal beyond attending meetings with other senior citizen groups and, in a general way, keeping members abreast of the proceedings through its house organ, *Retirement Life*.[21] The activities and decisions of congressional committees and subcommittees with authority to decide policy for federal retirees, on the other hand, are given frequent and voluminous attention by the organization.

FACTORS IN ORGANIZATIONAL VIABILITY

The three mass-membership groups included in this survey, despite differences in resources, goals and strategies, have in common a cluster of traits which serve to differentiate them from their coun-

20. *Retirement Life*, selected issues, 1956, 1960, 1971.

21. *Retirement Life* accounts of the White House conference were buried on pages 22, 15 and 20, respectively, in the issues of October and December 1971 and January 1972. Only the last of these editions contained more than six or eight paragraphs on the topic.

terpart organizations of the 1930s and '40s. In large part the difference consists in the fact that the newer groups are steadier and more persistent in their pursuit of substantive goals and less subject to internal and external disruptions. The point is well illustrated by noting the effect on the organization as a whole of the death of its founding leader—a significant event in the life of any group.

In the case of the earlier aging organizations, the demise of the founder was typically the occasion for profound organizational trauma, often followed by marked goal redefinition and agonizing reappraisals.[22] In contrast, among the groups under consideration here, the death of the founder was accommodated with no such traumatic results. The withdrawal of Aime Forand in the early 1960s in no way retarded the subsequent growth of his brainchild, the NCSC. The case of the NRTA-AARP is admittedly more complicated, since Dr. Andrus, without intending to do so, placed a severe strain on her organization during the last few years of her life—especially when, two years before her death, she sought to move its national headquarters from Washington, D.C., to her home in Long Beach, California. The effects of this, in terms of stagnating membership and organizational disruption, were not inconsequential. Yet, following her death in July 1967, the organization regrouped itself and proceeded to new levels of size and significance.

22. Sheldon L. Messinger, "Organizational Transformation: A Case Study of a Declining Social Movement," *American Sociological Review* 20, no. 1 (February 1955), pp. 3–10; Pinner, Jacobs and Selznick, *Old Age and Political Behavior*, *passim*.

NARFE—by far the oldest group under study—has, of course, survived numerous changes in leadership over its fifty years of operation.

Three developments seem to have an important bearing on this increased ability of senior citizen organizations to accommodate themselves to major internal and external changes. These are: (1) the growth of a technically proficient and competent bureaucracy composed of replaceable members; (2) an ability to generate substantial revenues not only from member dues, but from sources which are both more dependable and more elastic than dues income; and (3) the presence of a more benign and accepting political environment. The three groups under consideration, though largely similar to one another in these dimensions, are also in some respects different; this cross-cutting cannot be overlooked.

Bureaucratization

By insisting on adherence to the norms of competency, expertise and replaceable membership, organizations are capable of achieving high levels of rationality and efficiency. They can seek talent wherever it may be found, avoiding the dangers implicit in arbitrary exclusion of personnel on the basis of essentially extraneous criteria, such as age, race and sex. By becoming bureaucratized an organization better insures its survival in a modern, highly complex setting.

The attempt to impose bureaucratic standards on an organization composed of the elderly encounters at least one quite significant problem: namely, the rank and file, reversing the usual societal bias in favor of youth, may insist that the top executives themselves be persons of advanced age. For example, if a senior citizen leader were to suggest overtly that a person over age seventy may not be as well qualified to run a large organization as a person of similar background twenty years younger, he might endanger his own leadership status and risk disruptive internal strife. Yet, the fact remains that advanced age does exact a toll on persons, especially in terms of their ability to labor for long, grueling hours managing a large enterprise. Thus, bureaucratic demands and rank-and-file attitudes are in tension.

In the case of the two organizations with the fastest rates of growth, NCSC and NRTA-AARP, a way of resolving this dilemma has been found. Their formula informally guarantees that the top elective posts—in both cases, that of the president—shall be held by a person over sixty-five years of age, while those upon whom falls the main burden of administering the organization, though they be younger in age, may be considered for top positions on the staff. Bernard Nash was only in his mid-forties at the time of his appointment as NRTA-AARP executive director; Nash's immediate subordinates—introduced to the author in the course of recent interviews—are also comparatively youthful. Prior to his appointment Nash was deputy commissioner on aging and originator of the federal Foster Grandparents Program. On the other hand, the AARP president, Foster J. Pratt, is in his seventies.

A similar pattern has prevailed in the NCSC. The current president, Nelson Cruikshank, assumed his position at age sixty-six upon retirement as head of the AFL-CIO's Department of Social Security. However, the executive director, William Hutton, was appointed to office a decade ago when he was only forty-six. The NCSC's only full-time paid field representative, Ken Arvedon, is in his mid-forties. Arvedon and Hutton were obviously chosen on the basis of their vitality and sense of commitment, with old age not a determining factor.

This is not intended to suggest that aging organizations are predisposed against an individual in the over-sixty-five category for top executive posts, but rather that in becoming bureaucratized the groups in question have increasingly insisted on applying performance criteria under which advanced age confers no special advantages. In selecting persons to fill largely honorific posts—that is, those in which on-the-job performance is a less crucial factor—there is, of course, a continuing preference for over-sixty-five retirees.

Revenue supplementation

In an acute analysis of the factors which allow large lobbying organizations to survive, Mancur Olson, Jr., has suggested that potential members are not sufficiently motivated to join such a body simply by virtue of their agreement with its general principles and legislative goals. Since legislative victories won by the organization are likely to benefit the potential member whether he formally affiliates or not, the strictly rational person will elect not to do so, spending his dues money instead on that which seems from his standpoint to be a more immediately beneficial purpose. The survival of the organization is thus dependent more on its providing potential members with sought-after selective benefits, which can be bestowed on members at a reasonable charge and denied to nonmembers, with the surplus accruing from the transactions with members being used to underwrite the costs of lobbying activities.[23]

It was one of the chief sources of weakness in the older aging movements that the leaders were insufficiently aware of this important organizational fact. In commenting, for example, on the demise of the Townsend Movement as a true mass movement, Abraham Holtzman observed that:

Club members were increasingly frustrated by the impossibility of enacting their [Townsend pension] plan. At the same time, the benefits they and their fellows derived from the Social Security Act underlined the fact that old age security was accessible through other means than the Townsend plan.[24]

Although leaders of the Townsend Movement did eventually begin to offer a whole series of benefits unrelated to the basic political objectives—for example, Townsend Old Fashioned Horehound Drops, Townsend Club Toilet Soap, and Dr. Townsend's Vitamins and Minerals—their introduction came too late in the movement's development to arrest the drastic decline in membership, which began in the late 1930s.

A completely different pattern has prevailed in the case of the three groups currently under examination. While a political objective—the passage of Medicare—was central to the founding of NCSC, the organization

has never failed to appreciate the importance of providing selective benefits at attractive prices to members. In so doing, they have not only enlarged membership, but have also generated income. The organization offers a wide spectrum of services: travel, drugs, legal aid and so forth.

Moreover, as the semiofficial senior citizens arm of the American labor movement, the NCSC has relieved the regular labor officials of what might otherwise have been a distraction from their central concern with collective bargaining. In return, the larger industrial unions—particularly the auto workers, machinists, steelworkers, electrical workers and the AFL-CIO Industrial Union Department—have generously subsidized the NCSC budget. Of a total NCSC budget of $416,000 in 1971, fully 40 percent was contributed by sympathetic unions.[25]

The NRTA-AARP offers an equally clear illustration of how Olson's thesis applies to aging organizations. Although concerned from the outset with the political matter of state teacher pensions, the organization during its decade of most rapid growth—1958 to 1968—tended to minimize the lobbying aspects of its mandate and to concentrate on elaborating a. large range of selective benefits. Lobbying goals have become a major preoccupation only in quite recent years, beginning in late 1967 when Cyril F. Brickfield—whose experience during the previous decade had been that of counsel for the House Judiciary Committee—was named executive director. Brickfield stepped down from this post

23. Mancur Olson, Jr., *The Logic of Collective Action* (Cambridge, Mass.: Harvard University Press, 1965), pp. 60–61.

24. Holtzman, *The Townsend Movement*, p. 201.

25. Interview with William R. Hutton, January 1972.

two years later, having first overhauled the group's internal structure and smoothed the transition which began with the death of Dr. Andrus in July 1967. However, he has remained active in the organization as head of its six-man team of Capitol Hill lobbyists. At the state level the NRTA-AARP has also substantially increased its lobbying activity in the post-1967 era. This heavy commitment to achieving public policy goals would have been inconceivable in the absence of organizational surpluses generated in the service area.

The NRTA-AARP refuses to divulge the full magnitude of its service-generated income—its annual report to members essentially includes only income from member dues, which amounted to $3 million in 1971—but a rough idea of the sums involved is available from the AARP Form 990 filed with the Internal Revenue Service and from reports filed with the Securities and Exchange Commission. These statements indicate that for fiscal 1971, $1,027,672 was derived from the NRTA Insurance Plan, $2,301,378 from the AARP Insurance Plan, $63,825 from the NRTA and AARP Travel Service and an additional $1,000,000 in advertising revenue paid the organization by a Colonial Penn insurance subsidiary.[26] Member dues—$4.00 annually—evidently account for under 50 percent of NRTA-AARP operating revenue.

In the case of NARFE selective benefits have consisted in large degree of case work for dues-paying federal retirees and a modest range of economic services, such as a life insurance option.

A more benign external environment

A hostile and unreceptive political atmosphere was a basic conditioning factor in the environment of the aging groups of the 1930s and '40s. Francis E. Townsend's plan to pay each person over age sixty a pension of $200 per month financed out of a national sales tax was attacked on a wide variety of grounds. While the plan attracted the passionate support of many elderly persons—especially in California, Townsend's home base— it was acceptable to only a small percentage of the electorate: 3.8 percent, according to a 1936 Gallup poll. The plan was vigorously condemned by the Roosevelt Administration and met with hostility by the House Ways and Means Committee, where it died.[27]

Similarly, a pension scheme advocated in California by Robert Noble, leader of the Ham and Eggs group, proposed that the United States Congress deal with the Depression by issuing an unspecified amount of special scrip, the prompt spending of which was to be insured by having the scrip lose all its value after one year. The plan was roundly denounced by a host of California interest groups and, after an initial flurry of interest, became a political dead letter. In their efforts to significantly redistribute public revenues on behalf of relief specifically for the aging, the interest groups and mass movements of the thirties and forties found public opinion mostly arrayed against them.

During the past decade, however, the basic issue was not so

26. *Washington Post*, 13 February 1972, p. A21.

27. Putnam, *Old Age Politics in California*, p. 57; Holtzman, *The Townsend Movement*, p. 92.

much the redistribution of wealth as it was the distribution of a large, predetermined sum of money available through a variety of government channels. In the words of Binstock the "activities of aging organizations in national politics are hardly militant or radical. Their efforts do not reflect a vigorous pursuit of goals that could bring about a substantial 're-equalization' for the disadvantaged aged."[28] Within this scaled-down set of aspirations aging groups have labored, with increasing success, to gain acceptance as middlemen between the governmental funding sources—such as the Department of Health, Education and Welfare (HEW), the Office of Economic Opportunity (OEO), Department of Labor and Administration on Aging (AOA)—and the recipients. A particularly lucrative statutory basis for many of these middleman programs has been the 1965 Older Americans Act—especially Titles III, IV and V, under which the national government has distributed between $19 million and $23 million annually since 1969.

Another factor contributing to the more benign setting was the emergence in these years of what Theodore Lowi has termed "interest group liberalism." Lowi observes that John F. Kennedy, more than any other previous president, was inclined to encourage and reward group involvement in national policy-making, applying the principle of "participatory democracy" to the implementation, as well as to the formulation, of law.[29] The application of interest group liberalism principles to the old age

field was the logical corollary to their acceptance elsewhere at the federal level. Referring to the 1971 White House Conference on Aging, for example, Binstock remarks that:

The staff officially determined that business, labor, and consumers; the professions; religious, fraternal, social and service organizations; and community action organizations all deserved representation in formulating national policy toward the aging in the 1970's.[30]

Elected officials of both the Kennedy-Johnson and the Nixon administrations had come to accept the view that spokesmen for senior citizen organizations deserved not only to be heard when they spoke out, but in some cases even to be encouraged to express their policy preferences.

Given this more friendly atmosphere, aging groups often find themselves in a position to seek the best terms by shopping around among federal agencies. At the time of the establishment of the AOA, the National Council of Senior Citizens first nominated two of its most stalwart supporters—Charles Odell of the UAW and James O'Brien of the Steelworkers—for the post of commissioner. Both nominees were passed over in favor of William D. Bechill, a man with no strong and active ties with any of the aging organizations. When Bechill proceeded to allocate funds in ways which did not favor the NCSC, its leaders became highly critical of AOA. At the same time they shifted their pressure to Sargent Shriver, then head of OEO, insisting that he set up a task force on the "special problems of the elderly poor"; Shriver acquiesced. The task force, when established, consisted almost

28. Binstock, "Interest Group Liberalism," p. 278.

29. Lowi, *Liberalism*, pp. 79–82.

30. Binstock, "Interest Group Liberalism," p. 269.

exclusively of the NCSC and its allies, whose own interests were then given the most favored treatment in the subsequent letting of OEO contracts. For roughly the same reasons, the NCSC laid siege to the Department of Labor, with similarly favorable results.[31]

CONCLUSION

The present findings suggest that mass-membership bodies do, in fact, constitute politically viable entities which are capable of resolving their internal problems. The foundation for such organized senior power lies not only in an increasing benign climate of national opinion on aging questions, but also in their increased lobbying and internal managerial skills which have enabled them to make effective use of available resources. By supplementing their modest member-derived resources by subsidies from outside sources and by focusing their energies through efficient and goal-oriented bureaucracies, aging organizations are having an impact on the national political scene.

31. Ibid., pp. 273–277.

Age, Sex and Feminism

By Jessie Bernard

ABSTRACT: This paper attempts to delineate the relationship between age and sex as independent variables and certain issues related to feminism. Neither the dependent nor the independent variable is simple and unequivocal. Also, the relations among them cannot be precisely measured with data so far available. Only general trends can be traced and hypothetical interpretations of them offered. With these qualifications, the following conclusions seem acceptable. Although more older than younger respondents of both sexes tend—expectably—to be traditional on feminist issues, older men are more favorable than older women on such issues. Among women education seems to explain a good deal of the traditionalism associated with age. However, the historical circumstances in which the generation of women now in their forties were socialized may help to explain their anomalous positions on feminist issues today. The political implications of current trends lie in increasing acceptance of feminist positions.

Jessie Bernard, Research Scholar Honoris Causa, Pennsylvania State University, has written extensively in the areas of community, marriage, family and women. Her most recent books include: The Future of Motherhood *(Dial, 1974);* The Future of Marriage *(Bantam, 1972);* Women and the Public Interest *(Aldine, 1971);* The Sociology of Community *(Scott-Foresman, 1973); and, due in 1975,* Women, Wives, Mothers: Values and Options *(Aldine). She serves on many research institutes and editorial boards. One of her major concerns is that sociological paradigms be expanded to encompass the "other half" of the human species. She is also interested in analyzing and interpreting a variety of concrete research strands in order to discern what is actually happening in our society today. For the year 1974–1975 she will serve as Visiting Fellow at the National Institute of Education.*

TWO major distinctions have to be made as related to age as a variable: one between age and aging and one between age and education.

AGE, AGING AND EDUCATION

Age and aging

Because cross-sectional studies —usually in the form of surveys or polls—show older respondents of both sexes almost uniformly more conservative than younger ones, it is generally implicitly assumed that individuals become more conservative with age or that aging per se has a conservative effect. Actually, only longitudinal or before-and-after studies could tell us about the effect of aging per se on the attitudes and opinions of individuals. We have few, if any, such studies.

An interesting surrogate for such a study is one in which the present attitudes of a sample of eighty-nine fathers averaging 50 years of age are compared with their attitudes as they remembered them some 30 years earlier; the results suggest that the men did not become more conservative with time.[1] To be sure, as compared with their sons who averaged 20 years of age these men were, in fact, more conservative, suggesting that aging had slowed down, but had not inhibited, change. On all but 4 out of 17 items on a questionnaire the men were more permissive now than they remembered themselves as

1. Sylvia Clavan and Nicholas Robak, "Perception of Masculinity: Fathers and Sons" (Paper presented at the meetings of the Society for the Study of Social Problems, New York, New York, August 1973).

being in their youth.[2] On 3 of the remaining 13 items they had become more like their sons than they had been as they remembered themselves at their sons' age.[3] On the other 10 items the fathers, even when they had changed, remained nearer to themselves in their youth than to their sons.[4] They had not become more conservative than they had been in their remembered youth—except in the items referred to above—but they were nevertheless more conservative than their sons were. In brief, the effect of aging as measured— however inadequately—here was not to reverse attitudes or to prevent change, but only to slow it down. Exposed to the same influences as their sons, they had not become as permissive as their sons were, but more permissive— with the noted exceptions—than they had been in their youth.

Another surrogate-type study is the replicated Harris poll of women in 1972 as compared to the original poll in 1971. The two polls show

2. The 4 items dealt with premarital sexual behavior among girls. More men now than when they were young would think less of a girl if she: is agreeable to petting on a date; initiates necking and petting; agrees to sexual relations; and initiates sexual relations.
3. The 3 items dealt with helping wives with housekeeping and child care: help with cooking; help with feeding, bathing and diapering children; and help with taking care of children when wife is away.
4. Or, as on 4 items, they had come about half way between their positions in their youth and their sons' current position. One of these half-way items had to do with accepting the right of a girl to call to arrange a meeting. The other 3 referred to the acceptance of financial responsibility by women, that is: they would not think less of a girl if she agrees to a dutch treat; they would expect a wife to work before children were born; they would expect their wives to earn part of the regular family income.

that older women tended to approach the position of the younger women even over such a brief span of time as a single year. Thus, for example, if one compares the replies of women to a question on attitude toward efforts to strengthen or change women's status in society, one finds that in 1972, 41 percent of the women 50 years of age and over were catching up to the 46 percent of the women 18 to 29 years of age in 1971; so, also, had 42 percent of the women in their 40s. Women in their 30s had overtaken the 1971 18-to-29-year-olds; however, by that time the younger women had outdistanced all the others.[5] Again, then, although in cross-section the older women were uniformly more conservative than the younger, they had changed in a modern, rather than in a traditional, direction. In the absence, therefore, of convincing longitudinal data on the effect of aging per se on attitudes, no assumptions are made here that such an effect can be expected.

Age and education

The fact that more older than younger respondents in most surveys and polls tend to be conservative may be related more to their

lower level of education than to age itself. In fact, the Daniel Yankelovich polling agency told us several years ago that the really important gap was not so much the widely publicized generation gap as the less publicized education gap. There were, by and large, as many differences between young college and noncollege youth as between youth and their parents.[6] For, in general, less educated persons tend to be somewhat older, as well as more conservative, than the better educated;[7] conversely, older persons tend to be less well educated than those who are younger.[8]

6. Daniel Yankelovich, *Generations Apart* (New York: Columbia Broadcasting Company, 1969). Since the present paper was written, Daniel Yankelovich has released findings of a new study showing that between 1969 and 1972 the education gap was closing, especially on work-related items on a survey questionnaire. Noncollege youth in 1972 were approaching the position of college youth in 1968. Among women, however—although noncollege women were showing change—there was still a wide gap between noncollege and college women. Thus, almost half of the noncollege women—47 percent—rejected the woman's-place-is-in-the-home ideology, but among women entering college in 1972, almost three-fourths—74.4 percent—did. The Yankelovich data are from an interview reported by Stephan D. Isaacs, "A Rapid Change from Counter to Culture," *Washington Post*, 22 May 1974. The data on entering college women are from the American Council on Education.

7. Among male eighth grade graduates two-thirds—66.9 percent—were 35 years of age or over in 1972; among females, 70.1 percent. Among high school graduates the proportions 35 and over were, respectively, 53.3 and 56.2 percent. Current Population Reports, *Educational Attainment: March 1972*, series P-20, no. 243 (November 1972), p. 45.

8. In 1972 only a little over half—52.7 percent—of all women 35 years of age and over had completed high school; almost three-fourths—73.2 percent—of women 30 to 34 had. Only about two-thirds as many women 35 and over as women 30 to 34 had

5. Louis Harris and Associates, *The 1972 Virginia Slims American Women's Opinion Poll* (New York: Louis Harris and Associates, 1972), p. 2. In tabular form:

1971

18–29	46
30–39	40
40–49	39

1972

30–39	49
40–49	42
50+	41

Thus, any comparison of older with younger women involves comparing quite different populations. Any cross-section comparison of women of different ages tells one as much, if not more, about their schooling as it does about their age. Since the trend is in the direction of increased years of schooling for women,[9] it is also, inferentially, in the direction of greater acceptance by them of feminist views.

SEX DIFFERENCES ON FEMINIST ISSUES BY AGE

The significance of age differences—whatever may cause them —takes on salience when sex is also taken into account, for interesting differences show up with respect to feminist issues which involve political action.[10] Here, an unexpected, or at least unanticipated, finding is that more men than women tend to be sympathetic with the feminist movement.[11]

The 1972 Harris poll, for example, asked respondents about sympathy with efforts of women's liberation groups and found, overall, that 42 percent of the men replied in the affirmative compared to 39 percent of the women.[12] Another poll conducted in 1973 reported essentially the same thing. Almost half—46 percent—of the men compared to two-fifths—41 percent —of the women concurred in the statement that "while I might not agree with all their tactics, in general I agree with the goals of the Women's Liberation Movement."[13] Both sexes had gained in sympathy for the liberation movement, but men more than women.

More interesting than these overall differences was the difference between men and women by age, both with respect to strengthening women's status in society (shown in table 1) and sympathy with the efforts of women's liberation

---

had any years of college. The contrasts were, of course, even more marked between women 35 years of age and over and women under 30. More than twice as many 25 year old women as women 35 and over had had some college. Ibid., p. 45.

9. Thus, for example, whereas 5.8 percent of young (white) women 25 to 29 in 1972 had had only an 8th grade education or less, 17.8 percent of women 45 to 54 did. Conversely, whereas 4.6 percent of the younger (white) women had at least one year of college, only 2.8 percent of the older women did.

10. Among nonpolitical sex role issues are such issues as: men helping with the housework, sexual freedom, whether men or women have an easier life, and the like.

11. The generally positive male attitude toward women seems to be of fairly recent origin. Hazel Erskine has assembled the results of a series of polls from 1937 to 1969 on willingness to vote for a woman as president. Until 1955 more women than men replied affirmatively. From 1963 on, more men than women did. By 1969, 58 percent of the male respondents would be willing to

vote for a woman as president; only 49 percent of the women would. Hazel Erskine, "The Polls: Women's Role," *Public Opinion Quarterly* 35 (Summer 1971), p. 281. It may not be in voting and in legislation that women's rights suffer as a result of sex differences in political participation, but in the implementation of the laws and decisions and administrative rulings which result. It is here that age may make a difference. Although there is not yet available, so far as I know, any research on the bureaucrats and commissioners charged with executing the laws and rulings dealing with women, the expectation would be not unreasonable that older male administrators would be less vigorous than younger ones in scrupulously applying them.

12. While exceptions occurred among divorced and separated men, young men, low income men and city men, even among these exceptions the differences from other men were minimal.

13. Thomas C. Sorensen, "What Does a Woman Want?" *Parade Magazine*, 15 April 1973, p. 10. This poll was conducted by Daniel Starch and Staff, Inc.

		TABLE 1		

PROPORTION OF MEN AND WOMEN WHO
FAVOR EFFORTS TO STRENGTHEN
WOMEN'S STATUS IN SOCIETY,
BY AGE

	1971		1972	
AGE	MEN	WOMEN	MEN	WOMEN
18–29	53	46	61	56
30–39	37	40	47	49
40–49	52	39	50	42
50+	38	35	44	41

SOURCE: Louis Harris and Associates, *The 1972 Virginia Slims American Women's Opinion Poll* (New York: Louis Harris and Associates, 1972), p. 2.

TABLE 2

PROPORTION OF MEN AND WOMEN WHO
ARE SYMPATHETIC WITH THE EFFORTS
OF WOMEN'S LIBERATION
GROUPS, BY AGE

AGE	MEN	WOMEN
18–29	46	49
30–39	41	39
40–49	40	34
50+	42	34

SOURCE: Louis Harris and Associates, *The 1972 Virginia Slims American Women's Opinion Poll* (New York: Louis Harris and Associates, 1972), p. 4.

groups (table 2). Among the respondents in the 1972 Harris poll who were 50 years of age and over, the men were more favorable than the women; the difference was smaller among the respondents in their 30s and 40s. However, among those in their 20s the attitudes of the sexes had reversed themselves. Among them more women than men favored efforts to strengthen women's status in society and were sympathetic with the efforts of women's liberation groups.[14]

14. Of special interest is the position of the sexes on the abortion issue: men are more lenient than women. Judith Blake has summarized a series of polls on the subject from 1962 to 1969; in all of them there were more women than men who disapproved. Only in 1969 among those 45 years of age and over was the proportion of women who disapproved equal to that of men. Judith Blake, "Abortion and Public Opinion: The 1960–1970 Decade," *Science* 171 (February 1971), p. 544. In the *Parade* poll of 1973 considerably more men—57 percent—than women—50 percent—believed there should be no laws against abortion. Here, as with other issues, there has been an interesting shift: in this case a reversal of the sexes in attitude with age. Thus, in the 1973 poll far more women—68 percent—than men —52 percent—in the youngest age bracket —18 to 24—favored abortion; in the 40

THE SIGNIFICANCE OF SEX DIFFERENCES FOR FEMINIST ISSUES

The significance of sex differences in attitudes on feminist issues lies in the impact they may have by way of participation in the political process. Overall, participation increases with years of schooling (table 3). This is favorable toward feminist issues, since increased education is related to profeminist positions (tables 4 and 5), and the general trend in our society is in the direction of more years of schooling for both sexes.

The pattern of political participation by sex also favors feminist issues, both in the present and in the future. Until now, more men than women have tended to participate in all ages (table 6). Thus, even though women outnumber

to 59 age bracket there was rough agreement—54 and 53 percent; and only in the over-60 bracket did the old pattern remain, more men—62 percent—than women—35 percent—showing leniency. "What Does a Woman Want?" p. 10. Yankelovich found that among noncollege youth—sex not specified—the proportion viewing abortion as morally wrong declined from 64 to 48 percent between 1968 and 1972 (see footnote 6, above).

TABLE 3

VOTING HISTORY OF WOMEN BY YEARS OF SCHOOLING

	YEARS OF SCHOOLING			
VOTING HISTORY	EIGHTH GRADE	HIGH SCHOOL	COLLEGE	BEYOND COLLEGE
Registered to vote (year unspecified)	63	70	82	
Voted in 1970 congressional election	41	53	62	
Voted in 1968 presidential election	55	65	76	
Registered to vote in 1972 election	65.2	74.6	87.6	89.2
Voted in 1972 presidential election	51.5	66.2	83.2	85.5

SOURCE: Data on 1968 and 1970 elections: Louis Harris and Associates, *The 1972 Virginia Slims American Women's Opinion Poll* (New York: Louis Harris and Associates, 1972), p. 23. Data on 1972 election: U.S. Bureau of the Census, *Voting and Registration in the Election of November 1972*, series P-20, no. 253 (October 1973), p. 49, table 7.

TABLE 4

PROPORTION OF MEN AND WOMEN WHO ARE SYMPATHETIC WITH THE EFFORTS OF WOMEN'S LIBERATION GROUPS, BY EDUCATION

EDUCATION	MEN	WOMEN
Eighth Grade	45	37
High School	36	36
College	49	46

SOURCE: Louis Harris and Associates, *The 1972 Virginia Slims American Women's Opinion Poll* (New York: Louis Harris and Associates, 1972), p. 4.

men to a rather substantial extent in the politically most active years,[15] this advantage in numbers has been cancelled by a lower rate of participation. The result has been a plus

15. The sex ratio at conception has been estimated at roughly 150 males to 100 females. The greater fragility of the male fetus reduces this ratio to about 104 or 105 at birth. The continuing inferior male viability further reduces the sex ratio so that by the early 20s it has declined to rough equality. Thereafter, it continues to decline so that when the age bracket 65 to 74 has been reached, there are only 78 men left for every 100 women and by the age of 75 and over, only 64. Thus, in the ages when political participation is greatest for both sexes, there are potentially more women than men voters.

for feminist issues because of the more favorable attitudes of men than of women (tables 1 and 2).

However, changes seem to be in process. In the elections of 1968 and 1970, for example, although overall more men than women participated, the exceptions were all in the younger age brackets. By 1972 there were more exceptions and, again, they were all in the younger age brackets. In all three elections—one congressional and two presidential—young women were voting more than young men and, since young women favor

TABLE 5

PROPORTION OF MEN AND WOMEN WHO FAVOR EFFORTS TO STRENGTHEN WOMEN'S STATUS IN SOCIETY, BY EDUCATION

	1971		1972	
EDUCATION	MEN	WOMEN	MEN	WOMEN
Eighth Grade	40	36	38	42
High School	43	38	45	43
College	49	44*	62	57*

SOURCE: Louis Harris and Associates, *The 1972 Virginia Slims American Women's Opinion Poll* (New York: Louis Harris and Associates, 1972), p. 2.
* Includes post graduate work.

TABLE 6

POLITICAL PARTICIPATION OF MEN AND WOMEN, BY AGE

	REGISTERED				VOTED					
	1968–1970		1972		1968 CONGRESSIONAL ELECTION		1968 PRESIDENTIAL ELECTION		1972 PRESIDENTIAL ELECTION	
AGE	MEN	WOMEN	MEN	WOMEN	MEN	WOMEN	MEN	WOMEN	MEN	WOMEN
18–29	57	55			37	38	27	29		
30–39	84	76			75	77	64	59		
40–49	84	81			83	81	74	70		
50+	85	84			86	80	79	66		
18–20			57.9	58.3					47.7	48.8
21–24			58.6	60.3					49.7	51.7
25–29			66.0	66.2					57.6	58.0
30–34			71.6	70.8					62.1	61.7
35–44			74.4	75.1					65.9	66.7
45–54			79.9	78.9					72.0	69.9
55–64			81.1	79.4					72.4	69.2
65–74			82.9	75.1					73.2	64.3
75+			80.0	64.9					65.9	49.1

SOURCE: Data for 1968 and 1970: Louis Harris and Associates, *The 1972 Virginia Slims American Women's Opinion Poll* (New York: Louis Harris and Associates, 1972), p. 23. Data for 1972: U.S. Bureau of the Census, *Voting and Registration in the Election of November 1972*, series P-20, no. 253 (October 1973), p. 49, table 7.

feminine issues more than young men, this fact is a plus for feminist issues in the future. If women voted as a bloc, they could—for good[16] or for ill[17]—prevail and vote

16. During the early years of the suffrage movement it was argued that, given the vote, women would introduce a salutary force into the whole political process. The success of the Eighteenth Amendment was, in fact, attributed to the "woman's vote." A lingering belief that women would raise the level of political life remained until fairly recently. A Gallup poll in 1952, for example, found 59 percent of the women and 51 percent of the men believing that greater participation by women would reduce graft and corruption; 31 percent of the men and 47 percent of the women in the same poll believed that greater participation by women in government would mean better government. Yet, when satisfaction was recently expressed by some feminists that not a single woman was involved in the Watergate scandals, the cynical reply of others was that this was only an index of their lack of participation in positions of power. See, Geri Joseph,

"Women: Still on the Sidelines of Politics," *Washington Post*, 5 Aug. 1973. By 1969 there had been a letdown. Now only 26 percent of the women and 20 percent of the men believed we would be governed better if women had more to say in politics. These polls are summarized by Erskine in "The Polls," p. 282. As voters, women do show greater concern for humane values; they are "more responsive to issues with moral overtones"; Edmond Cosentini and Kenneth H. Craik, "Women as Politicians," *Journal of Social Issues* 28, no. 2 (1972), p. 218.

17. This aspect of the conventional wisdom with respect to the female electorate was stated by Maurice Duverger in 1955 as follows: "Women . . . have the mentality of minors in many fields, and, particularly in politics, they will accept paternalism on the part of men. The man—husband, fiancé, lover, or myth—is the mediator between them and the political world"; quoted by Cosentini and Craik, "Women as Politicians," p. 218. This, Cosentini and Craik note, "highlights what has become a virtual truism regarding women and politics." It undoubtedly has a modicum of validity for traditionalist women.

their convictions into practice. However, it is not likely that women—any more than men—will ever vote as a bloc; for, although they do differ from men on issues, they also differ among themselves, as well.

DIFFERENCES AMONG WOMEN ON FEMINIST ISSUES BY AGE

Since sexism pervades our entire society from cradle to grave, there are feminist issues for all ages.[18] Women, as well as men, take sides on all of them.

At the youngest age levels girls today are protesting the inequality of monies spent for boys and girls by boards of education for athletic equipment, training, coaching, sports and team uniforms; at the oldest age levels, Gray Panthers protest inequities in social security and pension rights. In the age brackets between these extremes, issues also vary. Among the younger

18. Women also differ by age on issues other than feminist ones. The 1972 Harris poll found, for example, that "Young women tend to be more troubled by the war, the economy, racial problems, the environment, and poverty, while older women are disturbed more by drugs, crime, unemployment and taxes." Harris, *Virginia Slims Poll*, p. 69. Interestingly, the set of issues of concern to young women paralleled that of the more affluent; thus, more women among those with incomes of $15,000 and over than among low-income women also showed concern "about the war, the economy, racial problems, the environment, welfare, and foreign relations." In general, on most issues young women, more than older women, tended to be in favor of change. More were in favor of gun control, were willing to pay to eliminate smog and pollution health hazards, did not feel blacks were moving too fast, felt blacks were justified in their demands, approved of busing school children to achieve integration, approved of more money for cities, favored welfare over defense expenditures and viewed themselves as liberal. Ibid., pp. 79 ff.

women they take the form of concern about: abortion, contraception, rape, child care, sexual mores and the like. Older women in the middle age range find divorce, child support and equal economic and professional opportunity more immediately pressing. These differences in major interest may be schematized, as in table 7. This table controverts two age-related allegations sometimes made against the feminist movement, one related to age directly and one related indirectly by way of occupation.

The directly age-related allegation against the feminist movement is that it neglects old women. It states that "women . . . sixty-five years of age and older. . . . are being ignored by the women's liberation movement" and asks "why is a socially sensitive movement like women's liberation neglecting its older sisters, leaving them to fend for themselves?"[19] The answer given is in terms of "ageism," a process "of systematic stereotyping of and discrimination against people because they are old, just as racism and sexism accomplish this with skin color and gender."[20]

The answer to this allegation is threefold. First, the feminist movement does not ignore older women. Resolution 147 of the February 1973 National Organization for Women (NOW) convention read:

Be it resolved that NOW establish a Task Force on Older Women, the functions of which shall include:

19. Myrna I. Lewis and Robert N. Butler, "Why is Women's Lib Ignoring Old Women?" *Aging and Human Development* 3 (1972), p. 223.
20. Ibid., p. 223.

TABLE 7

ISSUES OF MAJOR CONCERN TO WOMEN, BY AGE

GROUP	AGE OF LEADERS	ISSUES OF MAJOR CONCERN
Women's Equity Action League (WEAL)	Range: 29–67 Median: 47	". . . dedicated to improving the status and lives of *all* women. Our goal is equal participation in society with all the rights and responsibilities of full citizenship. WEAL works primarily in the field of education, legislation to achieve these ends. We seek to promote the economic well-being of women whether they work in the home, outside the home, or both."*
National Organization for Women (NOW)	Range: 26–55 Median: 38	The total spectrum of human issues, including, among others: poverty, minimum wage, child development programs, welfare, full employment, social security, equal opportunity, prostitution, needs of minority persons, sexuality and lesbianism, volunteerism, older women, rape, sports, marriage and divorce laws, the male mystique,† the conceptualization of sex roles.
Radical feminist— liberation—groups Antifeminist groups	Late 20s, early 30s‡ Same as NOW, roughly§	The conceptualization of sex roles.

SOURCE: Column two, WEAL and NOW: Maren Lockwood Carden, *The New Feminist Movement* (New York: Russell-Sage, 1974), p. 185.
  * WEAL flyer. Emphasis in original.
  † NOW Acts, p. 26.
  ‡ Personal estimate; actually, consciousness-raising groups do not have leaders.
  § Personal estimate.

(1) to investigate how women can document cases of age discrimination

(2) to give attention to a "supportive community" for older women: e.g., alternate life styles

(3) to promote affirmative action legislation to insure that employers have proportionate percentages of older women to develop a policy regarding the issue of equitable Social Security benefits for all women, including housewives, and

Be it further resolved that the Sixth Conference recommend that NOW Legal Defense and Education fund support test cases on discrimination against women on the basis of age, and

Be it further resolved that the Sixth National Conference of NOW go on record attacking the cult of youth which applies mostly to women.[21]

There is considerable agitation to correct the inequities for older women in the Social Security benefits system;[22] there are NOW members in the Gray Panthers;[23]

21. *NOW Acts*, Proceedings of the Sixth National Conference of the National Organization for Women (NOW), p. 10. In connection with the cult of youth, see, Inge Powell Bell, "The Double Standard," *Transaction* 8 (November-December 1970), pp. 75–80.

22. See, for example, Carolyn Shaw Bell, "Age, Sex, Marriage and Jobs," *Public Interest* 30 (Winter 1973), pp. 76–87.

23. Martha Gresham, "Report on a Gray Panthers Conference, October, 1973" *Vocal Majority* 4 (November 1973), p. 16.

and poverty is a major concern in the NOW agenda.[24]

The second answer is subtler. In the oldest age brackets specifically feminist issues tend to fade out. Sex roles have lost their saliency. Women tend to become more aggressive—Arlie Hochschild wonders where all that aggression was in their youth—and men more dependent. The consciousness-raising techniques do not operate very well among the truly old women.[25] It is, as the statement quoted above points out, so-called ageism, rather than sexism per se, which is salient in their lives—as it also is in the lives of old men.

Ageism is, indeed, a worthy cause—as are racism and exploitation of all kinds. It is part of the sexist ideology that women should come to the rescue of all ill-used people, cooperating in all worthy humanitarian causes. In the past they have tended to conform to this expectation, putting every other group's interests ahead of their own. There is a persisting temptation among feminists to continue in this admirable tradition. However, now they try to do it their way, which means a self-help way—in this context, a Gray Panthers way. When people are beyond self-help, they are a charge of the whole community. The feminist movement keeps us alert to this responsibility.

The second allegation—which is only indirectly related[26] to age—is

that the feminist movement is a white, middle class movement concerned only with professional and career women, with no concern for so-called working class women:

Women's liberation concentrates on middle-class women. It doesn't have much to do with lower-economic groups. The goal of most middle-class women is to get enough money to hire someone to clean her house. So middle-class women's emancipation from home is predicated on the notion that they can have a domestic to come in, and when you talk to them about emancipation of the domestic worker you are striking at their self-interests.[27]

First, whatever the goal of "most middle-class women" may be, the goal of the woman who is a member of the woman's liberation movement is not "to get enough money to hire someone to clean her

---

24. See, below, NOW resolution on poverty.

25. Gresham, "Report."

26. Older women differ from younger women occupationally, as well as educationally. More women 25 to 44 than 45 to 64, for example, are in professional, technical and kindred occupations and more are also in clerical and kindred occupations. Conversely, more of the women in the older than in the

younger age brackets are in service occupations.

27. Louis Ferman, quoted in William Chapman, "Over 40: 'No-Woman's Land for Jobs," Washington Post, 16 September 1973. Misconceptions of the feminist movement arise from lack of understanding of its total scope. A fragment here, a fragment there is snatched upon and taken for the whole. "The women's liberation movement is. . . . " No such grab bag approach does justice to it. The feminist movement is a great, amorphous, variegated, lumbering, capacious—entity, organism. Any more precise definition would be too limiting to express the nonspecificity of its multifaceted concerns. It embraces quarreling, bickering, differing persons who have in common a consciousness-of-kind which has to be experienced or empathized to be understood. They have also in common a conviction that human beings be dealt with as individuals on their own merits and not ascribed a status on the basis of preconceptions. All the statistics and polls and surveys are useless as sources of insight unless the critical click is heard. The click is the term used to refer to a phenomenon many women experience when for the first time they suddenly recognize, from something said or done in their environment, its sexist nature. It was first described in the first issue of *Ms*.

house." Quite the reverse: the literature on the women's liberation movement is filled with moral scruples and concern about the practice of hiring other women; strong objection has been expressed to the idea, especially among the younger women. Roxanne Dunbar, one of the outstanding leaders of the movement, has spent her life organizing women, especially in the South. The movement to organize domestic workers to improve pay and working conditions has had support from NOW. Women have made a strong case for defining poverty as a woman's issue, since most of those suffering from poverty are in fact women household heads and their children. Women have been more insistent than men that the contribution of the housewife be recognized both in status and in pecuniary reward. Indeed, all one has to do is examine the issues with which NOW is concerned, to see how erroneous is the conception of the feminist movement as class-biased.

At the February 1973 NOW conference one of the first resolutions to pass—no. 136—dealt with poverty as a woman's issue:

Therefore be it resolved that the National Conference designate 1973 as NOW's Action Year against Poverty, during which all NOW chapters, task forces (national and local) and members are strongly urged to focus their activities on strategies and actions to dramatize the problems of women in poverty and effect meaningful changes in the economic status of all women, and Be it further resolved that the national Task Force on Women in Poverty be designated as the coordinating group for NOW's Action Year against Poverty, and Be it further resolved that the top four legislative priorities for NOW in 1973 be

a) Revision of the Fair Labor Standards Act and similar state laws to provide for a minimum wage of at least $2.50 per hour, and extension of coverage under FLSA to include all workers, including domestics. (Note: This extension would incorporate these newly covered workers under the Equal Pay Act Provisions).

b) Passage of a comprehensive child development program, at least as good as the one vetoed by President Nixon last year, (including health, nutritional and educational components and providing for free services to low-income parents and a sliding scale for others).

c) A complete overhaul of the welfare program to provide for federalization of welfare in order to eliminate variations in requirements and payments, assurances that no custodial guardian or parent of pre-school or school age children will be required to work outside of the home and provision of supportive services including realistic job training. . . . [28]

It is admittedly true that working class women—as do old women, though for different reasons—sometimes find it difficult to work in the middle class style of the organized feminist groups. The feminists are well aware of this hurdle, and they make a determined effort to overcome it. They study in detail the specific behavioral differences which have an alienating effect on working class women in order to have their own consciousness raised and, hence, to be themselves better prepared to overcome the class-bound hurdles.[29]

28. NOW Acts, p. 7.
29. Especially noteworthy was a series of articles in the first volume of a feminist journal, The Furies. Among them were: Nancy Myron, "Class Beginnings," 1, no. 3 (March-April 1972); Ginny Berson, "Slumming It and the Middle Class," ibid.; Charlotte Bunche and Coletta Read, "Revolution

SEX ROLE DEFINITION AS A FEMINIST ISSUE

Although sex role definitions may have ultimate political implications—especially as symbolized in the Equal Rights Amendment (ERA)—they differ from more practical issues in that they are more profoundly personal and moral than political in nature. Here the relationship with age is equivocal, for it is not always the oldest women who are most likely to be traditionalists—as might be expected from the discussion so far—but women in their 40s. Education can explain some of the relationships reported, but generational factors may also be involved.

Three indexes of traditionalism in role definition are selected here: (1) preference for a status of dependency, (2) feeling that life under the traditional sex role definitions is easier for women than for men and (3) lack of sympathy for efforts of women's liberation groups.[30] In all three, women in their 40s tend to differ from both younger and older women (table 8). In the absence of other data available for explanatory purposes, I comment on only two possibilities, here: education and the peculiar circumstances under which this generation of women was reared.

Education seemed to be related to these indexes of traditionalism in a way similar to the way age was related to it. Young women and college-educated women resemble one another,[31] as do also women in their 40s and high school graduates (table 9). On the basis of the data available it is not possible to tease out the relative impact of these two variables—age and education—on traditionalism. Sooner or later, the technical researchers will apply their high power machinery to the problem; we will then learn precisely, to the last decimal, how much each one contributes to traditionalism. For the present, I evade the issue by concluding simply that education tends to make women think young.[32]

Begins at Home," ibid., no. 4 (May 1972). For a more extended discussion of feminism and class, see, Jessie Bernard, "Class and Feminist Issues," in *Women, Wives, Mothers: Values and Options* (Chicago: Aldine, 1975).

30. Harris, *Virginia Slims Poll*, pp. 4, 8. In the case of many of the other possible items available in this poll to serve as indexes, education seemed to be roughly adequate to explain differences. On 6 of the 10 items dealing with "certain feelings"—related to sex role attitudes—women in their 40s were out of line, differing from women both older and younger than they were.

31. A survey of 1,209 men and women in the Washington, D.C., metropolitan area in August 1973, showed the same resemblance. Asked which was more rewarding, a full-time job or running a home, the women responded as follows:

32. Karen Mason and Larry L. Bumpass in a study on women's sex role attitudes in the United States in 1970 based on data gathered in the Ryder-Westoff 1970 National Fertility study found education to be the most significant factor in sex role attitudes. However, they found no differences in sex role attitudes between women under 30 and those 30 and over. They concluded that whatever changes may have occurred have affected women over 30 as well as women under 30. "The age control. . . . provided

	18–29	SOME COLLEGE	30 AND OVER	NO COLLEGE
Running a home	39	32	48	52
Full-time job	22	18	16	16
Both rewarding	11	18	13	15
Can't choose	28	31	23	17

Jay Mathews, "The 'Best' Job: Housewife," *Washington Post*, 21 February 1974. See, also, footnote 6, above.

TABLE 8

TRADITIONALISM IN ROLE CONCEPTION OF WOMEN, BY AGE

ROLE CONCEPTION	18–29	30–39	40–49	50+
Want husband to take care of me:				
agree frequently	50	57	61	59
occasionally	21	19	18	13
hardly ever	26	21	17	23
not sure	4	3	4	5
Women have easier life than men:				
agree frequently	21	29	37	29
occasionally	23	27	22	19
hardly ever	54	42	39	49
not sure	2	2	2	3
Attitude toward efforts of women's liberation groups:				
sympathetic	49	39	34	34
not sympathetic	41	50	53	51
not sure	10	11	13	15

SOURCE: Same as table 3.

NOTE: In a 1973 poll far more women 40–59—58 percent—than women 18–24—37 percent—agreed that "in America, women mostly have an easier life than men"; Thomas C. Sorensen, "What Does a Woman Want?" *Parade Magazine*, 15 April 1973, p. 10. The responses for women 25–39 were not reported in this poll.

Years of schooling is only one differentiating characteristic of generations. It is at least a quasi-continuous variable and can therefore be dealt with as though it were a quantitative one. Yet, there are other differentiating characteristics which are harder to quantify or even to label. We speak of the depression generation or the wartime babies or the postwar babies, suggesting that the situation prevailing during the years of their early socialization leaves a mark on

in an attempt to discern whether more recent cohorts are more egalitarian in outlook. . . . provided no evidence of such intercohort difference, nor of possible aging effects." Mason and Bumpass, "Women's Sex Role Attitudes in the United States, 1970" (Paper presented at Meetings of the American Sociological Association, New York, New York, August 1973). Their measure of the age variable—under 30 and 30 and over——may have been too gross to ferret out nonlinear relationships.

them. Fortunately, there is a longitudinal study[33] which traces one such generation. Its findings are invoked here to help understand the women who were in their 40s in 1972. The study found that among women who lived in deprived households during the Depression of the 1930s, familism has been especially strong.

Glen Elder summarizes the findings of this study as related to traditionalism in women:

Our data suggests that receptivity to traditional roles is concentrated among women who grew up in deprived households that depended heavily upon the involvement of female members. From adolescence and the late 30's to middle age, a domestic life style in values and action is more characteristic of these women than of women

33. Glen Elder, *Children of the Great Depression* (Chicago, Ill.: University of Chicago Press, 1974).

TABLE 9

TRADITIONALISM IN ROLE CONCEPTION OF WOMEN, BY AGE AND EDUCATION

ROLE CONCEPTION	AGE AND EDUCATION			
	18–29	COLLEGE	40–49	HIGH SCHOOL
Want husband to take care of me:				
agree frequently	50	49	61	63
occasionally	21	19	18	17
hardly ever	26	29	17	17
not sure	3	3	3	3
Women have easier life than men:				
agree frequently	21	24	37	32
occasionally	23	25	22	22
hardly ever	54	50	39	44
not sure	2	1	2	2
Attitude toward efforts of women's liberation groups:				
sympathetic	49	46	34	36
not sympathetic	41	47	53	50
not sure	10	7	13	14

SOURCE: Same as table 3, pp. 4, 8.

from non-deprived homes. They were more involved in household chores, expressed greater interest in domestic activities, and, in the middle class, were more likely to marry at an early age. . . . The daughters of deprived families were most likely to stop working at marriage or when they gave birth to their first child; and (if from the middle class) to enjoy the common tasks of homemaking. The meaning of family preference centered first on the value of children and secondarily on the interpersonal benefits of marriage.[34]

The women who were in their 40s in 1972 were born between 1923 and 1932 and, hence, their earliest socialization occurred during the Depression, when many families were likely to have suffered deprivation. If Elder's analyses of his sample are valid for other women, this generational factor may help explain the traditionalism shown in table 8.

34. Ibid., chap. 8 (present quotation from manuscript version).

It is, of course, possible that findings reported in the Harris poll result from sampling errors. However, a combination of educational and childhood deprivation factors may, conceivably, have produced them.

Traditionalists, whatever their age, range from those who merely accept the sex status quo to those who are passionately and actively defensive of it. Not only do they not accept feminism, they aggressively fight it. Antifeminists have not been subjected to as much research as have the feminists; there is therefore relatively little firm data to report on them. While equal time is not called for, some attention to them is warranted.

ANTIFEMINISTS AND AGE

On the basis of a purely cursory examination of mainly journalistic reports, antifeminist leaders seem to come from Glen Elder's "children of the depression"—that is, they tend to be women in their late 40s and early 50s, with a range including the late 30s. The followers seem to be somewhat younger, corresponding in age to the women who participate in local consciousness-raising groups—that is, those who are in their late 20s and 30s. The leaders of three organizations—the Pussycat League, Happiness of Women (HOW) and Fascinating Womanhood—may serve as examples.

The most trivial and least significant is The Pussycat League, which was organized by Lucianne Goldberg "to answer militant feminism." Her book, *Purr, Baby, Purr: The Case Against Women's Liberation* stated its position: "The general thrust was that the kind of equality women's lib is talking about is a step down to any woman who enjoys being female. You can be in a man's world and be a female. . . . You can get more flies with honey."[35] Neither the author nor the book had any significant impact. Although the thesis of the book was vintage antifeminism, its facetiousness discounted the message it conveyed.

Both HOW and Fascinating Womanhood have strong biblical underpinnings. The HOW pamphlet, for example, states that "Man was divinely ordained to be the head of the family, God commanded Eve, 'thy desire shall be to thy husband and he shall rule over

thee.' " Still, in actual practice its leaders may be more symbolically, than actually, opposed to feminism. In a public debate, for example, Ms. Barbara Harris, a leader in HOW:

turned out to be an attractive young woman, who announced . . . that she was the mother of two children ('it's a sacred trust!'). . . . [Her position was] that women should be respected as the bearers of children, the family is sacred, the equal rights amendment would erase 'over 160' Federal laws from the statute book, and 'over 200' state laws protecting women would be wiped off in Arizona alone. . . . I don't see any reason not to have laws that protect women from having to pick up loads that weigh more than 30 pounds—extended to men too. Look at the number of them that have bad backs and hernias at the age of 40. . . . We want more and better protection, for men and for women.[36]

Precisely the feminist position. When asked if her husband made the final decision in her family, Ms. Harris replied, certainly not. Although a man was head of the family: "I think you have to make decisions together, in the interests of the whole family. After all, we both work. What I'm against is something like the ERA, because it would simply make us all men, or second-rate men, instead of being equal *as women*."[37] A woman who has a job, two children and shares decision making with her husband can hardly be viewed as a traditionalist in her conception of roles.

Helen B. Andelin, who is fifty-one and mother of eight, is the founder of a movement known as

35. Quoted by Jules Witcover, "McGovern's Mata Hari: Suspected Once, Ignored Often," *Washington Post*, 21 August 1973. Ms. Goldberg was later engaged by Republicans as a spy during the McGovern campaign. The comments of her male fellow journalists were not supportive. She was ignored, and "regarded as a pest." Apparently the click never occurred to her.

36. Michael Korda, "Liberation, U.S.A.," *Newsweek*, 16 July 1973, p. 17.

37. Ibid., p. 17.

Fascinating Womanhood. Her book with that title, which tells women how to please men by being feminine,[38] sold 250,000 copies. Its success led to the establishment of the Andelin Foundation which her husband, a dentist, left his own profession to run. It sells franchises —$10.00—for the privilege of offering an eight-week course based on the book.[39]

38. The tenets of Fascinating Womanhood are those which define traditional sex role conceptions: a wife must make her husband feel like a man; he must be number one; though marriage is a democracy, the man must be president; the ideal woman must be feminine, have a lovely character, find happiness in being a good homemaker and mother; women should retain a certain amount of childlikeness. Combined with complete understanding of her husband, these rules will help her find complete love. She fascinates, amuses and enchants him and arouses in him a desire to shelter and protect her. Both the meek and the overbearing husband undergo complete change under the influence of her new subservient behavior. No longer threatened, he becomes more tolerant and understanding himself. More love is needed in the world today, and this is not to be achieved by creating jobs for women or by Supreme Court decisions. An article on another antifeminist movement based on Marabel Morgan's *The Total Woman* (Old Tappan, N. J.: Fleming H. Revell, 1973) in *Newsweek*, 24 June 1974, elicited indignant letters from men as well as women. One protests the low opinion implied in *The Total Woman* of a husband "too insecure to accept criticism, so impotent he needs constant sexual stimulation and too selfish to take care of anyone's needs but his own. The real man-haters are not ardent feminists, but women like Marabel Morgan who apparently feel that women have all the strength and that men are too incompetent to survive without constant support and attention" *Newsweek*, 15 July 1974, pp. 6–7.

39. To receive a franchise a woman must be convinced of the principles of Fascinating Womanhood, experience them successfully in her own life—that is, she must have a happy marriage, have a good appearance and not be grossly overweight, use proper language, be a good housekeeper, not smoke and qualify as a teacher.

The followers of the antifeminist leaders seem to be the mirror image of the young women in consciousness-raising groups. However, instead of fighting against the sex role status quo, they fight to come to terms with it, to learn not only to live with it but to glory in it. One such group, consisting of fourteen women in a Fascinating Womanhood course, ranged in age from 25 to 52, eight being in the 28 to 38 age range.[40]

In response to essay questions, such antifeminist themes as the following showed up: the feminist movement is against Biblical teaching, against the will of God; it offers no effective solutions for happiness; "I am opposed to the movement in general and/or ignore or give it little attention"; it has gone too far beyond equal pay, the rest of its ideas are nonsense; I am for equal pay; the movement is based on confusion—people uninformed, uncertain and, therefore, ripe for propaganda; the members have lost sight of what it *really* means to be a woman; "I cannot relate to women's liberation, I have no desire to enter a man's world"; "The women in the movement are out for revenge because they are unhappy in marriage or, if single, because they have never had pleasant experience with a man"; "the movement is a reaction against superficial aspects of women emphasized in the past—that is, beauty and do-good organizations"; "the movement is part of an overall

40. Half of the women had had at least some college, four had a bachelor's degree; two-thirds of the husbands did. The fathers of half of the women had also had at least some college; the mothers of four of the women did. The data on Fascinating Womanhood were supplied by Ms. Josephine Carter, a participant observer.

scheme to destroy legitimate American values—that is, marriage and the family."

On the more positive side, the salvaging nature of the teachings of Fascinating Womanhood show up in the statement by a 29 year old mother of four, a high school graduate who married at age 17. After years of struggle against her status, she surrendered; she is now a happy housewife:

Fascinating Womanhood has meant a whole new life for me. I realize that women have suppressed men to the point of making them very unmasculine. I also realize that I enjoy living with a man that rules our home instead of me ruling it. For many years I have tried to put myself on the same level as my husband. The result was drastic. To the point of ruination of marriage, personality, heart and soul. Since my husband regained leadership, we are all so much more happy and content. I have no desire to work, study, or anything. My work is here at home and there are areas in my home that I can use my talents. My fulfillment in life is happy well-adjusted children and a happy husband. My husband takes pride in being the sole moneymaker. He also likes the new submissive me. He does not demand anything from me unfairly.

I am for equal pay. I am not for women working and pawning their children off on someone else to raise. The unmarried girl is one thing, the married girl is another. The will of God is that married women stay home and take care of their families. If all women live and act under the will of the Lord they will be blessed with happiness unlimited. I have yet to see a happy working woman. They are irritable, tired and bossy. Their kids are unruly brats or mental cases. I am a servant and comforter to my husband and in return I have received a love from him that is so deep he cannot put it into words. . . . The most important thing in my life is my family and I care for nothing else except the will of God in our lives.

A glance at table 2 suggests that the women in their 30s—as the women in this particular group were—consititute a sort of rear guard. They tend to resemble the older women—40 and over—more than they do the younger—18 to 29. On all three items in table 8 the break appears between those under 30 and those 30 and over.[41] On two of the items the nontraditional point of view has gained acceptance by about half of the young women. The trend seems thus to be in the direction of attenuation of the traditional role definition.

Basically, opposition to the feminist movement is opposition to the twenty-first century. It is a last-ditch stand against the demands of the modern world for a restructuring of roles. It is supported by women, reared in a particular historic context, who wish to remain protected and sheltered in the home, who want to invest their lives in their families. They feel threatened by the feminist movement.[42] They ignore it when they can and turn for leadership to women who can fight it for them. Whether or not their position is theologically, naturally, or scientifically best, they seem to be fighting a losing battle. They do not even have the total backing of men.

At the other end of the antifeminist scale is the phenomenon known as the Tiger Lady or Queen Bee syndrome. Within this category are the successful professional women who have made it in a

41. However, see footnote 31.
42. In the May 1972 issue of the *Reader's Digest* there appeared an article which revealed the feeling of threat many housewives were experiencing. "Women's libbers" were rocking a very comfortable boat. If they did not stop, men would catch on to the fact that women really were the favored sex and would cease to pamper them.

man's world and who do not wish to welcome their sisters as competitors or to change the rules in any way. "I made it, why can't you?" is their response to the arguments of the liberation movement for change.[43]

THE EQUAL RIGHTS AMENDMENT

The current throes of change in sex role definitions may be seen as analogous to the throes of change which the realignment of classes precipitated in the eighteenth and nineteenth centuries. The realignment of the status relations between the sexes involved in the new conceptions is as basic and profound as the transformation of the several estates or fixed stations in life into mobile classes. It taps wells of emotion as deep as, or deeper than, those tapped by the collapse of the conception of a natural order in which everyone was born into his or her proper station in life and forever after knew his or her place; in which men and women recognized their betters and accepted the privileges of those above them and their own deprivations as divinely ordained —that is, not to be questioned. The realignment in status between the sexes is certainly as great as the status realignment among age groupings which has also accompanied industrialization and urbanization.

The restructuring of sex roles today—the most fundamental change since the restructuring of society in the eighteenth and nineteenth centuries—is articulated in the Equal Rights Amendment. Although it appears to be archetypically a political issue— dealing as it does with a political goal and involving a basic political process—it is far more than a merely political issue. Although it is a one-time historical event, it is the culmination of a long process of restructuring our society to fit modern economic and technological conditions. It encapsulates the critical point in a long-time movement, precipitating a conflict which began to emerge over a century ago and has persisted—now latent, now manifest—ever since; it is a conflict personified, though by no means precipitated, by feminists and their opponents.

In and of itself the ERA does not mandate any role restructuring; it merely specifies that privileges and prerogatives, rights and duties, obligations and responsibilities be allocated without regard to sex per se. It is not, however, the specific details of the ERA which are most significant; they may well be left to experts on law and legislation, not to mention jurisprudence. It is more significant as a symbol of the changes in roles now in process in our society than as a statement of the actual changes themselves.[44]

---

43. For a perceptive analysis of the Queen Bee syndrome, see, Graham Staines, Toby Epstein Jayartne and Carol Travis, "The Queen Bee Syndrome," *Psychology Today* 7 (January 1974), pp. 55–60.

44. This fact is illustrated by the relatively trivial items sometimes seized upon as of momentous significance, for example, the prospect of shared toilet facilities. Even women who have travelled extensively on trains, planes or even buses without trauma find the idea fearful, unthinkable, in fact, much worse than the actual practice.

NCBA, Black Aged and Politics

By Jacquelyne Johnson Jackson

ABSTRACT: Taking the position that those who are both black and old are different from the aged or the minority aged, this paper is primarily concerned with providing background information on the National Caucus on the Black Aged, Inc. (NCBA) and selected demographic data on black and other aged to justify that position and hence, NCBA's existence. Black aged—who often experience multiple jeopardy from racism, ageism and poverty and, in the case of females, sexism—are beset with certain crucial problems differentiating them from other aged. Because NCBA is opposed to "artificial dissection of blacks," it is justifiably committed to the position that those problems can and must be resolved through effective political action involving NCBA and aging and aged blacks.

Jacquelyne Johnson Jackson is Associate Professor of Medical Sociology and member of the Center for the Study of Aging and Human Development at Duke University. Dr. Jackson, who received her Ph.D. from Ohio State University in 1960, is a founding member and currently Vice-Chairman of the National Caucus on Black Aged, Inc. and Technical and Training Director of the National Center on Black Aged. Having published a number of works about, and lectured widely on, both black aged and black females, she is committed to the need for more knowledge and understanding of homogeneous subsets within the black population.

OVER the years many old blacks now dead, as well as many yet alive, have been among the avant-garde of civil-rights and social activitists. Many others have been faithful followers. Yet, almost none of that activism has been aimed specifically or exclusively toward old blacks. This is not surprising for a number of reasons. For example, old blacks have been extremely sparse, both numerically and proportionally, within the black population. Much activism has been directed toward more global consequences of racial discrimination affecting blacks of varying ages, as in the case of voting disfranchisement. Racial discrimination itself has been, and remains, more vicious than age discrimination in its visibility, strength and devastating and debilitating effects. Finally, those most often responsible for molding black political activity have themselves been relatively unconcerned about particular adverse social conditions heaped upon those who were or are old and black.

Although various recent modifications in the types of phenomena indicated above all point toward emergent trends requiring greater political activity for and by old blacks precisely because they are old and black, relatively little concerted action in that direction has occurred. The most notable action has been that of the National Caucus on the Black Aged, Inc. (NCBA), an organization deliberately established in 1970—one year prior to the 1971 White House Conference on Aging (WHCOA)—to help improve qualities and quantities of life for aged blacks. NCBA's establishment and continued focus upon aged blacks as a specific race-age population subset deserving attention and political action have raised anew several highly charged political issues, one being the necessity for, and wisdom of, concentrating upon old blacks.

Since NCBA obviously believes in both the necessity and wisdom of such action, this presentation is primarily concerned with selected background data about NCBA and aged blacks which, in NCBA's view, justify that concentration. Although these data can be interpreted in varying ways by others, it should be clear from the outset that for NCBA aged blacks—who often experience multiple jeopardy from racism, ageism, poverty and, in the case of females, sexism as well—are beset with certain crucial problems which distinguish them, even if only in degree, from all white and nonblack minority aged, and that such problems can be resolved through effective and concentrated political action on behalf of and by aged blacks. Furthermore, NCBA believes that the resolution of such problems for aged blacks will necessarily benefit all other aged.

NCBA BACKGROUND

NCBA and WHCOA

NCBA—initially formed as an ad hoc group of various black and white professionals extremely concerned about aged blacks and/or inappropriate intrusions of partisan politics into, and the rigid overstructuring of, the then forthcoming WHCOA, as well as the planned underrepresentation of blacks within WHCOA—was, in the words of its first and continuing highly effective chairman, Hobart C. Jackson, born:

. . . out of concern, concern that the [WHCOA] would dilute the critical and special needs of the black and other minority aged, thereby weakening the effects of the total attack on the problems of the elderly of the nation. By highlighting this black segment, we reinforce and highlight the plight of all . . . The *Caucus* must forge its purpose into policy and its policy into action.[1]

During its first year of operation, NCBA set forth to translate purpose into policy, and policy into action.

Until Arthur S. Flemming—a former secretary of the Department of Health, Education and Welfare under the Eisenhower administration—became permanent chairman of WHCOA in midstream, NCBA met with considerable and open opposition. Most of the WHCOA staff appeared to be toiling diligently both to prevent any focus whatsoever upon aged blacks *qua* aged blacks and to minimize black participation—especially that of qualified blacks. Flemming's more equitable position,[2] coupled with certain NCBA pressure events,[3] enabled NCBA to succeed in its then principal objectives: (1) increasing black participation within WHCOA;

(2) officially setting forth, within a WHCOA special session report, needed recommendations for action to be taken over the next decade for old blacks.[4] Without NCBA, WHCOA would have had no concern about aged blacks *qua* aged blacks.

NCBA and the vast majority of WHCOA black delegates were very concerned about three major and

1. Hobart C. Jackson, "The White House Conference on Aging and Black Aged," in *Proceedings of Research Conference on Minority Group Aged in the South*, ed. Jacquelyne J. Jackson (Durham, N.C.: Duke University Center for the Study on Aging, 1972), p. 22.

2. Dr. Arthur S. Flemming—currently the U.S. Commissioner on Aging and Chairman of the Civil Rights Commission—was, and has remained, supportive of NCBA's efforts. His support has represented both political and moral acumen.

3. NCBA's pressure events included holding a Black House Conference on Aging several weeks prior to WHCOA and a picket by some of its members of the White House immediately prior to WHCOA, as well as other efforts intended to establish political clout.

4. *Report of the Special Concerns Session on Aging and Aged Blacks, 1971 White House Conference on Aging* (Washington, D.C.: Government Printing Office, 1972). Perhaps the two most controversial recommendations were those pertaining to (1) the setting aside of 11 percent—11 percent then being the approximate percentage of blacks within the total population of the United States—of all federal funds for research, training and services in aging for blacks over the next decade; (2) the reduction of the minimum age eligibility requirement for black males who qualified as primary beneficiaries of Old-Age, Survivors', Dependents and Health Insurance (OASDHI) under Social Security, so as to reduce existing racial inequities resulting from disproportionate life expectancies between black and white males—inasmuch as the former tended to become older at an earlier chronological age and to die earlier, on the average, than did the latter. For additional information about this Social Security proposal, see, especially, Jacquelyne J. Jackson, "Aged Negroes: Their Culture Departures from Statistical Stereotypes and Rural-Urban Differences," *Gerontologist* 10 (1970), pp. 140–145, reprinted in *Research Planning and Action for the Elderly*, ed. Donald P. Kent, Robert Kastenbaum and Sylvia Sherwood (New York: Behavioral Publications, 1972) pp. 501–513; and Jacquelyne J. Jackson, "Aged Blacks: A Potpourri towards the Reduction of Racial Inequities," *Phylon* 32 (1971), pp. 260–280. Also, for additional information on NCBA ideologies and developments prior to 1972, see, especially, C. Coiro, "Why the National Caucus on the Black Aged?" *Harvest Years*, 11 (1971), pp. 13–18; Hobart C. Jackson, "National Caucus on the Black Aged: A Progress Report" *Aging and Human Development* 2 (1971), pp. 226–231; and Hobart C. Jackson, "National Goals and Priorities in the Social Welfare of Aging," *Gerontologist* 2 (1971), pp. 226–231.

related issues. One was the insufficient attention given to minority groups, including blacks, in WHCOA's formation of issues and policy recommendations, as well as specific omission of references to blacks by major WHCOA speakers. The second was WHCOA black underrepresentation, even in comparison with other minorities; significantly, Native Americans and Spanish-surnamed groups were overrepresented.[5] The third was insufficient time and space for NCBA to present its recommendations

within the preliminary report of proceedings which delegates received at WHCOA's closing, as well as the general paucity of federally collected data about aged blacks.[6] Such political problems, however, generally plague black groups attempting to work within the established political system.

Also perturbing were certain undesirable episodes. For example, a WHCOA professional staff member seemed to persist in providing NCBA with misinformation in an effort to reduce its impact. Also, a Michigan black delegate was apparently persuaded to absent himself from WHCOA's Special Concerns Session on Aging and Aged Blacks, if he wished to be considered for scholarship support in a gerontological program at a Michigan university. Unfortunately, the individual absented himself without informing NCBA and without providing NCBA with any copy of his subcommittee's "Facilities, Programs, Services and Transportation" recommendations. Thus, NCBA recommendations—which became an official part of WHCOA proceedings in that area—were considerably weaker than planned. Furthermore, although NCBA had been advised earlier that its preliminary report could be modified, a later WHCOA ruling prohibited any

---

5. As indicated by H. Jackson: "Subsequent to the 1971 *White House Conference on Aging*, it was apparent that efforts to increase black participation in that Conference had met with moderate success inasmuch as approximately ten percent of the total delegation was black. Nevertheless, this represented slight underrepresentation as compared with the black proportion in the total United States population. As compared with the proportionate delegate strength of Asian Americans, American Indians, and Spanish-speaking persons, blacks were significantly underrepresented. According to the estimates of *The National Caucus on the Black Aged*, based upon racial and ethnic delegate data supplied by the *White House Conference on Aging*, the Conference had 1.62 black delegates per every 100,000 blacks in the 1970 U.S. population, 2.1 Asian American delegates per every 100,000 Asian Americans, 2.8 Spanish-speaking delegates per every 100,000, and 12.4 American Indian delegates per every 100,000 American Indians. Thus, while blacks were clearly underrepresented and Asian Americans were represented as expected by chance, Spanish-speaking persons and American Indians were overrepresented. One major effect of black underrepresentation was insufficient strength to ensure that specific policy recommendations seriously needed for black aged would receive sufficient attention in the various Sections of the *White House Conference on Aging*. Had it not been for the *Special Concerns Session on Aging and Aged Blacks*, many of the kinds of policy recommendations most important for black aged would have been overlooked completely, as in the case of nursing homes;" "White House Conference," pp. 23–24.

6. NCBA's efforts to obtain data useful in helping to determine the current demographic statuses of older blacks circa 1970 from such federal agencies as the Bureau of the Census and the Department of Housing and Urban Development were usually in vain; thus, undue reliance upon the previous decade's census, already ten years old, was necessary. In addition to the suggestion that more useful, readily available and current data should be produced by federal agencies—especially by the Census—NCBA felt then, and now, the need for vastly improved and more frequent censuses. Such recommendations were made to WHCOA.

change, thus making NCBA's final and preliminary reports identical.

NCBA and training programs

Even prior to WHCOA, NCBA was alarmed at the scarcity of black professionals interested in aging—a situation exacerbated by the absence of aging programs at black colleges and universities. NCBA labored to obtain such programs. Finding that available funding was hardly sufficient to launch a program at that time, NCBA carefully studied the problem and, then, opted for initiating a graduate training program at Fisk University. However, the funding agency chose to allocate funds among six different black institutions, including two within the same locale; the net result was that no institution received sufficient resources to fund its program. This political ploy, occurring a few months prior to WHCOA, was another instance of programming for failure.

In fact, some of the programs begun in 1971 are no longer functioning, and the functioning ones have generally been unsuccessful in reducing the scarcity of black professionals in aging. Moreover, the programs have usually overemphasized inappropriate undergraduate participation and low-level service delivery training and have underemphasized competent undergraduate preparation for further graduate and professional training—and, ultimately, competent aging specialists needed for basic research, planning and training. This ill-advised funding pattern of reaching out to the most deprived of the deprived can, however, be highly advantageous to whites seeking to curb professional black competition, even in aging.

Such a political tragedy is by no means uncommon or unexpected. A great tragedy is the extent to which blacks become pitted against blacks in the battle for or against excellence. In my judgment, aged blacks are too precious to be entrusted to incompetents—no matter what their color. Thus, those seriously and sincerely concerned about the black aged must ipso facto be concerned about the quality and quantity of black and other specialists on aging.

NCBA since WHCOA

Barriers to more effective action for old blacks, such as those proferred above, catalyzed NCBA's formation as a permanent and legally incorporated body in 1972. No other national organization has focused —nor is one likely to do so in the foreseeable future—upon aged blacks. Since 1972, NCBA activities, largely national, have included increasing awareness of, and forcing action upon, problems—particularly those of income, health and housing—confronting aged blacks.

Most NCBA activities have involved blacks and whites of varying occupations and ages. One major setting for dialogue has been the annual business meeting and conference held in May. In 1974 the theme of the annual meeting was "Black Aged, Black Churches, and Black Politics: Mutual Reciprocity." Federal funding received in 1973 enabled NCBA to establish its Washington, D.C., National Center on Black Aged. The primary objectives of the center include technical, training, research and legislative development and assistance to, and on behalf of, aged blacks.

Some individuals and groups have continued to pressure NCBA, either to expand to include all minorities, to disband or to function under the aegis of an existing organization presumably concerned with all aged, but controlled by whites. In fact, throughout its existence, NCBA has been repeatedly confronted with arguments against its very *raison d'être*. In addition to attempts to undermine or destroy it—emanating from some quarters unnamed here—NCBA has been informed that black aged are indistinguishable from nonblack minority and white aged. Why, then, is there a need for an organization focused upon old blacks?

In general NCBA has concluded that the fallacy of such arguments can best be explained by the theory of artificial dissection—that is, blacks are often treated as if their ascribed statuses of race, sex and age function independently in determining their composite social statuses. For example, black protest groups generally ignore the fact that some blacks are women, while women's groups generally ignore the fact that some women are black.[7] Both such groups are usually oblivious to old black females.[8] NCBA, however, remains cognizant of these interacting status determinants and, hence, of the futility of dissecting old blacks as if they were old or black. Old blacks *qua* old blacks differ from old nonblacks.

7. For further discussion of this issue, see, especially, Jacquelyne J. Jackson, "Black Women in a Racist Society," in *Racism and Mental Health*, ed. Charles V. Willie, Bernard M. Kramer and Bertram S. Brown (Pittsburgh, Penn.: University of Pittsburgh Press, 1973), chap. 7, pp. 185–268.

8. For a discussion of particular characteristics of this group, see, Jacquelyne J. Jackson, "Quadruple Jeopardy: Black and Female and Old and Poor," *NCBA News* 2, nos. 1 and 2 (1974).

BACKGROUND DATA ABOUT OLD BLACKS

Demographic data not only reveal heterogeneity among old— that is, 65 years of age and over —blacks themselves, but also differences of degree between them and nonblack aged—for example, in income—when categorical comparisons are made. However—although comparisons holding race constant are not presented to any significant degree within this context—in actuality common generalizations are really misleading and often prevent fuller knowledge and understanding of aging processes and patterns. For example, while it is claimed that females outlive males and that whites outlive blacks, some females outlive some males, some males outlive some females, some whites outlive some blacks and some blacks outlive some whites. Studies focused more closely on within-racial-group variation will—as I have suggested elsewhere[9]—aid us in unraveling aging, provided that appropriate comparisons of individuals, regardless of race, eventually become possible and feasible.

Aged black heterogeneity.

The approximately 1.6 million old blacks in the United States are homogeneous with respect to race. Beyond that, they are not all just alike. In fact, they are not even all just alike with respect to race, inasmuch as they have been differentially impacted by race and have exhibited differential responses to race. Although most are under 75 years of age, almost 8 percent are

9. Jacquelyne J. Jackson, "Social Gerontology and the Negro: A Review," *Gerontologist* 7 (1967), pp. 168–178.

85 or more years of age; a number are centenarians. Although almost three-fifths resided in the South in 1970, they are scattered throughout the United States, primarily within urban areas. Less than one-fourth were rural residents in 1970; of those, almost 93 percent lived in the South. The black aged sex ratio—76 males per 100 females— was less than that of the black population—90 males per 100 females—but slightly higher than the white aged sex ratio. Most males were married, and most females were widowed. Yet, each sex group contained individuals who had never married; who had married and were living with, or apart from, spouses; who were divorced; or who were widowed.

Most had received no formal education beyond elementary school, but many had. For example, in 1970 more than 33,000 were college graduates, and a number of them held graduate or professional degrees. Included in their numbers is Dr. Benjamin E. Mays, President-emeritus of Morehouse College and currently President of the Atlanta, Georgia, City School Board of Education, who is almost 80 years old.

Most were no longer active within the labor force, but some were still gainfully employed— sometimes fully, sometimes partially and sometimes irregularly so. The employed varied by occupational position as well, although most were not white-collar workers. One notable case is that of Arthur G. Gaston—a Birmingham, Alabama, businessman—who is not only self-employed, but whose payroll for his workers was more than $2.5 million in 1973.

Although the majority were poor, some were not. Black aged also varied by family composition, size and headship status, as well as by health, religion, leisure activities and other relevant traits.[10] In short, all aged blacks within the United States have never been, are not now and, in all probability, will never be all just alike.

Aged blacks and nonblacks

Race is the single most overriding difference between black and nonblack aged. Racial victimization is more serious than ethnic victimization. Inasmuch as blacks constitute a racial—and not an ethnic —minority, they differ from such ethnic minorities as Native Americans, Mexican-Americans, Puerto Ricans, Chinese-Americans, Japanese-Americans and Jews. Hence, as will be emphasized again later, blacks have recently been further disadvantaged by unwarranted political expansion of the concept of minority group. Minorities such as the aged, women, homosexuals,

10. For the most part this brief profile was extracted from a more detailed one presented in Jacquelyne J. Jackson, "Social Stratification of Aged Blacks and Implications for Training Professionals," in *Proceedings of Black Aged in the Future*, ed. Jacquelyne J. Jackson (Durham, N.C.: Duke University Center for the Study of Aging and Human Development, 1973). Specific census data source was U.S., Bureau of Census, *Census of Population: 1970 Detailed Characteristics*, Final Report PC(1)-D1, United States Summary (Washington, D.C.: Government Printing Office, 1973). For a bibliography containing works about additional traits mentioned, see J. J. Jackson, "Social Gerontology and the Negro"; J. J. Jackson, "Negro Aged: Toward Needed Research in Social Gerontology," *Gerontologist* 11 (1971), pp. 52–57; Jacquelyne J. Jackson, "The Blacklands of Gerontology," *Aging and Human Development* 2 (1971), pp. 156–171, reprinted in *Readings in Gerontology*, ed. V. M. Brantl and Marie R. Brown, (St. Louis, Mo.: C. V. Mosby, 1973), pp. 78–97.

Spanish-surnamed groups, the handicapped, the obese and so on *ad nauseam* have been categorized as minorities "just like the blacks." While admittedly some aged, some women, some homosexuals and so on are black, the concern of those groups, or those seeking to equate them with blacks, has not been with blacks. The overemphasis—and sometimes false emphasis—upon commonalities between blacks and groups "just like the blacks" is often racist. So be it—let blacks beware!

Unfortunately, detailed characteristics from the 1970 census were not available for specific nonwhite groups other than blacks. However, they were available for Spanish-surnamed groups—hereafter, Spanish—and whites. Thus, some comparisons between black, white and Spanish aged are possible.

Education and family

As shown in table 1, which contains selected educational and familial data, aged whites typically had at least an elementary school education, while aged blacks averaged less than an elementary school education. Although the differences were insignificant, blacks were better educated than the Spanish. A substantially larger percentage of white aged husbands with at least high school education were married to women with comparable education. Hence, to the extent that increased education facilitates adjustment to age, whites were more advantaged.

While residential stability—that is, same house occupancy in 1965 and 1970—was greatest among blacks, residing with spouse was less frequent—but statistically insignificant—among black females. Even though most black males lived with spouse, they were significantly less likely to do so than white or Spanish males. Black females were significantly more likely than white females to be family heads, while the reverse was true between black and white males. A similar, but insignificantly different, pattern characterized the black-Spanish comparison by family heads.

About one-third of the black and white, and somewhat fewer of the Spanish, females lived alone—or were primary individuals—while black males were far more likely than white or Spanish males to live alone. Minor children were more rare in white than in black or Spanish families. The average family size of 3.11 members in black female-headed families was highest, and both black and Spanish families were typically larger than white families.

Very significant is the fact that the greatest percentage of women who had never had any children occurred among blacks, with the black-Spanish difference being statistically significant. Parenthetically, it should be added that these differences in childbirth patterns are probably best explained by nonhealth factors. In any case, a critical distinction between the three groups is that black females were least likely to have children present. Fertility rates were also highest among Spanish, and not black, women.

Employment

Employment data for 1970 showed indistinguishable differences among the percentages of black, white and Spanish males within the labor force and a slightly

TABLE 1

SELECTED COMPARISONS OF BLACK, SPANISH AND WHITE AGED IN THE UNITED STATES, 1970

Characteristic	Black	Spanish	White
Median number of years of education			
Female, 65–69 years of age	7.0	6.2	9.5
70–74 years of age	6.7	5.9	8.9
75+ years of age	6.1	5.4	8.7
Male, 65–69 years of age	6.0	6.1	8.9
70–74 years of age	5.6	5.9	8.7
75+ years of age	5.1	4.9	8.4
Percent living in same house as 5 years ago	73.1	64.4	71.9
Percent married and living with spouse			
Female	26.1	30.8	34.5
Male	55.7	63.8	69.5
Percent of persons living in families as family head			
Female	17.6	12.4	8.6
Male	63.2	69.8	75.8
Percent primary individuals			
Female	32.2	22.6	36.2
Male	22.5	14.6	15.5
Percent with no dependent children under 18 years			
Husband (65+ years of age)-wife	89.4	86.8	97.2
Female family head	94.0	92.5	97.7
Average family size			
Husband-wife, head 65–74 years old	3.01	3.04	2.31
Husband-wife, head 75+ years old	2.74	2.72	2.24
Female family head, 65+ years old	3.11	2.99	2.45
Percent head, 65 + years of age, and wife without completed high school education	80.4	74.7	57.0
Percent females, 65+ years of age, who never had children	25.4	12.3	17.4
Fertility rate, females, 65+ years old*	2,908	3,914	2,515

SOURCE: U.S., Bureau of the Census, *Census of Population, 1970: Detailed Characteristics*, Final Report PC(1)-D1, United States Summary (Washington, D.C.: Government Printing Office, 1973).

* Per 1,000 women.

higher percentage of black females within the labor force than remaining females (see table 2). The lower median age of the Spanish aged group probably accounted for the somewhat higher fulltime employment pattern. Although unemployment similarities prevailed among the groups, a critical—but unanswerable—question is the proportion of the unemployed seeking work for work's sake, for needed income or for both reasons.

Although far greater similarities than dissimilarities characterize these groups by employment, occupational differences were apparent. For the total aged population employed within the civilian labor force, the modal male occupational category was craftsmen and kindred workers, followed by service

TABLE 2

EMPLOYMENT STATUSES OF BLACK, SPANISH AND WHITE AGED IN THE UNITED STATES, 1970

EMPLOYMENT STATUS, BY PERCENT	GROUP		
	BLACK	SPANISH	WHITE
Female, 65+ years of age			
in labor force	13.2	7.9	9.8
fulltime civilian labor force	41.6	58.1	49.0
part-time civilian labor force	48.6	30.9	41.5
unemployed civilian labor force	5.1	7.0	5.0
Male, 65+ years of age			
in labor force	23.5	24.8	24.9
fulltime civilian labor force	56.6	62.7	56.9
part-time civilian labor force	33.7	26.9	34.7
unemployed civilian labor force	5.6	6.4	4.3

SOURCE: U.S., Bureau of the Census, *Census of Population, 1970: Detailed Characteristics*, Final Report PC(1)-D1, United States Summary (Washington, D.C.: Government Printing Office, 1973).

workers—excepting private household workers. The corresponding female order was clerical and kindred workers, followed by service workers—again, excepting private household workers. The modal black male category, however, was service workers—27.8 percent—followed by nonfarm laborers—17.9 percent—which can be contrasted with the same mode for Spanish males—18.6 percent —followed by craftsmen and kindred workers—13.6 percent. Almost 52 percent of employed black females were private household workers, whereas the two highest Spanish female categories were (1) operatives, except transport, and (2) service workers, except private household workers —19.4 percent each. Thus, employed aged blacks differed from white and Spanish aged by occupational category.

Income

One crucial distinction among the groups was that of income. Black aged were typically poorer than white and Spanish aged.

Worse, income gaps between black and white aged have actually widened over the past several decades. Incidentally, a similar phenomenon has occurred between black females and males, with continuing higher incomes among the latter.[11]

Table 3 contains data about income and income sources in 1969 for the six race-sex groups under consideration. In addition to obvious differences in real monies, four related observations bear explicit statement. First, black females— poorest of all—had substantially lower incomes than white females and all males, while black males were significantly poorer than white males. Secondly, educational differences are insufficient in explaining income differences, inasmuch as blacks averaged lower incomes even when education is held relatively constant. For example, the mean difference between black and white female college graduates in 1969 was $1,729, and white male

11. See, e.g., Jacquelyne J. Jackson, "Are Black Women Created Equal to Black Men?" *Essence* (November 1973), p. 56+.

TABLE 3

INCOME AND INCOME SOURCES OF BLACK, SPANISH AND WHITE AGED IN THE
UNITED STATES, 1969

INCOME CHARACTERISTIC	GROUP		
	BLACK	SPANISH	WHITE
Median individual income			
female, 65–69 years	$1,170	$1,270	$2,594
70–74 years	1,098	1,248	2,305
75+ years	974	1,189	2,032
male, 65–69 years	1,956	2,659	5,959
70–74 years	1,711	2,101	4,630
75+ years	1,503	1,735	3,621
Percent persons with income under $2,000			
female	83.4	77.3	67.5
male	59.8	47.4	34.0
Percent persons without income			
female	14.0	21.0	13.0
male	5.9	5.8	2.9
Mean income by education			
female, 8 years	$1,380	$1,686	$1,738
high school graduate	1,953	2,466	2,910
college graduate only	3,151	3,311	4,880
postgraduate education	4,959	5,654	6,454
male, 8 years	2,599	3,524	3,765
high school graduate	3,572	4,808	5,917
college graduate only	4,555	8,412	11,252
postgraduate education	7,934	10,685	13,753
Median family income by family type			
husband (65+ years old)-wife	3,250	4,373	5,050
female, 65+ years old, head	2,904	3,897	5,772
Median income, unrelated individual			
female	1,237	1,499	1,791
male	1,511	1,817	2,210
Percent of all aged living in families in poverty	38.8	25.4	15.6
Percent of all aged unrelated individuals in poverty	71.7	58.1	48.8
Source of income, total aggregate income			
all families, head 65+ years old			
Percent earnings	60.3	58.6	50.2
Percent wages and salaries	56.1	51.5	40.4
Percent self-employed income	4.2	7.1	9.9
Percent Social Security income	25.3	19.8	21.1
Percent public assistance income	5.1	4.6	0.8
Percent other	9.3	17.0	27.9
families below poverty level, head 65+ years old			
Percent earnings	26.8	24.4	9.7
Percent wages and salaries	25.0	23.2	9.0
Percent self-employed income	1.8	1.3	0.7
Percent Social Security income	50.3	49.4	74.2
Percent public assistance income	16.7	19.4	7.2
Percent other	6.2	6.8	8.9

TABLE 3 (*continued*)

INCOME CHARACTERISTIC	GROUP		
	BLACK	SPANISH	WHITE
Percent of families, head 65+ years old, receiving income of specified types			
all families			
Percent earnings	61.6	59.4	54.5
Percent wages and salaries	58.2	55.1	46.6
Percent self-employed income	8.1	9.6	14.8
Percent Social Security income	77.2	74.7	84.3
Percent public assistance income	24.3	23.1	6.2
Percent other	26.4	37.5	60.7
all families below poverty level			
Percent earnings	40.8	32.7	20.5
Percent wages and salaries	37.1	29.3	14.6
Percent self-employed income	6.2	4.7	7.5
Percent Social Security income	78.2	73.9	87.0
Percent public assistance income	34.0	34.2	12.9
Percent other	13.4	15.8	22.5

SOURCE: U.S., Bureau of the Census, *Census of Population, 1970: Detailed Characteristics*, Final Report PC(1)-D1, United States Summary (Washington, D.C.: Government Printing Office, 1973).

college graduates averaged $8,101 more than their black female counterparts. Furthermore, the fact that Spanish aged were less educated, but better paid than black aged suggests that within the employment market blacks as a racial minority experience more severe economic discrimination than do Spanish as an ethnic minority. Also, geographical differences between the two populations do not account for income differences, inasmuch as the same pattern tends to prevail when comparisons are held constant by geographical location. Thirdly, not only were aged blacks more likely to be in poverty, but they were more dependent upon their own earnings than upon other income sources. Finally, the disproportionate distribution of income sources by total aggregate income, as well as by percent of families receiving income of spec-

ified types, indicated a considerable need for revising sources of both high dependable and increased income for aged blacks. This need has been only partially offset by the supplemental security income (SSI) program—begun in January 1974 and currently administered with varying degrees of success by the Social Security Administration—in which a chief problem has been enrollment of eligible aged blacks.

Mortality

Generally, very old blacks have represented a much healthier population than very old whites, due largely to greater operation of the survival of the fittest among blacks[12]—or, to rephrase the state-

12. For information on the racial crossover phenomenon, see, especially, Nathaniel O. Calloway, "Medical Aspects of

the Aging American Black," in *Proceedings of Black Aged in the Future*, ed. Jacquelyne J. Jackson (Durham, N.C.: Duke University Center for the Study of Aging and Human Development, 1973), pp. 50–56. See, also, R. G. Thornton and Charles B. Nam, "The Lower Mortality Rates of Nonwhites at the Older Ages: An Enigma in Demographic Analysis," *Research Reports in Social Science* 2, no. 1 (Tallahassee, Fla.: Florida State University Institute for Social Research, 1968); the authors examined mortality rates for specific nonwhite and white age groups between 1900 and 1961, and concluded that: "By age seventy-five . . . the life expectancy differential had reversed itself with whites having a life expectancy of 8.7 years and nonwhites one of 9.5 years. This crossing seemed to have occurred at about the age of sixty-eight." In a 1968 oral presentation before the Annual Meeting of the Gerontological Society, I commented that Thornton and Nam had: "contended that this phenomenon of racial reversal of life expectancy is probably not related to such factors as sex, cause of death, point in time, mortality measure, nor data error. Rather, the causal model 'which appears most consistent with the data' is one which does not rely on a biological explanation alone but which depends upon the interaction of biological and social variables." In a revised, published version of that presentation—"Aged Negroes: Their Cultural Departures from Statistical Stereotypes and Rural-Urban Differences"—I wrote that Herman Brotman, then an Administration on Aging statistician, had: " . . . suggested that data are too sparse and reporting too faulty to be able to even demonstrate such a pattern of racial reversal of mortality rates or life expectancies. He believes that, just as there is no significant difference by marital statuses between older whites and nonwhites, there is also *no* significant difference in their mortality rates or life expectancies. This, too, may be an issue in need of resolution. It is also highly probable that if older Negroes obtain significantly better preventive and other health care under Medicare, and if Medicaid is also extended significantly to the younger Negro population, this racial reversal, if it does exist, may well be erased." The above is cited in some detail in that Brotman's response in 1968 was triggered by my initial statement of my Social Security proposal, to wit: "Racial reversal or not, it is now the case that 1) most Negroes die earlier, 2) perceive of themselves as being 'old' earlier, and 3) are, in fact, *old* earlier than are whites." Hence,

ment, due to higher earlier mortality rates among blacks. Table 4 includes information on mortality rates from all causes of death for nonwhite and white females and males within the United States during 1950 to 1970; the data show that nonwhite females 75 and over had lower mortality rates than their white counterparts, excepting those 75 to 79 years of age in 1970. Nonwhite males 75 and over had lower mortality rates than their male counterparts in each of the years shown. The sharpest mortality decline over the two decades occurred among nonwhite females, and in 1970 the nonwhite female mortality rate of 775.3 was lower than the nonwhite male, white male and white female mortality rates. Inasmuch as the vast majority of nonwhite females are black, a logical conclusion would be that the overall black female mortality rate was lower than that of the remaining race-sex groups.

However, such a conclusion could be false—that is, the black mortality rate is not necessarily reflected accurately by the nonwhite rate. Specific black data for 1970 were not available at this writing. However, a comparison of

this serious and highly pragmatic proposal: the minimum age-eligibility for retirement benefits should be racially differentiated to reflect present racial differences in life expectancies. Interestingly enough, when Brotman—only a few days away from federal retirement—and I were members of a panel discussing aging in a June 1973 at the Duke University Conference, it was Brotman who informed the group about the existence of the black-white crossover in life expectancy; it was I who wondered why he now indicated belief in its existence, but questioned it in 1968. Finally, also see, P. Demeny and P. Gingrich, "A Reconsideration of Negro-White Mortality Differentials in the United States," *Demography* 4 (1967), pp. 820–837.

TABLE 4

MORTALITY RATES FROM ALL CAUSES OF DEATH FOR NONWHITE AND WHITE FEMALES AND MALES, UNITED STATES, 1950–1970, RATES PER 100,000 POPULATION

Age Group	Racial Group and Year									
	Nonwhite					White				
	1950	1955	1960	1965	1970	1950	1955	1960	1965	1970
Females										
All ages	990.0	875.9	870.0	824.3	775.3	800.0	774.4	800.0	800.5	812.6
60–64	3,240.0	2,872.4	3,020.0	2,723.7	2,218.8	1,620.0	1,385.7	1,360.0	1,249.5	1,222.9
65–69	4,240.0	3,348.5	3,470.0	4,220.7	3,129.5	2,520.0	2,304.4	2,150.0	2,071.3	1,924.5
70–74	5,160.0	4,472.4	4,740.0	4,371.7	4,488.4	4,260.0	3,718.0	3,580.0	3,321.6	3,134.1
75–79	6,840.0	6,156.8	5,880.0	5,472.5	5,782.2	6,990.0	6,396.3	6,080.0	5,587.1	5,349.8
80–84	8,170.0	6,892.2	8,480.0	7,128.2	7,421.5	11,250.0	10,528.4	10,650.0	9,657.9	8,869.4
85+	13,370.0	11,214.7	12,970.0	11,794.4	10,288.9	19,680.0	19,156.1	19,480.0	20,213.2	15,980.2
Males										
All ages	1,250.0	1,133.3	1,150.0	1,114.3	1,115.9	1,090.0	1,069.6	1,100.0	1,084.9	1,086.7
60–64	3,920.0	3,874.9	4,005.0	3,666.7	3,534.4	2,810.0	2,645.6	2,750.0	2,715.5	2,708.4
65–69	5,410.0	4,580.3	5,100.0	6,114.5	4,759.2	4,070.0	3,964.8	4,050.0	4,126.3	4,046.1
70–74	6,370.0	6,088.5	6,490.0	6,713.6	6,557.3	6,040.0	5,720.5	5,910.0	5,941.2	5,828.0
75–79	8,290.0	7,169.9	7,630.0	7,833.9	8,483.1	9,010.0	8,649.8	8,700.0	8,502.8	8,963.4
80–84	10,600.0	9,695.2	11,020.0	8,629.6	9,855.8	13,520.0	13,292.3	13,540.0	12,776.8	12,606.8
85+	16,020.0	13,766.7	15,240.0	13,070.7	11,405.2	22,120.0	20,063.6	21,750.0	22,243.4	18,551.7

SOURCES: Vital Statistics of the United States 2, *Mortality Data* 1953; 3, *Mortality Data* 1957; 2, *Mortality Data*, parts A and B, 1963; 2, *Mortality Data*, parts A and B, 1967 (Washington, D.C.: Government Printing Office); and U.S., Department of Health, Education and Welfare, Monthly Vital Statistics Report: Annual Summary for the United States 19, no. 3 (2 September 1971).

earlier mortality data for nonwhites and for blacks only showed that the nonwhite rate during the 1960s was usually lower than the black rate. For example, the black female mortality rates from all causes of death and for all ages in 1960—909.4—and in 1965—858.0—were higher than the respective nonwhite rates —870.0 and 824.3—and the respective white rates—800.0 and 812.6.

Such data, of course, reinforce the continuing need for NCBA and other interested parties to stress separation of relevant data by specific race-sex groups. During the past decade the Bureau of the Census has increasingly provided data separately for blacks. NCBA has engaged in several conferences with the Bureau about such data needs as increased sampling sizes for older blacks, as well as for those within the highest income groups, so as to permit more with-in group comparisons under conditions where such multiple variables as race, sex, age, education and income can be held constant. In addition, NCBA has participated in several conferences over the past few years with the National Center on Health Statistics concerning the need for specific health and related data for blacks only. Some favorable impact has occurred, with an example being the possibility of obtaining black life-table values for 1970.

NCBA is cognizant of the fact that some individuals and organizations have attempted to reduce racial separation of federal data. A serious conference devoted to establishing cogent federal policies regarding data needs by race-sex-age groups is needed. This need is urgent, since sound social planning requires basic social knowledge and periodic updating of that knowledge, as well as effective evalua-tion of programs which implement policies.

Institutionalization

Insufficient data prohibit succinct examination of existing major differences, if any, between the institutionalization of black and nonblack aged. However, available 1970 data showed, as expected, that the largest proportion so confined consisted of white females (see table 5). In fact, proportionately twice as many white females as blacks and white males were confined. Whites, rather than blacks or Spanish, were more likely to reside in homes for the aged. However, these data require age-adjustment, before inferences can be drawn about disproportionate representation of any group within homes for the aged or similar facilities. Other additional factors[13]

13. Jacquelyne J. Jackson, "Help Me Somebody! I'se an Old Black Standing in the Need of Institutionalizing!" *Psychiatric Opinion* 10 (1973), pp. 6–16. Also, see, James H. Carter, "Differential Treatment of the Elderly Black: Victims of Sterotyping," *Postgraduate Medicine* 52 (1972), pp. 211–214; and his "Psychiatry's Insensitivity to Racism and Aging," *Psychiatric Opinion* 10 (1973), pp. 21–25; L. L. Bachrach, "General Characteristics of Additions to Federally Funded Community Mental Centers during 1971," in *Statistical Note 87* (Rockville, Md.: National Institute of Mental Health, 1973); Robert N. Butler and Myrna I. Lewis, *Aging and Mental Health* (St. Louis, Mo.: C. V. Mosby, 1973); and Jacquelyne J. Jackson, "Compensatory Care for the Black Aged," in *Minority Aged in America*, Occasional Papers in Gerontology, no. 10 (Ann Arbor, Mich.: Institute of Gerontology, University of Michigan-Wayne State University, 1972). Incidentally, this compilation of conference presentations on various minority aged was scheduled for release prior to WHCOA; however, it was deliberately withheld until post-WHCOA, apparently because one of WHCOA's chief staff members felt that its release earlier would constitute an insult to her.

TABLE 5

PERCENTAGE OF AGED BLACKS, SPANISH AND WHITES IN INSTITUTIONS,
UNITED STATES, 1970

TYPE OF QUARTERS	BLACK		SPANISH		WHITE	
	FEMALE (%)	MALE (%)	FEMALE (%)	MALE (%)	FEMALE (%)	MALE (%)
Group quarters	3.5	3.7	2.1	2.7	6.6	3.4
Home for the aged	2.1	1.7	1.5	1.6	5.1	2.9
Inmate of mental institution	0.8	0.8	0.1	0.2	0.5	0.6
Rooming or boarding house	0.2	0.3	0.1	0.2	0.2	0.2

SOURCE: U.S., Bureau of the Census, *Census of Population, 1970: Detailed Characteristics*, Final Report PC(1)-D1, United States Summary (Washington, D.C.: Government Printing Office, 1973).

must also be considered in comparing racial patterns, for example: racial differences in institutional ownership and management; the aged individual's family background —presence or absence of spouse, age and number of individuals dependent upon the primary breadwinner attitudes of family members toward admission and speed of admission; advice patterns, such as those of physicians and social workers; year and location of initial institutionalization; and health status differences among black, white and other minority aged. Unfortunately, such data are yet sparse.

Housing

Comparisons of housing differences between black and white aged usually reveal differences in geographic characteristics, with black aged typically more likely to reside within central cities and low-income areas and in older and more substandard housing. They are also somewhat more likely to be in public housing. During the 1950s and 1960s, in particular, a number of older blacks experienced environmental uprooting, due largely to urban renewal and highway express construction projects which disproportionately affected black areas. Data about residential stability previously presented do not contradict greater involuntary housing mobility among old blacks.[14]

Political participation

In addition to such political differences between black and white

14. See, especially, L. Carey et al., "Some Identifiable Needs of Applicants to an Apartment Facility for the Elderly: Implications for Planning Services," *Gerontologist* 8 (1968) p. 38; M. W. Crocker, "An Analysis of the Living Arrangements and Housing Conditions of Old Age Assistance Recipients in Mississippi" (Ph. D. diss., Florida State University, 1968); Jacquelyne J. Jackson, "Social Impacts of Housing Relocation upon Urban, Low-Income Black Aged," *Gerontologist* 12 (1972), pp. 32–37; M. Powell Lawton and E. Krassen, "Federally Subsidized Housing Not for the Elderly Black," *Journal of Social and Behavioral Sciences* 19 (1973), pp. 65–78; P. L. Niebanck, "Knowledge Gained in Studies of Relocation: A Challenge to Housing Policy," in *Proceedings of the Research Conference on Patterns of Living and Housing of Middle-Aged and Older People* (Washington, D.C.: Government Printing Office, 1965); P. L. Niebanck and J. B. Pope, "An Overview of the National Relocation Population," in *The Elderly in Older Urban Areas* (Philadelphia, Pa.: Institute for Environmental Studies, University of Pennsylvania, 1965).

aged as larger proportions of elected and appointed governmental officials and of Republicans among whites, black aged have been less active voters than whites. However, they were more active than nonblack minorities. Data (see table 6) for the November elections of 1964, 1968 and 1972 show substantially larger proportions of white voters for each year. They also show, however, larger proportionate increases in voting among black female aged between 1964 and 1972 than among comparable black males and whites. Variations also existed within each race-sex group by age—for example, among black females the oldest were the least likely to vote, while the oldest white males were more likely to vote than white males under 35 years of age. Within each racial or ethnic group, males, rather than females, were more likely to vote.

While other observations can be derived from table 6, what is most important within the present context is the differential voting pattern among the aged: black aged being less active than white, but more active than other minorities. Similar patterns characterized

TABLE 6

PERCENTAGES OF PERSONS REPORTING VOTING IN NOVEMBER
1964, 1968 AND 1972, BY RACE AND SEX

YEAR, RACE AND SEX	AGE GROUP						
	21–24	25–34	35–44	45–54	55–64	65–74	75+
1964							
Black females	49.3	62.2	61.9	65.5	59.7	47.6	26.9
Black males	39.1	57.7	63.7	65.4	65.0	55.6	44.7
Nonwhite females	46.7	60.1	61.8	64.2	58.2	47.4	26.7
Nonwhite males	38.5	54.9	62.5	65.8	65.0	54.9	44.7
White females	51.6	64.8	72.8	75.2	74.2	68.0	51.3
White males	53.3	66.5	75.7	79.6	80.1	79.3	68.4
1968							
Black females	41.5	56.8	64.7	66.4	60.0	53.6	31.8
Black males	35.5	55.6	64.5	66.0	64.8	59.9	51.1
Nonwhite females	41.5	54.6	62.5	65.7	58.3	51.0	29.7
Nonwhite males	35.3	53.2	63.3	65.2	64.1	56.6	48.0
White females	52.6	63.3	71.0	75.1	73.8	68.5	51.1
White males	53.0	64.0	72.7	77.3	78.6	78.7	68.1
1972							
Black females	38.0	51.9	60.8	61.8	61.1	53.9	32.5
Black males	38.4	52.9	57.8	62.6	62.1	59.8	49.4
Spanish-surnamed females	32.0	33.7	43.0	41.7	33.2	24.8	—
Spanish-surnamed males	31.3	36.4	47.0	49.3	46.6	34.5	—
White females	53.8	61.2	68.0	71.1	70.2	65.3	50.6
White males	51.2	64.3	67.2	73.1	73.4	74.8	67.7

SOURCES: U.S., Bureau of the Census, *Current Population Reports*, Series P-20, no. 143, "Voter Participation in the National Election: November 1964" (Washington, D.C.: Government Printing Office, 1965); *Current Population Reports*, Series P-20, no. 192, "Voting and Registration in the Election of November 1968" (Washington, D.C.: Government Printing Office, 1969); and *Current Population Reports*, Series P-20, no. 253, "Voting and Registration in the Election of November 1972" (Washington, D.C.: Government Printing Office, 1973).

younger groups. Hence, while voting is obviously not the key to social status upgrading, it is a key. Greater emphasis upon more black aged political involvement, and less emphasis upon knitting, crocheting, singing and praying—that is, traditional senior citizens' activities—may well be in order for black aged; in fact, this represents an area of grave NCBA concern.

The recent film *The Autobiography of Miss Jane Pittman*, while a superb presentation, must not represent the most appropriate political model for blacks. On the one hand, it was commendable in that an old black woman finally took the plunge and "drank the water of freedom" at the age of 110. Yet, on the other hand, it was condemnable in that so many years passed before Miss Jane tasted freedom's water. Old blacks cannot wait so long to increase their active political involvement.

A part of that involvement could clearly include relevant distinctions between various minority groups. It is generally the case that various demographic traits—with the very important exception of race—distinguishing black, white and other minority aged are those of degree, not of kind. Inasmuch as the prevailing social definition of being black in the United States is one of kind, however, old blacks are different from old whites and other minorities. One crucial indicator of that difference is the fact that the Spanish, with less education than blacks, have a higher median income. Hence, attempts to subsume aged blacks under the categories of the aged or the minority aged should be avoided whenever those attempts are antithetical to black interests.

Most often, such attempts are without those interests. They are, instead, attempts to dilute further any specific focus upon problems of racism. As alluded to earlier, various recent attempts to expand the concept of minority group within the political arena to include the motley of nonblack women, the aged, obese persons and so on can be viewed, perhaps cynically—but quite realistically, if historical precedents are considered—as efforts to reduce attempts by blacks to upgrade their social statuses. These political counterplays are designed to overload the social system, which can only cope equitably with a limited number of upheavals at any given time. When overloaded, it responds less favorably to pressure groups with the least social status. Also, within specific pressure groups those who receive the least favorable response are again, those with the least status. Thus, the social system is responding to blacks less favorably now than it did in the past and least favorably to those who are black, old, female and poor.

Current arguments purporting the existence of the aged as a minority group[15] are quite unconvincing, but the vested interests of their proponents bear examination. Those seeking to create the aged as a minority could profit from the experiences of the National Women's Political Caucus and its various state affiliates. In 1972 the organization was highly unsuccess-

15. See, especially, Milton L. Barron, "Minority Group Characteristics of the Aged in American Society," *Journal of Gerontology* 8 (1953), pp. 477–482; Ewald W. Busse and Eric Pfeiffer, eds., *Behavior and Adaptation in Late Life* (Boston, Mass.: Little, Brown, 1969); and, as a related work, H. M. Hacker, "Women as a Minority Group," *Social Forces* 30 (1951), pp. 60–69.

ful in rallying women around sex while trying to deny or to ignore their racial and ethnic differences.

Since black aged are, and will be, both black and old, NCBA's specific focus upon them is highly justified as long as it continues to promote needed public awareness and relevant research, training, service delivery systems and political action. The need for greater public awareness of many adverse conditions confronting aged blacks should be obvious to aging professionals. Also, the serious gaps in available literature, especially in gerontological literature, should be noted. Most researchers have tended to concentrate upon nonblack aged[16] or to be interested in making racial or minority group comparisons,[17] while providing no significant comparisons of various black aged subsets.[18] Particularly absent from that literature and from most aging organizations is any concern about significant black aged political patterns.

16. Although this concentration upon nonblack aged has been most pronounced, literature specifically related to aged blacks has proliferated over the past several decades, as may be evident from the following references, given in chronological order, and with each being especially related to one or more sections of this presentation. References already presented were not repeated. G. Davis, "The Effects of the Social Security Act on the Status of the Negro" (Ph. D. diss., University of Iowa, 1939); A. T. Harris, "Analysis of Selected Socioeconomic Data for the Content and the Conditions under Which a Program of Education May Be Carried on by and for the Negro Adults of Chesterfield County, Virginia" (Ed. D. diss., University of Michigan, 1948); A. W. Caliman, "Personality Adjustment of Aging Women" (Ph. D. diss., Michigan State University, 1952); Edward Jackson, "Leisure-Time Activities of Negro Men, Aged Forty-Five Through Fifty-Four," (Ed. D. diss., Pennsylvania State University, 1955); Eugene G. Sherman, Jr., "Social Adjustment

of Aged Negroes of Carbondale, Illinois" M. A. thesis, Southern Illinois University, 1955); T. Talley and Jerome Kaplan, "The Negro Aged," *Newsletter of the Gerontological Society* 3 (December 1956); T. Bohanon, "Some Considerations of St. Louis' Negro Aged" (Unpublished manuscript, Washington University, St. Louis, Missouri, 1958); M. L. Hamlett, "An Exploratory Study of the Socioeconomic and Psychological Problems of Adjustment of 100 Aged and Retired Negro Women in Durham, North Carolina during 1959" (M. A. thesis, North Carolina College at Durham, 1959); Virginia Stone, "Personal Adjustment in Aging in Relation to Community Environment: A Study of Persons Sixty Years and over in Carrboro and Chapel Hill, North Carolina (Ph. D. diss., University of North Carolina, 1959); Walter M. Beattie, Jr., "The Aging Negro: Some Implications for Welfare Services, *Phylon* 21 (1960), pp. 131–135; J. A. Antenor, "An Exploratory Study of the Relation of the Adjustment of 100 Aged Negro Men in Durham, North Carolina, with Their Education, Health and Work Status" (M. A. thesis, North Carolina College at Durham, 1961); George Henderson, "A Study of Aged Negroes Receiving Old Age Assistance" (Detroit, Mich.: Detroit Urban League Community Service Department, December 1961); Dorothy Heyman and Frances Jeffers, "Study of the Relative Influence of Race and Socioeconomic Status upon the Activities and Attitudes of a Southern Aged Population, *Journal of Gerontology* 19 (1964), pp. 225–229; Mollie Orshansky, "The Aged Negro and His Income," *Social Security Bulletin* 27 (1964); R. E. Roberts, "Ethnic and Racial Differences in the Characteristics and Attitudes of the Aged in Selected Areas of Rural Louisiana" (M. A. thesis, Louisiana State University, 1964); George Henderson, "The Negro Recipient of Old-Age Assistance: Results of Discrimination," *Social Casework* 46 (1965), pp. 208–214; Aaron Lipman et al., "Miami Concerted Services Baseline Study," *Gerontologist* 5 (1965), pp. 256–258; Mercerdee E. Ball, "Comparisons of Characteristics of Aged Negroes in Two Counties" (M. A. thesis, Howard University, 1966); Abraham Davis, Jr., "Selected Characteristic Patterns of a Southern Aged Rural Negro Population" (M. A. thesis, Howard University, 1966); D. D. Dhaliwal, "A Sociological Description and Analysis of a Non-Random Sample of Low-Income Aged Negroes" (M. A. thesis, Howard University, 1966); Joe R. Geagin, "The Social Ties of Negroes in an Urban Environment" (Ph. D. diss., Harvard University, 1966); E. C. Hall,

"Analysis and Decomposition of the Distribution of Blood Pressure Level in a Population by Age, Race, and Sex" (Ph. D. diss., University of North Carolina, 1966); Jacquelyne J. Jackson and Mercerdee E. Ball, "A Comparison of Rural and Urban Georgia Aged Negroes" *Journal of the Association of Social Science Teachers* 12 (1966), pp. 30–37; Jacquelyne J. Jackson and Abraham Davis, Jr., "Characteristic Patterns of Aged, Rural Negroes in Macon County," in *A survey of Selected Socioeconomic Characteristics of Macon County, Alabama, 1965* ed. Beulah C. Johnson (Tuskegee, Ala.: Macon County Community Action Office, 1966), pp. 122–157; Aaron Lipman, "Preparation for Death in Old Age," *Journal of Gerontology* 21 (1966), pp. 426–431; D. W. Harper, Jr., "Socialization for the Aged Status among the Negro, French, and Non-French Sub-Cultures of Louisiana" (M. A. thesis, Louisiana State University, 1967); G. N. Kripalani, "Net Migration Response Differentials by Age, Sex, and Color for the U.S." (Ph. D. diss., University of North Carolina, 1967); Thomas F. Pettigrew, "The Negro Aged: A Minority within a Minority" (Unpublished manuscript, Institute for State Executives in Aging, Brandeis University, 1967); T. Lynn Smith, "The Changing Number and Distribution of the Aged Negro Population of the U.S.," *Phylon* 18 (1967), pp. 339–354; Stanley H. Smith, "The Older Rural Negro," in *Older Rural Americans* ed. E. Grant Youmans (Lexington, Ky.: University of Kentucky Press, 1967); Jeanne M. Thune, "Racial Attitudes of Older Adults," *Gerontologist* 7 (1967), pp. 179–182; S. Goldstein, "Home Tenure and Expenditure Patterns of the Aged, 1960-1961," *Gerontologist* 8 (1968), pp. 17–24; Joe R. Geagin, "The Kinship Ties of Negro Urbanites," *Social Science Quarterly* 69 (1968), pp. 660–665; Carl Hirsch, Donald P. Kent and Suzanne B. Loux, "Homogeneity and Heterogeneity among Low-Income Negro and White Aged," *Gerontologist* 8 (1968), p. 27; Jacquelyne J. Jackson, "Negro Aged and Social Gerontology, a Critical Evaluation," *Journal of Social and Behavioral Sciences* 13 (1968), pp. 42–47; Mark Messer, "Race Differences in Selected Attitudinal Dimensions of the Elderly," *Gerontologist* 8 (1968), pp. 245–249; Robert F. Morgan, "The Adult Growth Examination: A Preliminary Comparison of Physical Aging in Adults by Sex and Race," *Perceptual and Motor Skills* 27 (1968), pp. 595–599; S. Nadler and Marvin S. Schreiber, "Utilization of the Services of a Multi-Purpose Senior Center by Negroes Residing in a Public

Housing Project: A Descriptive Study of 100 Negro Elderly," *Gerontologist* 8 (1968), p. 39; Carolyn Rice, "Old and Black," *Harvest Years* 8 (1968), pp. 38–47; A. F. Brunswick, "What Generation Gap? A Comparison of Some Generational Differences among Blacks and Whites," *Social Problems* 17 (1969–1970), pp. 358–370; Jean Dominich, "Mental Patients in Nursing Homes: Four Ethnic Influences," *Journal of the American Geriatric Society* 17 (1969) pp. 63–85; D. S. Hays and M. Wisotsky, "The Aged Offender: A Review of the Literature and Two Current Studies from the New York State Division of Parole," *Journal of the American Geriatric Society* 17 (1969), pp. 1064–1073; M. A. Lambing, "Study of Retired Older Negroes in an Urban Setting" (Ph. D. diss., University of Florida, 1969); Aaron Lipman, "Latent Function Analysis in Gerontological Research," *Gerontologist* 9 (1969), pp. 33–36; Erdman B. Palmore, "Physical, Mental and Social Factors in Predicting Longevity," *Gerontologist* 9 (1969), pp. 103–108; Erdman B. Palmore, "The Aged Poor: Findings of Project FIND" (Washington, D.C.: National Council on Aging, 1969); Joe R. Geagin, "A Note on the Friendship Ties of Black Urbanites," *Social Forces* 49 (1970), pp. 303–308; R. J. Gregory, "A Survey of Residents in Five Nursing and Rest Homes in Cumberland County, North Carolina," *Journal of the American Geriatric Society* 18 (1970), pp. 501–506; Metropolitan Life Insurance Co., "Trends in Mortality of Non-Whites," *Statistical Bulletin* 51 (1970), pp. 5–8; Barbara J. Solomon, "Ethnicity, Mental Health, and the Older Black Aged," in *Ethnicity, Mental Health and Aging* (Los Angeles, Cal.: Gerontology Center, University of Southern California, 1970), pp. 10–13; J. J. Stretch, "The Development and Testing of a Theoretical Formulation That Aged Negroes with Differences in Community Security Are Different in Coping Reaction," *Gerontologist* 10 (1970), p. 54; Robert N. Butler, "The Public Interest, Report no. 2: Old Age in Your Nation's Capital," *Aging and Human Development* 2 (1971), pp. 197–201; J. W. Carey, "Senior Advisory Service for Public Housing Tenants," *Gerontologist* 11 (1971), pp. 264–267; Gerda G. Fillenbaum, "On the Relation between Attitude to Work and Attitude to Retirement," *Journal of Gerontology* 26 (1971), pp. 244–248; L. D. Hankoff, C. J. Rabiner and C. St. George Henry, "Comparison of the Satellite Clinic and the Hospital-Based Clinic," *Archives of General Psychiatry* 24 (1971), pp. 474–478; M. Heavenrich,

"Henry Remembered," *Aging and Human Development* 2 (1971), pp. 208–209; H. L. Hearn, "Career and Leisure Patterns of Middle-Aged Urban Blacks," *Gerontologist* 11 (1971), pp. 21–26; Jacquelyne J. Jackson, "Kinship Relations among Negro Americans," *Journal of Social and Behavioral Sciences* 16 (1971), pp. 5–17; M. M. Jenkins, "Age and Migration Factors in the Socioeconomic Conditions of Urban Blacks and Urban White Women," *Industrial Gerontology* 9 (1971), pp. 13–17; Richard A. Kalish, "A Gerontological Look at Ethnicity, Human Capacities, and Individual Adjustment," *Gerontologist* 11 (1971), pp. 78–87; Donald P. Kent, "The Negro Aged," *Gerontologist* 11 (1971), pp. 48–51; Donald P. Kent, Carl Hirsch and Sylvia K. Barg, "Indigenous Workers as a Crucial Link in the Total Support System for Low-Income, Minority Group Aged," *Aging and Human Development* 2 (1971), pp. 208–219; Donald P. Kent, "The Elderly in Minority Groups: Variant Patterns of Aging," *Gerontologist* 11 (1971), pp. 26–29; Donald P. Kent and Carl Hirsch, *Needs and Uses of Services among Negro and White Aged* (University Park, Pa.: Pennsylvania State University, 1971), vol. 1; Ronald Koenig, N. S. Goldner, R. Kresojevich and G. Lockwood, "Ideas about Illness of Elderly Black and White in an Urban Hospital," *Aging and Human Development* 2 (1971), pp. 217–225; Cary Lacklen, "Aged, Black and Poor: Three Case Studies," *Aging and Human Development* 2 (1971), pp. 202–207; U.S., Senate, Special Committee on Aging, *The Multiple Hazards of Age and Race: The Situation of Aged Blacks in the United States*, report prepared by Inabel Lindsay (Washington, D.C.: Government Printing Office, 1971); Helen Z. Lopata, "Social and Family Relations of Black and White Widows in Urban Communities," (Washington, D.C.: Department of Health, Education and Welfare, Administration on Aging, 1971); Helen Z. Lopata, "Widows as a Minority Group," *Gerontologist* 11 (1971), pp. 67–77; Joan W. Moore, "Situation Factors Affecting Minority Aging," *Gerontologist* 11 (1971), pp. 88–93; Erdman B. Palmore, "Variables Related to Needs among the Aged Poor," *Journal of Gerontology* 26 (1971), pp. 524–531; H. G. Richek, O. Chucalate and D. Klinert, "Aging and Ethnicity in Healthy Elderly Women," *Geriatrics* 26 (1971), pp. 146–152; Daniel I. Rubenstein, "An Examination of Social Participation Found among a National Sample of Black and White Elderly," *Aging and Human Development* 2 (1971), pp. 172–188; W. C. Swanson and C. L. Harter, "How do Elderly Blacks Cope in New Orleans?" *Aging and Human Development* 2 (1971), pp. 210–216; H. L. Sheppard, "Age and Migration Factors in the Socioeconomic Conditions of Urban Black and White Women," *New Perspective on Older Workers* (Kalamazoo, Mich.: W. E. Upjohn Institute, 1971); F. M. Wylie, "Attitudes toward Aging and the Aged among Black Americans," *Aging and Human Development* 2 (1971), pp. 66–70; M. L. B. Lambing, "Leisure-Time Pursuits among Retired Blacks by Social Status," *Gerontologist* 12 (1972), pp. 363–367; Daniel I. Rubenstein, "The Social Participation of the Black Elderly" (Ph. D. diss., Brandeis University, 1972); Herbert Shore, "The Current Social Revolution and Its Impact on Jewish Nursing Homes," *Gerontologist* 12 (1972), pp. 178–180; Lloyd C. Elam, "Critical Factors for Mental Health in Aging Black Populations," in *Ethnicity, Mental Health, and Aging* (Los Angeles, Cal.: Gerontology Center, University of Southern California, 1970); Ira F. Ehrlich, "Toward a Social Profile of the Aged Black Population in the United States: An Exploratory Study," *Aging and Human Development* 4 (1973), pp. 271–276; Audrey Faulkner and E. Dodson, "The Black Aged as Good Neighbors: An Experiment in Volunteer Service," *Gerontologist*, 13 (1973), p. 99; *Final Report of Delivery Services to the Tampa Model Cities Aged: A Demonstration Project* (Tampa, Fl.: University of Florida Aging Studies Program, 1973); M. A. Heisel and M. E. Moore, "Social Interaction and Isolation of Elderly Blacks," *Gerontologist* 13 (1973), p. 100; Jacquelyne J. Jackson, "Family Organization and Ideology," in *Comparative Studies of Blacks and Whites in the United States*, ed. Kent S. Miller and Ralph M. Dreger (New York: Seminar Press, 1973); Jacquelyne J. Jackson, "Black Behavioral Science Roles in Black Health in the United States," *Black Lines* 3 (1973), pp. 25–35; H. Roy Kaplan, "Self-Derogation and Social Position: Interaction Effects of Sex, Race, Education, and Age," *Social Psychiatry* 8 (1973), pp. 92–99; R. McCaslin and W. R. Calvery, "Social Indicators in Black and White: Some Ethnic Considerations in the Design and Delivery of Services to the Elderly," *Gerontologist* 13 (1973), p. 88; A. T. Meyerson, J. Z. Moss and R. S. Belville, "The Elderly Patient in a Psychiatric Acute Care Clinic of a General Hospital," *Gerontologist* 13 (1973), p. 56; E. Percil Stanford, "A case Study of Aged Blacks in a Suburban Community," *Gerontologist* 13 (1973), p. 67.

SUMMARY

This presentation was primarily concerned with the provision of selected background data about NCBA and about aged blacks which can be used to justify the position that aged blacks represent a legitimate population subset, because they are both old and black, and that such problems as racism, ageism and poverty adversely affecting many of them—again because they are both old and black and, in many instances, poor—warrant NCBA's existence. That is, NCBA needs to exist not only because it is most aware of the peculiar meanings of being black and old, but also because—through its interdisciplinary framework and under the guidance of its humane chairman, Hobart C. Jackson—it has found a way to merge scholarship, services and action where its *central* concern is upon those who are old and black and who are black and growing old.

---

17. Some relevant works available on nonblack aging and aged minorities include: H. Marian, "The Filipino Immigrant in the United States," (M. A. thesis, University of Chicago, 1934); R. Ross, Social Distance between First and Second Generations Japanese in Los Angeles," (M. A. thesis, University of Southern California, 1939); V. R. Acquino, "The Filipino Community in Los Angeles" (M. A. thesis, University of Southern California, 1952); W. C. Chen, "Changing Socio-Cultural Patterns of the Chinese Community in Los Angeles" (Ph. D. diss., University of Southern California, 1952); Y. Kimura, "A Comparative Study of the Collective Adjustment of the Issei, the First Generation Japanese in Hawaii and in Mainland United States since Pearl Harbor" (Ph. D. diss., University of Chicago, 1952); S. Cho, "Correlation of Cultural Assimilation of Two Groups of Issei Women" (M. A. thesis, University of Washington, 1953); W. Y. Kanagwa, "A Study of Old Age Assistance Recipients of Japanese Ancestry under Honolulu County Department of Welfare" (M. A. thesis, University of Hawaii, 1955); R. K. Dare, "The Economic and Social Adjustment of San Francisco Chinese for the Past 50 Years" (M. A. thesis, University of California, 1959); P. S. Staniford, "Values of Some Issei Japanese of Manapepe Valley, Kauai" (M. A. thesis, University of Honolulu, 1961); John Modell, "The Japanese American Family: A Perspective for Future Investigations," *Pacific Historical Review* 37 (1968), pp. 67–81; J. Rush, "The Generation Gap as Analyzed by Reference Group Behavior and Effect on Solidarity of Chinese Community of Sacramento," (M. A. thesis, Sacramento State College, 1969); J. H. Burma, ed., *Mexican-Americans in the United States: A reader* (Cambridge, Mass.: Schenkman, 1970); Frances M. Carp, "Communicating with Elderly Mexican-Americans," *Gerontologist* 10 (1970), pp. 126–134; L. Grebler, J. W. Moore and R. C. Guzman, *The Mexican American People: The Nation's Second Largest Minority* (New York: Free Press, 1970); S. Yen, "Aging and Mental Health in San Francisco's Chinatown," in *Ethnicity, mental health, and aging* (Los Angeles, Cal.: Gerontology Center, University of Southern California, 1970), pp. 7–9.

18. For further discussion on this point, see, Jacquelyne J. Jackson "Social Gerontology and the Negro."

Age and Political Alienation: Maturation, Generation and Period Effects

By Neal E. Cutler and Vern L. Bengtson

ABSTRACT: Trends in political alienation may be defined in terms of one or more of three age-related explanations reflecting different aspects of change over time. These may be posed as the following set of hypotheses: (1) trends in political alienation represent cumulative effects of maturational processes—aging—of subgroups within the population; (2) trends in political alienation represent the flow of successive generational cohorts through the population; (3) trends in political alienation reflect political and historical events or periods which affect all members of the population in a similar fashion. The purpose of this research is to discern the plausibility of these hypotheses by analyzing data on political alienation via the technique of cohort analysis. An analysis of three nationwide political attitude surveys revealed that, of the three possible explanations, the historical or period effect best explains changes in political alienation across the years 1952 to 1968. Much less marked is a trend attributable to generational effects. No maturation or aging effects were evident.

Neal E. Cutler is Associate Professor of Political Science and Chief of the Social Policy Laboratory of the Gerontology Center at the University of Southern California. Professor Cutler, who received his Ph.D. in Political Science from Northwestern University, was a Woodrow Wilson Fellow and a Senior Fulbright-Hays Research Scholar. He is author of Aging and Generations in Politics: The Conflict of Explanations and Inference, Towards a Political Generations Conception of Political Socialization and several other books and scholarly articles.

Vern L. Bengtson is Associate Professor of Sociology and Chief of the Laboratory for Social Organization and Behavior at the University of Southern California. Professor Bengtson, whose research has been primarily in the area of adult socialization, intergenerational relations and the social-psychological aspects of widowhood and retirement, is currently Principal Investigator of research on "Socio-Cultural Contexts of Aging: Implications for Social Policy." His publications include The Social Psychology of Aging and articles for scholarly journals.

THE initial focus of the present research concerned the question: "is there a generational basis to recent patterns of political alienation?" Yet, consideration of this question quickly led to two much larger areas of inquiry. Analysis of generational phenomena in social and political behavior is part of a much larger issue in which generation, maturation and specific period or situation factors can each account for the existence of changes and trends. Similarly, political alienation represents only one facet of the larger phenomenon of alienation in several contexts.

Given the larger issues in which our inquiry is embedded, the purpose of this first section is to indicate more specifically the limitations of our efforts in the present article. The main thrust is to present a brief overview of recent analyses of political alienation as a subset of alienation in general. This discussion is confined to a consideration of these studies which deal with the aging and generational aspects of political alienation.

AGE, GENERATIONS AND POLITICAL ALIENATION

Alienation is a concept which has occupied the serious attention of social commentators and analysts for dozens, if not hundreds, of years; moreover, this attention represents innumerable schools and fields of philosophy and behavioral science. As both Durkheim and Marx noted, alienation represents one important interface between certain aspects of social structure on the one hand and characteristic responses at the individual level of attitudes and behaviors on the

other.[1] Despite—or perhaps because of—the long history of interest in the concept of alienation, there is no universally accepted definition of alienation in terms of the psychological state it represents or the social-political object toward which it is directed.[2]

The importance of the topic of alienation, combined with the variability of approaches to its conceptualization and study, has led to a large variety of empirical studies. A bibliography on the subject compiled in 1969 by the National Institute of Mental Health, for example, cites two hundred twenty-five articles.[3] Schwartz's recent discussion of the relationship of political alienation to political behavior cites over fifty separate studies as being germane to the topic.[4]

Consequently, there have been attempts to systematically outline the main dimensions of alienation, both conceptually and operationally. In his now classic review of previous usages of the term, Seeman identifies five analytically distinguishable dimensions of the concept: powerlessness, meaninglessness, normlessness, isolation and self-estrange-

1. Emil Durkheim, *Suicide: A Study in Sociology* (Glencoe, Ill.: Free Press, 1951; for a discussion of the Marxian view of alienation, see, the discussion in T. Bottomore, *Selected Writings in Sociology and Social Philosophy* (New York: McGraw-Hill, 1956).
2. William Martin, Vern Bengtson and Al Acock, "Alienation and Age: A Context Specific Approach," *Social Forces* 53 (1973), pp. 67–84.
3. National Institute of Mental Health, *Social Aspects of Alienation* (Washington, D.C.: Government Printing Office, 1969).
4. David C. Schwartz, *Political Alienation and Political Behavior* (Chicago, Ill.: Aldine, 1973), chap. 1.

ment.[5] More recently, Seeman has added the concepts of loneliness and cultural estrangement to this typology.

Martin, Bengtson and Acock have attempted to refine the total conceptualization of alienation beyond the Seeman typology by specifying the institutional target of alienation.[6] As these writers maintain, a focus on the psychological modes of alienation—powerlessness, estrangement and so on—leaves unanswered the important question of "alienated from what?" Consequently, they employ a structural-functional conception of society in which alienation may be described in terms of the social institution toward which the alienation is directed: political, economic, educational, religious and familial. When these five institutional contexts of alienation are combined with the original five dimensions of alienation reported by Seeman, a typology representing twenty-five different context-specific types of alienation is created.

Also, as Schwartz has argued, the degree of relationship between alienation toward the political system and alienation toward other institutional targets must be empirically established, not simply assumed. The different modes and institutional contexts of alienation may have different antecedents, different trends and different behavioral consequences. Thus, as these investigators have argued, social analysts may have to model and analyze the different manifestations of alienation separately[7] rather than

to employ a unidimensional construct.

Within this extensive conceptualization of alienation the present study occupies a small corner. As our title indicates, we are concerned with alienation from the political system. The particular attitudinal indicators employed jointly represent two of the modes of alienation cited by Seeman: (1) *powerlessness*, the expectation on the part of the individual that there is little probability that his own behavior can or will affect the goals he seeks; (2) *estrangement*, the belief or perception on the part of the individual that he does not or cannot identify with the political system.

As a further limitation on the scope of the present research, attention will be focused on a trend analysis of political alienation with special reference to age and generational sources of observed trends. While there have been many studies of political alienation at the individual level and some discussion of trends or group patterns of political alienation, there have been very few studies which have specifically attempted to investigate the possible maturational and generational sources of these trends. There are three hypotheses which can be asserted regarding alienation and time-related contrasts; the remainder of this section will outline these hypotheses and review the issues germane to an analysis of this kind.

Maturation—life-cycle—effects and alienation

The hypothesis that maturation or aging may be related to changes in political alienation is represented by many analyses which

5. Melvin Seeman, "On the Meaning of Alienation," *American Sociological Review* 24 (1959), pp. 783–791.
6. Martin *et al.*, "Alienation and Age."
7. Schwartz, *Political Alienation*, p. 6.

may be characterized as youth and politics studies. Many examinations of student protest cite the alienation of the young person as a major source of personal and group political activity. For example, in a significant report of several analyses of student political activity in the Chicago area in the mid-1960s, Flacks refers to the "revolt of the advantaged" in discussing the role played by alienation in the political activity of wealthy and well-educated upper middle class students.[8] Formal participation in the political system has been withheld from people under the age of twenty-one—recently changed to the age of eighteen. To the degree that alienation does represent powerlessness, therefore, it should not be unexpected that analyses such as those by Friedenberg and by Kenniston, Whittaker and Watts indicate that a major social locus of alienation in American society is represented by youth.[9]

At the other end of the age continuum several studies have presented examples and explanations of the political alienation of the elderly. Reviews of political participation in American and European contexts have documented the drop in participation after the age of sixty or so.[10] The estrangement of the elderly individual from politics may be one manifestation of a more general disengagement of the individual from a variety of social roles. Thus, as derived from disengagement theory, political alienation may be a natural consequence of the aging process.[11]

That the youngest and the oldest member of society may represent the typically most alienated sectors of society has been noted by several studies. For example, the data of Martin et al. suggest a curvilinear relationship between alienation and age, with the middle-age group the least alienated on most of the twenty-five dimensions compared.[12] Similarly, Miller, Brown and Raine found increasing levels of estrangement in both young and older Americans and concluded that "age-linked conflict in America has become a curvilinear phenomenon."[13] Perhaps the most elaborate formulation of this general issue is the "center-periphery" conceptualization by

8. Richard Flacks, "The Liberated Generation: An Exploration of the Roots of Student Protest," *Journal of Social Issues* 23 (1967), pp. 52–75.

9. Edgar Z. Freidenberg, "Current Patterns of a Generational Conflict," *Journal of Social Issues* 25 (2969), pp. 21–48; Kenneth Kenniston, *The Uncomitted* (New York: Dell, 1965); David Whittaker and William A. Watts, "Personality Characteristics of a Nonconformist Youth Subculture," *Journal of Social Issues* 25 (1969), pp. 65–89.

10. Herbert Tingsten, "Age Groups in Politics," in *Political Behaviour*, ed. Tingsten (London: P. S. King and Son,

1937), pp. 79–119; Lester W. Milbrath, *Political Participation* (Chicago, Ill.: Rand McNally, 1965), p. 134; Anne Foner, "The Polity," in *Aging and Society: A Sociology of Age Stratification*, vol. III, ed. Matilda White Riley, Marilyn Johnson and Anne Foner (New York: Russell Sage, 1972), pp. 118–132.

11. Elaine Cumming and William Henry, *Growing Old* (New York: Basic Books, 1961); Vern L. Bengtson, *The Social Psychology of Aging* (Indianapolis, Ind.: Bobbs-Merrill, 1973). Disengagement as an explanation of old age alienation is argued in: Thomas J. Agnello, "Aging and the Sense of Political Powerlessness," *Public Opinion Quarterly* 37 (1973), pp. 251–259.

12. Martin et al., "Alienation and Age."

13. Arthur H. Miller, Thad A. Brown and Alden S. Raine, "Social Conflict and Political Estrangement, 1958–1972" (Paper presented at the Annual Meeting of the Midwest Political Science Association, Chicago, Ill., 1973), p. 59.

the Norwegian sociologist Johan Galtung.[14]

Galtung argues that the members of any sociopolitical system may be characterized as being closer to the center or more to the periphery of that system. Among the political attributes which are associated with location along the center-periphery axis are access to channels of political communication, political resources, political participation, extremity of political orientations and the degree to which the individual can realistically believe he can have an impact on affecting or changing the system—that is, political alienation.

Galtung and his colleagues employ an additive index to identify the social location of any respondent along the center-periphery gradient. One of the component variables in the index is age, for which under twenty-five and over fifty-five are scored as being indicators of periphery status. In arguing that in most political systems the young and the old do not have the resources or the access required to affect the system significantly, Galtung's position is consistent with studies of youth and the elderly cited above. A curvilinear relationship between age and political alienation should be expected, since the alienated young would become less alienated as they move into the age status which typically brings the greatest number of personal and social resources. Moreover, according to

14. Johan Galtung, "Foreign Policy Opinion as a Function of Social Position," *Journal of Peace Research* 1 (1964), pp. 206–231; J. Galtung, "Social Position, Party Identification, and Foreign Policy Orientation," in *Domestic Sources of Foreign Policy*, ed. James N. Rosenau (New York: Free Press, 1967), pp. 161–193.

this maturational view, the aging individual might exhibit increased feelings of alienation as those resources and status are lost or taken away through disengagement or decline.

Generational effects and alienation

Evidence can also be cited which supports a generational hypothesis concerning trends in political alienation. Such labels as the beat generation or the lost generation allude to groups of individuals whose alienation was brought about by combinations of circumstances which affected members of the generation throughout their lives, not only in the young and the elderly life-stages. This orientation is consistent with the thesis developed several decades ago by Manheim regarding generations as sociopolitical "entelechies" reflecting enduring social groupings.

Something of a paradox emerges when we examine closely the empirical analyses of generational aspects of political alienation. Much of the research which we have classified as youth and politics studies—studies which see alienation as a characteristic orientation of youth—also refers to the political alienation of new generations. For example, in the Flacks' study already cited, the author attempts to construct a social, psychological and historical analysis of the student protestors of the mid-1960s. One conclusion of this analysis is that, in terms of political alienation and political activity, the birth cohort of which the university students in 1965 were a part does indeed represent a distinct generation. This distinctiveness, in turn, is the product of the interaction of cohort-specific sets of historical and social circumstances.

Another genre of studies relevant here are those which may be referred to as generation gap studies. Typically, these are analyses of young people as compared with their own parents or the older generation in general. There are a variety of views of current and recent gaps in the political relations between young and old. Some of these studies see the differences as temporary gaps which will close as the young attain the status and responsibilities of adults. Generation gap studies of this kind are thus supportive of a maturational view of political alienation. One review of generation gap studies, however, has identified a group of theorists who see a great gap between the current youth and the current adult generation.[15] For these analysts the alienation of the younger people is so great and so strongly connected to a political system which is seen as inhumane and unjust that it cannot be expected that the alienated youth will mellow into traditionally involved adults.

In a review of several studies relevant to this question House and Mason report conflicting explanations of the social sources of changes in national levels of political alienation.[16] Some writers argue from a regional perspective that it is the residents of the American

South and West who constitute the new alienated; other analysts reviewed by House and Mason refer to the alienation of youth and minorities as a response to the nation's involvement in Vietnam, racism, increasing impersonalization of society and the dominance of profit-making values over human values. This latter source of the polarization of generations has been documented in Inglehart's cross-national study of five Western European countries, as well.[17] While this view supports the great-gap perspective concerning distinctive generational bases of political alienation, it has been disputed by Scammon and Wattenberg, who have attributed recent trends in alienation to the "unyoung, the unpoor, and the unblack."[18]

Period—historical—effects and alienation

Recent trend analyses of political alienation and estrangement have yielded mixed results in testing a third hypothesis, that of historical or period trends in alienation. Based on a correlational analysis of data spanning from 1952 to 1968, House and Mason concluded that trends in political alienation in the United States reflect aggregate "period effect" changes in the population as a whole; such trends, they argue, do not represent any simple aggregations of changes in any identifiable age, region, sex, education or income group.[19] Un-

15. Vern L. Bengtson, "The Generation Gap: A Review and Typology of Social-Psychological Perspectives," *Youth and Society* 2 (1970), pp. 7–31.

16. James S. House and William M. Mason, "Trends in Some Survey Measures of Political Alienation in America, 1952–1968: What Do They Mean?" (Paper presented at Annual Meeting of the American Sociological Association, New York, New York, 1973).

17. Ronald Inglehart, "The Silent Revolution in Europe: Intergenerational Change in Post-Industrial Societies," *American Political Science Review* 65 (1971), pp. 991–1007.

18. Richard Scammon and Ben J. Wattenberg, *The Real Majority* (New York: Coward, McCann and Geoghegan, 1970).

19. House and Mason, "Trends in Some Survey Measures," p. 14.

fortunately, the structure of the House and Mason analysis did not allow for the direct assessment of the three effects described here— maturation, generation and period effects. In an analysis of political estrangement over the years 1958 to 1972, Miller, Brown and Raine statistically eliminated any period effects by standardizing estrangement scores to the earlier time period.[20] The subsequent comparison of the remaining two effects, maturation and generation, yielded mixed results: it was concluded that the estrangement of the older age groups represents maturational influences, while the estrangement of younger persons represents a possible generational effect, "since young people today are being socialized into a society which is, on the whole, considerably more negative toward the government than it was fourteen years ago."

In sum, we may observe that there is no single, clear explanation of recent trends in political alienation, especially concerning the question of the dynamics of the generational or maturational forces which might lie beneath those trends. That is, because several studies have looked at the main effects of maturation, generation and period factors as independent explanations, we have little evidence concerning the *relative importance* of each of the hypothetical explanations in accounting for patterns of political alienation. Therefore, an empirical analysis designed to directly identify maturational and generational effects in the context of possible historical or period effects seems to be necessary. The following section briefly describes the background and mechanics of the cohort analysis technique by which this test can be carried out.

COHORT ANALYSIS

In the analysis of historical trends undertaken in the context of age analysis, three general kinds of effects may be operative: (1) a generational or cohort effect, (2) a maturational or aging effect and (3) a situational or period effect. The first two effects are typically easy to confound and difficult to unravel, since each is measured by the same variable: age. Since the same datum—the age of the respondent in an interview study—is used to measure two competing effects or explanations, it becomes the obligation of the analytic methodology to uncover the distinctions.

A person's age indicates how many years he or she has been alive; thus, it is a measure of maturation which includes acquisition of knowledge and skills, experience, roles and responsibilities. In sociological terminology, a person's age is a good—albeit imperfect— indicator of his life stage.[21] At the same time, a person's current age can be used to discover the year in which he was born. This in turn is an indicator of generational effects, since people born into the same age cohort and raised during the same historical era may, under certain circumstances, consciously or

20. Miller *et al.*, "Social Conflict," p. 75.

21. Vern L. Bengtson and K. Dean Black, "Intergeneration Relations and Continuities in Socialization," in *Personality and Socialization*, ed. K. Warner Schaie and Paul Baltes (New York: Academic Press, 1973), chap. 9; Vern L. Bengtson, "On the Socialization of Values: Cohort and Lineage Effects in Intergenerational Transmission" (Paper prepared for the Annual Meeting of the American Sociological Association, New York, New York, 1973).

unconsciously behave or view the world in a characteristic fashion.[22]

In cross-sectional studies representing a single point in time percentages or correlations relating age to an attitude or behavior cannot be unambiguously interpreted in either aging or generational terms.[23] Only a few human attributes can be unambiguously interpreted in this way; formal education is an example. Years of formal schooling for most people does not change over the course of the life span. Thus, a study of a given population which shows a strong correlation between age and education should probably not be interpreted in maturational terms; more likely, age is in this case an indicator of generation. The often-noted negative correlation between age and education certainly does not indicate that as people age they somehow lose their education. Clearly, such a correlation means that more recent generations have a more extensive educational experience.

Such an explanation could not be validly fashioned in the case of age and political alienation. As the discussion in the previous section has illustrated, both generational and maturational explanations are plausible explanations of levels of political alienation. Therefore, a knowledge of the relationship between age and political alienation based upon a single study produc-

ing data from one point in time cannot provide the evidentiary base from which a choice between the competing explanations of age and generation can be made.

Cohort analysis represents an approach to the problem which facilitates the choice between competing, plausible explanations.[24] A cohort analysis of attitudes—as adapted from the demographers' use of cohort analysis in conjunction with census data—starts out with a sequence of attitude surveys taken over a period of time. Each survey within the set is sorted by age in such a way that several birth cohorts can be traced across time by looking at the appropriate age group in the sequence of surveys. To trace the 1920 to 1924 birth cohort across a series of surveys taken every ten years, for example, the analyst would look at the 26 to 30 age group in the 1950 survey, the 36 to 40 year olds in the 1960 survey and the 46 to 50 age interval in the 1970 survey. Or, to reverse the language, the 1920 to 1924 cohort is 26 to 30 years old in 1950; it is 36 to 40 years old in 1960, and 46 to 50 years old in 1970.

When each of the attitude surveys is stratified into the appropriate age intervals, it then becomes possible to trace a number of different generational or birth cohorts across the span of history represented by the sequence of surveys. Consequently, although each separate survey represents attitudes at a single point in time, the juxtaposition of a sequence of surveys, sorted or stratified according to the

22. Karl Mannheim, "The Problem of Generations," in *Essays on the Sociology of Knowledge*, ed. and trans. by Paul Kecskemeti (London: Routledge and Kegan Paul, (1952), pp. 276–322.

23. Neal E. Cutler, "Aging and Generations in Politics: The Conflict of Explanations and Inference," in *Public Opinion and Political Attitudes* ed. Allen R. Wilcox (New York: Wiley, 1974), pp. 410–462.

24. Norman B. Ryder, "The Cohort as a Concept in the Study of Social Change," *American Sociological Review* 30 (1965), pp. 843–861; Riley *et al.*, *Aging and Society*, chap. 2.

appropriate age intervals, can be used to construct a more dynamic picture of the generational cohort changes, if any, over time.[25]

A cohort matrix of the kind described here—as presented in table 1 in the following section of this paper—provides the opportunity to evaluate the three kinds of effects enumerated at the beginning of the present section. The analyst can observe the behavior of a number of different generational cohorts across the time span of the sequence of surveys. Individual cohorts may be selected for particular scrutiny or the attitude and behavior pattern of each cohort may be compared with the patterns of each of the other cohorts.

The aging effects can be observed in the same data matrix in either or both of the following ways. Since each of the surveys will have been sorted into the same set of age intervals, the analyst may choose to look at the 21 to 25-year olds in each of the survey years; for purposes of comparison, he may also look at the 61 to 65-year olds in each of the years. If it is hypothesized that there is a distinctive attitude or behavior pattern associated with each of these mat-

urational life stages, then—despite historical changes—21 to 25-year olds or 61 to 65-year olds should closely resemble one another across time. A second way of observing maturational effects would be to look at the pattern of attitudes within each individual birth cohort as the cohort ages over the time span represented by the sequence of attitude surveys. In this way it might be determined not only what the general aging pattern is, but also if maturational processes are similar or different for the succession of generational birth cohorts.

The identification of generational effects and aging effects might be considered to be the main outcome of the kind of formal cohort analysis described here. Yet, in seeking to understand these trends, a third time-oriented effect must also be considered as a plausible hypothesis rivaling the two main alternatives. Trends and fluctuations across the cohorts and the age groups may simply reflect large scale changes produced by specific situations and events so pervasive that all age groups and all generational cohorts respond in a similar fashion. If every person in a population reacted in an identical way to the event of a war, depression or scandal, then the trend fluctuation for that specific historical period should be interpreted as a period effect.

The existence of dominant and pervasive societywide events which precipitate period effects does not imply that every cohort and age group will have the same attitude level or percentage; differences across groups will exist since each age or cohort group had a different starting point prior to the event of the period. However, the general trend or pattern for each

25. For extended discussions of cohort analysis see: William M. Evan, "Cohort Analysis of Survey Data: A Procedure for Studying Longterm Opinion Change," *Public Opinion Quarterly* 23 (1959), pp. 63–72; Neal E. Cutler, *The Alternative Effects of Generations and Aging Upon Political Behavior* (Oak Ridge, Cal.: Oak Ridge National Laboratory, 1968), chap. 4; Norval D. Glenn and Richard Zody, "Cohort Analysis with National Survey Data," *Gerontologist* 10 (1970), pp. 233–240; Herbert H. Hyman, *Secondary Analysis of Sample Surveys* (New York: Wiley, 1972), pp. 274–290; Matilda White Riley, "Aging and Cohort Succession: Interpretations and Misinterpretations," *Public Opinion Quarterly* 37 (1973), pp. 35–49.

TABLE 1

AGING, MATURATION AND PERIOD TRENDS IN POLITICAL ALIENATION, 1952 TO 1968, PERCENT AGREEING WITH ITEM

AGE	YEAR BORN	"PUBLIC OFFICIALS DON'T CARE"*				"PEOPLE LIKE ME HAVE NO SAY"†				"POLITICS IS SO COMPLICATED"‡			
		1952	1960	1968	COHORT MEAN	1952	1960	1968	COHORT MEAN	1952	1960	1968	COHORT MEAN
21–28	1924–31 (E)	29	26	36		31	10	31		75	51	66	
29–36	1916–23 (D)	35	22	41		28	26	34		69	65	73	
37–44	1908–15 (C)	30	19	35	28.7	25	25	37	31.3	67	56	67	69.0
45–52	1900–07 (B)	31	25	38	30.7	29	29	40	31.0	70	57	72	65.7
53–60	1892–99 (A)	39	26	50	35.0	35	27	49	34.3	71	61	72	65.3
61–68	1884–91	48	25	61	39.3	40	32	54	36.7	73	48	77	69.3
69+	—1884	51	39	57	40.3	41	37	53	40.0	82	67	79	66.0
Total		36	25	44		31	27	41		71	59	71	

* "I don't think public officials care much what people like me think."
† "People like me don't have any say about what the government does."
‡ "Sometimes politics and government seem so complicated that a person like me can't really understand what's going on."

group will be similar, and that pattern, found to a greater or lesser degree in all groups, will be known to document historical period effects rather than the effects of the aging process or the effects of generational learning and socialization experiences.

POLITICAL ALIENATION IN AMERICA, 1952 TO 1968

As indicated earlier, the measure of political alienation employed in the present analysis embodies the notions of estrangement and powerlessness perceived by the individual as representing his relationship to the political system or the government. Specifically, three items were taken from the series of nationally representative presidential election attitude surveys undertaken by the Center for Political Studies of the University of Michigan.[26] The following items appeared in each of the presidential election surveys for the years 1952, 1960 and 1968: (1) "I don't think public officials care much what people like me think;" (2) "people like me don't have any say about what the govenment does;" and (3) "sometimes politics and government seem so complicated that a person like me can't really understand what's going on." Taken together, affirmitive response to the set of items indicates both the estrangement which the individual

feels toward government and politics and the powerlessness he feels to modify or change the situation.[27]

Table 1 presents the percentage of agreement for the items for the total samples in the three historical periods, as well as for various age and generational and cohort groups. Evidence of an interesting trend in political alienation is indicated by the totals for each item across the sixteen-year period. For each of the three indicators one can see that political alienation dropped in the period 1952 to 1960 and that, in every instance, alienation substantially increased over the years 1960 to 1968. The general trend is one in which the level of political alienation in 1968 is somewhat greater than that of 1952 and much greater than in 1960.

As a first interpretation, therefore, it could be argued that the similarity of the pattern across the

26. The data utilized in this report were made available by the Inter-University Consortium for Political Research. The data were originally collected by the Center for Political Studies of the Institute for Social Research, University of Michigan, under a grant from the National Science Foundation. Neither the original collectors of the data nor the consortium bear any responsibility for the analyses or interpretations presented here.

27. As pointed our earlier in this paper, what is defined as a kind of alienation and what is defined as a component of alienation is still an open question. The three items employed here are considered as a measure of political alienation, a conclusion reached also by House and Mason, "Trends in Some Survey Measures." While the originators of this set of items at the University of Michigan refer to them as "political efficacy," more recently, Michigan analysts have referred to efficacy as a subcomponent of political alienation; see: Angus Campbell et al., The American Voter (New York: Wiley, 1960); Miller et al., The same items, however, have alos been analyzed and referred to as political effectiveness, political anomie and political potency in the following studies, respectively: Elizabeth Douvan and Allan M. Walker, "The Sense of Political Effectiveness in Public Affairs," Psychological Monographs 70 (1956); Charles D. Farris, "Selected Attitudes on Foreign Affairs as Correlates of Authoritarianism and Political Anomie," Journal of Politics 22 (1960), pp. 50–67; Robert E. Agger, Marshall N. Goldstein and Stanley A. Pearl, "Political Cynicism: Measurement and Meaning," Journal of Politics 23 (1961), pp. 477–506.

set of three items indicates an historical period effect in political alienation in the United States during this sixteen year period. In any trend analysis, however, examination of the responses of the total sample may not be a true indication of the underlying sociopolitical attitudinal process operating within the population during this period —that is, a pattern which is apparent for the total population might contain significant subpopulation trends some of which could be quite different from the overall pattern. It is to an examination of this possibility that we now turn.

The previous section noted that cohort analysis allows for the examination of three kinds of effects within the same set of data: a period effect, a generational effect and an aging effect. Although the similarity of the sixteen-year trend for the three indicators of political alienation suggests the existence of a period effect in these data, before such an explanation can be accepted, the data must be examined for evidence of either or both of the other two competing interpretations —a maturational effect or a generational effect.

Two questions may be posed concerning the presence of a generational pattern in these data. First, are the various generational cohorts substantially similar or substantially different in their overall level of political alienation across the 1952 to 1968 period? Second, do these cohorts respond to the stimuli of social and political events during this sixteen-year period so differentially that one should conclude that some kind of a generational effect is operative?

The question concerning the overall level of political alienation

across the sixteen-year period may be answered by looking at the average alienation percentage for each of the generational cohorts for which we have the complete set of three observations: the averages are included in table 1 and are graphically displayed in figure 1.

A first interpretation is that there appear to be some differences in the overall or average alienation level for the different generational groups. At least for the "don't care" item and the "no say" item it appears that the more recent generational cohorts—those born in 1916 or later—have slightly lower levels of political alienation then those born in earlier years.

Before accepting even this evidence of possible generational effects, however, it must be noted that a person's perception of his relationship to the political system has been found to be strongly associated with one's level of educa-

FIGURE 1

COHORT AND PERIOD TRENDS IN POLITICAL
ALIENATION, 1952 TO 68

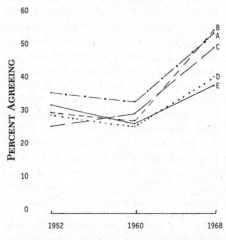

"People like me don't have any say about what the government does."

tion.[28] Furthermore, as was noted in the previous section, in the United States educational attainment itself has been increasing in the population in generational terms—that is, each successive generation has a higher aggregate level of education than the previous one. Consequently, the observation that the more recent generations have become less politically alienated may be accurate in descriptive terms, but in terms of an understanding of the sociopolitical processes which affect alienation, the apparent cohort differences in political alienation may be simply due to the fact that the more recent generational cohorts are better educated.

To test this possibility we divided each of the national samples into high and low education groups—the completion of high school being the dividing line—and then constructed a separate cohort matrix, as in table 1, for each of the two education groups. Although space limitations prevent the presentation of these additional sets of data,[29] the results of the education-by-cohort analysis can be easily summarized. As expected, levels of political alienation are in fact associated with levels of formal education for every one of the generational cohorts in the three national samples: the more educated groups are in each case approximately twenty percentage points less politically alienated than the less educated groups.

The specific test of cross-generational differences is also illuminated by the educational analysis. The average alienation levels across the cohorts, when strat-

ified by education, are not very different from one another. Furthermore, of those differences which do exist even within the high education or the low education subsamples, the patterns do not indicate any systematic generational differences. In summary, the apparent generational interpretation—that the cohorts born 1916 or later have lower levels of political alienation—does not hold true when the several generations are standardized in terms of educational attainment.

The second generational question posed above focuses on the pattern of response of each generational group to the sixteen years of history represented in these data. Even if the overall levels of political alienation are similar for different cohorts, differences in the 1952 to 1968 pattern of political alienation should be considered as at least tentative evidence that historical or generational socialization experiences are producing some kinds of generational similarity among the members of a birth cohort.

The data for the whole samples in table 1 and figure 1 dramatically indicate that for these measures of political alienation, all of the generational cohorts responded to the stimuli of 1952 to 1968 in an almost identical fashion. No matter what the starting level of political alienation in 1952, it was followed by a drop in 1960 and, then, an upsurge in 1968. Thus, it may be concluded that although each successive cohort evidences slightly lower levels of alienation, there is only slight evidence that patterns of political alienation in the United States across the years 1952 to 1968 can be usefully interpreted in generational terms.

Examination of the possible mat-

28. For example, see, Milbrath, *Political Participation*.

29. Tables available from the senior author upon request.

urational effect as an explanation of the trends in political alienation also poses two related questions. First, across all of the cohorts for which the complement of three observations is included in the data, is the pattern of sixteen years of aging similar or different? Second, given various theories concerning differential maturational processes at different stages in the life cycle, are there any identifiable differences in the aging patterns as found in the earlier years as contrasted with the later years?

Examination of the total sixteen-year period, as well as closer examination of the subsets of eight-year aging shifts, indicates quite clearly that for all three of the political alienation items and across all of the generational cohorts the pattern of aging is virtually identical. As noted previously, the general trend in political alienation in these years was one of a decrease between 1952 and 1960, followed by an increase between 1960 and 1968—with the 1968 level being higher than the initial level of 1952. With few exceptions, the identical pattern is found for each age group and across all three political alienation items.

Therefore, in response to our two questions concerning the possibility of a maturational or aging effect producing differences in the political alienation response to the events of the 1952-1968 period, the data indicate that in neither case are such differences present. With two minor exceptions—for which a difference of a few percentage points would produce the basic pattern—the pattern of aging was the same for all groups. In particular, it should be pointed out that those groups entering the analysis in their younger years do not have a

different pattern of aging and alienation as compared to those entering the analysis in their later years.[30]

To further substantiate this conclusion we may again consider the results of the separate analysis of these data by high and low education groups. Since education is known to be correlated with political alienation, the effects of aging might be different for the two education groups. The pervasiveness of the pattern already discovered is reinforced by the separate education data. The combination of two education strata, three alienation items and five cohort groups measured across the 1952 to 1968 period produces thirty separate examples of the pattern of aging across this sixteen-year period. In twenty-six of these thirty the already identified pattern is found. Of the remaining four instances— all found among the high educa-

30. Agnello, in "Aging and Political Power-lessness," has concluded from his own analysis of two of these three alienation items that the patterns provide evidence of a maturational effect over the years 1952–1968. This conclusion is unfortunately based on a data scoring system which Agnello adapted from Crittenden's earlier study of political party identification. At least two studies, however, have found the conclusions reached by the Crittenden method to be in error. In addition, Agnello's analysis suffers from a technical problem: in 1968 the alienation items were asked only in the post-election interview; 14 percent of the original sample did not participate in the post-election interview and were thus not asked in the questions. Agnello erroneously based his 1968 analysis on the total number of cases in the original sample. The dispute over the data scoring system may be found in the following: John Crittenden, "Aging and Party Affiliation," *Public Opinion Quarterly* 26 (1962), pp. 648–657; Neal E. Cutler, "Generation, Maturation, and Party Affiliation: A Cohort Analysis," *Public Opinion Quarterly* 33 (1970), pp. 583–588; Norval D. Glenn and Ted Hefner, "Further Evidence on Aging and Party Identification," *Public Opinion Quarterly* 36 (1972), pp. 31–47.

tion respondents—it is again basically a case of difference of a few percentage points accounting for a deviation from the basic pattern.

Therefore, the predominant period pattern is found to be pervasive among all the cohort groups. There is no evidence of a process of aging which produces, or is in other ways related to, political alienation among adults during the period studied. At least for this period of sixteen years of aging in the 1950s and 1960s, aging in the younger years of the life cycle and aging at the older end of the life cycle does not produce differences in the way in which political alienation changed; rather, the basic pattern found for the total population is that which is descriptive of the component age groups within the population.

SUMMARY AND CONCLUSION

Using data from three nationally representative attitude surveys in which a set of identical survey items were included, this research has presented a cohort analysis of political alienation over the years 1952 to 1968. The cohort analysis approach facilitates the investigation of three interrelated phenomena: a period effect, an aging effect and a generational effect. The focus of this article has been to determine the relative importance of each of these effects in understanding political alienation in the United States over the sixteen-year study period.

The results of the cohort analysis have been rather clear. The basic finding is that political alienation, measured as powerlessness and self-estrangement, decreased between 1952 and 1960 and, then, substantially increased between 1960 and 1968—the latter increase yielding a higher level of political alienation in 1968 than in 1952. In other words, important period effects are evidenced in these data on alienation.

Second, maturational and generational effects are important alternatives to the acceptance of the conclusion that such national patterns truly reflect the response of the whole population to the events of the period under study. Such trends could be the consequence of unique generational groups entering the population while other generational groups are dying out of the population. Or, what appears to be a response to a situation or historical period may, in fact, be nothing more than the additive consequences of an aging population.

This cohort analysis of political alienation indicates that neither a maturational nor a generational effect provides alternative interpretation of the patterns of political alienation found in these data. To the contrary, the analysis appears to strengthen the period effect interpretation. While there are some generational differences in the overall level of political alienation expressed over the 1952 to 1968 period, these differences are small and appear to be the result of the different educational composition of the different educational groups rather than indicators of the existence of clearly identifiable generational groups. Furthermore, the analysis indicates that each of the generational groups responded to the events of the 1952 to 1968 period in an identical fashion—that is, the same pattern as already noted for the population as a whole is repeated.

Examination of the maturation effect was accomplished by looking at how each cohort aged over the sixteen-year period. The analysis yielded no differential pattern of political alienation associated with maturation across different stages in the life cycle. Although various theories of aging may predict that social and political attitudes may change differently in the older years as compared to the younger years, these data do not indicate any differences in the pattern of response of groups of people of different ages to the social and political conditions of the 1952 to 1968 period.

This research included the application of educational controls to the cohort analysis. This was done for two interrelated reasons: (1) previous research has indicated the strong association between education and the attitude of political alienation; (2) the education level of the United States has been increasing over the past sixty years, so that the different cohort groups in the analysis have different educational compositions. Any cohort analysis, therefore, should be careful not to confound such compositional effects with the main effects of period, generation and maturation.

The cohort analysis by education group reinforced the patterns found earlier. For each of the three indicators of political alienation, those respondents with at least a completed high school education were about twenty percentage points less alienated than those with less education. Yet, despite the different absolute levels of political alienation, the changes associated with maturation and generation were virtually identical to those already documented for the total population. The level of political alienation dropped between 1952 and 1960 and, then, increased between 1960 and 1968. With few exceptions, this was the pattern found for both high and low education groups within each of the five generational cohorts and for each of the three measures of political alienation.

Aging and Conservatism

By NORVAL D. GLENN

ABSTRACT: The notion that aging beyond adolescence and young adulthood leads to conservatism is part of the conventional wisdom, and there are theoretical reasons to believe that certain dimensions of biological, social and psychological aging contribute to some kinds of conservatism. For instance, with the assumption of family responsibilities, a diffuse liberalism-humanitarianism is likely to be overshadowed by concern for specific others. Or, aging persons may become more conservative in the sense that their attitudes and values become more resistant to change, because each subsequent experience is a smaller proportion of the total background of experiences. Empirical evidence on the topic is not definitive; moreover, in view of intransigent methodological problems which plague the study of aging effects, the evidence may never be definitive. However, cohort analysis of United States survey sample data reveals that in recent years persons aging beyond young adulthood and beyond middle age have tended to become more liberal in many respects, in conformity with general societal trends. However, these people have tended to become more conservative in a relative sense since their liberalization has not kept pace with changes in the total adult population. Although the evidence suggests that attitudes probably become somewhat less susceptible to change as people grow older, there is scant evidence for any other contribution of aging to conservatism.

Norval D. Glenn is Professor of Sociology at the University of Texas at Austin. Formerly on the faculties of Miami University and the University of Illinois at Urbana, he is co-author of Transformation of the Negro American and is author of journal articles in the fields of racial and ethnic minorities, social stratification, urban sociology, political sociology, aging and the life cycle and the sociology of science. He is on the editorial boards of the American Sociological Review, the Public Opinion Quarterly and the Social Science Quarterly.

THE belief that people tend to become more conservative as they grow older is part of the conventional wisdom. This assumption is prevalent among social scientists, as well as the lay public. Indeed, there seem to be few other generalizations about human behavior and thought processes on which there is such widespread agreement.

In recent years, however, some students of aging and the life cycle have challenged the aging-conservatism thesis or have pointed out that it may not be valid without major qualifications. Even if older people as a whole are more conservative than younger people, it does not necessarily follow that the aging process accounts for the difference. The older people's crucial formative experiences were different and occurred when the society was different in many ways from the society in which the younger people's basic values and personality characteristics were formed. Therefore, the older adults were not necessarily less conservative when they were young adults than they are now. Even if the older adults had become more conservative on the average as they grew older, aging would not necessarily have been the cause. Rather, general social and cultural changes in the society—period influences—could have brought about the change.

Another difficulty with the aging-conservatism thesis is the variation in definitions of conservatism used by persons who set forth the thesis. Conservatism may be defined in terms of a system of values and beliefs about the nature of reality, or it may be defined simply as resistance to change, reluctance to take risks, cognitive rigidity or some similar characteristic. Obvi-

ously, aging may lead to conservatism in one of these senses, but not in the others. Unfortunately, statements about aging and conservatism often leave the latter term undefined.

The term aging is also somewhat ambiguous. In its most elementary sense aging is simply passage of time after birth, but psychological effects are rarely attributed to the passage of time per se. Rather, biological and social changes which tend to accompany chronological aging are believed to exert influence toward conservatism. For both theoretical and practical reasons it is important to know which of these changes, if any, tend to make people conservative. Clearly, ambiguity of both aging and conservatism makes the simple form of the aging-conservatism thesis too vague and imprecise for social scientific discourse.

Therefore, I must delineate several dimensions and discuss several meanings of the concepts aging and conservatism before I discuss the theoretical bases of the aging-conservatism thesis and the empirical evidence relating to it. Since research on this topic is in its infancy and is faced with some unusually obstinate methodological problems, I can provide little in the way of scientific truth to replace the conventional wisdom. However, I hope to encourage the reader to develop a more skeptical, analytic and sophisticated manner of thinking about aging and conservatism.

DIMENSIONS OF AGING

When the term aging is used without a modifier, the referent is usually chronological aging or simply the passage of time after birth. As chronological aging occurs, a predictable sequence of biological changes occurs in the organism. However, the rate of biological aging varies among individuals, presumably for both environmental and hereditary reasons. Another process imperfectly correlated with chronological aging is social aging, the characteristic sequence of changes in status and roles during the lifespan—or, to translate from the jargon, the relationships of the individual to others and the behavior the others expect of him or her tend to change in a predictable and characteristic fashion as chronological aging occurs. Social aging is similar to biological aging in that its rate varies among individuals; it differs in that its sequence of changes varies considerably among societies and somewhat among subcultures within a society.

A crucial aspect of social aging is passage through the stages of the life cycle. The term life cycle has somewhat different meanings to different authors, but it is usually conceived of as a series of stages demarcated by a number of significant life events, starting with birth and including entry into school, completion of formal education, entry into the labor force, marriage, birth of first child, exit of last child from the household, retirement and, finally, death. According to one school of thought, conservatism results from passage into the middle or later stages of the life cycle.

Psychological aging entails the characteristic sequence of changes in personality—including attitudes, values and behavioral tendencies —associated with chronological aging. This process is presumably to a large extent a consequence of biological and social aging. Therefore, its rate varies a great

deal among individuals, and its sequence of changes varies somewhat among societies. If persons typically become more conservative as they grow older, that change is an aspect of psychological aging. Of course, a shift to conservatism could be an aspect of psychological aging in some, but not in other societies, or it could occur only in certain social and demographic categories within a society.

The concept of aging can be decomposed further, because biological, social and psychological aging consist of several dimensions which are not perfectly correlated. That is, each stage of each kind of aging consists of several changes which charactistically occur together, but do not always do so. For instance, a person who is prematurely gray-haired may retain the physical vigor characteristic of young adulthood; or, a man may first become a father in his late fifties, thus combining a "young adult" role with roles characteristic of late middle age.

DIMENSIONS AND CONCEPTIONS OF CONSERVATISM

One of the simplest and most prevalent definitions of a conservative is that he or she is a person who resists or opposes change. Conservatism in this sense has many dimensions; opposition to change may not be general, but may be specific to certain kinds of change. The conservative in this sense may be an active opponent of change or may simply have values, attitudes and beliefs which resist influences for change affecting many other people in the society. Significantly, most other conceptions of conservatism in some way involve change or attitudes toward change.

For instance, if conservatism is defined in terms of attitudes other than those toward change, those attitudes which are becoming—or those which in the long run have become—less prevalent may be considered conservative; in such a case attitudes which are becoming more prevalent are considered liberal. That is, conservatism and liberalism in this sense are defined by the direction of long term change. Which specific attitudes are considered conservative is relative to time and place; yesterday's liberalism will tend to be today's conservatism. This conception of conservatism does not presuppose a high degree of consistency among different conservative attitudes or view conservation as a well-integrated ideology.

Other definitions of the attitudinal content of conservatism are not relative to time and place. The writings of Edmund Burke may be used as the model for conservative political philosophy, for instance, and Burke's conception of conservatism may be used to analyze political thought in any society at any time. Constant, nonrelative definitions of the attitudinal content of conservatism vary considerably, but they often include a high valuation of social order; a resistance to change which is perceived as a threat to order; emphasis on authority and obedience; and a generally restrictive, rather than permissive and tolerant, attitude toward human behavior. Conservatism in this sense is different from a general resistance to change, because change in a restrictive direction is favored.

Conservatism is sometimes viewed as an antiegalitarian philosophy or as resistance to change which would benefit disadvantaged segments of the population. Thus, for persons not disadvantaged, this conservative-liberal distinction is essentially the distinction between self-interestedness and humanitarianism. Conservatives in this sense do not consistently emphasize restrictiveness more than liberals, since they tend to oppose government regulation of business. A related distinction is between realism and idealism, in the popular rather than philosophical sense—that is, liberals tend to believe in the attainability of egalitarian ideals, whereas conservatives tend to believe that human nature and the exigencies of human existence inevitably lead to a great deal of inequality and human suffering.

Another important conception of conservatism is that it is unwillingness to take risks. The cautiousness may be restricted to one's personal decisions and behavior or it may be generalized to include advocacy of caution on the part of collectivities of which he or she is a member.

Each of these conceptions of conservatism involves many dimensions. For instance, if the content of conservative attitudes is defined by the direction of long term change, conservatism has as many dimensions as there are attitudes on which there has been change. If conservatism is defined in terms of restrictiveness, there are different dimensions according to the kinds of people and the kinds of behavior to which the restrictiveness applies.

SOME THEORETICAL CONSIDERATIONS

There are theoretical reasons to believe that several of the dimensions of aging may lead to conservatism in one sense or another. For instance, such aspects of biological aging as a decline in energy and loss of brain tissue could be linked directly or indirectly to cautiousness, attitudinal rigidity and a tendency to resist change. Adapting to change requires at least some expenditure of energy; furthermore, it requires a certain degree of cognitive flexibility for which the neural basis may be insufficient at an advanced stage of biological aging.

Some biologically based loss of flexibility and adaptability as the person reaches senescence and approaches death is hardly in doubt, but my main concern here is with changes which occur from adolescence and young adulthood through middle age and the stages of advanced maturity short of senescence. At these stages of aging the influence of biological aging on personality is likely to be overshadowed by the influence of social aging.

For instance, passage from the earlier to the middle stages of the life cycle, via marriage and childbearing, may account for a tendency for persons to shift away from liberalism-humanitarianism. Although individuals vary along a general dimension from altruism to self-centeredness, they may vary even more in the focus of their altruistic concerns, and the latter variation may be associated with stages of the life cycle. Any altruistic impulses of the unmarried adolescent or young adult are likely to be rather diffuse, being directed perhaps to minorities or to disadvantaged people in general. With the assumption of family responsibilities, however, any general humanitarianism is likely to be overshadowed by concern for specific others. If one's family is not among the disadvantaged, the interests of one's family and of disadvantaged persons will be to some extent competing, and if one must choose between these competing interests, he or she is likely to favor the interests of the family.

If, as is typical for males in the United States, a person experiences upward mobility in income and occupational prestige during young adulthood, his self-interest becomes more opposed to egalitarian ideals. Therefore, it is reasonable to expect some weakening in the average level of liberalism-egalitarianism from young adulthood to middle age. However, any antiegalitarian effect of the upward mobility of young adults may not be simple, direct and uniform. For instance, the extent to which persons attain their expected status may be more important than the amount of mobility; moreover, anticipation of upward mobility may often be as destructive of egalitarianism as the mobility itself.

The mere accumulation of experiences may make the individual more conservative in the sense of being less susceptible to changes in attitudes, beliefs and similar elements of personality. To illustrate how this change may occur, let us assume an oversimplified model of attitudinal development whereby one's attitude on a controversial issue is determined by the mean of all of the pro and con stimuli to which the person has been exposed. The second or third stimulus may change the mean considerably, but the twentieth or the fiftieth can have relatively little effect. In fact, attitudes do not develop in such a simple fashion. Yet, there may be a tendency for the effects of stimuli to diminish with the number of preceding relevant stimuli. If the number and intensity of stimuli and experiences do not vary appreciably from one year to another, the effect of a year of living on one's attitudes may be roughly a function of the proportion of the time the person has lived which that year constitutes. If so, each subsequent year will tend to have somewhat less effect than the year before.

There may be a tendency for attitudes to stabilize after young adulthood because social and geographic mobility become less frequent; thus, the changes in social influences associated with mobility occur less often. Therefore, if the attitudes of middle-aged and older people typically change less during any given period of time than the attitudes of young adults, the reason may be that the former are less exposed to influences for change, not that they respond less to the influences to which they are exposed.

Some conservatives believe that experience tends to lead to more accurate views of human nature and society and, hence, to acceptance of conservative tenets. For instance, if—as one kind of conservatism would have it—people are by nature evil and must be restrained by law and other social institutions, then accumulative exposure to unrestrained human nature should tend to convert one to conservatism. Of course, only a conservative is likely to believe that any conservatism associated with aging is simply an aspect of wisdom born of experience.

There are also theoretical reasons to believe that certain dimensions of aging may at some stages exert influences against one or more of the forms of conservatism. For instance, in industrial societies the more advanced stages of aging typically entail sharp losses in affluence, authority and prestige; therefore, it is in the interests of most old people to work for a more equitable distribution of rewards and resources. Of course, old people may advocate change for the benefit of themselves, but remain conservative in regard to broader questions of distributive justice. Furthermore, such factors as identification with younger relatives and increased ideological rigidity may prevent widespread liberalization which might have otherwise resulted from downward mobility in old age.

Although childbearing may at first be an influence against liberalism-humanitarianism, as the children grow older they may tend to influence their parents in a liberal direction. Conservative or moderate parents with liberal offspring can lessen intergenerational conflict and dissonance within the family by accepting some of the liberal values; or also, they may simply find their children's liberal arguments persuasive. Grandchildren may also be agents for resocialization in a liberal direction.

THE EMPIRICAL EVIDENCE

Regardless of which of the more common definitions of conservatism is used, the preponderance of evidence from contemporary Western societies shows that at any point in time older people as a whole are more conservative than young adults. For instance, national survey data collected in the United States during the past twenty years rather consistently show elderly people as a whole to be more conservative than middle-aged people and the latter to be more conservative than young adults. Among the conservative characteristics positively associated with age are cautiousness, restrictive standards of sexual behavior, opposition to school desegregation, opposition to interracial and interreligious marriage, advocacy of harsher treatment of criminals, Republican party identification and voting for conservative candidates for public office.[1] If conservatism is defined in terms of the direction of long term change, older people are more conservative on the average than younger adults on virtually all dimensions covered by the data, even though some of the differences are not large.[2]

The association of conservatism with chronological age is important in itself, but it provides no convincing evidence on the effects of the biological, social and psychological aging processes. As I point out above, present young adults may differ from present older adults because their formative experiences were different. For instance, older people have less formal education on the average, and many dimensions of conservatism vary inversely with amount of education. Therefore, in some respects older people may be more conservative only because they have less education. If conservatism is defined by the direction of long term change, one must take into consideration the fact that

older people grew up in a society more conservative by present standards than the society in which young adults received their early socialization.

Since the people who are born during a given period of time and who experience each stage of chronological aging together are called a birth cohort, attributing the variation in conservatism by age to variation in formative experiences is called the cohort interpretation, as contrasted with the aging interpretation. Cross-sectional data— for one point in time—can be, and have been, analyzed to throw light on the relative credibility of the two interpretations. However, such evidence can never be the basis for a definitive choice between the two.

For instance, if it can be shown that older and younger adults with the same amount of education differ little or not at all in conservatism, the cohort interpretation gains credence. Yet, the relationship between age and conservatism might reappear if some variable in addition to education were held constant. Furthermore, years of schooling are not strictly comparable from one birth cohort to another, since both the content of education and the selective processes in the educational system have varied through time—and most kinds of formative experiences can be measured and statistically controlled even less precisely than amount of education.

In view of the inadequacy of cross-sectional data, there would seem to be a need to see how people have changed as they have grown older. Although longitudinal data are much rarer than cross-sectional data, a few panel studies have measured the attitudes of the

---

1. See, Matilda White Riley and Anne Foner, *Aging and Society: An Inventory of Research Findings*, vol. 1 (New York: Russell Sage Foundation, 1968); also, recent issues of the *Gallup Opinion Index*.

2. This statement is based on findings from a study of aging and conservatism I recently completed with a grant from the National Science Foundation.

same individuals at two or more widely separated points in time. For instance, panel studies have investigated changes in the attitudes of college graduates within a few years of graduation.[3] These studies have generally found little or no change in a conservative direction; however, since the society as a whole moved in a liberal direction during the periods covered, the data do not prove that an aging influence in a conservative direction was not offset by general societal influences—period influences—in a liberal direction. It is apparent, then, that longitudinal data from a panel study are not necessarily superior to cross-sectional data for the purpose of discerning the effects of aging. Whereas cross-sectional data confound aging effects with cohort effects, longitudinal data confound aging effects with period effects.[4]

Some of the most fruitful research on the effects of aging has utilized a technique, called cohort analysis, in which cross-sectional and longitudinal data are examined simultaneously. Sets of cross-sectional data are juxtaposed so that birth cohorts can be traced as they grow older. For instance, one ten-year birth cohort can be traced over a twenty-year period by looking at the age ranges of 30 to 39, 40 to 49 and 50 to 59 in cross-sectional data for 1950, 1960 and 1970. If the different sets of data contain comparable measures of some dimension of conservatism, one can tell whether or not the cohort as a whole became more conservative as it grew older.[5] If the adult population as a whole remained stable from 1950 to 1970 or if it became more liberal, then any trend toward conservatism in an aging cohort is rather clearly an aging effect. If, however, the trends in the aging cohort and in the total population are in the same direction, the evidence concerning aging effects is ambiguous.[6]

3. For instance, see, Andrew M. Greeley and Joe L. Spaeth, "Political Change Among College Alumni," *Sociology of Education* 43 (1970), pp. 106–113.

4. For a lucid treatment of the research problems resulting from the confounding of these effects, see, K. O. Mason, W. M. Mason, H. H. Winsborough and W. K. Poole, "Some Methodological Issues in Cohort Analysis of Archival Data," *American Sociological Review* 38 (1973), pp. 242–258. The authors introduce a method for separating aging, period and cohort effects which is useful for certain special cases, but is not a general solution to the problem posed by the confounding of the different kinds of effects. The problem encountered here is an example of the identification problem, which arises when one variable in an analysis is a perfect function of two other variables. In this case, age is a perfect function of period and cohort. Since any aging effect will appear in a statistical analysis as an interaction between period and cohort, tests for statistical interaction have been proposed for detecting aging effects. Although a lack of interaction is evidence against an aging effect, not all interactions between period and cohort should be considered aging ef-

fects. As I point out below, differences in the formative experiences as well as in the ages of cohorts may lead them to react differently to period influences.

5. One must make sure, of course, that measured change in an aging cohort is not a result of changes in the composition of the cohort rather than of changes among the surviving cohort members. Since differential mortality changes somewhat the sex and educational composition of aging cohorts, it is advisable to standardize the different sets of data for each cohort to one sex and one educational distribution. See, Norval D. Glenn and Richard E. Zody, "Cohort Analysis With National Survey Data," *Gerontologist* 10 (1970), pp. 233–240.

6. As I have pointed out elsewhere— Norval D. Glenn and Ted Hefner, "Further Evidence on Aging and Party Identification," *Public Opinion Quarterly* 36 (1972) pp. 31–47—use of trends in the total adult population as estimates of period

The evidence is usually ambiguous. I know of no cohort analysis of attitudinal data in which aging cohorts consistently moved counter the trend in the total adult population. I know of only one analysis in which aging cohorts tended to become more conservative while the total adult population remained stable. More typically, aging cohorts—including those aging into their sixties and seventies—follow societal trends, although usually the younger cohorts change more than the older ones.[7]

A more or less typical pattern of change is shown in table 1. These data on attitudes toward Red China illustrate how the positive relationship between age and conservatism may typically come about. In 1954 the cohorts were almost uniformly negative toward Red China. As attitudes generally became more favorable, the younger cohorts changed more than the older ones, thus producing the negative relationship between age and favorable attitudes shown for 1964. I tend to believe that this typical pattern of

influences has a major deficiency: namely, the component of the trends due to mortality does not reflect any influences likely to impinge on aging individuals. However, mortality effects are usually small and can be separated from other components of trends in the total adult population.

7. This generalization is based on my own recent research and on data reported by Stephan J. Cutler and Robert L. Kaufman, "Cohort Changes in Political Attitudes," (Paper presented at the Annual Meetings of Gerontological Society in Miami Beach, Florida, 1973), and by William Evan, "Cohort Analysis of Attitude Data," in *Computer Methods in the Analysis of Large-Scale Social Systems*, ed. James M. Beshers (Cambridge, Mass: Joint Center for Urban Studies of the Massachusetts Institute of Technology and Harvard University, 1965). The one exception is a cohort analysis of political self identifications reported by Evan.

TABLE 1

PERCENTAGE OF PERSONS WHO SAID THEY APPROVED OF ADMISSION OF RED CHINA TO UNITED NATIONS, BY BIRTH COHORT, 1954 AND 1964

DATE OF BIRTH	1954	1964	CHANGE
1925–1934	7.3	21.2	+13.9
1915–1924	8.4	18.8	+10.4
1905–1914	5.9	14.8	+ 8.9
1895–1904	6.1	9.4	+ 3.3
1885–1894	5.0	9.1	+ 4.1

SOURCE: Gallup Surveys of the United States population. The raw data were obtained from the Roper Public Opinion Research Center, Williamstown, Massachusetts.

NOTE: The 1954 percentages are standardized to the sex and educational distributions shown by the 1964 data.

change in aging cohorts reflects the tendency for attitudes to become less responsive to influences for change as persons grow older.

There are, however, two alternative explanations. It is possible that aging exerts some influence against liberalism-permissiveness and/or liberalism-egalitarianism, but that the strength of this influence in recent years has not been strong enough to offset completely the period influences in the opposite direction. So long as period influences are in a liberal direction, the empirical consequences of an aging influence toward attitudinal rigidity and of a relatively weak aging influence toward conservative values would be identical. In such a case no technique of data analysis can distinguish one kind of effect from the other. However, during a period of conservative reaction a rigidity influence would lead older people to change less than younger people, whereas an influence toward conservative values would lead older people to change more than younger ones. Few periods of conservative reaction have been covered by cohort analyses, but the rather tenuous evidence available suggests that older cohorts tend to change less than younger ones regardless of the direction of change.

One may also give a cohort, rather than an aging, interpretation of the tendency of older cohorts to change less than younger ones—that is, the older cohorts may change less not because they are older, but because their early socialization left more deeply ingrained values. The younger cohorts grew up in a period of very rapid change, and perhaps they were socialized to greater attitudinal flexibility; to a tentative, rather than a firm, adherence to attitudes and beliefs. If so, present young cohorts will continue to be very responsive to influences for change as they grow older. This interpretation would be supported if it could be shown that aging cohorts do not become less responsive to influences for change of a given strength, but no one has devised a means for precisely measuring the strength of influences for change at different times.

So far, it may seem to the reader that little is known about aging and conservatism and that little is knowable, in view of the methodological problems which plague research on this topic. However, I should not emphasize areas of ignorance and ambiguity to the exclusion of the firm knowledge which has been gained. For instance, cohort analysis of United States survey sample data gathered during the past thirty years makes clear two basic and important facts: (1) according to almost any constant definition of conservatism, people have typically become less, rather than more, conservative as they

have grown older, in conformity with general societal trends. For instance, people who are now in their fifties and sixties are as a whole distinctly more permissive and egalitarian than they were when they were in their thirties and forties. Therefore, the notion that people develop a high degree of attitudinal rigidity in early and middle adulthood must be rejected. (2) Cohorts who have aged into and beyond middle age during the past three decades have become more conservative in a relative sense— —that is, relative to the total adult population and probably relative to prevailing definitions of conservatism and liberalism. Whereas aging cohorts have changed in the same direction as the total adult population, those aging beyond young adulthood have generally changed less than the total population. Perhaps this increase in the relative conservatism of aging persons explains why one study shows an increase in conservative self identifications in aging cohorts, but not in the total population.[8] Paradoxically, people may become more likely to consider themselves conservative and to be considered conservative by others while, according to a constant definition of conservatism, they become less conservative.

Much of our present ignorance about aging and conservatism grows out of the recency of scientific interest in the topic, not out of intransigent methodological problems. For instance, all of the research I have discussed has used only data on chronological age and has not attempted to separate empirically the effects of biological, social and psychological aging. However, it would be relatively

8. Evan, "Cohort Analysis."

easy to incorporate measures of life cycle stage into cross-sectional, cohort and panel studies. Data on dimensions of biological aging have been collected in several panel studies of very old people and could be used in studies of younger people.

In conclusion, the topic of aging and conservatism is a virgin research area in which much remains to be learned. We have only recently begun to ask sophisticated questions about the topic and to recognize the methodological difficulties which stand between us and definitive evidence. We may never reach a state of certainty concerning all of the causal relations among the various dimensions of aging and conservatism, but we should move substantially toward that elusive goal in the next few years.

Age Groups in American Society and the Rise of the Young-Old

By BERNICE L. NEUGARTEN

ABSTRACT: The age distributions of industrialized societies are rapidly changing, thereby altering the traditional relations between age groups. Some observers think ageism is increasing in the United States; others, that it is decreasing. In either case, stereotypes of old age are now changing with the rise of the young-old—that is, the age group 55 to 75, who constitute 15 percent of the population—who are relatively healthy, relatively affluent, relatively free from traditional responsibilities of work and family and who are increasingly well educated and politically active. This group will develop a variety of new needs with regard to meaningful use of time and for maximizing the opportunities for both self-enhancement and community participation. The young-old have enormous potential as agents of social change in creating an age-irrelevant society and in thus improving the relations between age groups.

Bernice L. Neugarten has been Professor of Human Development at the University of Chicago since 1964, Chairman of the Committee on Human Development from 1969 to 1973 and Director of the Graduate Training Program in Adult Development and Aging since 1958. She is a former President of the Gerontological Society, consultant to the National Institute of Child Health and Human Development and is now a member of the Council of Representatives of the American Psychological Association. She was a member of the Technical Committee on Research and Demonstration for the 1971 White House Conference on Aging and in 1972–1973 was a member of the Technical Committee on Aging Research of the Department of Health, Education and Welfare. In 1971 she received the Kleemeier Award from the Gerontological Society for outstanding contributions to research on aging and in 1973 received a similar award from the Ethel Percy Andrus Gerontology Center, University of Southern California. She has coauthored or edited seven books and has written more than seventy research papers, monographs and review articles, most of them dealing with adult development, middle age and aging and the relations between age groups. Among the books are Society and Education, Personality in Middle and Late Life, Middle Age and Aging, Adjustment to Retirement *and* Social Status in the City. *She has been an Associate Editor of* Human Development *and of the* Journal of Gerontology.

OURS is a society characterized by longevity. While the natural limits of the human life span have probably not changed since ancient times, an ever increasing number of persons now live to age 80 or 90, thus approaching what appears to be the natural, probably genetically fixed limit. Put in different words, advances in biomedical science and other social, political and economic changes have resulted in a redistribution of deaths so that deaths now occur much less frequently at the beginnning of the life span—in infancy and childhood—and more frequently at the end—in old age. Continued medical advances are expected to add only a few more years to average life expectancy, and most biologists—a few to the contrary notwithstanding—believe that no major scientific breakthrough or anti-aging treatment is likely to appear within the next two decades to produce a dramatic extension of the life span. Nevertheless, because more people live to old age, the numbers of older persons in the United States will continue to rise sharply. Future numbers cannot be translated directly into future proportions, because future birth rates—and, therefore, the future total population—are uncertain; however, the numbers of older people can be accurately predicted because these persons are already born. At present, 20 million persons are aged 65 and over; the number will grow to 28 million by 1990 and to 40 million by 2020; the pulse, or swell, in numbers will be due to the aging of large cohorts of people who are presently young.

The age distribution of a population is both the result and the cause of pervasive changes in economic, political and other aspects of social organization. Some of the implications become obvious enough when a developing nation in Asia, Latin America or Africa is compared with an economically developed society such as our own. In the former, during the period 1965 to 1970, roughly 41 percent of a national population was under age 15 and only 3 percent was over age 65. By contrast, in the developed nation the parallel figures were 27 percent under 15 and 10 percent over 65.[1]

RELATIONS AMONG AGE GROUPS

The relative numbers of young, middle-aged and old affect every aspect of life, particularly the relations among age groups. In most societies in most periods of history an equilibrium becomes established whereby all age groups receive an appropriate share of goods and services and an appropriate place for their different world views. Unusual circumstances sometimes arise, however, in which relations among age groups become strained and customary modes of accommodation are no longer regarded as equitable.

For instance, in some countries the appearance of large numbers of older persons has been relatively sudden—as in United States within the past fifty years—and dislocations have occurred because these societies have been unprepared— that is, unprepared by prevailing value systems which determine human priorities—to meet the newly emerging needs. In the United States a sizable proportion of older people have suffered from

1. P. M. Hauser, "Extension of Life: Demographic Considerations" (Paper presented at the Twenty-Fifth Annual Conference on Aging, Institute of Gerontology, University of Michigan, Ann Arbor, Michigan, 12 September 1972).

inadequate income, poor housing and a host of other social and economic ills; thus, they have constituted a disproportionately disadvantaged group. A large minority of needy aged grew up who created acute problems in the fields of social and medical welfare. Although our Social Security program was established in the late 1930s it is only within the last decade that a wide range of remedial and palliative public and private programs have been initiated.

It is perhaps equally cogent that fluctuations in birth rates in the United States have also led to an enormous population pulse of young persons who are presently 15 to 25. With the growth of technology and an economy which provides insufficient work opportunities, and with a system of secondary and higher education which fails to provide meaningful experience for a growing minority of young people—particularly those from low occupational levels—the problems with regard to the young may be as serious as those with regard to the old.

IS AGEISM INCREASING OR DECREASING?

Some observers believe that not only inequities, but conflicts, between age groups are increasing in the direction of both young and old; that a new age divisiveness is appearing; and that new antagonisms, which can be called ageism, are growing. Some have said that the Western world is entering a period of social change not unlike earlier eras marked by struggles for political and economic rights; however, the present struggle is for age rights, and it is being joined not only by the young, but also by the old who might otherwise become its victims. Some

decry the trend toward age segregation, pointing to the high school and college as age ghettoes for the young and to age-segregated residential areas—whether new retirement communities or deteriorated neighborhoods in the inner city where the old are left behind—as age ghettoes for the old. Just as anger toward the young was on the rise in the 1960s, with the attention drawn to the youthful law offender, the student activist and the hippie, so these observers believe that anger toward the old may rise in the 1970s as a growing proportion of power positions in the judiciary, legislative, business and professional arenas are occupied by older people; as the number of retirees increases and Social Security taxes rise; and as the economic burden is perceived—rightly or wrongly—as falling more and more upon the middle-aged taxpayer.

Other observers take a more optimistic view. They point to new attempts to integrate the young into the adult society—as witnessed by the lowering of the voting age from 21 to 18; to the greater permissiveness toward the new life styles of the young; to the deference given to their technical expertise. In the other direction, they point to the fact that while a substantial minority of older persons has been economically disadvantaged, there has been a regular rise in overall purchasing power in the hands of older people; that in the past five years Social Security payments have increased nearly 70 percent—although inflation has offset much of this gain; and that the proportion of older persons who are poor has dropped dramatically. In this view age-segregated communities, at least for that large majority of older persons who are not poor, are a sign of the greater permissiveness toward the new life styles of the old, for older persons move into these communities by choice and are therefore responding to the new options being offered them. In some segments of American society older people are becoming a visible and contented leisure class, helped along by a change in national values from instrumentality to expressivity and from a work ethic to a leisure ethic.

Regardless of the special problems of the young and the question of whether ageism is waxing or waning, it is true that in the United States—as in other industrialized societies—both young and old must adapt to new phenomena resulting from added longevity. Moreover, all members of society must adapt to multigenerational families, retirement and trends toward gerontocracy. From this perspective, increased numbers of older persons—whether they are needy or affluent—poses the problem of major social readjustments, and their presence leads to the need for new alignments among all age groups.

CHANGING PERCEPTIONS OF THE LIFE CYCLE

The relations among age groups are also influenced by changing perceptions of the life cycle and the periods of life. Age groups have become increasingly differentiated over time. For instance, it was not until the seventeenth and eighteenth centuries, with industrialization, the appearance of a middle class and formal educational institutions, that childhood became a discernible period of life with its special needs and characteristics.[2] The concept of adolescence can be

2. P. Aries, *Centuries of Childhood* (New York: Vintage Books, 1962).

viewed as an invention of the twentieth century. Now, a case is being made for a new stage called youth; this stage has appeared only in the last few decades as the transition from childhood to adulthood has been increasingly prolonged, resulting in a free-choice period between high school and first job or marriage for a growing number of young persons.[3]

Also, in the past few decades middle age has become a newly delineated stage in the life cycle, due not only to increased longevity and improved health, but also to the historically changing rhythm of events in the family cycle. Since the turn of the century marriage and parenthood occur earlier; children—whose births are spaced closer together —grow up and leave the home earlier. Thus, before retirement there is now a period, which begins around 40, when most parents consider themselves to be middle aged. The perception is widely shared that persons no longer move abruptly from adulthood—the period of full commitment to work and family responsibilities—into old age, but that they go, instead, through a relatively long interval during which family responsibilities are diminished, work continues, even though specific work roles may change—for example, women reentering the labor market in their 40s and 50s—and physical vigor remains high.

THE YOUNG-OLD

It seems likely that we are presently undergoing still another

3. *Youth: Transition to Adulthood*, Report of a panel of the President's Social Science Advisory Committee, J. S. Coleman, Chairman (Washington, D.C.: U.S. Government Printing Office, 1974).

changing perception of the life cycle and that still another meaningful division is appearing: namely, a division between the young-old and the old-old. Although chronological age is not a satisfactory marker, it is nevertheless an indispensable one. So, at the risk of oversimplification, the young-old come from the group composed of those who are approximately 55 to 75—as distingushed from the old-old, who are 75 and over.

There is undoubtedly overlap between the middle aged and the young-old. Indeed, in terms of self-perceptions, many persons call themselves middle aged until their 70s, thereby expressing a sense of continued youthfulness and/or a denial of aging. However, putting aside self-perceptions—which tend, at best, to be inconsistent from one group to another—the young-old are distinguishable primarily by the fact of retirement. Granted that the use of a single life event as the criterion is arbitrary, retirement is nevertheless a meaningful marker with regard to the young-old, just as the departure of children from the home is a useful marker with regard to middle age.

This 55 to 75 grouping is not one to which we have been accustomed. Ever since the beginning of our Social Security system, we have used age 65, not age 55, as the economic—then, as the social and psychological—marker of old age. For various other historical reasons a set of stereotypes have grown up about old age which are based primarily upon the old-old. Moreover, although the stereotypes of older persons as sick, poor, enfeebled, isolated and desolated have been greatly overdrawn even for the old-old, they have become uncritically attached to the whole group

over 65. These stereotypes are only now beginning to yield to reality.

For one thing, 65 as a marker of economic old age is becoming less consistent. While eligibility for Social Security benefits has only recently been set at 62, by 1973 the number of retirees drawing Social Security benefits who are 62 to 64 and who are not disabled had already grown to over 1.5 million. In some occupational groups eligibility for pensions is determined not by chronological age, but by the number of years of service. It is not unimportant also that the wide array of federally supported services provided through the Older Americans Act go to persons aged 60 and over rather than 65 and over.

Age 55 is beginning to be a meaningful lower age limit for the young-old because of the lowering age of retirement. Many workers are now voluntarily retiring just as soon as they think they can live comfortably on their retirement incomes —for examples, auto workers who exercise their option to retire at 55. In other industries where overall employment is declining, the downward trend in age of retirement is dramatic—whether most retirements are voluntary or involuntary. The 1970 census showed that a significant drop in the proportion of all men in the labor force occurs by age 55, when 81 percent of 55- to 64-year-olds are in the labor force, as compared to 92 percent of the next younger age group.

Whether this trend toward earlier retirement will continue in the future depends upon a large number of other factors: rates of economic and technological growth, the number of young workers, the number of women workers, increases in part-time work opportunities and a possible share-the-work movement.

Most observers predict, however, that the downward trend will continue over the next two or three decades.[4] By and large, then, the young-old will increasingly become a retired group.

It is already a relatively healthy group. While the data have not been aggregated in the appropriate age categories, table 1 shows that about 15 percent of 45- to 64-year-olds need to limit their major activities because of health, while under 40 percent of all those 65 and over must do so. If the young-old group were differentiated in these data, the proportion with health limitations would probably be between 20 and 25 percent.

OTHER CHARACTERISTICS OF THE YOUNG-OLD

Because of the enormous diversity of life styles among the young-old, meaningful differences are obscured in aggregated data of the type shown in table 1. Nevertheless, the gross characteristics of this age group are worth noting.

At present the young-old group numbers roughly 31 million and constitutes more than 15 percent of the total population—as compared with the old-old, who constitute less than 4 percent. Their proportion is expected to remain about the same over the next three decades—depending, of course, upon birth rates and total size of population.

Because mortality rates for women are lower, women outnumber men by a sizable proportion; this imbalance is expected to grow even larger. Nevertheless, because most men marry women somewhat younger

than themselves, the young-old as a total group are more like their younger, than their older, counterparts with regard to marital status and family relations. About 80 percent of the young-old men and well over half the women were married in 1970 and living with their spouses. The rates of widowhood are, of course, very different for the two sexes; about 7 percent of the men, but over 30 percent of the women, are widowed. By far the common pattern is husband-wife families living in their own household—some 70 percent owning their own homes—and only a very small number moving from one house to another within a five-year interval. Of married men living with their wives, 95 percent are heads of their households. In other words, very few such couples live in households where a child or a relative is the head of the household.

The young-old see their children frequently, often living near to at least one child. They expect that when they grow to advanced old age and can no longer manage for themselves their children will come to their aid—not financially, for the government is looked to as the expected source of financial and medical assistance, but emotionally. As a number of studies have shown, assistance and services are being exchanged across generational lines, and affectional ties are strong. Thus, the family continues to be an important part of daily life.

It is noteworthy that a large proportion of young-old have a living parent. The estimate is that one of every three 60-year-olds had a living parent in 1972; furthermore, this proportion will increase, because the numbers of old-old are growing faster than the numbers of young-old. Although the care of an aged parent poses problems, the fact that a

4. A. J. Jaffe, "Has the Retreat from the Labor Force Halted? A Note on Retirement of Men, 1930–1970," *Industrial Gerontology* (Spring 1971), pp. 1–12.

TABLE 1

CHARACTERISTICS OF THE YOUNG-OLD AND THE OLD-OLD, 1970

CHARACTERISTICS	YOUNG-OLD		OLD-OLD
	55 TO 64	65 TO 74	75 AND OVER
Numbers: Total (millions)	19	12	8
men	9	5	3
women	10	7	5
percent total population	9	6	4
percent increase 1960–1970	19	15	43
Projections, 2000: Total	22.5	16	12.5
men	10.5	7	4.5
women	12	9	8
percent total population*	9	7	5
percent increase 1970–2000	21	31	64
Marital status (%)			
men: married, wife present	82	75	56
widowed	4	11	28
women: married, husband present	64	44	19
widowed	20	42	68
Living arrangements (%)			
men: heads of household†	95	93	86
in institutions	1	2	7
women: heads of household§	27	42	51
in institutions	1	2	11
same house as in 1965	72	73	71
moved, same county	16	15	16
In labor force (%)			
men	81	32	12
women	42	14	5
Median income			
All white families (age of head)	$10,680‡	$5,260§	
only husband worked	9,150	5,740	
husband and wife worked	13,400	9,730	
Percent who were poor			
1967	—	29.6§	
1971	11.6	21.6	
1972	10.8	18.6¶	
Median years schooling completed			
men	10.2	8.7	8.3
women	10.8	9.0	8.6
projected, 1990 (M + F)	12.3	11.9§	

TABLE 1 (*Continued*)

CHARACTERISTICS	YOUNG-OLD		OLD-OLD
	55 TO 64	65 TO 74	75 AND OVER
Health status (%)			
limitation or inability to carry on major activity:			
men	17[II]		43§
women	14[II]		35
Political behavior			
highest of all age groups on overall participation	X#		
highest of all age groups on voting			X§**

* Based on Series E census projections; birth-rate, 2.1. This is higher than the actual birth-rates of the past two years.

† Head of family or primary individual.

‡ The comparable figure for 45 to 54-year-olds is $12,580.

§ Data refer to total group 65 and over.

¶ The percent poor has dropped further since 1972, due to the 20 percent increase in Social Security benefits in 1973, the 11 percent cost-of-living increase in Social Security in 1974, and the Supplemental Security Income system in 1974 which provides minimum incomes for those aged 65 and over.

‖ Data refer to total group 45 to 64.

For the age group 51 to 65; data are corrected for income and education. See, S. Verba and N. H. Nie, *Participation in America* (New York: Harper and Row, 1972).

** Data are corrected for income; See, Verba and Nie, *Participation.*

parent is still living usually contributes to a sense of youthfulness in the young-old child.

The economic status of the young-old is less easily summarized. Income from work is a major factor in economic status, and for most persons income drops precipitously upon retirement. In 1970 the average income for white families was about 15 percent lower for the 55 to 64 age group than for the 45 to 54 group; it dropped to half the latter amount for those over 65. These are data for different groups of persons rather than for the same persons at different ages; therefore, the statistics may be deceptive with regard to change over the life span. Nevertheless, if present trends continue, the adjustment to lower incomes for

most persons may be timed closer to age 55 than to age 65. The anticipation of a longer period of life at a reduced income may affect monetary savings plans in young adulthood, just as it affects pension plans; however, such consequences are presently unpredictable.

Neither can the economic position of this age group relative to other age groups be easily determined. While income drops sharply for most persons upon retirement, current money income is only part of total economic resources—for instance, government in-kind transfers, such as Medicare, value of rent to homeowner, net worth holdings, tax adjustments, intrafamily transfers and other components need to be included in assessing economic status.

The relative economic status of the young-old compared to other age groups is similarly unpredictable for future decades, for the distribution of goods and services among age groups and the degree to which direct income payments to retirees will outweigh the provisions of services—indirect income—remain to be seen. Whether or not affluence will be increasingly equalized by age is an open question, even though the trend has now been toward improved economic status for older people.

It is likely that economic hazards for both the young-old and the old-old will be reduced in the near future, even if economic status is not equalized with that of younger groups. The rise in Social Security payments, the new cost-of-living increases which protect against inflation, and the new federalization of the welfare system—the Supplemental Security Income system which makes the income of the poorest old people somewhat more adequate than before—together constitute one major step forward. Second, it is almost certain that a form of national health insurance will soon be instituted to meet an increasing proportion of health costs for persons of all ages; for older persons it will be a marked improvement over Medicare. Third, private and public pensions and profit-sharing plans have spread. Currently, the need for improving their operation is recognized in Congress and elsewhere. To the extent that these and other changes occur, the major threats to economic well-being of older persons will be effectively diminished—with the outcome that the future young-old will be much more financially secure than their predecessors.

The young-old are already much better educated than the old-old, but the more important fact is that in the near future they will be in a less disadvantaged position in comparison to the young. So marked are the gains in educational level in successive cohorts of the population that by 1980 the average 55-year-old will be a high school graduate; by 1990 this will be true of all the young-old as a group. Furthermore, with the anticipated growth in higher education for adults, whether degree-oriented or not, and the even greater growth in what the Carnegie Commission calls "further education"—that is, education, both part-time and full-time, which occurs in settings other than college campuses and which is not aimed at academic degrees— it can also be anticipated that the educational differences which presently exist between young, middle-aged and young-old will be much reduced.[5]

With regard to political participation there is no evidence that age blocks are forming or that a politics of age is developing in the United States.[6] A quite different picture emerges, however, when general political participation and voting patterns are examined. Verba and Nie show that, when their national data are corrected for income and education, overall political participation—for example, voting, persuading others to vote a certain way, actively working for party or candidate, working with others on local problems—is highest for the age group 51 to 65. It falls off only

5. Carnegie Commission on Higher Education, *Toward a Learning Society* (New York: McGraw-Hill, 1973).

6. A. Campbell, "Politics through the life cycle," *Gerontologist* 11, no. 2 (Summer 1971), pp. 112–117.

a little for persons over 65.[7] For voting alone—and, again, when the data are corrected for income levels—the peak is the period after age 65. Thus, the young-old group are a highly active political group as compared to other age groups, and within the electorate as a whole they are disproportionately influential.

WHAT WILL THE YOUNG-OLD WANT?

These, then, are some of the characteristics of that 15 percent of the total population who are the young-old. As a group they are markedly different from the outmoded stereotypes of old age. Although they are relatively free from traditional social responsibilities of work and family, they are relatively healthy, relatively affluent, and they are politically active.

A vigorous and educated young-old group can be expected to develop a variety of new needs with regard to the meaningful use of time. They are likely to want a wide range of options and opportunities, both for self-enhancement and for community participation.

They will probably want a wider range of options with regard to work. Some will opt for early retirement; some will want to continue working beyond age 65; some will want to undertake new work careers at one or more times after age 40. They are likely to encourage those economic policies which hasten the separation between income and work and which move toward the goal of providing retirees with sufficient income to approximate their preretirement living standards.

We are already seeing a trend which will probably accelerate: a wider range of life patterns with regard to the three related areas of

7. S. Verba and N. H. Nie, *Participation in America* (New York: Harper and Row, 1972).

work, education and leisure. More middle-aged and older people are returning to education, some because of obsolescence of work skills and others for recreation or self-fulfillment. Plans are now going forward in various parts of the country to create inter-generational campuses with housing for older people, and in this and other ways to help bring into reality the so-called learning society.

The needs of the young-old in housing, location and transportation will be increasingly affected by the decisions they make with regard to the use of leisure time. The large majority will be living independently, apart from children and other relatives. This fact, combined with the desire to find interesting things to do, will lead them to seek environments which maximize options for meaningful pursuits. The extent to which age-segregated communities will increase depends, presumably, upon the extent to which the young-old will be provided opportunities for meaningful community participation in their present locations.

The vast majority will be living as married couples, but the large number of widows and single and divorced will probably lead to the formation of more group households composed of nonfamily members. At the same time, many will want housing arrangements which make it possible to maintain an aged parent at home. Perhaps an incentive system will be undertaken whereby family care of an old-old relative will not only be possible, but even remunerative. Family interactions of other types may also increase rather than decrease. Some observers predict that as the more instrumental aspects of life—education, income maintenance, health services—are increasingly shifted to other social institutions, the family may become more, rather than less, important within the expressive aspects of life—that is, in providing lasting emotional ties, and a sense of identity and self-worth.

The young-old are also likely to want greater options with regard to cultural enrichment, community participation and local political involvement—in general, for what might be called an age-irrelevant society in which arbitrary constraints based on chronological age are removed and in which all individuals, whether they are young or old, have opportunities consonant with their needs, desires and abilities. Over all, as the young-old articulate their needs and desires, the emphasis is likely to be upon improving the quality of life and upon increasing the choices of life styles.

THE YOUNG-OLD IN 1990

If the young-old in the 1970s have moved far from the stereotypes of old age, what can be said of those who will constitute the young-old in the 1990s? The group will include those who are presently 30 to 40 years old, those who are actively participating in the major political and cultural movements which are presently altering our traditional social institutions. This age group includes those who challenged government leaders over the issue of a land war in Southeast Asia in the 1960s; those who were involved in the civil rights movement, the Women's Liberation movement and the antipollution movement; those who are now activists in an era during which corporate enterprise has come under attack as the result of the consumer movement and the office of the presidency has come under attack as the result of Watergate.

These are parents of school-age children at the time when the public schools are being challenged to provide better outcomes for disadvantaged groups and when the issues of desegregation and busing have become personal issues. These are persons who have grown up in an age of organ transplants, legalization of abortion, the problems of cities, crime, the energy crisis. Furthermore, they have come into political maturity in an age when persons look increasingly to government—whether federal or local—not only to provide essential services and to protect citizens from harm, but also to improve the quality of their lives.

These experiences and these attitudes, combined with their higher educational and occupational levels, will probably lead the future young-old to exert a potent influence upon government. Compared to the young-old of the 1970s, the young-old of the 1990s are likely to wield their influence through direct political action and to make demands of both the public and private sectors to bring the benefit structure in line with their raised expectations.

THE OLD-OLD

This focus upon the young-old is not meant to denigrate the old-old, nor to neglect their needs. For one thing, the number of those over 75 is growing at an increasing rate. Their legitimate claims upon the society are at least as compelling as those of other age groups.

Their needs for meaningful ways of spending time, for special housing and for transportation will depend in large measure upon health status. Probably an increasing minority will remain active and productive and, because this is true, increased options in all areas of life will be important. The majority will probably live independently, but they will need both supportive social services and special features in the physical environment to enable them to function as fully as possible. Not only will the old-old require health services geared toward slowing physical and mental deterioration, but social services designed to prevent unnecessary decline in the individual's feelings of self-worth and dignity. In this respect opportunities for social interaction and social contributions will continue to be important.

For the old-old, as the probability of illness increases, some will require nursing home care; others who wish to remain at home will require new forms of home health services. There is no denying the fact that at the very end of life there will be a shorter or longer period of dependency and that increased numbers of the old-old will need special care, either in their own homes or in institutional settings. Thus, a larger share of the service budget of the nation will go to the old-old.

With regard to persons who are terminally ill or incapacitated, society will continue to face the problems of providing the maximum social supports, the highest possible levels of care and comfort, the assurance of dignified death and an increasing element of choice for the individual himself or for members of his family in deciding how and when his life shall end. The future will probably see the spread of educational programs aimed at the public at large, as well as at various professional groups, for achieving a "best death" for each individual.

THE FUTURE ROLES OF THE YOUNG-OLD

To return now to the broader question of the relationship among age groups in a modern society and to the broader historical perspective: the role of the older person vis-à-vis other age groups has undergone a major transition. Although the point has often been exaggerated, it is true that as a result of a slow historical process the older person is no longer the repository of wisdom which he may have been in simpler and more stable societies. More recently, he is also moving away from the role of economic producer—or the role of worker, as we have usually used that term. He has now become the user of leisure time. In that new role the young-old may be regarded as the first age group to reach the society of the future. Will they experiment with what some observers would call their truly human condition— the condition of freedom from work and freedom from want?

If our portrait of the young-old is correct, then, with their relative good health, education, purchasing power, free time and political involvement, they are not likely to become the neglected, the isolated or the expendables of the society. Will they, instead, become the social contributors, as well as the self-fulfilled? Will they be the first to create, on a large scale, new service roles and to offer their services to the community without regard to direct financial remuneration?

If, as seems presently true, the young-old will not form a strong age-group identification of their own, they might become the major agents of social change in building the age-irrelevant society. If they create an attractive image of aging, thus allay the fears of the young about growing old, and if they help to eradicate those age norms which are currently meaningless and those age attitudes which are currently divisive, they will do the society an untold service. Theirs is an enormous potential.

Aging and the Future of American Politics

By ROBERT H. BINSTOCK

ABSTRACT: Trends suggesting a dramatic increase in the proportion of aging Americans have brought attention to the possibility of gains in "senior power." Consideration of this possibility is most appropriately focused on voting and interest group politics, the political activities which have bases in large categories of citizens. Examination of electoral politics suggests there is no sound reason to expect the aging will gain power by voting more cohesively in the future. The most powerful likely result for interest group politics is that organizations based on aging members, consumers, clients, and subjects for study will have credentials to participate in the politics of a broader range of interest group arenas than they do now. At most, some roles in the political system may be exchanged, and some aging citizens as well as aging interest groups may achieve incremental gains in the playing out of what Lowi has characterized as interest-group liberalism. A more important political implication of increased numbers of the aging is the concomitant increase in services and facilities they will need. If government responds to those needs, however, it will be because of pervasive ideological considerations and not because it is pushed to do so by so-called senior power.

Robert H. Binstock is Stulberg Professor of Law and Politics at Brandeis University. In 1967–68 he served under President Lyndon Johnson as Director of the White House Task Force on Aging. He has written a number of articles on the politics of the aging and the policies that affect them. His books include Feasible Planning for Social Change, America's Political System, *and* The Politics of the Powerless. *He is co-editor of* The Handbook of Aging and the Social Sciences *which is scheduled to appear in 1975.*

SEVERAL contemporary trends suggest a dramatic increase during the next few decades in the number and proportions of Americans who will be regarded, by society and by themselves, as aged. Because of these trends, journalists and scholars have begun to consider the implications of aging for the future of American national politics. The possibilities discussed have ranged from gains in so-called senior power to the emergence of gerontocracy—literally, rule by the aged.[1]

While the terms senior power and gerontocracy are provocative, they do little to focus a serious discussion of the aging in American politics. To consider how much political power the aging are likely to have in the future—or even to assess the contemporary extent of senior power—requires some specification of referrents. In short, one must ask: power for what?

Since discussions of senior power have been generated by the possibility of substantial increases in the proportion of aging citizens, the most immediate issues for attention should center on those political activities—voting and interest group politics—which have their bases in large categories of citizens. The issues implicit in discussions of senior power and gerontocracy would seem to be: (1) does and will "the aging vote" determine the outcome of elections and (2) do or will organizations based on the existence of millions of aging members, consumers, and clients have significant power in the conflicts and accommodations that take place in American interest group politics? To focus on electoral and interest group politics is to emphasize selected sources of power in the American political system at the expense of others. Nonetheless, these are the most relevant political dynamics to consider when analyzing the prospects for mass-based power.

THE PRESENT AND FUTURE AGING

The prevailing custom for counting senior citizens in the United States is to include all persons 65 years of age and older, and to exclude the rest. This practice is slowly eroding as government and industry gradually lower the chronological ages at which persons are defined as old in relation to retirement policies, pension benefits, service eligibility, and various other regulations. The Age Discrimination in Employment Act of 1967, administered by the U.S. Department of Labor, goes so far as to define the older worker as 40 years of age and older.[2] At the moment, however, 65 is still sufficiently prevalent to be used as the yardstick for a contemporary profile of the chronologically aged.

In 1974 about 10 percent of the American population is 65 years and older. These persons constitute approximately 15 percent of those who are old enough to vote, and they do, in fact, cast about 15 percent of the votes in national elections.[3]

Stimulated by these figures, many observers of the political scene feel that senior citizens are, or at least could be, a powerful force in contemporary American politics. In building up this case, they assume

1. At its 1974 annual meeting, for instance, the American Association for the Advancement of Science sponsored a symposium on "The 1990's and Beyond: A Gerontocracy?"

2. P.L. 90-202.

3. These percentages are calculated from tables appearing in U.S., Department of Commerce, *Statistical Abstract of the United States, 1973* (Washington, D.C.: Government Printing Office, 1973), pp. 31, 379.

not only that numbers is an important source of power in American politics, but also that masses of citizens can be led to cohesive political behavior on age-based interests.

Trends of two different types suggest possibilities that the current proportions of aging citizens and voters may increase substantially in the years ahead. Demographic trends could lead to a greater percentage of persons who are chronologically aged—65 years and older. Trends in retirement from the work force at earlier ages could lead a great many Americans younger than 65 to confront the social and economic problems that are commonly faced by the chronologically aged. Consequently, many retirees as young as 55 or so may come to regard themselves, and to be regarded by society, as within the category of "the aging."

The percentage of Americans who are chronologically aged could grow considerably by the year 2000 or beyond. Until then it will remain approximately the same as it is now. All of the people who will be old enough to vote between now and the early 1990's have already been born; plausible assumptions about declining mortality rates due to biomedical advances do not change the picture substantially. Whether the age structure of the American population will be significantly altered by the year 2000 or some more remote decennial marker depends primarily on fertility rates in the years ahead. Zero or sub-zero population growth rates over the next several decades could result in a dramatic increase in the proportion of persons 65 and older in the 21st century. Or by then, a currently implausible biomedical discovery for prolonging life may have been identified and widely implemented for a period of time sufficient

enough to alter drastically our current rate of mortality. While low fertility rates in the past few years indicate that a substantial increase in the proportion of the chronologically aged is possible by the year 2000, this trend would need to continue for some time for such a change in age structure to be reliably projected. The trend may well continue, but an increase in the percentage of chronologically aged is currently a matter for conjecture, not prediction.

Trends increasing the proportion of younger "retired-aging" persons seem more reliable,[4] though not susceptible to quantitative projection. Many workers are now opting for early retirement when they anticipate a comfortable retirement income. Others seem to retire early because of pressures generated by various factors in labor force activity. Some of these factors are: the relatively high rate of technological obsolescence among workers in their 50's and early 60's; increasing relocation of major firms; cyclical unemployment, and stagnation of certain sectors of the economy. While the extent of retirement at ages younger than 65 has not been quantitatively projected for the future, it is probably safe to assume that the phenomenon will continue and increase.

With the trends toward early retirement, millions of persons in their 50's may face problems now associated with the chronologically aged, such as the economic dependency that comes from living on a reduced, fixed income in an inflationary economy. Inadequate housing, lack of access to transportation, and other problems stemming from inadequate purchasing power may

4. J. A., Jaffe, "Has the Retreat from the Labor Force Halted? A Note on the Retirement of Men, 1930–1970," *Industrial Gerontology* 9 (Spring 1971), pp. 1–12.

emerge. If they choose to re-enter the labor force they may find it extremely difficult to obtain employment. And they will no longer have the social roles and the various forms of status that work provides. At the same time, the retirement status of these younger retirees may lead the rest of society to assign to them the stereotypes of aging. For along with images of physical aging and the infirmities associated with old age, retirement status is one of the chief means of identifying the aging in American society.

A future in which young retirees perceive themselves, and are perceived by society, as being in a category with the chronologically aged is not at all implausible. Such a future is especially possible in the contexts of economic and social aging. It may, in turn, have political implications if the younger retired-aging and the chronologically aged come to share economic and social aspirations and problems.

Even the most sophisticated modes of prediction cannot yield a reliable guess as to the numbers and proportions of the chronologically aged or the younger retired-aging who will inhabit America in the year 2000 or at some later date. If there is no dramatic increase in the proportion of aging citizens, there will be no political implications. But if we assume that the proportion of the aging—in one sense or another—will increase dramatically, what differences will it make for American politics? On the basis of contemporary data regarding the political participation of persons in their 50's and older, we can assume that—whatever their number—at some future date they will be highly active.[5]

5. For a summary of literature on political participation and aging, see, Matilda White

Will this change existing patterns of electoral and interest group power in national politics?[6]

CONTEMPORARY ELECTORAL POLITICS

The most important general assertion to be made about the contemporary electoral power of the aged is that there is no "aging vote."[7] The political attitudes and partisan attachments of the aged are diverse and notable for their stability. To be sure, one can identify instances in which the percentage of older persons voting for a party or a particular candidate has switched markedly from one election to the next. But in such instances the switches have been paralleled by comparable shifts among middle-aged and younger voters; age is not an important variable for explaining voting swings. In short, there is no evidence to indicate that aging-based interest appeals can swing a bloc of

Riley and Anne Foner, *Aging and Society* (New York: Russell Sage Foundation, 1968), vol. 1, pp. 463–479.

6. Here, the discussion is necessarily confined to national politics for reasons of space. It can be generally asserted that the electoral behavior of the aging in state and local politics is approximately the same as in national elections, although aging voters seem to respond more homogeneously than usual to certain municipal referenda propositions. For one of the few scholarly treatments of contemporary aging interest groups in state politics, see, John C. Henretta, "Political Protest Among the Elderly: An Organizational Study" (Ph.D. diss., Harvard University, 1973).

7. For more detailed discussions of the political attitudes and voting behavior of the contemporary aging, see, Angus Campbell, "Politics through the Life Cycle," *Gerontologist* II, no. 2 (Summer 1971), pp. 112–117; Elizabeth B. Douglass, William P. Cleveland and George L. Maddox, "Political Attitudes, Age, and Aging: A Cohort Analysis of Archival Data," *Journal of Gerontology* (1974).

older persons' votes from one party or candidate to another.

That presumed old-age interests do not form the basis for a cohesive voting bloc should not be at all surprising. Even to the extent that older persons identify as aging, it is a relatively new identity, negative in effect; and only one among many (usually stronger) competing identities.

Various studies suggest that a substantial proportion of older persons, ranging from 40 to 65 percent, do not perceive themselves as old or aged. Data suggest that most of these persons are relatively well-off, ranking high in socio-economic status and health. Apparently they wish to avoid identification as aged because they feel that it would lead others to regard them as old, different and perhaps deviant. To the extent that they are concerned with problems and grievances linked to old age, some fragmentary evidence suggests that they do not perceive these problems as stemming from the fact that they are aged.[8]

Even comparatively disadvantaged older persons, who are most likely to identify as aged, do not tend to see their income, health, housing, safety, and transportation problems as primarily aging problems. No systematic studies dealing directly with this question exist. Nonetheless, general scholarship in the field of developmental psychology as well as political science indicates that even if the disadvantaged aged see their problems as age-related problems, they see them in other contexts as well. A full life cycle of socialization, experiences and attachments—family, schooling, ethnicity, occupation, income, residence, peer and other associations—presents a multitude of sources for group identification and perceptions of special interest. It would not be unreasonable to infer that many of those who identify as aged—even those responsive to the special needs of the disadvantaged aged—would have stronger competing identifications and interests. Presumably these competing factors substantially dilute a response to attempts to mobilize a cohesive voting bloc, even of the disadvantaged aged, based on their special interests.

FUTURE ELECTORAL POLITICS

For these reasons it should be clear that even a 100 percent increase in the proportion of chronologically aged voters during the next several decades would not likely, in itself, engender a cohesive aging vote that could determine the outcome of elections. In some remote future, beyond the year 2020, the generational cohorts who enter the ranks of the chronologically aged may be sufficiently homogeneous in their political attitudes and attachments to respond to aging-based interest appeals by voting cohesively. But all of the generational cohorts that will reach 65 years of age between now and then have displayed already their political heterogeneity. As Campbell has expressed it:

Because each age cohort includes people who differ profoundly in many important conditions of life it is not likely that any age group will be very homogeneous in its attitudes. The evidence which national surveys provide us does in fact demonstrate that attitudinal differences between age groups are far less impressive than those within age groups.[9]

---

8. A summary of the literature on age identification can be found in Riley and Foner, *Aging and Society*, pp. 303–305.

9. Campbell, "Politics through the Life Cycle," p. 117.

This seems to hold as true for the 18-year-olds who cast their ballots in the 1972 national election as it does for older age cohorts.[10]

While the emergence of the younger retired-aging would not be likely to provide the basis for a decisive aging vote bloc, it could engender greater electoral cohesion based on aging interests. One can speculate that passage into retirement status, with its attendant problems and interests, at a comparatively early stage in the life cycle could lead to the development of an aging identity that takes on political strength and meaning through the reinforcement of time and experience. But to suggest that such a development could provide the basis for an aging vote that would determine the outcomes of elections is to go beyond the bounds of reasonable conjecture.

If one considers that a person retiring at 50 spends almost as much of his life in retirement as he does at work, it is reasonable to expect that retirement status can play as significant a role in the formation of his political orientation as does his occupational identity. Moreover, the distribution of occupations within any age cohort is highly diverse. The status of retirement, in contrast, is relatively uniform despite variations in other characteristics of retirees. Thus, while occupational identities lend heterogeneity to political orientations, retirement identity developed through a substantial number of years might well engender homogeneity. The common experiences of retirement could be a cohering factor in the electoral behavior of the younger retired-aging.

Lest such speculation be regarded as wholly fanciful, it should be stated that nothing that is known about political socialization through the life cycle precludes such a development. While it is often assumed that the political orientation of adults is largely determined by childhood political socialization, the evidence available contradicts this. The research literature indicates that there are no bases for saying: (1) whether childhood learning of political attitudes endures throughout life, or basic orientations acquired during childhood structure the later learning of specific issue beliefs; (2) whether adult socialization mediates or even replaces childhood learning of issue beliefs, even acknowledging that socialization takes place throughout the life cycle; (3) under which circumstances political socialization affects political attitudes and behavior; or (4) under which circumstances, if any, planned efforts at socialization can be effective.[11]

To the extent that retirement status may provide some measure of commonality in the political orientation of persons under 65, translation of this latent group bond may be accelerated by broader politicizing forces. Heightened public controversy over governmental policies that distribute resources among Americans in relation to age and work force status, could bring to the surface any tendencies that the younger retired-aging—and perhaps the chronologically aged—may have for perceiving their political self-interest in terms of conflict be-

10. For a report on the youth vote in the 1972 national election, see, *Congressional Quarterly Guide to Current American Government, Spring, 1973* (Washington, D.C.: Congressional Quarterly, Inc., 1973), p. 24.

11. A thorough discussion of the state of scholarship on political socialization can be found in Donald D. Searing, Joel J. Schwartz and Alden E. Lind, "The Structuring Principle: Political Socialization and Belief Systems," *American Political Science Review* 67, no. 2 (June 1973), pp. 415–432.

tween old and young. Some precedence for this can be found in the nationwide Townsend Movement of the 1930's[12] and the California Ham and Eggs movement, which began in the Depression and extended into the 1950's.[13]

Signs that public policy issues may be debated increasingly in age-distribution terms are already evident. Perhaps the most notable example is the contemporary spate of magazine and newspaper articles that identify Social Security payroll deductions as regressive taxes and not—as was widely accepted for many years—premium payments into an old-age insurance program.[14] That Social Security is not an actuarially viable insurance program has been clear to economists and other professional analysts for at least two decades; for some time they have technically categorized the program as an income transfer from the productive to the unproductive. Even the Secretary of Health, Education, and Welfare proposed to Congress in 1972 that the Social Security trust fund be fully expended since it has no use as an ongoing resource for making benefit payments. But it has been in 1974, when the impact of inflation on middle class and working class pocketbooks has become a popular concern, that syndicated columnists have begun to politicize the program by writing about "the Social Security rip-off."[15]

Continuing politicization of age-distributive programs would not in itself lead to more cohesive electoral behavior. Whether aging-based political orientations might result in greater senior power depends upon the presence or emergence of leadership to cohere any existing potential for electoral power, or for other forms of political influence based on a large category of citizens.

Organizations built on aging-based interests are currently active in national politics. What kind of power do they have, and what do they use it for? Will trends in the aging population change the power and goals of these interest groups? Will new aging-based organizations with different objectives emerge in the decades ahead?

CONTEMPORARY INTEREST GROUP POLITICS

While literally hundreds of organizations participate in the politics of national decisions affecting the aging, only ten are more or less exclusively preoccupied with issues related to aging.[16] The power of these organizations is derived from the existence of more than 20 million older Americans. Three of the organizations—described by Henry Pratt elsewhere in this volume— are mass-membership associations. The other seven deal with the aging as consumers, clients, and as subjects for study. Four of these are trade associations, another is

12. See, Abraham Holtzman, *The Townsend Movement* (New York: Bookman Associates, 1963).

13. See, Frank A. Pinner, Paul Jacobs and Philip Selznick, *Old Age and Political Behavior* (Berkeley, Cal.: University of California Press, 1959).

14. See, for example, Roger LeRoy Miller, "Social Security: The Cruelest Tax," *Harper's Magazine* 248, no. 1489 (June 1974), pp. 22–27.

15. This particular phrase was one of the

milder bits of hyperbole in a syndicated column by David B. Wilson, "The Golden Age is Really Golden," *Boston Globe,* 7 January 1974, p. 19.

16. For detailed sources and a fuller treatment of the politics of contemporary aging interest groups, see, Robert H. Binstock, "Interest-Group Liberalism and the Politics of Aging," *Gerontologist* 2, part 1 (Autumn 1972), pp. 265–280.

a professional society. Still another is a loose confederation of social welfare agencies, and a coalition of individual professionals, activated just several years ago, is attempting to bring special attention to the plight of black older persons.

The bases provided by millions of older members, consumers, clients, and subjects provide these interest groups with sufficient credentials to participate in most formal and informal national policy processes. Indeed, in the classic pattern of American interest group politics, public officials and other politicians feel it incumbent upon them to invite these groups to participate in most policy activities related to aging. Because of this legitimacy they have essentially three forms of power available to them.

First, they have ready, informal access to public officials—to Congressmen and their staffs, to career bureaucrats, to agency and department heads and occasionally to the White House. Consequently, they can put forth their own proposals and work to block the proposals of others. To be sure, their audiences or targets may often be unresponsive, but access provides some measure of opportunity.

Second, their legitimacy as aging interest groups enables them to obtain public platforms in the national media, in Congressional hearings, and at pseudo-events such as the 1971 White House Conference on Aging. From these platforms they can exercise power by initiating and framing issues for public debate. They can bring attention to conditions in nursing homes, point up the double-jeopardy to which black older persons are exposed or ask whether biomedical breakthroughs in the prolongation of human life are desirable, given the qualitative problems of existence for the aging in the United States. And of course, they can use such platforms to register public support or opposition on any issues that have already been framed.

A third form of power available to these groups, particularly the mass-membership organizations, might be termed the electoral bluff. As indicated earlier, the votes of aging persons cannot be swung in a cohesive bloc through an aging-based interest appeal. Most politicians—certainly national politicians—recognize this and do not develop special appeals to the aged as the central issues of their electoral campaigns. Nonetheless, they wish to avoid offending the aged and therefore are disposed to favor proposals for providing incremental benefits to older persons. The interest groups, with their access to politicians and their platforms for framing issues, are in a key position to interpret the interests of millions of aging voters whom politicians do not wish to offend. By virtue of their symbolic role in representing millions of aging citizens, the mass-membership organizations are particularly credible in interpreting the interests of the aging. Whether the interpretations are accurate is never tested politically. Within moderate limits, public officials are responsive to the interpretations of the interest groups; and the interest groups keep their interpretations within these moderate limits, never putting forth radical proposals that might force politicians to call the bluff of the aging vote.

Given these forms of power, what do the interest groups do with it? The activities of the aging organizations in national politics are hardly militant or radical. They do articulate and support many demands favorable to the interests of elderly persons. But their efforts do not reflect a vigorous pursuit of major policies that could bring about substantial changes in the fundamental status of the aged in American society.

In briefly reviewing the contemporary political activities of these organizations, it is worth distinguishing broadly between two types of policies and programs,[17] because the manner in which the aging organizations engage with them are rather different. One type can be characterized as direct income transfer policies and programs: those designed to place additional purchasing power in the hands of explicitly designated population groups, defined by income and demography, through specific conditions embodied either in legislation or in implementing administrative regulations and guidelines. This group includes Social Security, Old Age Assistance, veterans' benefits, Federal Civil Service Retirement Benefits, Railroad Retirement Benefits, Rent Supplements, Medicare, and Medicaid. The other type can be termed middleman policies and programs: those that fund and empower public and private organizations to develop and operate properties, and to carry out services such as training and education; research; planning, program development, technical assistance and coordination; and social, health and recreational services. These include the Hill-Burton Act, a variety of volunteer and paid community services or action programs, the

Older Americans Act, Manpower Training and Development, innumerable programs administered by the National Institutes of Health and the National Institute of Mental Health, and literally hundreds of others.

In the politics of direct income transfer programs, the various types of aging organizations pursue somewhat divergent objectives suitable to their interests, but all involve incremental adjustments in existing programs. The mass-membership organizations adopt policy positions and present testimony on income transfer programs favoring increases in size of benefits, extension of eligibility for benefits to a greater number of persons, extention of conditions and time periods for which benefits are due, and relaxation or elimination of conditions that determine eligibility for benefits. The trades associations, particularly the three health care organizations, are especially concerned with ways in which income transfer provisions affect their organizational operations. They favor benefit increases and extensions of eligibility that will enable their enterprises to function more profitably or more smoothly— in the case of non-profit organizations. They are most active in seeking adjustments in the rules that govern their roles as vendors in the income transfer process: procedures for third-party payments and standards regarding the kinds of institutions in which beneficiaries can be eligible for transfer purchasing power. The National Caucus on the Black Aged formulates proposals for distributing a greater proportional share of direct income transfer payments to black than to non-black older persons. The confederation of social welfare agencies and the professional society of researchers, edu-

17. Still a third type not considered here is policies which are purely regulatory, such as the Age Discrimination in Employment Act of 1967. For a thoughtful discussion of considerations which need to be taken into account in distinguishing among types of governmental programs, see, Martha Derthick, *The Influence of Federal Grants* (Cambridge, Mass.: Harvard University Press, 1970), pp. 5–8.

cators, and service providers do not participate in income transfer politics except to insert occasional statements into the public record.

In general, the activities of the aging organizations in relation to direct income transfer issues have largely been efforts to obtain incremental adjustments in existing programs. The organizations have not put forth strong proposals for major new policies and programs for redistributing purchasing power to the aged—they did not, for instance, play a strong role in the passage of Medicare.[18] That the organizations' activities are directly responsible for bringing about changes they seek in direct income transfer programs is doubtful. Nonetheless, adjustments consonant with those sought by the organizations are continuously effected.

In the politics of middleman programs, the aging organizations have many behavioral features in common. They seek to create new programs that would provide funds and authority more or less exclusively to aging organizations. Within existing programs that already make funds and authority available to a fairly broad range of middlemen, they attempt to earmark, or otherwise lay claim to, an established share for aging organizations. They search, without much success, for some authoritative administrative mechanism—typically termed a means of coordination—to increase greatly their leverage for carving out shares for aging organizations within middleman programs.

Proposals of the aging organizations regarding middleman programs rarely present details on means

18. See, Theodore R. Marmor, *The Politics of Medicare* (London: Routledge and Keegan Paul, 1970).

through which problems of the disadvantaged aged might be solved. Vague substantive content is offered, designed to provide sufficient rationale for including aging organizations among the middlemen that share in a program. When highly specific proposals are set forth by the aging organizations, they deal with two types of matters: (1) they suggest rule changes designed to increase the probability of aging organizations' winning a share of middleman programs, and (2) they set forth detailed proposals for maintaining or increasing funds authorized for programs in which aging organizations have already established a share. The only essential differences among the aging organizations in all this activity concern which of them should be receiving middleman shares from which sources and how much each should get.

Our aggregate result of these organizations' activities in the politics of middleman programs is that they have been successful in creating a domain of program funds and authority that is available more or less exclusively to aging organizations. Moreover, they have successfully laid claim to established shares for aging organizations within domains that make funds and authority available to a fairly wide spectrum of middlemen. No single organization or faction of organizations has succeeded in dominating these activities or in excluding the others. Each of the organized interests has managed to gain access to an adequate source and supply of rewards. While the organizations engage in conflict as they seek to advance their own shares, they have managed to arrive at a fairly stable pattern of reward distribution and accommodation.

In summary, the aging organizations have sufficient power to maintain themselves and their interests, but the goals articulated and sought by these organizations are not suitable to redress fundamentally the economic, biomedical, and social problems of the severely disadvantaged aged—let alone change the general societal status of the aged. While they probably would not have sufficient power to achieve such goals even if they sought them, the very incentive systems that create and sustain their organizational viability—interests of their members and the pursuit of their trades and professions—preclude them from testing the extent of their power to achieve fundamental changes for the aging. In short, these organizations are similar to those in many other arenas of interest group activity that have been examined by students of American politics.[19]

FUTURE INTEREST GROUP POLITICS

If the next several decades bring substantial increases in the proportions of chronologically aged and younger retired-aged citizens, will aging-based interest groups have more power, and will they exercise what power they have for different purposes than they do now? Will new types of aging interest groups emerge? Will they have different political objectives?

An increase in the proportion of chronologically aged persons would probably have little effect upon interest group politics. The legitimacy provided by greater numbers of members, consumers, clients and subjects would probably enhance the capacity of the interest groups to gain access to public officials and to obtain platforms for framing public policy issues. The size of the electoral bluff would be more impressive. The contemporary interest groups and any new ones that join them would have more security in their efforts at organizational maintenance. They would probably succeed in establishing a larger domain of funds and authority to divide among themselves through conflict and accommodation. But unless the political orientations of the chronologically aged undergo considerable change, there is no reason to expect that aging interest groups would vary significantly the nature of their objectives. In order to prosper, the organizational leaders must maintain a modicum of harmony between their political activities and objectives, on the one hand, and the needs, problems, and aspirations of their constituencies on the other.[20]

The development of a younger retired-aging constituency, even with political orientations based on a stronger aging identity, is only somewhat more likely to change the activities of aging-based interest groups. A common aspiration among them to find new social roles and identities may well give rise to additional organizations based on constituencies of aging members, consumers, and clients. But as Bernice Neugarten points out elsewhere in this volume, the "young-old" are likely to desire a

19. The classic work on interest groups is David B. Truman, *The Governmental Process: Political Interests and Public Opinion* (New York: Alfred A. Knopf, 1951). A more recent treatment is Herman Ziegler, *Interest Groups in American Society* (Englewood Cliffs, N.J.: Prentice-Hall, 1964).

20. One of the more useful theoretical treatments of the relations between external organizational behavior and the incentive bases which maintain the organization can be found in Peter B. Clark and James Q. Wilson, "Incentive Systems: A Theory of Organizations," *Administrative Science Quarterly* 6 (March 1961), pp. 129–166.

wide range of options and opportunities. Therefore, organizations developing in response to this common need for meaningful activities will probably be numerous, but diverse in nature and unlikely to have a shared basis for working alliances. Their political relevance would probably be negligible.

To the extent that there is group cohesion focusing on the problems of economic dependency in retirement and its attendant difficulties, the aging-based interest groups—particularly the membership organizations—may be forced to put forth stronger age-redistributive policy proposals in order to maintain their legitimacy and to avoid the threats of new organizational competition. If their proposals do not seem too radical to the politicians of the day, the latter may continue to acquiesce to the bluff of the aging vote. In the unlikely event that the proposals are so radical that the politicians feel forced to call the electoral bluff, the subsequent power of the aging-based interest groups will decrease or increase sharply, depending on whether a decisive aging vote materializes on that critical election day in the future. More likely, as indicated by our consideration of electoral behavior, there would be no pivotal bloc of aging voters on that day; the power of the aging-based interest groups would subsequently decline.

THE PROSPECTS FOR SENIOR POWER

Since contemporary attention to the implications of aging for the future of American politics has been generated by trends suggesting increases in the proportion of aging citizens, this discussion has focused largely on aging voters and the behavior of interest groups based on mass constituencies of the aging. Before touching on other political dynamics that could have implications for aging and the future of American politics, what can one conclude about the possible consequences of an increased aging population for senior electoral power and senior interest group power?

The aging do not vote cohesively to determine the outcome of contemporary elections. Are they likely to do so in the future? Although a number of possibilities have been raised, there is no sound reason to expect that in the immediate or remote future the aging will wield decisive power in determining the outcomes of national elections. Even if the proportion of aging Americans were to double, the most powerful consequence one can reasonably imagine is that politicians might woo the aging vote as assiduously as they now woo the vote of organized labor. But even this is most unlikely. The organizational structure of unions provides a far stronger—though hardly reliable—mechanism for swinging votes than any aging-based interest group is likely to develop.

The aging-based interest groups have some power by virtue of their ready access to public officials and other politicians, their opportunities to obtain public platforms for framing policy issues and their discreet exercise of an electoral bluff. They use this power to support incremental benefits for the aging and to carve out and divide among themselves the middleman's share in government programs which provide services and facilities for the aging. If there is a substantial increase in the number of members, consumers, clients, and study subjects that form the bases for these organizations' power, what is likely to happen?

The most powerful consequence

that one might realistically suggest is that the aging-based interest groups will have credentials to participate in a broader range of interest group political arenas. Currently they are only legitimated for invitation and access to arenas that are clearly labeled as relevant to the aging or to some category of disabled adults. But with substantial increases in the numbers of citizens they symbolically represent, these groups may find the doors of more general policy forums thrown open to them. Even as the 1971 White House Conference on Aging could not be conducted without prominent representation of business and labor interest groups, the aging-based interest groups may become welcome and sought-after guests at major forums dealing with issues central to business and labor.

To suggest these possibilities is to intimate that a substantial increase in the proportion of aging will have little impact on the basic nature of American politics. To be sure, some roles in the system will have changed if aging voters are wooed a bit more than some other category of voters, and if aging-based groups take some other interest's seat at the many bargaining tables of interest group politics. Some aging citizens as well as the aging organizations will achieve incremental gains in the playing out of what Theodore Lowi has characterized as interest-group liberalism.[21]

If one looks briefly to forms of power other than voting and interest groups, are there alternatives for increased senior power in national politics? No, not very strong ones, unless there are sweeping changes in the nature of American society.

While government and corporate elites are comparatively advanced in age and may well continue to be, they do not wield their power on behalf of aging-based interests. Ad hoc protest groups of the aging have demonstrated some capacity to influence the outcome of minor decisions in local politics, such as the reduction of public transit fares for senior citizens. Like most groups mobilized around ad hoc purposes, they have not provided the base for longer-lived protest organizations.[22] One can never exclude the possibility that a nationally-focused ad hoc protest—a march on Washington by senior citizens—might be successful. But given the obstacles of logistics, economics, and group cohesion, the odds of any success seem formidable.[23]

A less conservative approach to prediction than the rather rudimentary modes of projection implicit in this discussion can yield a variety of futuristic scenarios involving the aging in American politics. For instance, one can posit the emergence of the so-called no-growth economy, which has been the focus of fashionable intellectual speculation in the past several years,[24] and find that cleavage between the economically productive and the non-productive is the central political conflict of the day. Surely the political behavior of

21. Theodore J. Lowi, *The End of Liberalism* (New York: W. W. Norton, 1969).

22. Perhaps the only exceptions are those groups developed through the organizing tactics of Saul Alinsky; see, his *Reveille for Radicals* (New York: Random House, 1946).

23. The experience of the Poor People's Campaign in 1968—when they established Resurrection City in Washington—provides an informative picture of the difficulties to be surmounted in a march on Washington. See, Nick Kotz, *Let Them Eat Promises: The Politics of Hunger in America* (Englewood Cliffs, N.J.: Prentice-Hall, Inc., 1969).

24. See, for instance, "The No-Growth Society," *Daedalus* 102, no. 4 (Fall 1973).

the chronologically aged and the younger retired-aged would be exceptionally cohesive in such a setting. To consider whether that cohesion would provide a basis for power in the no-growth society would be to lead oneself through an endless series of fanciful speculations.

Of all the imaginable political implications of growth in the numbers and proportions of aging citizens, the most serious can be found in the impact that their presence will likely have on the need for public services and facilities. The needs of the contemporary population of aging citizens—in physical and mental health care, social services, educational opportunities, recreational and community activities, appropriately designed housing—far outstrip the available personnel and facilities available to meet them. Yet it is already established policy of the American government to undertake responsibility for meeting these needs.[25] With millions of additional aging citizens, the gap between government's official policy and its capacity to implement that policy will be enormous. As this situation emerges, the politics of federal resource allocation may lead to a retrenchment in, or abrogation of, policies committing government to help meet all these needs. If government responds positively to the challenge of expanding services and facilities, it will be because of pervasive ideological considerations and not because it is pushed to do so by senior power.

25. See, U.S., Senate, Committee on Labor and Public Welfare, Subcommittee on Aging and the Special Committee on Aging, *Post-White House Conference on Aging Reports, 1973* (Washington, D.C.: Government Printing Office, 1973).

Book Department

INTERNATIONAL RELATIONS

RAYMOND ARON. *The Imperial Republic: The United States and the World, 1945–1973.* Pp. vii, 339. Englewood Cliffs, N.J.: Prentice-Hall, 1974. $10.00.

The original French edition of this book won the prestigious Prix des Critiques in 1973. The English translation will widen the circle of its readers, especially in the United States. It is one of the most balanced and most perceptive appraisals of the role of the United States in the postwar world that has been written by anyone, American or foreign. Raymond Aron, in the grandiloquent words of a French journal, might have been the "French Kissinger," but instead he "has chosen to be Raymond Aron." For this his many admirers should be grateful.

Professor Aron takes Nixon's visit to China in February, 1972, as symbolizing the end of the postwar inter-state system and the President's new economic policies of August, 1971, as marking "the end of the postwar monetary system." The two parts of his book, of about equal length, deal with these two themes—one with the political role of the United States in the

inter-state system, the other with the economic role of the United States in the "world market." The first role was that of paramountcy, marked first by success and then by failure; the second was that of dominance, characterized by both privileges and constraints.

In this new work, as in previous writings, Professor Aron sees many successes and many failures in U.S. foreign policy. On the whole he believes that U.S. policy toward Europe, especially during the Truman era, was correct and effective. In Asia, American policy was far less successful. "It was in Asia far more than in Europe that the American republic assumed the imperial burden." The concept of containment "developed without losing its defensive connotation into 'globalization' and 'militarization' as a result of the Korean campaign," and these trends became more marked as the United States experienced the agonies of Vietnam. On the whole, the United States had more success in dealing with developed than with developing countries. Aron obviously deplores "the counterrevolutionary role now played by the United States in Latin America, and in some cases in other parts of the

213

world as well." But he is "unable to take the revisionist thesis very seriously," either with regard to the origins of the cold war or with regard to the influence of the Pentagon and the "military-industrial establishment" on the course of U.S. foreign policy.

Although Professor Aron refrains from any extended analysis of the American domestic scene, and has little to say about the impact of domestic pressures and developments on foreign policy, he does comment on the lack of knowledge of much of the American public and many members of the Congress on foreign policy questions, and on the role of the press, the intellectuals, and the universities in creating "the climate in which the president and his advisers live." He believes, however, that "Basically, foreign policy is the preserve of the president, his private advisers . . . and the vast civilian and military organizations in charge of immense interests closely interrelated with those of other nations." He is sparing in his comments on the Watergate affair, which in his view is "as specifically American as the Dreyfus affair was specifically French"; but he believes that as a result of Watergate "President Nixon's authority is bound to be impaired to some degree and that the Senate is bound, temporarily at least, to exert more influence on United States foreign policy than it has since 1939." He is obviously not happy with this trend. Indeed, he frankly confesses that "it is on Richard Nixon and Henry Kissinger that a European pins his hopes for a foreign policy governed by reason."

Clearly Aron harbors doubts as well as hopes about the future role of the United States in both the inter-state system and in the world economy. "The Imperial Republic must find a middle way between globalism and isolationism." Neither in the political nor in the economic realm is it capable of carrying the imperial burden which it tried to carry in the immediate past. But it is still a major actor on the world's political and economic stage,

and it cannot escape continuing involvement and commitment.

                    NORMAN D. PALMER
Department of Political Science
University of Pennsylvania
Philadelphia

DOUGLAS E. ASHFORD. *Ideology and Participation.* Pp. 300. Beverly Hills, Calif.: Sage, 1974. $7.00.

PATRICK J. MCGOWAN AND HOWARD B. SHAPIRO. *Comparative Study of Foreign Policy.* Pp. 256. Beverly Hills, Calif.: Sage, 1974. $7.00.

Ashford attempts to revitalize the notion of ideology as a useful concept for understanding political activity. He brings a wide-ranging diversity of ideas from comparative political analysts, psychologists, anthropologists, philosophers, and others to bear on the problem of ". . . how psychological and cultural elements of individual and group behavior relate to manifestations of their shared values, especially as they appear in political life." In addition, he is primarily concerned with developing a conception of a "working ideology" which can deal with the interaction of political ideas and behavior at both the level of the individual citizen and the collectivity.

The closest Ashford comes to a compact definition of a working ideology is the statement, "I am using 'ideology' to refer to both the activity individuals can attach to political ideas and the norms found in collective endeavor intended to manifest political ideas." In the ensuing arguments, Ashford, drawing on specific propositions and findings from several disciplines and heavily peppering the discussion with substantive examples, condemns past pejorative uses of the term ideology and proceeds to develop his own concept. The basis for his conception of a working ideology is the extent to which political values affect variation in the behavior of individual citizens and variation in collective behavior based on institutional norms. Thus, his notion of congruence of behavior between individual and institutional levels emphasizes relational aspects ". . . of how men as citizens individually and collectively relate to one another in a political system."

The notion of working ideology is linked to other theoretical formulations involving status, political culture, and the developmental literature. His arguments at various points are suggestive of hypotheses on the effects of dimensions of a working ideology conceived as a cross-level, behavioral phenomenon.

However, suggesting directions for the conceptualization of ideology and its utility for understanding political life is not the same as presenting analysis based on a developed conceptual product. Though Ashford has outlined a direction for further theoretical effort, it is far from clear that his path will disentangle the confusion he seeks to order. The linkages between ideas or values and behavior; between individual and collective levels of analysis; and, between ideology as a social science concept and ideology as a normative or prescriptive program all remain sticky, clouded problems. Ashford's directions are informed and stimulating, but construction of a specific theoretical vehicle, based on the concept of ideology, useful for further empirical analysis, remains illusive.

Using the well-known Berelson and Steiner survey of scientific findings on human behavior as a model, McGowan and Shapiro attempt an heroic review of findings extracted from over 200 "representative" empirical studies, published in the English language from 1955–1972, in order to assess the field they call the "comparative study of foreign policy." The findings are organized under 118 propositions which are in turn categorized according to an organizing framework which views foreign policy behavior (official acts of nation A to control B) as a function of four sets of variables: (1) attributes of the external environment of the actor (other nation's policies, systemic changes); (2) attributes of the actor (nine factors ranging from psychological and elite background variables to societal, cultural, and historical variable types); (3) the dimensions of the decisionmaking process as intervening variables linking the two preceding categories and the dependent variable (foreign policy behavior); and (4) feedback from policy behavior to the actor and to the international environment of the actor.

The authors provide a vital service to foreign policy analysts by (a) comprehensively describing the state of foreign policy studies as of 1972, (b) highlighting gaps in the cumulative knowledge about this field, and (c) suggesting research directions for the rest of the decade.

However, comprehensiveness was not achieved without costs. The treatment of particular findings is brief, often to the point of being superficial. Secondly, the organizing framework offers little promise of serving a classificatory function beyond the immediate purposes of McGowan and Shapiro. Finally, a set of criteria by which a valid comparison can be recognized remains largely unspecified, thereby leaving the "comparative study of foreign policy" unbounded and without a separate identity as a field of inquiry.

Overall, the limitations noted do not prevent this survey from significantly contributing to the study of foreign policy as a tool facilitating review and synthesis.

MICHAEL E. AKINS
University of Pennsylvania
Philadelphia

ABRAM CHAYES. *The Cuban Missile Crisis: International Crises and the Role of Law.* Pp. v, 157. New York: Oxford University Press, 1974. $5.95.

Commissioned by the American Society of International Law, Professor Chayes of the Harvard Law School has reviewed the much publicized 1962 confrontation between the United

States and the Soviet Union in terms of the role played by international law. Even more precise was the question put by the Society: *how* did international law affect the positions of the antagonists? To this question a fair and adequate answer is given. Along the way, as illustrative of the different legal issues, the varying ways of treating them, and the institutional biases and objectives motivating the many personalities involved, highly useful bibliographical references are listed. Having granted these credits, it is necessary to observe that the presentation is so short that peripheral issues to the basic crisis are either ignored entirely or are greviously slighted.

Not only does Chayes' view of the intricasies of crisis management benefit from the advantage of hindsight, but some of the documents relied on are similarly subject to challenge. The position of the Office of the General Counsel of the Defense Department as of 1962 is made known by a letter to Chayes dated 1971. Another letter, written in 1968, explains the content and the circumstances of drafting the memorandum for the Attorney General in August, 1962, regarding the legality of remedial action against the threat of a missile base. (The August brief, elaborating upon the Monroe Doctrine, was dismissed by President Kennedy who realized that the famous Doctrine was a unilateral statement of policy and by no means a rule of international law.)

The utility of the United Nations as a forum when Ambassador Adlai Stevenson demanded a yes or no answer about the emplacement of missiles and displayed enlarged photographs to the UN Security Council, "was as effective in generating support for and neutralizing opposition to the United States as any other action in the week of crisis." But Stevenson's proposal to consider a "trade" of missiles in Turkey for those in Cuba was not publicly adopted by the United States and hence not advanced at the UN, although it ultimately materialized.

Chayes devotes extensive coverage to the problem of obtaining the support of the Organization of American States for the decision to quarantine Cuba from further importations. As the Russian freighters were en route to the Caribbean, President Kennedy announced the quarantine before the OAS took action. The Organization's subsequent approval, declared to be unanimous, in fact had some negative votes and abstentions on parts of the final resolution.

The answer to the Law Society's question, from Chayes, is that "the men responsible for decision did not ignore legal considerations." "They made a considerable effort to integrate legal factors into their deliberations." He asserts that law operated "substantially, but not decisively" as a constraint upon American actions. "The significance of legal justification for decision-making is greater and more complex than is customarily supposed." And, if justification is another word for public accountability, in a democratic-representative society it can have a profound effect.

WILLARD BARBER
University of Maryland
College Park

OTTO HIERONYMI. *Economic Discrimination Against the United States in Western Europe, 1945-58.* Pp. xvi, 232. Geneva, Switzerland: Librairie Droz, 1973. No price.

CHARLES P. KINDLEBERGER. *The World Depression, 1929-1939.* Pp. 336. Berkeley: University of California Press, 1973. $10.00.

Otto Hieronymi's book is essentially the history of the economic relations between the United States on the one hand and Western Europe on the other during the period of economic readjustment after World War II. It deals with the facts of those relations and the governmental policies affecting them. Hieronymi writes clearly, dispassionately and with a minimum of theoretical and econometric obscurity.

The frame of reference of this book is the U.S. policy at the end of the war in favor of a new international monetary system (to be institutionalized in the International Monetary Fund), increased international investments (to be institutionalized mainly in the International Bank for Reconstruction and Development), and liberalized nondiscriminatory trade (to be institutionalized in the International Trade Organization or the General Agreement on Tariffs and Trade). Hieronymi appropriately denotes this as a "universalist" approach.

The Western Europeans gave only grudging support to this approach, which was detailed in the *Proposals for the Expansion of World Trade and Employment*, issued by the U.S. Government in 1945. When it became fully apparent, in 1947, that Western Europe was either unable or unwilling to follow the "universalist" policies of restoring equilibrium in the balance of payments and reducing trade restrictions, the United States acceded in large measure to the pressures for special capital movements (conspicuously, Marshall Plan aid) and the continuation, or indeed extension, of discriminatory monetary and trade restrictions against the United States. The large tariff reductions resulting from the GATT negotiations of 1947 "universalist" in principle, were largely nullified by the quantitative trade restrictions and exchange controls, but the devaluations of 1949 were in keeping with the "universalist" objective. On the other hand, the impetus given to European integration by certain policies associated with the Marshall Plan, particularly the Code of Trade Liberalization, the European Coal and Steel Community, and the monetary clearing arrangements culminating in the European Payment Union, furthered the move toward what Hieronymi calls "group discrimination" against the United States.

Significantly, Hieronymi states that it is "the conclusion of this study that discrimination as such was not a major factor in eliminating the so-called dollar shortage, or more accurately in improving the balance-of-payments posi-

tions of the individual Western European countries" (p. 218). On the other hand, "the scare of the dollar shortage and the discrimination it engendered helped shape the permanent integration of Europe . . ." (p. 220).

This reviewer agrees with the author that the multilateral and nondiscriminatory trade and payments policy advocated by the United States was blunted, and continues to be blunted, by the discriminatory policies pursued by the Europeans and avidly imitated by others. Hieronymi's book is a valuable addition to the scholarly works in this field.

"The explanation of this book [*The World Depression, 1929–1939*] is that the 1929 depression was so wide, so deep and so long because the international economic system was rendered unstable by British inability and United States unwillingness to assume responsibility for stabilizing it . . . " (p. 292). Specifically, Kindleberger cites (a) the lack of a relatively open market for "distress goods," particularly primary products; (b) the drying up of international counter-cyclical long-term lending; and (c) a closely-related financial factor, the failure of the United States, alone or in concert with a few other countries, to "discount" financial assets in return for internationally liquid funds.

These conclusions derive from Kindleberger's highly readable general review of economic events in the decade after World War I, his detailed description of the decline from 1929 to 1932, and his examination of recovery efforts up to 1939. The author touches on practically all of the factors that have been cited by others as giving rise to and accelerating the Great Depression. For example, with respect to the 1929 stock market crash: "One should not be dogmatic about it, but it is hard to avoid the conclusion that there is something to the conventional wisdom which characterized the crash as the start of a process. The crash led to a scramble for liquidity . . . " (p. 127). Earlier, the stock market had attracted funds away from international lending, which had been essential to the brittle and tentative international monetary equilibrium that had been established after 1925.

Like most other analysts, Kindleberger finds the international monetary-financial events of the spring and summer of 1931 the clue to the deepening of the depression: bank failures in Germany and Austria, French reluctance to lend to the Germans while the Austro-German Anschluss was being considered, British inability to meet the requests for conversion of sterling into gold, the lack of U.S. foreign lending. These and other elements are described in dramatic detail. President Hoover's efforts to arrange a moratorium on intergovernmental payments, eventually successful, put him in a good light. Even so, Britain let the pound float in September 1931 and effectively rang down the curtain on London as the world financial center. As Kindleberger says, "For the world economy to be stabilized, there has to be a stabilizer, one stabilizer" (p. 305). Britain stepped out; the United States did not step in. President Roosevelt's sabotaging of the 1933 World Economic Conference revealed how far the United States was from providing leadership.

The description of the recovery efforts of the 1930s is provided against an implicit Keynesian backdrop: easy money could not overcome pessimistic expectations by businessmen, which expectations could be improved only by expanded aggregate demand, which could be provided only by substantial government deficit spending. In the United States, it was April 1938 before this approach was consciously accepted. Roosevelt was by inclination even more of a budget-balancer than Hoover.

On the international front, floating exchange rates, currency blocs, exchange controls, quantitative controls, higher tariffs, tariff discrimination, and strings on foreign investment devastated the international economy. Expansionist policies were only the timid tariff reductions started on Cordell Hull's initiative after 1934, the hesitant stabilization of dollar-pound-franc rates under the Tripartite Agreement of 1936, undertaken mainly to provide political "cover" for French devaluation, and the 1934 establishment of the U.S. Export-Import Bank.

Kindleberger recognizes that he might be overemphasizing the international monetary-financial factors in trying to explain the course of events in the United States. The United States would have had a depression without external stimulus or reinforcement. For other countries, more heavily involved in international trade and finance, Kindleberger's explanation has more cogency.

Is the world still subject to such a world depression? One may question whether there is really an open market for "distress goods," if supply should seriously overshoot demand in some lines. The International Bank for Reconstruction and Development has not dared to operate counter-cyclically, so it is quite possible that international counter-cyclical lending could dry up, unless the U.S. Government provided or guaranteed large international loans. On the international monetary front— the third of Kindleberger's pegs— the International Monetary Fund is technically able to "discount," as a bank of last resort, but both the European Economic Community and the United States have veto power over the expansion of Special Drawing Rights, which are the contemporary international device for providing liquidity. Would the leading central banks fill the gap?

This reviewer agrees with Kindleberger that present formal international arrangements (IBRD, IMF and the General Agreement on Tariffs and Trade) provide means—which did not exist earlier—for avoiding another great world depression. But without U.S. leadership they would not be effective.

JOSEPH D. COPPOCK
The Pennsylvania State University
University Park

CHALMERS JOHNSON. *Autopsy on People's War*. Pp. vii, 118. Berkeley: University of California Press, 1974. $5.75.

From a penetrating mind and in trenchant style, here is a work far more provocative of thought than one would think likely in so little space. The author brings to bear years of interest and his acquired sophistication concerning modes and facets of revolutionary struggle. He emphasizes revolutions in the present century, particularly the Chinese Communist experience and selected Maoist doctrines. He views great, modern revolutions as paradigms, having an impact on latent and developing forces for change—especially propensities to use violence for political and socio-economic transformations—each during the ensuing generation. Although he acknowledges what he calls Communist China's relations on "two levels" with several countries in Southeast Asia (support to selected insurgents yet improved relations with established governments, policies since 1969 being described on pages 76–84), the author asserts that the era of people's wars inspired by the Chinese design and abetted by the PRC, are mostly over; the time for autopsy is said to have arrived.

Another theme, apparent particularly near the start and in his concluding chapter, is that too much attention has been paid to the socio-economic and other tensions ("reductionism") preceding revolutions. Johnson stresses rather what revolutionaries think they are accomplishing—strategically as well as critically and antagonistically. One expects this in a treatment of Mao-influenced and aided people's wars—the recognized importance of ideology. Yet every such struggle modifies the paradigm, even as Mao found adaptation of the Leninist guidelines necessary.

Chapter seven on "Spinoffs from the Doctrine" presents a perceptive interpretation of urban guerrilla purposes. Their tactics are explained as derived from conditions in which revolutionaries lacking mass support try to precipitate interventions which may create revolutionary situations. The author points out that modern revolution entails a crisis for the development of a state, that successful transformations through struggle result in enlarged state power. A more analyzed distinction is needed, however, between revolutions that open the way to the fuller integration and modernization of traditional or transitional systems—for example, Tsarist Russia, Nationalist China—and the problems confronting revolutionaries in rather centralized, technologically powerful states. If, in the latter half of this century, the more broadly observed problems of humanly willed, corrective change in so-called advanced countries grow increasingly critical, the experience being gained may have some prospective significance for countries intent at earlier stages on industrialization. If this seems like a partial return to "reductionism," one can say that there are long stretches between major revolutions in the same societies; obviously there are many modes of intervening changes. I see nothing intrinsic about the study of causal forces and conditions that precludes attention to revolutionary ideologies and strategies. Probably Johnson agrees with this; his objection rather is against the frequent assumption that revolutions are necessarily progressive, or are always vindicative catharses of discerned causal trends.

ALLAN B. COLE

The Fletcher School of Law
  and Diplomacy
Tufts University
Medford
Massachusetts

STEWART STEVEN. *Operation Splinter Factor: The Untold Story of America's Most Secret Cold War Intelligence Operation*. Pp. 249. New York: Lippincott, 1974. $7.95.

Operation Splinter Factor, according to the author, was conceived by Allen

Dulles, director of the Central Intelligence Agency of the United States from 1953 to 1961, bleak years indeed in the period of the Cold War. Its purpose was to drive a wedge between the Eastern European satellites of Russia and the Kremlin. For the Communist parties in Poland, Czechoslovakia, Hungary and Bulgaria were hopelessly divided between those who believed that close ties with the Soviet were necessary to protect them from Western "imperialism" and who took the hard Communist line, and those who, while still loyal to Communism, worked to retain their national sovereignty not wanting to become Russian "colonies."

The Dulles plan was ingenious. The idea was to get the hard-core party into power and thus make life so miserable for the people that they would revolt and thus break up the Russian "empire" which in those years was on the defensive and by no means sure of itself in foreign relations. As a result of American action, people on the liberal side suffered horribly and, in the end, Moscow infiltrated with hosts of secret agents and police, and used their raw power to establish their party in control. Up to that point the American operation went according to schedule, but that was as far as it went. The people would not or could not forge the expected revolution. The author claims that 100,000 men, women and children, mostly innocents not knowing what was going on, suffered directly; as many as 1,000 were killed, and uncounted thousands went to prison or labor camps, or were deprived of their property and means of livelihood. Steven concludes that Operation Splinter Faction was "politically unproductive, unnessarily barbarous and unquestionably a failure." He divides the blame between Stalin and Dulles, the former who was made to believe that many of his erstwhile brother Communists were acting as double agents for the Americans, and the latter who did not care what happened to the "national" Communists as a result of the adventure. Progress and stability in the satel-

lite countries were set back at least a generation.

Central in the operation was Lieutenant Colonel Jozef Swiatle, a high-ranking Polish Communist who defected and came over to the American side. He worked up and down the East European area fomenting trouble and undermining the anti-Russian Communists to carry out Dulles' objectives. (*Mirabile dictu*, he ends up in the United States under the benevolent protection of the CIA). Then there were also Noel Field and his family, American Communist sympathizers who disappeared behind the Iron Curtain because Stalin was made to believe that Field was a double agent in Dulles' employ. Field actually thought that he was defecting to Russia: little did he know what and how it happened. But, again *mirabile dictu* when the Communists saw their mistake they were released with $40,000 compensation each for their pains. Several of them now reside in the United States but not Noel and his wife who took residence in Budapest.

Steven's book contains a lot of "tall" history, much of it understandably still incomplete and undocumented. In fact, his background descriptions of developments are more important than his specifics. His main characters, even Dulles, emerge pale and almost unreal. However, if one peruses the sources listed at the end of the book, one is impressed by the breadth, if not the depth, of his research. He utilizes books already written in the general field, some historical papers now available, and newspaper stories. Not much comes from tightly-closed files and tightly-closed lips of CIA agents and others in espionage circles.

So while this book cannot be considered the last word for this segment of the Cold War, it is certainly an eye-opener. It goes to show how a few men without restraints and control, backed up by government, in behalf of a "just" cause can manhandle the destiny of thousands of innocents, and how brutal and utterly diabolic is the modern world of espionage. It merges into and sometimes is actually legalized terrorism.

HAROLD F. ALDERFER
Professor Emeritus of Political
    Science
The Pennsylvania State University
University Park

YAN-LI WU. *Raw Material Supply in a Multipolar World.* Pp. ix, 55. New York: Crane, Russak & Co., 1973. $4.95.

In this short, rather expensive, analysis of raw material supply in the world, Wu is concerned with the curtailment of supplies on major United States' allies. Discussion of particular raw materials is limited to such strategic items as iron ore, copper, lead, zinc, bauxite, petroleum and uranium. The author argues that the supply of critical materials needs to be given greater consideration when the validity of existing free world alliances is assessed. Major sources and the security of supplies for each ally are outlined, the routes by which the materials reach the importing nation are discussed, and the strategic issues raised by each import pattern are evaluated.

Wu raises a number of interesting points. He asserts, for example, that a nation can only have a high degree of security if it aligns with other nations which collectively can achieve independence in resource supply. Most of the major allies have a high import dependency, and these nations are particularly vulnerable to short term curtailments in supply. He discourages investment in any long term contracts with "unfriendly" nations. Allies must, therefore, search for alternative supplies, improve relations with key importers, and find new alternative technologies and substitute materials.

Linked to this concern with sources of raw materials are many strategic questions over supply routes. Wu regards the Soviet Union as perhaps the greatest threat to allied resource supplies. The Mediterranean supply routes are particularly vulnerable and there are dubious benefits for the western alliance in reopening the Suez Canal and increasing trade movement in the Mediterranean.

Wu's assessment is a welcome analysis of the role of raw materials in world affairs. This is not, however, a complete or exhaustive study. Given the assumptions about demand and the strategic nature of resources, a more thorough discussion of the extent and location of raw materials could have been expected. Additional maps on location and commodity routings of materials would also have enhanced the description. The role of international corporations in raw materials movements and the vulnerability of exporting nations to economic sanctions and tariffs needs to be evaluated. One might also question the underlying assumption that existing alliances should be maintained and that so-called "friendly" nations will not place some restrictions on raw material movements. In short, Wu's book raises many provocative questions but the full complexity of the issues is not treated sufficiently.

WILLIAM M. ROSS
Cook College
Rutgers University
New Brunswick
New Jersey

ASIA, AFRICA AND LATIN AMERICA

DAVID C. BAILEY. *¡Viva Cristo Rey!: The Cristero Rebellion and the Church-State Conflict in Mexico.* Pp. xiii, 346. Austin: University of Texas Press, 1974. $10.00.

The Cristero Rebellion of 1926–1929 climaxed Mexico's century-long Church-State conflict. Based on his doctoral dissertation, David C. Bailey's work is an analysis of this attempt to bring down the regime established by the Mexican Revolution and restore to Catholicism a major role in determining

Mexico's national destiny. Skillfully condensing a vast amount of material on the nineteenth century liberal-conservative struggle over the role of the Church, Bailey demonstrates that by the time of the Revolution of 1910, Mexican Catholicism, responding to Pope Leo XIII's encyclical *Rerum Novarum,* supported a social reform program not unlike that proposed by the revolutionaries. Yet the leaders of the revolution were convinced that the Church was the congenital foe of progress and, in drafting the Constitution of 1917, included severe restrictions on the Church and clergy. After nine years of government temporizing, in 1926 President Plutarco Elías Calles ordered strict enforcement of the Constitution's anticlerical provisions; thereupon, the Mexican episcopate suspended public worship. Simultaneously, lay Catholics, having previously been organized by a militant and disciplined youth movement, rose in armed rebellion in various parts of the country.

This bloody rebellion, and its ultimate settlement in 1929, form the main substance of the author's account. But Bailey's greatest service has been to reveal how resorting to arms produced internal disputes within Mexican Catholicism that profoundly affected both the nature of the rebellion and its final conclusion. Moreover, he gives justifiable credit to United States Ambassador Dwight Morrow for his role in arranging the Church's de facto settlement with the government of Mexico. In the process he answers critics of United States policy by demonstrating that her primary concern was the promotion of a Church-State *modus vivendi* that would strengthen the Mexican nation.

Although the book is sometimes burdened by detail, and Bailey lacks a touch for making his characters come alive, his is a solid, well researched scholarly study. He is particularly deft in drawing upon polemics from all sides of the controversy without becoming the captive of any one persuasion. Certainly he makes wise use of the available manuscript, archival, and newspaper collections in both the United States and Mexico. With this book the University of Texas Press adds to its reputation for publishing quality works on the study of Latin America and makes a good case for publishing doctoral dissertations.

LARRY D. HILL
Department of History
Texas A & M University
College Station

J. C. BEAGLEHOLE. *The Life of Captain James Cook.* Pp. v, 760. Stanford, Calif.: Stanford University Press, 1974. $18.50.

This biography is the culmination (and alas the termination) of the life work of New Zealand's greatest historian. It is based on J. C. Beaglehole's superb editions of Cook's *Journals,* Banks' *Journal,* and his sundry other publications relating to the exploration of the Pacific. It is difficult to imagine this book being supplanted as the standard Life of Cook, at least in this century, for Beaglehole made the life and voyages of Captain James Cook uniquely his own field of study; seldom does such an important figure become so much one historian's property.

Cook spent eight and one half of the last ten and one half years of his life (1728–1779) on three epic voyages. His main accomplishments in the area of discovery are well known: his long and arduous travels in the extreme south, which finally put to rest any notion of a habitable southern continent; his explorations in the far north of the Pacific, which convinced him there was no northern passage to the Atlantic; his numerous discoveries of Pacific islands, among them Hawaii, where he met his death. But Beaglehole also brings out the importance of Cook's voyages for the sciences of cartography, astronomy, and navigation, and the value of his detailed descriptions of society, as yet virtually untouched by Europeans, in New Zealand, Tahiti, Hawaii, and Tonga. Cook himself emerges as serious, relatively humane, extremely thorough, humorless, in one of Beaglehole's felicitous phrases "the genius of the matter of fact." Perhaps such a man was needed for such laborious work as Cook's. His accomplishment was to fill in many gaps on the map of the world, and for this work the conquistador bravado of the earlier explorers would have been of little use.

The merits of the book are legion. It is based on documentation from all over the world. Stanford University Press has made a superb book, complete with maps and agreeable illustrations, of which four are in color. Beaglehole's leisurely account is marked by a polished style and a mordant (according to his son "antipodean") wit. Biographies and travel narratives are usually popular; as a life of a very great explorer this book should sell well. It deserves to become a classic not just in the literature of exploration but also in the wider field of historical biography.

M. N. PEARSON
University of Pennsylvania
Philadelphia

HENRY BIENEN. *Kenya: The Politics of Participation and Control.* Pp. vii, 215. Princeton, N.J.: Princeton University Press, 1974. $10.00.

This is a brief, well written, adequately informed, and highly controversial case study of Kenyan politics in the post-independence period. Having argued in a similar case study of Tanzania (*Tanzania: Party Transformation and Economic Development,* 1970) that TANU, the governing party, is organizationally incapable of rapidly modernizing its society, Professor Bienen has moved on to neighboring Kenya to demonstrate that modernization can occur without a viable mass-based national party.

According to Bienen, the Kenyan example necessitates a revision of Huntington's model of political decay in changing societies. As we all know, this model posits that social change leads to increased political participation that then causes increased demands on political institutions, which if they are not institutionalized and thus capable,

leads to political instability and decay. Bienen seeks to demonstrate in this book (1) that Kenya is a rapidly changing society, (2) that there is genuine mass political participation—especially at the local-rural level, (3) that while the Civil Service is strong, the ruling party, KANU, is very weak, and (4) that nevertheless, Kenya is a stable, increasingly prosperous nation-state in which the government (Civil Service) has authority and delivers real services to the people.

The core of Bienen's book is built around three long chapters that respectively describe and analyze the administration, party politics, and ethnicity and class factors in Kenyan political behavior. There is much to be learned from these chapters, particularly by readers not very familiar with the Kenya case. The volume begins with a discussion of the concept of political participation and concludes with an analysis of the bases of support for the regime. The author has chosen to write a short book and thus can be charged with sins of omission as well as commission.

With regard to omissions, how a general book on Kenyan politics can be written without an examination of political corruption and the role of non-Kenyans in the decision-making process (see pp. 17–18) is beyond this reader. I was also disappointed by Bienen's failure to make systematic and frequent comparisons to Tanzania, a country he knows well and which contrasts in so many interesting respects with Kenya.

Errors of commission abound as well. First, the methodology is not convincing. Bienen collected his information by residence, wide reading, "interviews" with an unknown number of Kenyan leaders, and by conversations with other specialists on Kenyan affairs. Not a single table of data in this book was generated by the author, and there are twenty-one such tables! Apter's *Gold Coast in Transition* was published in 1955. Reading the two books at the same time would suggest that the study of African politics has not changed in nineteen years.

Second, because of his methodological weaknesses, which relate primarily to impressionistic data gathering, Bienen repeatedly makes unsubstantiated (in this book) and controversial (to me) generalizations. Instances are (p. 64) that the Kenyan Civil Service is an effective vehicle for political participation because it is an efficient communicator of rural demands to central decision-makers and (p. 112) that turnover among MPs gives individual Kenyans "the feeling that there is a response possible to poor, that is ineffectual, representation."

Third, conceptual confusions abound. Participation, a key concept to the study, is defined in a tautological and vacuous manner (see p. 17). Except for one footnote (p. 129), Bienen fails to distinguish between diffuse regime support and what can be significant dissatisfactions over specifics, thereby vitiating the relevance of the public opinion data he presents. Bienen never defines political stability, yet he thinks Kenya is stable. It is true that Kenya ranks as one of the most stable African regimes in terms of *elite stability*, but comparative data show that it is one of the most unstable African states in terms of *communal instability* and *turmoil* (*Black Africa: A Comparative Handbook,* 1972, pp. 128–130). How stable, then, is Kenya?

Finally, the values Bienen uses to evaluate the performance of the Kenyan regime are debatable, but he does not attempt to justify them. Bienen admires the performance of the Kenyatta government because it has been "stable," because GNP per capita has increased nicely, and because the Civil Service is efficient. During the period 1963–1972 the Republic of South Africa was as stable as Kenya, the South African economy grew even faster than Kenya's, and its Civil Service is notoriously efficient. Is the South African regime to be preferred over Kenya's, or more fairly, is Kenya's system to be judged better than Tanzania's?

Obviously, Professor Bienen has written a controversial book, which I also think is a bad book. If you are interested in Kenya or in the study of African politics, the book merits a careful reading, for Professor Bienen is a serious scholar and any serious book about Kenya is bound to be both interesting and controversial.

PATRICK J. MCGOWAN
Syracuse University
Syracuse
New York

KANG CHAO. *Capital Formation in Mainland China: 1952–1965.* Pp. xiii, 178. Berkeley: University of California Press, 1974. $12.00.

Professor Chao's latest book on the Chinese economy is another important contribution to the quantitative analysis of economic development Chinese style. Using a different approach than other economists who have attempted to take the measure of that salient variable in modern economic growth—capital formation—Chao has constructed a reasonably reliable series covering China's investment process to the eve of the Great Proletarian Cultural Revolution. These data then become the framework for his analysis of the role of capital formation in China's developmental process and provide a quite useful addition to the limited statistical arsenal of the China watcher.

In constructing a comprehensive gauge of Chinese fixed capital investment, Chao employs the commodity flow method, an approach different from earlier major attempts made by western economists to measure capital formation. Instead of starting with official data on investment and then adjusting them for conceptual differences and valuational shortcomings, he takes into account each investment component and capital goods item generated in the period under review, building the aggregate through summation. The data come from various Chinese publications (investment data are more reliable since there is no incentive to exaggerate them) and from countries exporting capital goods to China. With this foundation Professor Chao constructs, first, a solid investment series for the period 1952–57; then he builds a tentative series for the period 1958–65. The latter series is refined since it appears to overstate gross fixed investment for the years 1960–65, due to a biased sample. Meticulous estimation by another method yields a more reliable series and then the two parts form a quite useful set for the entire period. The result is a much more dependable series in quality and coverage than was formerly available.

Professor Chao's work reveals a fluctuating rate of capital formation starting at over eight percent in 1952 and rising to a peak of 43.4 percent in 1959. The post-Great Leap Forward decline to 9.4 percent in 1962 is followed by recovery to 22.3 percent by 1965. These data confirm the contour of capital formation already known and reveal an extremely high rate in the peak years even for developed countries. Even in the other years, omitting the rather low rates in 1952, 1962, and 1963, the rates are quite pronounced for a country of China's backwardness.

China's socialist planning system seems successfully to have generated large amounts of saving to sustain high investment rates. This was accomplished through controls over wages and consumer prices, taxation and procurement programs in the countryside, and the direct use of surplus rural labor for road-building and water conservation projects. Thus it would appear that China's level of investment was an important function of its transformed economic institutions.

In China, capital formation has played a significant role in its economic development. Conventional economic wisdom points to the twin thrusts of investment: demand- and capacity-creation. For China it is the latter role that is effectively carried out, demand being readily controlled by the state; and given the wide gap between China's technology and that of the advanced nations, the rapid rate of investment has facilitated the filling in of

that gap and propelled her development.

As he has in other works, Professor Chao has again provided a most useful tool for looking more closely at China's economic performance over an important fifteen-year span of the Chinese revolution. Extension of this work to cover the last decade would further help to answer significant questions which the fascinating process of Chinese economic development poses.

CHARLES HOFFMANN
State University of New York
Stony Brook

EDWARD GONZALEZ. *Cuba Under Castro: The Limits of Charisma.* Pp. ix, 241. Boston, Mass.: Houghton Mifflin, 1974. $5.95.

Most extant works on Castro's Cuba stress *either* his coming to power and the reasons which brought about a social revolution in Cuba *or* the accomplishments and problems of the post-1959 regime. Because he covers both facets at approximately equal length, Edward Gonzalez' new book is probably the most complete and balanced treatment of the Cuban Revolution that we have yet had. Although the author is clearly no enthusiast for Castro, the book is also about as balanced and "objective" in an ideological sense as one is likely to get.

Professor Gonzalez' analysis places heavy stress on the political. Thus he attributes the radicalization of the Cuban Revolution primarily to three substantially political causes: the generational rebellion against the "old political class"; nationalism; and the guerrilla experience in the Sierra Maestra.

The Castro regime itself is viewed as an extension of *fidelismo* and the guerrilla experience—for example, in its elitism and in its behavioral style, which Gonzalez characterizes as the "Sierra Maestra complex." That is, he sees Cuba since 1959 as an attempt by a charismatic leader (the "socialist caudillo") and his close associates of the Sierra Maestra campaign to instill "charismatic-hardship communism" in Cuba by mobilizing Cuban society from above essentially through reliance on revolutionary will-power.

The book presents little new data or "inside" information, although its insights do partly derive from two brief visits to Cuba by the author during the late 1960s. At times the prose seems somewhat discursive and repetitive. The major limitation for most, however, may be precisely its heavily political emphasis. Thus, as the author acknowledges, there is little attention paid to the accomplishments of the regime in such areas as social policy, structural change, and the forging of a new Cuban nationhood.

Other facets of the Castro regime do nevertheless receive extended and perceptive treatment, including Soviet-Cuban relations, the political context of economic decision-making, the internal politics of the regime—seldom treated so extensively elsewhere—and, above all, the central role of Castro as charismatic leader as well as the increasing limits on the exercise of that charisma. The author concludes with the assessment that a new era, marked by the increasing bureaucratization and Sovietization of the regime, began about mid-1970 and that these trends are likely to be accentuated in the near future.

Gonzalez' emphases and interpretations will not find favor with everyone. But as a provocative, comprehensive political study of the Castro regime and its origins, this book is the best available.

ROBERT H. DIX

Rice University
Houston
Texas

KENNETH W. GRUNDY. *Confrontation and Accommodation in Southern Africa: The Limits of Independence.* Pp. xxi, 381. Berkeley: University of California Press, 1973. $12.50.

ALBIE SACHS. *Justice in South Africa.* Pp. 288. Berkeley: University of California Press, 1973. $9.00.

Kenneth Grundy observes that southern Africa does not command the attention it deserves. Apparently only major crises provide the magnet drawing attention to a trauma in process. If, in the fullness of time, the course of events will make southern Africa the focus of worldwide concern, at least a fund of knowledge and analysis will be available. For this the "Perspectives on Southern Africa" series, published by the University of California Press, deserves the highest commendation. The volumes under review are the tenth and twelfth in that series.

Confrontation and Accommodation in Southern Africa provides an analysis rooted in the systems approach. The region is treated as a whole, not country by country. The leading characteristics of the system (or more properly the southern African sub-system) are: the dominant role of the Republic of South Africa; the pattern of relationships of an economic, transport, political and diplomatic character; and the inherent conflict within the sub-system arising out of the roles of race and economic imbalance. Race is so salient an issue that one is required to contrast the role of black-led and white supremacist states. Black African states conscious of their incapacity and of the power of white-controlled states are faced with a choice of living within the rules of the system, or of isolating themselves from it, or of seeking to change it. Thus, Malawi has adopted the first option, Botswana the second and Zambia the third.

For its part South Africa has sought to reinforce the system through an "outward policy," entailing normalization of diplomatic relations with black Africa, dialogue, and a measure of internal adaptation to permit African diplomats in the Republic.

Writing in the early 1970s Grundy concludes ". . . that the situation, currently, is moving in the direction beneficial to the white-governments. . . . Revolutionary black Africa has become defensive . . . pessimism prevails. . . ." However, the author also warns that "The debilitating realities of domestic racial exploitation and privilege will ultimately take their toll."

Kenneth Grundy's use of the systems approach is a felicitious one on several scores. It organizes data in a clear and useful manner. It provides ordering concepts which illuminate our understanding of the intrastate relations of the sub-system and are suggestive of the way in which influence from outside the sub-system can penetrate it.

Since this study has been written changes have taken place—the outward policy has been de-emphasized, Lesotho has abandoned efforts to adapt to South African values, and Portugal has begun on a very different role. Nevertheless the factor of South African dominance continues and with it the characteristics of the sub-system endure.

Albie Sachs' study is very different from Grundy's in approach. *Justice in South Africa* provides a primarily historical analysis with emphasis on the role of racial ideology. The author traces the development of judicial institutions, with emphasis on that of the influential Cape province experience. The contributions of the major jurists are discussed. Sachs makes an unassailable case that the administration of justice, even more than the law, lays bare the racial prejudice of South Africa's judicial system.

In the early days of the Cape, the standards of justice were rough, inconsistent and unsophisticated. As late as the early 19th century the legal system was in a "sorry state" but achieved an "allegedly 'near perfect' condition" at the century's end. In the Orange Free State and Transvaal the developing legal system was characterized by democratic values for white men but also served as an instrument of rule over Africans.

The author allows that judges often inhibited and tempered the racist violations of individual and group rights. Invariably such stands were undercut by new laws which entrenched ever more stringently the modalities of white supremacy. The author supplies penal statistics which reveal the full extent to which law and, through law, the courts have become instruments of racial suppression. The problem is that they have been unable to stem the almost inexorable thrust towards white supremacy and have typically acceded to this trend. This judgment may be obvious but it needs to be restated with the supporting evidence which this book contains.

J. LEO CEFKIN
Department of Political Science
Colorado State University
Fort Collins

A. G. HOPKINS. *An Economic History of West Africa.* Pp. ix, 337. New York: Columbia University Press, 1973. $15.00.

The writing of economic history has an unfortunate tendency to lag behind the writing of other forms of history. It is much more difficult to popularize, and becomes ever more difficult as it becomes more technical. Yet, while more popular political history tends to deal with the pretexts for historical change, economic history invariably supplies the underlying causes. An economic history of West Africa has long been needed, and this attempt to supply it constitutes one of the most important publications in African history for many years.

This is essentially a work of synthesis. Hopkins utilizes the research of anthropologists, geographers, economists, political and economic historians to survey the economic history of West Africa from neolithic times to the present. He uses the concept of the market as his integrating theme to carry him through pre-colonial times, the era of the slave trade, the period of "legitimate" commerce designed to replace that trade, the colonial "open economy," the strains in and modifications to the open economy in the late colonial and decolonization period. It is a limiting approach and one that causes him to skimp on much social change that is crucial in the understanding of economic history. Modern education, for example, scarcely receives a mention, and yet contributed both a rapidly developing "want" of modern times and a vital conditioner of economic change. Modern urbanization is likewise virtually ignored, together with the economic and social strains associated with it.

But limiting though it is, his approach offers splendid rewards. His pre-colonial study argues convincingly for a "formalist" rather than a "substantivist" approach, thereby stripping away much of the mystification of the anthropologists, and concluding that African economic responses in the pre-colonial period can be understood in terms of a modified western economic theory. Current research in Central African economic history tends to support this view. Equally illuminating is Hopkin's survey of the modern period: his examination of the "imperial balance sheet" is judicious; he explains much technical work in development economics; and he never loses sight of the political change which economic change invariably underpinned.

Yet many will find this an irritating book. It pursues, particularly in its earlier sections, a severely historiographical approach. It repeatedly sets up and hacks down straw men. Nor does it wear its scholarship lightly, for the apparatus academicus constantly obtrudes. But it is a stimulating, if wayward, work, full of insights, full of suggestive lines for further research, full of comparative material from elsewhere in the world, and not without flashes of wit. And after being stimulated and irritated by turns, the reader receives a magnificent reward at the end, in the most comprehensive bibliography on the economic and related history of the area yet published.

JOHN M. MACKENZIE
Lecturer in African History
University of Lancaster
England

RAGHAVAN IYER. *The Moral and Political Thought of Mahatma Gandhi*. Pp. xiii, 449. New York: Oxford University Press, 1973. $12.50.

Saint or Politician? The dimensions of ethics and politics implied in the question are commonly supposed to be dichotomous alternatives. A basic thesis of Iyer is that for Gandhi these dimensions are inseparable. In this extensive, intensive and sensitive exposition of Gandhi's basic concepts, he supports this thesis. " 'Gandhism' stands for a distinct attitude toward politics and society . . . a particular ethical standpoint . . ." (p. 13). Iyer's work is a systematic exploration of Gandhi's concepts with metaphysical presuppositions and ethical and political precepts, attempting to make explicit that which is implicit in Gandhi's action and writing. Iyer's assumption is that Gandhi, as well as a man of action, was also an original and creative, though not systematic, political thinker. Gandhi's presuppositions are exposed: modern civilization is corrupt; politics can be purified. Following Iyer's treatment of Gandhi's assumptions about vows, human nature, progress and perfectibility, ethical precepts for political action are analyzed: conscience, heroism, truth, nonviolence, Satyagraha, self-rule, and self-reliance.

Iyer makes clear the power and originality of Gandhi, although he is careful to point to some difficulties. However, his final assessment that Gandhi "was mainly a political moralist who wrote from the standpoint of the rebel . . ." (p. 374), is unconvincing. Iyer indicates the fundamental importance of the "Constructive Programme" as a dimension of Satyagraha and tellingly demonstrates that this was more than rebellion. ". . . Gandhi concern[ed] himself with the possibilities of setting up a nonviolent police force, or nonviolent army, peace brigades and the like . . ." (pp. 186–7). Further, "[Gandhi] later pointed out that all this constructive work should be 'for its own sake. And yet be sure that it will develop the quality required for nonviolent responsible government' " (p.

306). There is an inconsistency here to be worked out.

Iyer presents a significant study of the ethical and political thought of Gandhi, even though the eclectic nature of the study, putting Gandhi in the context of both Western and Indian traditions of political theory, tends to detract from the central argument. Also, more careful attention to the use of primary sources would be helpful: complete information in "Notes"—for example, p. 396, H(arijan), Oct. 8, 1938 instead of H(arijan), Oct., 1938; greater accuracy in distinguishing both direct and indirect quotes—for example, p. 90, N. 2; N. 9; p. 92, N. 19; p. 120, N. 16; p. 167, N. 74.

In the field of Gandhian studies this is one of the most thorough attempts through reference to the primary sources to develop a systematic exposition of Gandhi's thought. Iyer has convincingly shown that Gandhi was an original political thinker. He has suggested the timeless and universal importance of Gandhi's assertion of ". . . politics as a branch of ethics" (p. 50).

STANLEY W. CROKER
Callison College
University of the Pacific
Stockton
California

ILPYONG J. KIM. *The Politics of Chinese Communism: Kiangsi under the Soviets*. Pp. 232. Berkeley: University of California Press, 1974. $12.50.

Broadly, this work seems to fall into two parts, the four chapters which are on Mao's concepts, the structure of soviet government, and leadership behavior, and the last three which are on mass mobilization, local government, and cadre training. The latter part is to me the more interesting. In the chapter on local government the author gives a detailed account of the party and government structure from the county down to the village level. To mention a few highlights, government was always by committee, whose members were elected for a few months at a time in order that more people could be elected to serve in turn. Good communication between one committee and another was strongly emphasized, and one device to facilitate it was for some member at one level to serve also in a committee at the level above it. Still another feature of the soviet system was the designation of a model unit among the committees at each level, for the purpose of setting a norm and urging the units to greater efforts. Even some minor points are significant. Thus, the Communist practice of allotting three to five acres of good land per sub-district (*hsiang*, how many there were in a county?) is reminiscent of the well-field system in ancient China. Did Mao get his idea from history? If so, would it not be an illustration of Mao's indebtedness to tradition, even though for different reasons neither Mao nor his detractors would concede such a link?

As Kim points out, the operational details varied greatly from one soviet area to another. It is therefore even more striking that certain basic institutions prevailed in all of the regions. From the viewpoint of mass organization, perhaps two of the most important were the poor-peasant corps and the tenant-farmer unions. The former took in not only poor farmers but manual and handicraft workers as well and reached the broadest possible range of the masses. It served primarily as a channel through which the masses could articulate their grievances and receive government attention. The tenant-farmer union, on the other hand, recruited only landless peasants but pursued a variety of tasks including issuing propaganda, promoting cultural standards of the workers, and strengthening the soviet government in general. Although Kim fails to explain the reasons behind this *modus operandi*—that is, narrower basis of recruitment but wider scope of activities—there is no doubt that he has touched upon some key aspects of the process of Communist organization. Still a third important device was the inspection system which existed at all levels and whose primary aim was to ensure that policy directives from above would be vigorously pursued at the lower levels. Taken together, these three institutions probably contributed much to the Communist success in mass organization.

Since all tasks had to be performed by men, the training of the cadres received much Communist attention. Special handbooks were issued on the methods of selecting the cadres. Each party committee above the county level maintained its own school, in addition to various short-term courses, in-service classes and special training programs sponsored by all party and government units. A common aim of all of these courses was the integration of theory and practice: all cadres were urged to become the living models of the way in which theory and action could be synthesized. Quite logically, the promotion of a cadre also depended on his ability to cultivate the masses and develop support among them.

The author also has a tendency to overstate his case occasionally. It is, of course, one thing to involve the masses in discussion and another thing to let them make policy decisions. The latter is inconceivable even in democratic countries and there is no reason to believe that it was done under Mao in Kiangsi. Kim's repeated assertion that the masses did participate in the formulation and execution of policy is therefore puzzling.

Like many writers on modern China, the author accepts as a fact that gentry members invariably oppressed the peasants. The reality was probably more complex. Strictly speaking, the term "gentry" refers only to the civil service degree-holders under the imperial regime. Not only did their number decline steadily after the revolution of 1911 but with rapid advance of urbanization in China the surviving members increasingly moved with their families into the cities. Although this process

has never been studied methodically, it is nevertheless safe to assume that the "gentry" of the 1930s differed greatly from that of a decade ago. Since we are not even sure of the meaning of this word, it is hardly scientific to consider the exploitation of the peasants by this class as a proven fact.

Despite lapses like these, Kim's book is valuable to students of the Communist movement.

YI CHU WANG
Queens College
The City University of New York
Flushing

JAMES B. MAYFIELD. *Rural Politics in Nasser's Egypt: A Quest for Legitimacy*. Pp. xvi, 288. Austin: University of Texas Press, 1971. No price.

Studies of non-Western societies are, generally speaking, easily divided along disciplinary lines: the political scientist above, in the councils and agencies of the government; the anthropologist below, in the tribe, village or quarter; the economist in the national pocketbook. Findings, while frequently illuminating about the sector or subsystem examined, and sometimes theoretically noteworthy, do not usually provide a reliable understanding of cumulative changes, a basic concern for those students interested in modernization. The reason for this is that none of the sectors or subsystems is independent of one another, and the development of each is integrally tied, albeit in complex and in some cases indirect ways, to the development of the others. Not only have the broader patterns not been properly examined, but even the points of subsystem articulation have been neglected. For this, the specialized disciplines, with customary methodological approaches not always appropriate for unconventional studies, are partly to blame. Having divided up the social landscape, they continue to be ill prepared to move beyond their turf in quest of the overall patterns and inter-system dynamics.

What, then, is required? Students must focus attention upon the points of articulation between the subsystems and sectors, and must be shameless enough to appropriate the necessary methodology, if need be even from a mix of other disciplines. The political scientist must deign to leave the capitol for the provinces, and the offices of officials for the meeting places of ordinary citizens. The anthropologist must gird himself to look beyond the traditional social life and exotic customs to the intrusions and influences of extra-local forces. The economist must look to the people behind and the political and cultural forces in tandem with economic institutions.

Professor Mayfield, a political scientist, attempts exactly this in his study of Nasser's Arab Socialist Union and its impact upon the peasants of rural Egypt. His background chapters on the political history of the fellahin, on personality and culture of the fellah, and on village politics indicate a willingness to search beyond disciplinary boundaries for useful approaches and substantive clues. And that he visited 79 villages (p. 131, note 30), interviewed 47 school teachers (p. 152, note 1) and "250 . . . officials, fellahin, and private citizens" (p. 184), indicates that he made efforts to see what was happening "on the ground." The basic purpose and approach of the study is just what is required.

All the more disappointing, then, is the book coming from this promising study. Most surprising is the complete lack of systematic data, the text instead consisting of references to the literature, to official documents, anecdotes and "apt illustrations." Statements such as "after careful analysis of some 250 interviews with officials, fellahin, and private citizens, I have come to the conclusion that . . ." recur, but are not documented by the presentation of data. The description as set out is impressionistic, and this reviewer cannot but fear that it is superficial.

Perhaps the inadequate conceptualization and outmoded theoretical assumptions did not provide an effective stimulus. "Legitimacy," "political culture," "socialization," "communica-tion," and "modernization" are invoked, but, never satisfactorily defined or related to begin with, they result in a hash of imprecise jargon. The search for "political culture" degenerates into an impressionistic grasp at attitudes. Assumptions of consensus as the basis of political systems, attributions of institutional success to the filling of needs, assertions of the prime role of political socialization are all indications of functional theory ill-used. This book is a sad primer on how opportunity for studying the impact of national politics at the local level can be squandered.

PHILIP CARL SALZMAN
McGill University
Montreal

FRANK D. MCCANN, JR. *The Brazilian-American Alliance, 1937–1945.* Pp. x, 527. Princeton, N.J.: Princeton University Press, 1973. $18.50.

American scholars have begun to produce a plethora of important studies of Brazil, and Frank McCann's history of U.S.-Brazilian relations during the Estado Novo period of the Getúlio Vargas dictatorship rightfully deserves a place among those studies. Like many of his contemporaries, McCann's work is the product of several field trips which provided the basis for a dissertation and later substantial revision.

Given its approach and the context of its discussion, this study is definitive in its coverage of Brazilian relations with the outside world during the period 1937 to 1945. No other scholarly work does so well. In fact, heretofore, few serious studies on the topic were available to student and scholar alike. Further, this study is interesting reading. It is nicely written. As such, it is descriptive, covering events and details exhaustively in chronological order. There is no theoretical framework, no set of propositions that have been verified through systematically organized data. Instead we have here an historical account, carefully documented as a consequence of the author's thorough research in archives found in Rio and Washington.

The eight-year time frame embraced by this study is described over fifteen chapters. McCann begins with portrayals of Vargas and Roosevelt, then delves into the roots of their policies and actions in order to demonstrate how they maneuvered themselves into positions establishing an alliance between Brazil and the United States. The author examines the relationship of Brazilian Ambassador Oswaldo Aranha and Sumner Wells, U.S. Assistant Secretary of State. Then he turns to Brazilian domestic affairs, showing how Vargas repressed the neo-fascist integralist movement as well as an incipient German Nazi movement in the country. He attempts to demonstrate that while Vargas headed an authoritarian dictatorship, he neither endorsed the axis powers nor became a puppet of the United States, a position which runs counter to many interpretations of this period. McCann then looks at efforts to establish the security of the Western Hemisphere in the face of German influence and penetration, and here he is able to describe the consolidation of the U.S. position in Brazil, a process which culminated in a series of economic and military treaties between the two nations. This process was one of intense competition between Germany and the United States to control the Brazilian market, with the U.S. strategy being oriented to the use of reciprocal trade agreements to generate outlets for U.S. agricultural and industrial surpluses. In effect, the U.S. objective aimed to open the door to U.S. capital penetration in Brazil, whereas the Brazilian response was oriented to the maintenance of a neutral position between Germany and the United States, a position through which Brazilian economic nationalism could be preserved. The author's analysis also moves to military questions as related to international strategies of the axis and allied powers. This culminated in a U.S.-Brazilian military alliance and eventually in Brazil's declaration of war against Germany and Italy, and the sending into battle of a Brazilian division of soldiers. All this is described by McCann who aptly shows how the flush of victory along the German-Italian front was utilized by Vargas to build national spirit at home.

In a summary assessment of the era, McCann affirms that U.S. policy had ensured Brazilian superiority over Argentina, had maintained U.S. military bases in the country, and had prevented the European powers from providing military assistance. Several conclusions are apparent. First, the Vargas regime was not ideologically motivated; it increasingly moved toward a combination of technology and economic nationalism in establishing a basis for the developmental nationalism which pervaded the Brazilian political economy after 1945. Second, the U.S.-Brazilian union was a consequence of Brazilian desires to offset shifting relationships between the United States and other Spanish-speaking nations, especially Argentina which desired to establish dominant leadership not only over the River Plata region but all of South America. Third, the alliance, the war, and all the related developments resulted in a modification of Brazil's dependency with the outside world, away from England especially but also Germany and toward the United States. McCann stresses this as a major theme in his book: Brazil, he states, became "subservient, very nearly a dependency, to the United States." In freeing itself from British domination (it cut its financial ties with the British Rothschilds in favor of Wall Street), Brazil attempted to ensure its own hegemony over South America, an effort which its military leaders continue to pursue today. Thus, McCann provides us with a solid understanding of the subservient, dependent relationship which also characterizes today's ties between Brazil and the United States.

RONALD H. CHILCOTE
University of California
Riverside

BURTON PASTERNAK. *Kinship and Community in Two Chinese Villages*.

Pp. ix, 174. Stanford, Calif.: Stanford University Press, 1972. $8.50.

DAVID K. JORDAN. *Gods, Ghosts and Ancestors*. Pp. 163. Berkeley: University of California Press, 1972. $7.50.

One of these studies of Taiwanese villages is concerned with lineages, the other with religion. Pasternak's is a comparison between two villages, one "traditional," the other go-ahead; one rich, the other poor. In the rich village the many associations were not lineage-based. The poor one was dominated by the lineage said to descend from the first settler 200 years ago. Pasternak rejects theories which ascribe lineage formation to the requirements of defense or of irrigated rice-growing; both necessitate co-operation, but this need not be confined to agnates. In fact, it was precisely for defense against Hokkien raids that Tatieh, the rich village, organized a neighborhood association. It is where there is no external threat, and no competition for land, he argues, that single-lineage communities can be expected to develop. He examines studies of mainland Chinese and concludes, unsurprisingly, that the principles of kinship and neighborhood will be combined in different proportions in any given community. His writing is by no means easy to follow, and he has an irritating way of describing villages as "playing down" or "de-emphasizing" kinship as if people did this as a concerted policy.

Jordan's study of religion was made not a hundred miles from Chungshe, Pasternak's poor village, but among Hokkien. He sees Taiwanese folk religion as essentially a means of protection against misfortune and remedy when it strikes. Little attention is paid to ancestors, a fact which he accounts for by the assertion that corporate lineages were "apparently lacking in Taiwan from the beginning." Various gods are worshipped on a transactional basis; offerings create the obligation to return protection and good will. Every three years

the superior gods of an area inspect their territory, and they and their lower-ranking colleagues move in their palanquins in a procession which visits every village; the order of precedence agreed among the inferior deities reflects the political strength of their worshippers at a given time.

Misfortune is less often ascribed to the displeasure of gods than to the influence of unhappy ghosts, particularly those of girls who have died too young to be married and so (from the point of view of the community) have failed to make their contribution to the continuance of a family. They grow up in the spirit world, and eventually demand a husband, making this known by inflicting sickness on some member of their natal family. Some of them want more: to be worshipped as gods (little gods), and speak through the mouth of a medium. Jordan observes that in recent years it has become common for them to attack the families of their affines.

His theoretical conclusions concern the anomalies in a belief system that can make gods of people who are by definition deviants, and the changes in the ascription of responsibility for a family's misfortunes. He reminds us that it is in fact the community that interprets the wishes of gods and ghosts, that the irregularities which these beings punish—or rather seek to have rectified—differ as the norms accepted by the community change. Thus apparent contradictions need never destroy the beliefs; only external forces can, and no doubt eventually will.

LUCY MAIR

London
England

RUBEN E. REINA. *Paraná: Social Boundaries in an Argentine City*. Pp. xi, 390. Austin: The University of Texas Press, 1974. $10.00.

Scholars in cultural and urban anthropology should be rewarded by delving into this book by Dr. Ruben E. Reina of the University of Pennsylvania. Argentine-born and educated through high school, the author received his higher education in the United States, earning the Ph.D. at North Carolina. He admits that "the hardest part . . . is to immerse himself in the study of a culture of which he has been a part." Yet he achieved enough objectivity in his book that fellow-Argentines who study it, as the author hopes will happen, may have their pride wounded. To the busy reader, I recommend the last two chapters and the Epilogue.

Paraná is an administrative center, capital of the Province of Entre Ríos. The author chose that city as his subject because it contributed importantly to the consolidation of Argentina in the mid-19th century, because urban development, industrial expansion, and modern political revolution have not changed it radically, and because the culture of the city retains the early families as the core of the traditional elite group. Yet the author strives through his informants to whom he gives generous space, to portray a dynamic of social mobility and opportunity for the wide-ranging middle class, and even those of lower social standing who manage to obtain adequate education.

The glorious gaucho tradition of *Martin Fierro*, and the lustrous profession of teaching are emphasized by Dr. Reina. Dr. Arturo Frondizi, third generation Argentine of Italian heritage and President, 1958–62, who was reared in Entre Ríos, relished discussing his younger days and recalling his father's teaching career in talking to this reviewer when the latter was American Ambassador to Argentina. Author-statesman Domingo Sarmiento, in the 1880s, invited a group of U.S. teachers to Argentina, thus starting cultural exchange and virtually enshrining their profession.

The author has brought professional skill and integrity to bear on a subject of limited appeal. The result is an enlightening picture of one Argentine city. While one should resist overgeneralizing, Reina's following opinions are revealing: "In Argentina and in Paraná, quiet disbelief, social dissatisfaction, individual apathy, and psychological uprootedness underlie the way of life and affect interpersonal relationships." "The social structure is more deeply rooted in history than the value system."

As a diplomat and political scientist, I have found Argentina to be a challenging subject. Perhaps the following quotations from Dr. Reina's informants will enlighten others as they did me: "We have everything that is necessary to be an excellent nation, but I believe we lack spiritual fortitude." "From the beginning of our independence, we have continuously been searching for a savior." "The old generation of intellectuals came to an end during Peron; those who were in formation during that period were corrupted; the present generation is the product of an anarchic situation." "Apariencia (appearance) is the basic dynamic of our life style in Paraná." "Schools . . . are divorced from the dynamics of neighborhood life." "Learning to trust is our major task."

R. RICHARD RUBOTTOM
Southern Methodist University
Dallas
Texas

FRANK A. STONE. *The Rub of Cultures in Modern Turkey—Literary Views of Education.* Pp. x, 184. Bloomington: Indiana University, 1973. $16.00.

Professor Stone presents the first book in English about modern Turkish literature, a subject on which the reader would have to search to find a half-dozen learned-journal articles (but listed in his Bibliography). The title reflects his central interest in the interaction of ideas propagated by two sets of writers, conditioned by their respective backgrounds, which he identifies as the Bosphorus Civilization and the culture of Anatolia. Representatives of the former are urban in background, from not only Istanbul on the Bosphorus but also cities on the Aegean and Black Sea coasts. What is most interesting about their writing is their motivation: to acquaint the literate elite—mostly urban—with the plight of the village folk of Anatolia whose development out of traditional patterns into modernity these writers believe has been willfully neglected by the ruling elite. Our author does not distinguish between the urban writers who rely on first-hand experience and those who exploit their imagination and the writings of others (Greenwich Village and Hollywood writers of "westerns"), but does identify the authors who are products of villages and Village Institutes, one of whom, Mahmut Makal, has been most famous of all for over twenty years.

The subtitle alludes more to Stone's interest in education and the fact that some ruralite teachers have been outstanding writers than to the general acquaintance of literary figures with this field or their impact upon it. Because of the standardization of scholastic procedures, classroom use of contemporary literature is exceptional rather than standard operation. Whereas schools in the early years of the Republic of Turkey were agencies of indoctrination, both general and vocational education now are focused on preparation for freedom of choice and action. Thus, in a free society, writers more than educators are agents of reform.

Among the 134 pages of text, there are some thirty-four pages of quotation from the 143 works by sixty authors with whom Stone deals (not counting more than fifty works of criticism and biography in Turkish). Even without turning to the twenty-two pages of footnotes and fifteen of bibliography, one is impressed by the vast amount of material which the author has surveyed and interpreted. He regrets that so few of the works have been rendered into English; the reviewer regrets that these few are not identified. For a subsidized publication, the book is overpriced. Libraries should own it; many readers should learn from and enjoy it.

DONALD E. WEBSTER
Claremont
California

MARTIN KING WHYTE. *Small Groups and Political Rituals in China*. Pp. 279. Berkeley, Calif.: University of California Press, 1974. No price.

When the Chinese Communists came to power in 1949, they wanted to totally unify and mobilize the entire Chinese population, responsive to their demands. For this purpose they initiated certain organizational innovations and activities—known as the small-group political study and mutual-criticism rituals in which a large percentage of the population regularly participates.

Mr. Whyte's book pursued a scholarly examination of these political mechanisms of both social control and mass mobilization in China. The primary data used in this study are intensive (more than 700 hours) interviews the author conducted in Hong Kong in 1968–69 with 101 refugees who had left mainland China during the previous few years. Whyte explored the significance and effectiveness of these obligatory small-group and political rituals in the daily lives of officials, students, workers, peasants and inmates of corrective labor camps. He then presented comparative case-studies constructed from the above-mentioned interviews to illustrate the range of successes and failures of these practices.

The author's overall conclusion is that China's small-group political study and mutual-criticism rituals have succeeded in getting people to drop old habits and to undertake new tasks, thereby promoting new Communist order and preventing opposition. But they have been less successful in achieving their avowed goals of creating a true unity of thoughts and wills among the participants (800 million population). The fact that the Mao regime still relies upon the carrot-and-stick technique of materialistic incentives and sanctions to motivate the entire population to high commitments and efforts tends to support the author's conclusion. Indeed, Chairman Mao Tse-tung as China's "infallible" supreme leader has achieved rapid, drastic and far-reaching revolutionary changes in his country's social structure and way of life for the past two decades. But, as Mao apparently realizes on the eve of his twilight years, he has been expecting much more than what is humanly possible.

In the absence of the more reliable, on-the-spot and first-hand original data, the methodology taken by the author seems to be a most effective way of doing scholarly research on the effectiveness of the Peking regime's small-group and political rituals. In short, the book is a remarkable contribution to the growing library of volumes of studies on contemporary China.

TAI SUNG AN
Department of Political Science
Washington College
Chestertown
Maryland

EUROPE

STEPHEN F. COHEN. *Bukharin and the Bolshevik Revolution: A Political Biography, 1888–1938.* Pp. xv, 495. New York: Alfred A. Knopf, 1973. $15.00.

In recent years there has been a notable scholarly revival of interest in "Old Bolsheviks." Warren Lerner's study of Karl Radek, "the last internationalist," and Sidney Heitman's bibliography of Nikolai I. Bukharin's writings come readily to mind. And now we have Dr. Cohen's biography of Bukharin.

Let me say at the outset that this book—originating as a doctoral dissertation at Columbia University—is, within its limits, an outstanding achievement. The author does succeed in restoring Bukharin to his rightful place both as a noteworthy Marxist ideologist and as political leader during the Revolution and the first decade of Soviet power. Dr. Cohen is correct in regarding his work "as a contribution to the ongoing effort by various scholars to revise the customary interpretation which views the Bolshevik revolution after Lenin chiefly in terms of a Stalin-Trotsky rivalry."

The documentation is vast even though many Soviet archival materials on Bukharin are still unavailable for scholarly inspection. Hence Dr. Cohen sensibly acknowledges that his work should not be looked upon as "definitive."

From this reviewer's point of view, a little too much emphasis is placed upon Bukharin's attempted ideological refutations of the anti-Marxist Austrian school of economics led by Böhm-Bawerk, Menger, and von Wieser. Bukharin, in Dr. Cohen's presentation, is not entirely convincing in his supposed theoretical demolition of Austrian marginalism. On the other hand, it might have been fruitful if the author had expanded his coverage of Bukharin's months of emigration in the U.S.A. (centering in New York) during 1916 and 1917. Bukharin's impressions (or lack of same) of American life and institutions would make revealing reading, I am sure.

Perhaps weakest are the pages dealing with Bukharin's formative years. The influence of Bukharin's father upon his son's literary and cultural development, "the background of Bukharin's prominence as a Bolshevik literary critic," is surely far from unique. Many educated Russian middle-class fathers of the time fostered similar tastes in their children without turning them to "Bolshevik" literary points of view. Bukharin's "lepidopteral knowledge" is also certainly not so unique as Dr. Cohen would make out. After all, Bukharin's contemporaries Vladimir Nabokov and André Gide were avid butterfly collectors too. And before leaving the subject of Bukharin's family, I think it is misleading not to capitalize "orthodox" (as is done twice on p. 6) if Russian Orthodox is intended. But these comments should not detract too much from the solid merits of Dr. Cohen's study.

The book is enriched by numerous illustrations, including a 1928 photograph of Bukharin "pledging to young Communists to quit smoking." At the risk of sounding frivolous, I wonder if the "genial" pipe-smoking Stalin was ever photographed taking a similar pledge?

All in all, this is a book to be recommended to scholar and layman alike.

DAVID HECHT
Department of History
Pace University
New York

CRAUFURD D. W. GOODWIN. *The Image of Australia: British Perception of the Australian Economy from the Eighteenth to the Twentieth Century.* Pp. 255. Durham, N.C.: Duke University Press, 1974. $8.75.

This is an excellent and exceedingly useful book designed to tell one how United Kingdom commentators thought they saw the Australian economy from earliest times to the era of the Great Depression, with emphasis on the criticisms of public economic policy, private economic conduct, and the Australian response to both. It is too bad the focus of the book is not wider for even the evidence cited shows that there was also a steady flow of social and cultural criticism, and while economic specialists may be well satisfied with Goodwin's book, students of Australian history at large will want to call for another and more comprehensive study before they are satisfied that all the perceptions, critical and otherwise, have been reviewed. However, it clearly emerges that the U.K. criticisms of Australia were fiercest and most dogmatic when ignorance of Australia actualities was most comprehensive. Goodwin's demonstration that "the Brits" (as they are called today) *were* persistently ignorant will bring an appropriately sardonic response from contemporary Australian readers. But then when has ignorance not been a large component of the discussion of public affairs?

By and large the book is very intelligently executed within its defined limits, but every so often one feels that Goodwin's knowledge of Australian history is deficient. Illustratively the policy struggle over the land, into

which the British critics blundered, whether between the squatters and the Imperial and colonial governments or later on as a three-cornered struggle of the pastoralists, the crop agriculturalists, and the self-governing colonies, does not come through with proper vividness. In fact, the persistence of controversy over the land and its uses throughout Australian history is not emphasized. It is, again, the case that while the British attacks on Australian urbanization, persistent throughout Australian history, are noted, and the support for them from Australians devoted to the pastoral interest taken into account, it is not pointed out how this anti-urban sentiment in a highly urbanized country led to a weird underemphasis on the cities in Australian history, a mis-orientation only today beginning to be repaired.

Even more noticeable is the inadequacy of the account of the policy controversies of the Great Depression years. As it stands the account is little more than a "buttering up" of the late Douglas Berry Copland and the so-called Premiers' Plan. Even so it is not as fully documented as the bibliography allows. But no attempt is made to depict the opposition to Copland and others, and the Premiers' Plan, right or left, of which there was a good deal from both angles; nor is anything made of the very important fact that Australia was ruled by a Labor Government from 1929 to 1931 which was unable to establish the legitimacy of its innovative proposals, lost as a consequence the support of its "loyal" and dissenting constituency in the Parliament, and fell not least because more or less in despair it embraced the Premiers' Plan.

Nevertheless, this is a book all thoroughgoing students of Australian history can (and should) read with profit.

C. HARTLEY GRATTAN
University of Texas
Austin

HOLGER H. HERWIG. *The German Naval Officer Corps: A Social and*

Political History, 1890–1918. Pp. viii, 298. New York: Oxford University Press, 1973. $19.25.

L. L. FARRAR, JR. *The Short-War Illusion: German Policy, Strategy and Domestic Affairs, August-December 1914.* Pp. viii, 207. Santa Barbara, Calif.: American Bibliographical Center, 1973. $4.75.

These two books offer an interesting and useful contribution to the study of German history during the period up to and including the First World War, but for different reasons.

Holger Herwig presents an unusual but highly relevant aspect of German naval policy during the generation which began with the ambitious program of Tirpitz to construct a large and powerful battle-fleet. He looks at the personnel policies of the navy with reference to the social composition of the officer corps, their educational background and the social environment in which they circulated. The result is a fascinating description based on extensive archival findings of what working conditions were like in the German navy, and of the social values which determined the attitudes and behavior of the officer corps. Every angle of the problem is covered with careful detail even to the extent of providing us with information on the navy's exclusive views on the subject of marriage by their officers and of the significance of duelling. One becomes aware of the obsessive interest shown by Kaiser Wilhelm II in appointments within the service and in his position of supreme war lord as revealed in his habit of checking the logbooks of his submarine commanders. Some light is also thrown on the political outlook of the officer corps, particularly their strong antipathy towards the SPD.

The German naval officer corps was, however, far from being a cohesive body. Herwig's main thesis is the differences and antagonisms in the relationship between the various grades of the corps, and how these tensions were increased by the conditions of war and contributed to the mutinies in the navy

during 1917–18. The first half of his book deals separately with the three groups of executive officer corps, the engineer-officer corps and finally the deck-officer corps. The executive officer corps showed the most exclusive tendencies in their lack of real contact with other personnel, which created resentment on the part of the engineer corps whose importance and role in the navy had grown correspondingly with their increase in size during the 19th century and the greater dependence of the navy on technical specialists. In Herwig's view, all these issues reflected the rigid divisions of Wilhelmine society.

The latter part of his book examines how the neglect of personnel questions by Tirpitz and the internal differences within the navy leadership over recruitment policy created problems which came home to roost during the First World War. The initial appeal to patriotism neutralized these tensions only temporarily, for the length of the War imposed an added strain on relations within the officer corps and brought old grievances to a head. Holger Herwig has produced an excellent piece of historical research; the only point which detracts from the merit of his work is the absence of a conclusion summarizing his results and emphasizing the general themes which emerge from his detailed analysis.

The Short-War Illusion is a book of a contrasting kind. It looks at the problem of the immediate war aims of the belligerent powers in the last months of 1914. The author does not pretend to offer new information on a subject which has already been amply covered by other historians, for his aim is "a synthesis and interpretation of recent scholarship." The novelty and value of his book is that it provides a political-science approach to a problem which has caused much controversy among historians since the early 1960s. Using a conceptual framework relating to the nature of international relations and in particular war diplomacy at the time, Lancelot Farrar argues that the initial belief that the War would be short-lived was unfounded because the military preconditions for such a war did not exist. The governments involved had revolutionary political aims, while their domestic political circumstances as well as material factors militated against a brief war. This book is a refreshing antidote to some of the more turgid tomes on the outbreak of war in 1914.

GEOFFREY PRIDHAM
University of Bristol
England

RUDDOCK F. MACKAY. *Fisher of Kilverstone.* Pp. 539. New York: Oxford University Press, 1973. $19.25.

This carefully researched book traces the career of Admiral of the Fleet Sir John Fisher from the time he joined the British Navy at the age of thirteen in 1854, to his last acid criticism of England's "fossilizing" military power in 1920, the year he died at the age of seventy-nine. Fisher's name is linked essentially to the remodeling of the British navy as a modern instrument of war in the period prior to the First World War. It is Fisher who will always be identified with the introduction of a new, more powerful battleship, the *Dreadnought,* in 1906. It is Fisher who, in the early stages of the First World War, reluctantly approved Churchill's ill-fated scheme for a British attack on the Dardanelles. And it is Fisher, with his iconoclastic attacks on naval tradition and bitter personal feuding, who remains the most controversial figure in British naval history since the days of Nelson.

In charting Fisher's career, Mackay portrays the technical and strategic transformation of a navy still operating within the traditions set down in the Napoleonic Wars. Fisher, with his demonic energy, challenged outdated traditions, demanded experimentation and the application of scientific advances. But Mackay also notes that Fisher, blinded perhaps by his own self-confidence, failed to institute a General Staff for the navy, a failure

which hobbled British strategy in the Great War.

With the outbreak of war in 1914, Fisher, age seventy-four, was recalled to duty as First Sea Lord. At the Admiralty, Churchill called for a naval strike at the Dardanelles; and, against his best strategic judgment, Fisher yielded to his superior's demand. Only after the disastrous campaign was underway did Fisher resign (May, 1915); but the damage was done, and Fisher must share the blame with Churchill. Mackay suggests that Fisher's failure was due to "strain, near-exhaustion, natural deviousness, and temporary loss of confidence."

Mackay has presented a judicious, cautious, and detailed account of Fisher's life. But certain larger questions go unanswered. For example, Fisher's support for the new *Dreadnought* is presented in detail; but the question as to whether this leap ahead in the arms race helped or hindered Britain over the next decade is ignored. Fisher's disdain for limitation in the conduct of war (his willingness to shoot German prisoners if necessary) is cited, but passed over. Finally, whether some deeper flaw of character was responsible for Fisher's failure to oppose Churchill on the Dardanelles issue is overlooked. Still this is a solid and valuable study, oriented to the student of naval history more than to the student of general political or social history.

EDMUND S. WEHRLE
The University of Connecticut
Storrs

MICHAEL MALLET. *Mercenaries and their Masters: Warfare in Renaissance Italy.* Pp. i, 284. Totowa, N.J.: Rowman and Littlefield, 1974. $15.00.

Readers of this very valuable book should not be mislead by the sub-title. The author is interested in the position of mercenaries in Italian society, not in the details of battles and campaigns. In fact, a little more attention to military history would have been helpful to the general reader; a reference to the "War of Ferrara" is not very enlightening to one who is not a specialist in 15th century Italian history. On the other hand, there is a mass of detail, much of it drawn from hitherto unused sources, on the recruitment, financing, organization, and behavior of Italian mercenary armies.

The author's main thesis—that Italian mercenary armies were necessary, relatively effective, and usually reliable—is fully supported by the evidence. By 1300 no European government could function without hiring soldiers. The real problem was to keep the hired soldiers under control, and the "Free Companies" were as dangerous to 14th century France (or Greece) as they were to 14th century Italy. The great condottieri of the 15th century could keep their troops under control and were, on the whole, loyal to their employers. They were also men of good family, often lords of small principalities, often well-educated, and no more unscrupulous than the popes and princes whom they served.

Italian mercenaries were as good soldiers as those of any other country. At least Charles the Bold of Burgundy made great efforts to obtain Italian companies, and Charles, with all his faults, was a good military organizer. The main trouble with Italian armies was that Italian states were small. No state could support a very large army, and alliances of states found it hard to combine their troops effectively. (Incidentally, my one serious disagreement with the author would be over the estimates of the size of Italian armies, that he has accepted; some of them seem much too large).

The Italians faced the problem of civilian control of the military; some of the most interesting pages in the book deal with the administrators sent out by the cities to work with—and keep an eye on—the military leaders. And, as always, there was the problem of finance. By far the biggest expense was the pay of troops, even though wages declined in the 15th century. Fortifications came next; costs for *materiel* were relatively low. But the overall burden

on governments was tremendous. One interesting result of expenditures on war was that money was transferred from rich cities to smaller places. Urbino would not have been a center of the Renaissance if its lord, Federigo la Montefeltro, had not been a famous commander. One wonders if similar transfers of wealth from richer to poorer areas did not take place in trans-Alpine countries.

JOSEPH R. STRAYER
Princeton University
New Jersey

ALBERT MARRIN. *The Last Crusade: The Church of England in the First World War.* Pp. viii, 303. Durham, N.C.: Duke University Press, 1974. $9.75.

Can we look back to call anything the "last crusade" while "Christians" Protestant and Catholic kill each other's babies in Ireland? At least the author finds a difference in World War I and later wars in which England has been engaged.

Nationalism has the power to overwhelm everything binding men in different nations together, he says. "The clergy of all the major denominations of the West threw their support, material no less than moral, behind the war efforts of their respective countries, while Catholic, Protestant, and Jewish laymen slew their coreligionists with as little compunction as atheists slew their fellow nonbelievers."

How did the Church of England respond to the crisis of 1914–1918, World War I? That Anglican body represented the status quo, the establishment, in many ways. It did not exactly welcome the war. But Belgium was entitled to help by treaty, and gentlemen, you know, honor their pledged word. Call it a "scrap of paper?" That would prove you are not to be trusted in anything.

During the first weeks of the war, many feelings of guilt and shame were expressed. Had we not been drifting away from God, sinning with the tide?

Was there perhaps divine displeasure at disestablishment of the Episcopal church in Wales? Does not this war represent a judgment, a punishment, from God?

The author found no anti-German sentiment in the prewar church; rather Germans were admired as exemplars of moral conduct and intellect. But Germans burned the university library at Louvain, used dumdum bullets, made Britain itself a theater of operations by bombardment of East Coast towns—so "we" look at the sins of Germany. They are many! With Germany seen as the most sinful nation, it now becomes possible to blame her for the war, a premeditated crime. We call names; Germans are "Huns," the Kaiser is Attila. And they don't think like we do—we go for individual liberty while they submerge the individual in the state!

He who cherishes human life, if he is to resolve his own inner tensions, must assert the validity of the cause. Then, if our side is the exemplar of "pure principles," the other side must be motivated by their opposites! To a degree not easy for the secular-minded, the devout man can radicalize a conflict. Soon you are at war with the Devil—while you represent God! Allied war aims took on apocalyptic overtones. The Allies were fighting a crusade against antichrist, to kill war by eradicating the doctrine of state idolatry, the spirit of aggressiveness, and the disease of militarism.

Now total victory only can satisfy— you cannot consider a compromise peace. You must have abject surrender. So do what is necessary to achieve it—does not the end justify the means?

The clergy saw hope for peace in a "league of nations." Perhaps man could give loyalty of nationalistic intensity to a "One World" government?

Finite man finds difficulty in faithfully representing the infinite, the universal, the eternal.

ROLFE L. HUNT

New Rochelle
New York

DAVID W. MILLER. *Church, State and Nation in Ireland: 1898–1921.* Pp. 579. Pittsburgh, Pa.: University of Pittsburgh Press, 1974. $14.95.

The relations among church, state, and nation in Ireland underwent fascinating changes during the first two decades of the present century. Reference is to the Roman Catholic Church, the state structure in control of the island, and the Irish nation, the networks of nationalist-minded Irishmen. This account of those complexities in readjustment begins with the recovery of the nationalist movement in the late 1890s, and it continues until the eve of Irish ratification of the treaty with the United Kingdom and the outbreak of internecine fighting between the pro- and anti-treaty Irish factions. As the author states, "it is a remarkable story in which the Church protected, and indeed augmented, her interests—the fervent devotion of her people and the institutional conditions which, she believed, fostered that devotion—up to the last hours of the old order and yet entered the new order with those interests intact for the future as well."

Based upon a careful sifting of available printed and manuscript sources, this is a tangled story of intrigues, conspiracies, negotiations, misunderstandings, deceptions, and violent and nonviolent aggressions. In 1898, a well-established British regime controlled the state, and the nation consisted of a sharply divided Irish Parliamentary Party and its sympathizers. By the end of 1921, the British had maneuvered Irish representatives into signing a treaty setting up what became for a while a twenty-six-county Free State with status in the empire similar to that of Canada. This meant the abandoning, at least for the time, of the idea of an independent thirty-two-county republic. It also meant the continuation of a high degree of control by the British over Ireland's politico-economic affairs. In accepting this compromise, members of the Dail Eireann (Irish parliament) precipitated two years of civil war and subsequent bitterness in the twenty-six counties as well as more than a half-century of agitation and periodic conflict in the six-county British enclave, Northern Ireland.

Against the background of changing Anglo-Irish politico-economic relations, Miller sets forth quite objectively incident after incident of Roman Catholic hierarchical involvement in the affairs both of the Irish state and nation and of the United Kingdom's relations with Ireland. "In the years covered by this study the Church so played out her role in the Irish political system that she achieved, for a half-century at any rate, a position in the new political order that might be the envy of churchmen throughout the world." This was especially the case in education. By 1900, the "national" schools of the country had lost all of their originally legislated pretense of being nondenominational. Local school managers were almost always parish priests or, in non-Catholic areas, other clergymen. Such managers had autocratic control of hiring and firing teachers and of prescribing curricula. Efforts at about that time by the Irish National Teachers' Organization to work out some degree of protection for teacher tenure resulted in the blacklisting of its members for several years and the forcing of Protestants to form their own teachers' union. Thus, religiously segregated education on all levels had become the accepted pattern. The only exceptions were some of the technical schools and Trinity College (Dublin) and The Queen's University (Belfast).

Miller does not contend that the Irish state under the British or as Free State or Republic functioned as a theocracy, "but it is a State in which the Church has had considerably more influence than any ordinary interest group." He attributes the church's success to the objectivity with which it strengthened relationships available to it and did not fully identify itself with the changing phases of state and nation. "Within the 'given territory' in which the Nation could successfully supplant the State, the Church, in the period of this study, made the Irish political system serve her interests with consummate skill and determination."

This is a valuable contribution to a difficult and neglected aspect of Irish history. I trust it will inspire volumes dealing with the preceding and subsequent periods.

ALFRED MCCLUNG LEE
Professor of Sociology and
  Anthropology Emeritus
Brooklyn College and the
  Graduate Center
The City University of New York

NICHOLAS ORME. *English Schools in the Middle Ages.* Pp. 369. New York: Barnes & Noble, 1973. $25.00.

BERYL SMALLEY. *The Becket Conflict and the Schools: A Study of Intellectuals in Politics.* Pp. 258. Totowa, N.J.: Rowman and Littlefield, 1973. $13.50.

The history of education in Britain has been receiving increased attention during the past two decades. A broad treatment of the Middle Ages, however, has not resulted from this renaissance, and, except for specialized articles and monographs, the area was dominated by A. F. Leach's *The Schools of Medieval England* (1915, 1916). Possibly, the rising criticism of Leach was a factor in the publication of Orme's study.

The author is well aware of the contemporary conviction that the history of education encompasses not only schools, but also "family life, social conditions, religious ideas and the tasks and preoccupations of adulthood" (p. 1). Nonetheless, he has concentrated on the schools, inasmuch as "the work of the schools is relatively well documented and, since it was more formalized, far easier to construct. It also provides an operational base for the wider study of the life and education of medieval man" (*ibid.*).

The content is concerned with the interrelationship of education and the various components of English society, as well as curriculum, instruction, and life in the medieval schools from the twelfth century to the sixteenth. The appendix consists of a convenient alphabetical listing of schools (1066–1530), with an indication of sources of information, and a well-classified bibliography. The maps and illustrations are useful aids to the reader.

Orme's basic thesis is not novel: "The Church was the original center of literacy, and the need for a literate clergy was the principal cause of the appearance and existence of schools in England until the sixteenth century" (p. 56). However, he does supply details of greater or lesser significance and analyses of the schools in their social milieus. There is appropriate mention of the secular studies, the long school day, benefactions, violence, and punishment. It is particularly interesting to take note of the teaching of Latin composition through *vulgaria*—"allusions to the life and interests of the time" (p. 99)—in other words, discussions of "relevant" topics. The documentation is derived from primary sources, while the secondary literature is subjected to critical scrutiny.

The Smalley work is specialized in temporal scope but broad with regard to ideas in politics and society. Essentially, it analyzes the relation of the papacy to the schoolmen and their teachings concerning the state and the ecclesiastical power. Miss Smalley also discusses the role of the Seven Liberal Arts in the dissemination and indoctrination of theological arguments and propaganda. What was at stake was the doctrine expounded by St. Thomas Becket, of clerical privileges and immunities *vis-à-vis* the royal throne. The author documents competently the teachings and behavior of the masters, and points up the changing attitudes among English scholars toward the martyred Becket. In her own words, "This is the fullest study of elusive data which has appeared thus far" (p. 14).

L'affaire Becket exerted a noticeable impact on the academic thought of the twelfth century, political theory, and church development. It "marked high tide in the claims of *sacerdotium* against *regnum*. It was excited and

noble while it lasted. By the end of the century it had begun to pall" (p. 239). The bored professors of theology turned to the study of other religious issues.

The monograph by Miss Smalley, author of *The Study of the Bible in the Middle Ages*, contributes greatly to the understanding of the medieval academia, ecclesia, and patria. If it deals in some detail with the familiar John of Salisbury, it also presents the lesser known Herbert of Bosham. While written in a somewhat colloquial style, it is a solid work of scholarship which will doubtless remain standard for some time to come.

Those who are interested in the history of education and related fields will learn much of value concerning medieval education from both volumes.

WILLIAM W. BRICKMAN
University of Pennsylvania
Philadelphia

R. M. PUNNETT. *Front Bench Opposition*. Pp. vii, 500. New York: St. Martin's Press, 1973. $17.95.

In the Seventeenth Century opposition to the King's Government in Britain stopped being considered as treason and became an accepted parliamentary activity; although it was not until many years later that it became known as His (or Her) Majesty's Loyal Opposition. By now, with the development of parties, the position of the Opposition in Parliament has become formalized and its leader and some of its whips receive official salaries.

This book contains a short history of how the change took place, but is mainly an excessively detailed description—based chiefly on the period 1951–1972—of how the process now works. As the author points out, the origins of formal opposition were different in the present two main parties and the procedures adopted to provide for it reflect this difference. Starting in the Eighteenth Century as a cabal of ex-Ministers who came together to discuss tactics, it developed in the spacious days of the Nineteenth Century into dinner parties where policy was discussed; but it was not until the Twentieth Century that formal meetings of what came to be known as the "Shadow Cabinet" took place. Whereas in the Conservative and Liberal Parties this was naturally a body appointed by the leader, the Labour Party, which had never been in office and placed emphasis on its democratic origins, when its numbers after the 1922 election made it necessary, naturally turned to an elected Parliamentary Committee.

In 1955 Attlee announced that in the future he would appoint Members of the Parliamentary Committee, and other leading M.P.'s to specific "Shadow" departmental posts on which they would lead the Party in debate and the Conservatives, when they returned to opposition, followed suit. This went further than either Party had gone before but of course Front Bench speakers had specialized in different subjects before. After the 1931 election, when the Labour Party was reduced to a handful of Members, some of those who became the leading Party spokesmen had to learn completely new subjects. Tom Williams, for instance, a coal miner, was the Party's spokesman on agriculture and became a very successful Minister of Agriculture in the 1945 Government.

Dr. Punnett describes both the advantages and disadvantages of this system: among the former the clarification of who represents the official opposition point of view and the knowledge which specialization can bring when a "Shadow" becomes a real Minister; although as he points out, with the aid of statistics, this is by no means certain to happen. Among the disadvantages are that it weakens the power of choice of an incoming Prime Minister and enlarges the gap between front and back bench Members. On the whole, however, he takes a conventional view of the value of the British system of opposition as providing criticism of government action and an alternative with some preparation to take its place and mentions a number of proposals, such as Civil Service assistance and extra salaries for Shadow Ministers, to make it more effective. It is clear that much of his information and opinions are direct reflections of the views expressed to him in interviews with those who have held these positions.

Dr. Punnett has not examined in any depth how far the British system of formal opposition accompanied by strong Party discipline is suitable for the problems of present day government; however, in a short appendix he describes the alternatives of other democratic systems. Compared with the American system the British has the undoubted advantage of a legislature in which ministers can be continuously called to account for their policies and administration and an incoming Prime Minister who will rarely arrive at his desk without staff and totally inexperienced in the machinery of national government. On the other hand, the average Member of Parliament has retained little power over the processes of legislation and most of the time lacks the inside knowledge to make his criticisms effective. To some extent this is changing with the growth of Select Committees investigating various aspects of government policy. Our Select Committees in Britain tend to be less partisan than the House itself and this development would, therefore, lead to a growth in the power of the legislature vis-a-vis the executive; but this could only occur if the present power of the party machines were diminished. Opposition would then no longer be an almost automatic reaction to government proposals, but the processes of decision making would be more publicly explored.

Austen Albu

Sussex
England

Stanley Suval. *The Anschluss Question in the Weimar Era: A Study of Nationalism in Germany and Austria, 1918–32.* Pp. ix, 240. Baltimore, Md.: The Johns Hopkins University Press, 1974. $12.50.

Stanley Suval addresses himself to two questions—Austria's postwar efforts to join Germany or find her own national identity, and the more general question of nationalism's influence on Austria's foreign policy. Though the subtitle suggests that the author included the entire postwar period, he in fact has not discussed the immediate postwar months. The pre-Versailles period plays a vital role in the Anschluss story, but since it is so extensive, it could not properly have been included here. While in the heady days of 1918 and 1919, the Anschluss advocates had hoped to achieve union on the basis of an idealistic interpretation of the right of national self-determination, Anschluss efforts became an integral part of German and Austrian diplomacy for peaceful revisionism after 1919.

The author approaches his subject topically, examining first Austria's desire and determination for union, emphasizing Social Democratic methods of propaganda and agitation, as opposed to the middle class's approach towards institutional harmonization through study groups and laws. Later the author deals with the Anschluss as a foreign policy issue. He illustrates quite clearly that the German government "had no Anschluss policy" (p. 127), but rather placed that issue behind the problem of the Rhineland occupation, reparations and the eastern border. Even though the author claims, as do most students of Anschluss, that the majority of Austrians favored union, he spends a considerable amount of time discussing the many interest groups and individuals who opposed the union. This reviewer considers it fallacious to assume that the majority of Austrians at any time had more than an emotional commitment to union and would have been willing to make the sacrifices in foreign and domestic affairs which union would have required.

Throughout, the author contrasts the two trends in the Anschluss movement—public, often highly emotional, Anschluss propaganda, versus generally calm and reserved diplomatic efforts which were, it seems, based on the assumption of minimal chances of success. Finally the author discusses Austrian pro-Anschluss sentiment ver-

sus Austrianism—the development of an Austrian national identity.

Mr. Suval makes extensive use of German and Austrian diplomatic sources and of published works. Even though he lists many newspapers and periodicals, these sources, this reviewer believes, might have been exploited more extensively to obtain a fuller reading of public and party sentiments. Mr. Suval's work constitutes a valuable addition to the continuing examination of the Austro-German Anschluss question.

FREDERICK DUMIN
Washington State University
Pullman

UNITED STATES

LELAND V. BELL. *In Hitler's Shadow: The Anatomy of American Nazism.* Pp. 135. Port Washington, N.Y.: Kennikat Press, 1973. $7.95.

SANDER A. DIAMOND. *The Nazi Movement in the United States, 1924–1941.* Pp. 380. Ithaca, N.Y.: Cornell University Press, 1974. $15.00.

Although history is what happened and historians give short shrift to what did not, failures sometimes reveal as much as successes. In analyzing the failure of American Nazism, these two books help us understand the United States and Germany during the 1930s. The wisdom of hindsight can, however, become the distortion of anachronism. While the horrors of German Nazism are difficult to forget, American Nazism seems almost unreal: one is tempted to wonder less why it failed than how it existed at all. This view is partially justified by these studies which agree on the unlikelihood of its successes. Yet such a conclusion distorts the 1930s since both American Nazis and Americans took American Nazism seriously. These works tell us why.

The two books are similar in subject, chronological organization, analytical approach, and broad conclusions, but differ in specifics. In style Bell is popular and Diamond scholarly, although both are clear and well organized. While their main focus is American Nazism during the 1930s, Bell offers a postwar chapter and Diamond includes considerable discussion of German governmental policy and relations between the two countries. Diamond's study is four times as long and provides considerably more detail. Both authors utilized extensive secondary works, German official documents and some American Nazi publications, but Diamond's original sources are more extensive and only he gained access to some—though not all—unpublished American Nazi documents. Both books are footnoted, Bell's at the end of chapters, Diamond's at the bottom of pages. Although Diamond's is more extensive and useful, informative introductions are offered by both, but only Bell suggests brief conclusions. Both books have complete indexes. The two works can be highly recommended but to different audiences: Bell to the nonspecialist who might then turn to Diamond; Diamond to the specialist who seeks the definitive study.

The history of American Nazism during the 1930s can be recounted briefly. American Nazi activity before 1933 had been fragmented and notably unsuccessful. Hitler's accession to power galvanized American Nazis into action which resulted both in new organizations—above all, the Friends of New Germany (FONG) founded in July 1933—and the first serious opposition—including Congressional investigation. When the FONG's leaders quarreled and the German government disavowed it in December 1935, American Nazism seemed to be waning. But Fritz Kuhn revived it by founding the German-American Bund (Bund) in March 1936 and meeting Hitler in August 1936. Bund's success was, however, met not only with increased American opposition but also official German disavowal in February 1938. Kuhn nonetheless persevered, only to be arrested in spring 1939, sentenced to prison in November 1939, and the Bund was disbanded on the day after Pearl Harbor.

The main participants were the German government, American Nazis, German-Americans, and the American public, press and officials. Although considerable disagreement existed among German factions over American affairs, most doubted that a distinct American Nazi party could be effective. Their main concern was to avoid complications with the United States and they consequently disavowed first the FONG and then the Bund. Thus the prevalent belief that American Nazis were German agents proves to be fallacious.

American Nazis are the focus of both books. The leaders were mostly German nationals who were members of the German Nazi Party, while the rank and file were either German nationals who had arrived since the war and were not members of the German Nazi Party or recently naturalized American citizens born in Germany. They were remarkably similar in place of origin, age, purpose and vocational background. Most had arrived since the war; most were Catholics from Baden, Bavaria and Württemberg; many hoped to remain but returned to Germany in the late 1930s; most were youthful; few were professionals and about half were skilled and half unskilled; and about two-thirds were unemployed during the depression. Very few—perhaps around 10 percent—were either Americans of German extraction or naturalized Americans who had immigrated before 1914. Justice Department records indicate that maximal Bund membership was around 8500 with some 5–6000 sympathizers. Organization was modeled on the German Party, all of whose parapheralia was aped. Like the German Party, the American movement experienced sordid leadership conflicts until it was finally dominated by Kuhn. German ideology was taken over—German superiority, anti-Semitism and anti-Communism—and supplemented with anti-Negro racism. The methods were familiar: mass meetings, parades, sensationalism, and violence. Germany was idealized and the United States attacked. Although ideology, economic pressures and fear-hate probably contributed, the compulsion for comradeship in an alien land may have been the major appeal. Thus American Nazism tells us more about German emigrés than American immigrants.

Americans of German origin who themselves or whose ancestors had immigrated before World War I proved unresponsive. However incomplete the melting pot, German-Americans identified themselves enough as Americans to reject the Nazi claim that they were only "Germans *in* America." The positive appeal of America had been reinforced by the sometimes traumatic warning of anti-German sentiment during World War I. Ultimately German-Americans may have resisted for the same reason recent immigrants responded: Nazism was more German than American.

The American public, press and officials became increasingly hostile after 1936. Since this reaction was due less to fears of an indigenous takeover than to Hitler's international successes and the tendency to perceive American Nazis as Hitler's agents—the notorious "fifth column"—it is a more accurate barometer of American anxieties than American Nazi success.

American Nazi success is better measured in terms of its own goals, namely, establishment of an organization, official German sanction, mobilization of German-Americans, and influence on American foreign policy. The first objective was achieved despite personal squabbling and financial problems. Far from supporting, the German government disavowed and sought to squelch the movement. Pre-1914 German immigrants refused the appeal; at most a thousand of the several millions joined. The Bund even failed with recent immigrants; only one-two percent of the four hundred thousand responded. The greatest effect was upon the American public, press and government but was negative: the more the Bund raged, the more the opposition grew. American Nazism was consequently a nigh total failure.

This failure can be explained at several levels. Bund organizational and leadership problems contributed but were probably not crucial. Its foreign ideology and manifestations were perhaps more significant since they alienated many Americans. Conditions were probably the main factor: although plagued by problems, Americans were not yet desperate enough to resort to fascism. German Nazi international successes insured American Nazi failure. With professed friends like Hitler, the Bund did not lack enemies and those who wanted to awaken Americans to the Nazi menace could have found no better agent than the Bund. This is the paramount significance of American Nazism.

L. L. FARRAR, JR.
Department of History
Lewis and Clark College
Portland
Oregon

DAVID W. BRADY. *Congressional Voting in a Partisan Era: A Study of the McKinley Houses and a Comparison to the Modern House of Representatives.* Pp. xi, 273. Lawrence: University Press of Kansas, 1973. $10.00.

In recent years, the 1890s have attracted numerous students of American political behavior. Aided by computer-assisted statistical analysis, they have sought to understand the decade's massive voter realignments, its new political institutions, and its distinctive patterns of legislative behavior. And while full understanding has remained elusive, the result has been a growing body of more precise information and more rigorously tested generalizations.

To this body of knowledge, political scientist David Brady has made a significant but in some ways disappointing contribution. Seeking to measure and explain the high levels of partisan voting in the fifty-fifth and fifty-sixth Houses of Representatives (1897–1901), he devotes a chapter each to a computer-assisted determination of party cohesion on significant rollcalls, a statistical correlation of voting behavior with congressional-district characteristics, and a comparison of leadership mechanisms at the time with those of other periods. Through these operations, he establishes that party cohesion was exceptionally high and that, in all likelihood, this was related both to the turn-overs generated by shifting voter loyalties and to newly developed institutional arrangements giving party leaders great power over the selection and presentation of issues. What remains unclear is how this behavior differed from that of the immediately preceding and following periods, and what seems less than convincing is Brady's argument that high cohesion reflected a situation in which both national and party cleavages had been realigned along an industrial-agricultural continuum. On this the evidence is at best ambiguous, and it is only with considerable strain that the author imposes the framework on the diversities of the Midwest, the behavior of states like New York, and the persisting intraparty tensions.

Indeed, one of the book's major weaknesses is its uncritical acceptance of a class-sectional framework that most historians now regard as mistaken or inadequate. In recent years, such scholars as Paul Kleppner, Richard Jensen, and Samuel McSeveney have amassed an impressive array of both quantitative and qualitative evidence to show that the Republican successes of the 1890s were due less to their identification with a rising class than to their capture of formerly Democratic ethnic groups, their formulas for restoring prosperity, and their ability to blunt class conflict and develop pluralistic appeals. Fitted into this scholarship, Brady's voting configurations would almost certainly take on new meanings. But of its existence and relevance, he seems totally unaware: mute evidence, perhaps, that even in the quantification fraternity interdisciplinary barriers remain high.

ELLIS W. HAWLEY

University of Iowa
Iowa City

WILLIAM R. CORSON. *Consequences of Failure*. Pp. 215. New York: W. W. Norton, 1974. $7.95.

This is an important—and highly disturbing book. Perhaps it is important *because* it is disturbing, and because, if widely read, it will lead to policies which will negate much of what the author says might otherwise come to pass. If Mr. Corson—a retired U.S. Marine officer and a man already known for his critical comments on the American policy in Vietnam—is correct, then there is little cause for optimism about the future of the United States, a future, he says, made especially bleak as a result of our involvement in the Vietnam war.

The purpose of Corson's book is to examine the "consequences of failure" of America's course of action in Vietnam. Indeed, Corson emphasizes that it is not a defeat that we have suffered there, but that it is a "military failure." He spends several chapters in a comparative examination of the "phenomenon" of such failure, discussing how Rome, Spain and Great Britain coped with certain of their military disasters and why military failure occurred in Ireland during the period from 1916 to 1922. In each of the examples cited by Corson, "failure resulted from incorrect strategy in that it did not take into consideration the prevailing 'objective conditions'—those circumstances beyond the nation's immediate control that have a direct bearing on the accomplishment of its objectives" (p. 72). These circumstances, says Corson, are the "attitudes, sympathies and loyalties of the armed forces; the state . . . of public opinion; and the international situation . . . " (*Ibid*). And, he says, military failure can be described "in detail," we can "identify its turning point," and we can "identify and predict its path" once that turning point has been reached (*Ibid*).

Corson views the consequences of our Vietnamese failure from the following perspectives: the impact of drugs, dissent and racial discrimination on the future of the military; the cautious role of the government in its approach to domestic problems as a result of the war (and in the process of this consideration he makes a scathing attack on the bureaucracy, offering three steps to "prevent the emergence of the American Bureaucratic State" (p. 121); the attitudes of Americans, especially those of youth and the middle class; and the impact of the war on the economy which, Corson says, has been to create on the part of American citizens an acceptance of "creeping fascism." The consequences of failure, Corson says, thus take on the following parameters: "a social and institutional structure in serious disarray; a lack of confidence in our leaders; an unwillingness to face the sacrifices we must make to solve our nearly overwhelming domestic problems; and a condition of environmental disequilibrium that affects the quality of daily life in a thousand ways, ranging from mindless violence to class conflicts and widespread dissatisfaction with America's cultural and ethical value system" (pp. 148–149).

In the end, however, Corson offers his readers a "formula" for overcoming failure: we must acknowledge that we have in fact failed; we must take whatever small steps are necessary to prevent disaster, even before all the information we might need is in; and we must repair the damage done to our institutions and environment—all of which will require great sacrifices from the American people. Corson suggests, further, three outcomes which are likely to occur during Mr. Nixon's "generation of peace," and he predicts that the first—and most pessimistic—is *most* likely to occur. His last chapter ends with a suggestion of how to overcome failure by using the military to help solve local community problems, and, in addition, becomes a plea for aiding the Vietnam veteran.

In this book, as in his earlier books, Corson writes with passion and states his case convincingly. His tone is often sarcastic. It seems, too, that he bases his statements often upon casual analysis and what from a scholar's viewpoint might be considered insufficient evidence. His generalizations are often sweeping. But all of this is not to deny the importance of what Corson is saying. The book, although hardly the most scholarly ever written on matters related to the Vietnam war, should receive wide attention. For, as Corson himself puts it,

This war will provide a remarkable case study of how "little" decisions lead to big problems. It will be unfortunate if we as a nation are so eager to forget Vietnam that the war—and especially Nixon's management of the withdrawal from it—does not receive the rigorous analysis it deserves, because it would deny us of an important opportunity to understand and learn from the methods by which executive decisions are made (p. 27).

EARL R. KRUSCHKE
California State University
Chico

ROBERT A. DIVINE. *Foreign Policy and U.S. Presidential Elections, 1940–1948.* Pp. xii, 352. New York: New Viewpoints, 1974. $12.50. Paperbound, $4.95.

ROBERT A. DIVINE. *Foreign Policy and U.S. Presidential Elections, 1952–1960.* Pp. x, 359. New York: New Viewpoints, 1974. $12.50. Paperbound, $4.95.

Robert Divine of the University of Texas is probably the most prolific historian of American foreign policy at work today. The author of several excellent books on the era of Franklin Roosevelt, he has moved in the two volumes under review to a study of the impact of foreign policy during presidential campaigns since 1940. It is an important study—not because it produces any startling new information, but because it shows a learned and mature scholar re-examining conventional wisdom and leaning toward more critical interpretations. No radical, Divine has nonetheless produced two volumes which will help narrow the debate between "revisionist" and "traditionalist" historians of recent American diplomacy.

Divine is clearly disturbed by the results of his research. "Ideally," he writes, "a presidential campaign should be a great educational experience, in which would-be leaders make clear the issues confronting the nation and offer positive programs to the voters." The reality, however, is different. Whether it be FDR promising not to send the sons of American mothers into any foreign wars in 1940, Republicans calling for "liberation" instead of "containment" in 1952, or John F. Kennedy bewailing a nonexistent "missile gap" in 1960, Divine describes contests where the nominees try not "to enlighten the voter, but instead to appeal to his emotions by oversimplifying and frequently distorting complex world problems." Afterward, according to Divine, victorious presidents "turn diplomatic issues back to the small cadre of experts who repair the damage and strive to preserve their domain from the ravage of political discussion for another four years" (Vol. I, pp. x–xi).

But do the experts actually "repair the damage?" Is the simplistic rhetoric of the campaign so different from the private thinking of statesmen? Do the slogans only serve to get men elected—and without much adverse effect on subsequent diplomacy? Divine is not sure. On the one hand, he says that the system works, that despite distortions and duplicity "the American electorate displayed an innate wisdom in choosing its Presidents for qualities of international leadership. The people tended to cut through the charges and countercharges to seek the man they felt was most capable of leading the nation in a hazardous world" (Vol. I, p. xi). On the other hand, Divine is careful to show that the electoral process provided little choice in candidates or policies. In 1948, when Truman flailed the 80th Republican Congress for "doing nothing" domestically and shrewdly managed the Czech and Berlin crises to his own advantage, Thomas

Dewey chose not to challenge the Democratic record in foreign policy. Thus, writes Divine, "in 1948 the democratic process failed to offer the American voter choices and alternatives in the crucial area of foreign policy; all he could do was ratify the policy of containment or throw away his vote on the eccentric and unstable Henry Wallace" (Vol. I, p. 276). Similarly, despite television debates over Quemoy/Matsu, missile gaps, and Cuba, the 1960 contest between Kennedy and Nixon produced even less enlightenment. "Both men," Divine argues, "offered themselves to the voters as ardent Cold Warriors, differing only in their assessment of how well the United States was doing in the mortal contest with the Soviet Union. . . . For all the rhetoric of a new generation of leadership, Kennedy . . . simply expounded the doctrines of Dean Acheson and John Foster Dulles in his constant description of a world divided between slavery and freedom and in his relentless hammering at the need to get the nation moving again in world affairs" (Vol. II, pp. 286–87), Divine also contends that there were little real differences in foreign policy between Roosevelt and Willkie and Roosevelt and Dewey; nor did Eisenhower and Stevenson disagree fundamentally in their two campaigns. FDR and Eisenhower ("I shall go to Korea!") simply presented themselves more effectively.

Divine's two volumes are predominantly narrative history, smoothly written, grounded upon previous scholarship, as well as extensive research in manuscript and oral history collections. Although Divine occasionally profits from political science insights with regard to voting behavior and electoral analysis, he uses statistics and jargon sparingly, and graphs not at all. Some of his insights, such as the contention that Kennedy nearly lost the 1960 election through maladroit handling of foreign policy issues, are historian's surmises not subject to rigid proof. It is a study aimed at historians and the general reader, not a treatise on who votes for whom.

If the reviewer may indulge himself, Divine makes one fascinating observation about the 1944 campaign that has relevance to 1972 and the scandals surrounding Watergate. Throughout that wartime contest some of Thomas Dewey's supporters made not-so-veiled insinuations about FDR's responsibility for the Pearl Harbor disaster, even charging the President with censorship for refusing to publish the Navy's report of its investigation of the Japanese attack. Dewey himself had been told by a high-ranking officer that the Navy had cracked the Japanese codes in 1941 and thus Washington had knowledge of the Pearl Harbor operation ahead of time. The Republican candidate seriously considered making these facts public. General George C. Marshall then intervened, telling Dewey that publication of the Navy report would have a "calamitous" effect on the war effort. Japan would learn that its cables were being read and quickly change codes. Dewey accepted the rationale of national security and remained silent. According to Divine, because so many million Americans came to believe in Roosevelt's culpability after subsequent Pearl Harbor investigations in 1945–46, "a dramatic revelation that Roosevelt was reading secret Japanese messages and still was unprepared for the attack on Pearl Harbor might have had a devastating impact on the election" (Vol. I, p. 147). This is not to suggest that General Marshall played John Mitchell's role in "covering up" for his chief, but it does add an ironic wrinkle to present arguments about "national security" versus political advantage.

In sum, Divine's study deserves wide reading.

JOHN GARRY CLIFFORD
Department of Political Science
University of Connecticut
Storrs

DOUGLAS F. DOWD. *The Twisted Dream: Capitalist Development in the United States Since 1776.* Pp. vi, 315. Cambridge, Mass.: Winthrop Publishers, 1974. $8.95.

Professor Dowd argues that the United States has entered the first stage of a deep and growing crisis, attributable squarely to the nature of the capitalist economic system. Capitalism is a dynamic force that must constantly expand, and this expansion entails exploitation. At home, the result is racism; abroad, the consequence is imperialism. The problems of inadequate health care, destruction of the environment, drugs and crime, poverty, sexism, decaying cities, militarism, foreign wars, and the deteriorating morale of the people, especially the young, are all caused by "rampant capitalist imperialism and racism."

As the crisis grows, Professor Dowd sees a move toward either the Left or the Right, an American brand of Socialism or Fascism. The fascist solution is more likely "unless those who would bring socialism educate and organize around that vision." *The Twisted Dream* is both an effort to make the American people aware of the historical development of the capitalist system and a plea for a more humane alternative.

Individuals who believe that Marx, Veblen, and the Union for Radical Political Economics offer the most persuasive insights into the character of the American economic system and who subscribe to the New Left school of historical interpretations, represented by William A. Williams, Gabriel Kolko, Noam Chomsky, and others, will welcome and applaud this book. Those who fail to share these ideological and historical predilections will find little of value.

WILLIAM M. LEARY, JR.
University of Georgia
Athens

RICHARD FITZGERALD. *Art and Politics.* Pp. ix, 254. Westport, Conn.: Greenwood Press, 1973. $14.50.

In this book Richard Fitzgerald has given us an interesting series of examples of the relationship between art and society. He deals with five American graphic artists, Art Young, Robert Minor, John Sloan, K. R. Chamberlain, and Maurice Becker, who became artistic contributors to *The Masses* and *The Liberator*, two radical periodicals of the early twentieth century. Through an analysis of their lives and cartoons he helps us to understand some of the problems of adaptation of radically minded artists in our society.

The modern Western artist generally has found his niche on the fringe of society where he cultivates his artistic freedom at the expense of wealth and power. Some of the artists have taken on commercial work in order to make a living. Others have allied themselves with radical groups and tried to use their art for political goals. But, as this book demonstrates, neither of these forms of adaptation works out very well in our society. Fitzgerald, using case histories, gives us an indication of the uneasy relationship between art and radical politics in recent American history. At the conclusion of the book we can begin to comprehend why the integration of the American artist and his work into Socialist or Communist parties has never been fully accomplished.

Fitzgerald includes sixty examples of illustrations and cartoons by the five artists, and it is in his analysis of these that he is at his best. He not only discusses the content of these works, but the form and style as well. The drawings are powerful examples of art in the service of political propaganda—at first the vaguer kind of bohemian socialism of *The Masses* and later the more ideologically constrained work of the hard line *Liberator*. The author's treatment of the history of the epoch and the biographies of the artists tends to be perfunctory. We get a notion of the social, psychological, technical, and artistic context of these artists' work, but a convincing analysis of the relationship between these factors and the art in question is not accomplished. Nevertheless, Fitzgerald has performed an important service in

outlining some of the more significant parameters of the artist's role in our society and, with exemplary illustrations of their art work, how one group of artists adapted to it.

DENNISON NASH
University of Connecticut
Storrs

ANDREW M. GREELEY. *American Politics in the 1970s*. Pp. 430. New York: New Viewpoints, 1974. $12.50.

Father Greeley is a sharp, intense political analyst who really knows what's happening. This rich menu of bold ideas compels serious attention of practical politicians and theoreticians. Strong, provocative statements are supported by substantial documentation. At times the prose blazes with sound suggestions on a wide range of issues. The style is peppy and invites rapid reading. It cuts away all the mushiness connected with these themes and puts them across in direct, forceful terms.

The major convictions are: 1) coalition politics is the pulsebeat in this business and serves as an indispensable instrument to reach all voters and solve stubborn social issues; 2) the New Issue is that people want *in* on the political and social decision-making process; 3) the American public is bored and weary with the leader who has simple, magic answers. The urge to emphasize critical passages is irresistible; whether reshaping an old idea or advocating a brand-new approach, the message comes across:

The large majority of the American electorate is neither "liberal" nor "conservative" (94).

Indeed, political pluralism is probably more the result of social pluralism than its cause (13).

The American Catholic population has finally "made it" in American society (191).

The skilled political leader maintains a balance between making things happen and sustaining the coalition that supports him (230).

American blacks, then, tend to be integrationists, cultural pluralists, and cautious militants (331).

As a national political director, I sense, the author would produce winning candidates. Throughout, social continuity and change are stressed. Pointing to failures—organizational and tactical—of both political parties, Father Greeley opens some new doors to solutions. Government must become more humane, responsive and responsible. The power of social elites is slim. Skilled compromise moves the political mountains, not intransient ideologues. The center of our politics can be shaped towards new directions and dimensions. Leaders must learn how better to manage conflict and serve as change agents. Carefully, exhaustively covered are the positive roles of ethnics, black-white political coalitions, weaknesses of bureaucrats, protest movements, potentials of average citizens, radicals, liberals and even the city manager movement.

This is a hopeful book. Now and then portions of a chapter are choppy and uneven but overall Father Greeley introduces new facts and reexamines the old, tired issues systematically. The rules of our political game need some revisions. His surveys are tight and exact. Myths are assaulted with logic. Problems are solved with insight and reason. It truly is most rewarding reading.

R. J. NOVOGROD
Long Island University
The Brooklyn Center
New York

ROSE BASILE GREEN. *The Italian-American Novel: A Document of the Interaction of Two Cultures*. Pp. 415. Cranbury, N.J.: Fairleigh Dickinson University Press, 1974. $18.00.

Rose Basile Green's *The Italian-American Novel: A Document of the Interaction of Two Cultures* presents a stimulating and a useful study of the autobiographical sketches and later of the fiction developing from these accounts, of the history and progress of one ethnic group in its complex and varied role as immigrant to an estab-

lished but still evolving culture in the United States. In addition to its merit as a study and a competent guide to one important area of literature, the book should interest students of American civilization, particularly those looking for first hand accounts of immigrants. The story, as depicted, involves detailed synopses and informative sketches of the work of some seventy writers, many of whom are little known and are presented as worthy of a hearing. Well-known figures, such as Mario Puzo and Francis Pollini, appear in a new and illuminating perspective, as part of a tradition that has existed within and as a part of our literature, but without the due recognition Green seeks so ably to provide.

Surveying the writing of Italians coming to America in the late nineteenth century, and later, of second and third generation writers of Italian descent, writing from the standpoint of native Americans established within the culture pattern of the United States but still aware of or in some cases subconsciously influenced by their particular heritage from the old country, Green illustrates her thesis that the interaction of cultures tended to produce a unique product of major significance and one which, in a literary sense, has received too little attention. The reading public, trained to acceptance of the self-proclaimed excellence of the literary East, has, in the author's opinion, tended to accept literature of Puritan–Anglo-Saxon lineage to the exclusion of others. Green's work is based on the assertion of Bernard Devoto, whom she identifies as the first writer of Italian descent to become a major figure in American literature, that American letters must consider the writing of all representative groups rather than focusing exclusively on the established coterie of New England and its offshoots.

Green seems to overlook the possible significance of class and even sectional background in terms of the type of fiction emerging, and this makes the generalizations and categories established difficult to trace. However, despite this, she does focus on the obvious importance of the Italian-American writer, and she documents with skill her conclusion that overall, the Italian-American novel exhibits an emphasis on human values, struggle for success, optimism, plus a flair for well-made plots. The book is a veritable mine of information conveniently assembled and beautifully indexed. It serves well to establish its "ultimate aim" of presenting "the contribution of the Italian-American novelist to the mainstream of American literature."

DOROTHY RUDY
Montclair State College
Upper Montclair
New Jersey

SIMON LAZARUS. *The Genteel Populists.* Pp. ix, 303. New York: Holt, Rinehart and Winston, 1974. $8.95.

This is a provocative book. The author examines the populist ideal of suspicion of corporate power and of corporate subversion of government power. Present Populists promote the identical themes of their antecedents of the 1890s, namely, the necessity of big government to regulate huge corporations and direct democracy so the people may have the opportunity to initiate reforms and to recall corrupt officials.

Mr. Lazarus doubts the efficiency of many government regulatory agencies and states that they are currently functioning in behalf of corporations and not the people. The Nixon economic policy (NEP) results only in higher prices and more government powers used to assure increasing corporate profits. The powerlessness of the people, concludes the author, is amazing.

Projected populist reforms are an exercise in politics without power. In order to be successful, reformers must dramatize their message by stagecraft and secure the appropriations necessary to achieve their goals. In their efforts to restore pageantry to the populist movement the author lauds the work of Ralph Nader's "Public Citizen" and John Gardener's "Common Cause" movements.

The farmers, who initially furnished the Populists ideals and leaders, have joined corporations in their control of agricultural products and the market. In fact, agriculture and labor have identical goals—"internal political autonomy and external market powers" (p. 134). Even the poverty-welfare folk through the National Welfare Rights Organization (N.W.R.O.) seek to capture the legislative and administrative arms of the welfare system.

If the populist reformers are to succeed, the author contends, they must make sure their crusade is one of a vision for the whole society, not for a particular group. These reformers are presently focused on consumer and environmental protection and the integrity of our electoral system. (Unfortunately the movement is controlled by minorities, not by the public.) Public good must be weighed over private gain.

Not only are the executive and legislative branches of our government involved but the judicial is equally concerned. Indeed, the author argues convincingly, that all of the United States Supreme Court late initiatives—"race, reapportionment, prayer in schools, protection for accused criminals—have gravely imperiled the Court as an institution" (p. 251). Fortunately the judges have not been deterred from doing what, in their opinion, the Constitution provided that they should do in these matters.

In the legal profession the author finds faults. The law, he states, was made to embody the commands of the people but lawyers are using their talents to aid centers of private power to evade those commands. His conclusion that the legal system is not a dedicated instrument of democracy but is, in fact, a tool of selfish interests will not be generally accepted by legalists nor by scholars outside of the legal profession.

GEORGE OSBORN
Gainesville
Florida

ARTHUR S. LINK et al., eds. *The Papers of Woodrow Wilson, 1907–1908*. Vol. 17. Pp. viii, 647. Princeton, N.J.: Princeton University Press, 1974. $22.50.

What impresses one as Wilson's career moves closer to the high point of Progressivism is the height of the world he inhabits. Melancton Williams Jacobus, Cleveland Hoadley Dodge, Paul Van Dyke, and Viscount James Bryce are just several of numerous figures concerned for Princeton and all education, and beyond that for social stability and control. They make careful recommendations for celebrations, lectures, and appointments. The world of popular figures scarcely enters their correspondence. Youth is to be served, but hardly consulted. Women, it should be noted, are vital to their principles and the expression of those principles.

Nevertheless, there are circles above them as well as below them. Wilson's plan to end the regal student clubs in favor of "residential quads" which mix aristocrats with plebes rouses fear and resentment. In Hartford, Connecticut, center (a Wilson supporter notes) of "New England ideas and New Haven prejudices," the *Times* sees Wilson's scheme as a blow to individual freedom, and the *Courant* warns it will create "a pretty commotion" among Princetonians. It does, among trustees, alumni, faculty; and though Wilson is first approved by the trustees, they finally accede to pressure, and Wilson, defeated, contemplates resigning the presidency.

At the other end of the spectrum, Wilson refers to a ship steward as one of "the vulgar" but he also writes urging education as possible for all beyond elementary and high school grades. Such a policy will help "fertilize" democracy. Wilson is present at the celebration of the Jamestown Exposition, July 4, 1907. Also present is Charles Evans Hughes, made famous and governor of New York by his successful investigation of life insurance practices. The popular crowd cheers Hughes as the next President to

be. Wilson himself speaks on the Founding Fathers, protests too much government (a hit at President Roosevelt), and recommends clearly defined corporate obligations, with penalties for transgression. Only so, he says, can we escape socialism:

I have not seen much of Mr. Roosevelt since he became President, but I am told that he no sooner thinks than he talks, which is a miracle not wholly in accord with an educational theory of forming an opinion (p. 519).

Wilson repeated this thought several times, evidence that he had polished it in his mind for public display. He protested that he was not interested in holding public office, but a "Credo" he prepared for a group of conservative Democrats August 6, 1907 (pp. 335–338) suggests it was much on his mind. Wilson led an admirably well-balanced life. It was dedicated to family, to the wearing business of the university, and the production of educational and other essays, as well as a major series of lectures, delivered at Columbia University, on American constitutional government. He also began his battle over the location of the new Graduate School. The course of his crucial differences with Dean West is given in detail, and must continue in a subsequent volume.

LOUIS FILLER

Antioch College
Yellow Springs
Ohio

DIANE RAVITCH. *The Great School Wars: New York City, 1805–1973. A History of the Public Schools as a Battlefield of Social Change*. Pp. xviii, 449. New York: Basic Books, 1974. $12.95.

This volume may eventually be recognized as a seminal work, not only for New York's educational history, but for the city's general history as well. Like all New York's serious historians, Diane Ravitch found its original sources incredibly diffuse; its secondary literature, meagre. This explains why a definitive, scholarly history of the city has yet to be written. Most historians concentrate on a given period, such as the American Revolution, or a limited sphere, such as education or the City Council. Diane Ravitch's book offers insights into New York's general history because it does not concentrate exclusively on educational themes: its story is developed within the broad context of the city's political and social history.

Her principal thesis, in fact, is that each major turning point of its school system was inextricably interwoven into the city's political and social history. Each coincided with a great tide of immigration, with the public school the "battleground where the aspirations of the newcomers and the fears of the native population met and clashed." The first "great school war," for example, grew out of the Catholic clergy's efforts to obtain public funding for schools of their faith. This attempt failed, but the controversy destroyed the Public School Society, an aristocratic philanthropic group that provided free education to poor boys, and unexpectedly established a decentralized school system, with control over autonomous districts vested in powerful locally elected school boards.

But great weaknesses soon appeared in decentralized, politically controlled boards—"involvement in partisan politics, the lack of uniformity from district to district, the narrow perspective of local boards [and] the constant jostling between local boards and the central board." These glaring defects became the concern of a new generation of school reformers in the late 19th century, as the city encountered an unprecedented wave of immigration from Southern and Eastern Europe. Regarding school district officials as unfit to cope with the new wave of immigrant children, the reformers demanded a centralized system, managed by professionals rather than patronage-hungry politicians. A total reform victory was followed by a "remarkable burst of energy and innovations," an immense, multi-faceted venture into new areas. A partial list of new programs included classes for children with physical and mental defects, over-age children, and non-English speaking pupils; manual and vocational training; evening and summer schools; adult education; and after-school use of school buildings. Reformers regarded the broadening of school services into these new areas as a democratization of education.

The last "school war" followed a giant wave of Black and Puerto Rican immigration. Originally minority group leaders demanded integration. This became increasingly difficult to achieve when white pupils were reduced in numbers to a third of the school population. With some encouragement from philanthropic foundations, federally funded antipoverty units, some members of the academic community, several civic associations, McGeorge Bundy, and Mayor John Lindsay, the militants changed course and demanded total control over local schools. After the most devastating teachers' strike in local history, they obtained a compromise plan of decentralization rather than community control. The difference was vital, for under community control the winners of each local election would have gained power to administer the schools in accordance with their own ideology. Under decentralization, power was not completely dispersed among thirty-odd districts, but shared with central authorities. This meant the retention of the *common school*, a school "supported by all, controlled by all, and which propagates no particular religious, ideological, or political views." Ironically, decentralization was instituted in response to demands for "accountability," "efficiency," and "improved teaching," the very reasons offered for centralizing the schools seventy-five years previously!

Diane Ravitch carefully considers the charges directed at public schools by "revisionist" historians—that they provided a handle for the rich to control the poor and that they were an "educational disaster" for the poor. Her text reveals that the Public School Society (see above) was an elitist group, but that before its demise it advocated *common schools,* enrolling children of all backgrounds, offering equality of opportunity, eroding social castes, and serving the needs of a democracy. Furthermore, both movements for decentralization tended to be proletarian, shifting power towards lower socioeconomic classes. The "disaster" hypothesis comes closest to the mark among first generation immigrants, but becomes less plausible among succeeding generations. By 1940, for example, large-scale trans-Atlantic immigration was long past, and the immigrants' children attended schools regarded as a model for the nation, attracting teachers of unusually high caliber and recording achievements far above national norms.

This volume fills an enormous gap in the city's educational history. During the controversy preceding decentralization, for example, the Bundy report never referred to the city's half century of decentralized schooling, and few disputants on the subject, if any, publicly recognized it. With the publication of *The Great School Wars*, the lessons of the past will be readily available, and it will become increasingly difficult to ignore them.

Historians have disproved many details in Parrington's *Main Currents in American Thought*, but have accepted his major thesis—that American literature is a vital aspect of this nation's historic development rather than a collection of *belles lettres*. Probably many fewer of Diane Ravitch's facts will be refuted than Parrington's. What is more, scholars are not likely to demolish her principal theme—that the city's educational history reflects its demographic, political, and social history.

FREDERICK SHAW
    Bureau Head
    Educational Program Research
    Brooklyn
    New York

DAVID REES. *Harry Dexter White: A Study in Paradox.* Pp. 506. New York: Coward, McCann & Geoghegan, 1973. $12.50.

Harry Dexter White was an economist, one of the many academicians who came to Washington during the New Deal. Joining the Treasury Department in 1934, he soon became the Director of Monetary Research, was appointed as assistant to Secretary Henry Morgenthau on the day after Pearl Harbor, and became Assistant Secretary in 1945. During the war years White supervised the Treasury Department's international financial arrangements, including the controversial shipments of gold to China and currency for occupied territories. He played a major role in the formulation of the Morgenthau Plan for postwar Germany and the proposals which led to the establishment of the International Monetary Fund and the World Bank. In 1946 he resigned from the Treasury to become the first American executive director of the Fund. Then Whittaker Chambers and Elizabeth Bentley testified before the House Un-American Activities Committee, accusing White of passing classified information to Russian agents. White appeared before the Committee to defend himself in August, 1948. Three days after his appearance, White died of heart failure, but the controversy surrounding him, and the accusations made against him continued throughout the McCarthy era.

Rees' study of White's career in the Treasury Department and of American foreign economic policy during World War II should be welcomed by scholar and layman alike. It is commendable for its attention to detail and skill in presentation. Rees deals with the complex economic issues handled by White on their own merits and against the background of the times, without becoming bogged down with the Communist issue. He finds White a commendable public servant whose decisions were based on the objectives and realities of the time and White's conception of the best alternative to serve the American national interest. Herein Rees finds his paradox, for his assessment of the Communist issue agrees with that of Lord Robbins, that White was "a sentimental and highly indiscreet fellow traveler." He was both patriot and traitor, both dedicated public servant and dupe of Russian espionage.

The White controversy continued long after his sudden death in 1948. In 1953 Harry Truman felt compelled to answer charges made by Eisenhower's Attorney General, Herbert Brownell, regarding the former President's promotion of White to the International Monetary Fund. Little evidence has been added since that time, and Rees offers nothing new. While the study will not aid those seeking to vindicate or condemn White, it should not be dismissed, for its merit lies in its analysis of White's career and his impact on wartime economic policy.

DONALD B. SCHEWE
Franklin D. Roosevelt Library
Hyde Park
New York

JOHN SNETSINGER. *Truman, the Jewish Vote and the Creation of Israel.* Pp. xv, 207. Stanford, Calif.: Hoover Institution Press, 1974. $6.95.

This is an account of the policy of the Truman Administration relative to the creation of the State of Israel. The story begins essentially with the advent of Mr. Truman to the Presidency in April 1945 and it ends basically with the election of 1948, in which the "issue" of Israel was fully exploited. Following a brief introduction, the author plunges into his story, the nodal points of which center on the attempts in 1945–1946 to find a solution of the Palestine through the work of the Anglo-American Committee of Inquiry, the partition Resolution of November 29, 1947, the abandonment of the British mandate in Palestine and the proclamation of Eretz Israel on May 14, 1948, and the Palestine conflict which ensued.

Few who are familiar with the politics of the day will contest the author's contention that President Truman was not an unalloyed believer in the cause of the Jewish State, that in his early White House years, he pursued an ambivalent policy relative to Israel, sometimes following the advice of the experts in the Departments of State and Defense, and at other times that of Democratic politicians who wished to cultivate Jewish voters through the pursuit of pro-Zionist policies. Only during his last three years in office, so the author contends, did Mr. Truman follow a consistent, pro-Zionist policy, from which he did not deviate. Mr. Truman called for the establishment of a Jewish state when Democratic prospects looked dim in the Congressional campaign of 1946, reversed that policy early in 1948 at the onset of the Czechoslovak crisis, and assumed an increasingly pro-Zionist position with the approach of the 1948 Presidential campaign and recognized Israel immediately after the proclamation of independence. As the author well notes: "Truman's Palestine-Israel policy offers an extraordinary example of foreign policy conducted in line with short-range political expediency rather than long-range goals" (p. 140).

It is difficult to quarrel with the author's basic thesis, which is well buttressed with careful research among the Truman papers and consultation with many who played roles in the development of policy during the Truman period. The author might well have used materials conveniently available in the volumes on *The Foreign Relations of the United States* to fill out some of the gaps in his work during the immediate post World War II period. Similarly, he might well have extended his story to the end of the Truman Administration. The story of the pressure politics which Mr. Snetsinger has told is a very important one and it should be widely read and pondered.

HARRY N. HOWARD
Bethesda
Maryland

MICHAEL USEEM. *Conscription, Protest, and Social Conflict.* Pp. v, 329. New York: John Wiley & Sons, 1973. No price.

Having subtitled his book "The Life and Death of a Draft Resistance Movement," Michael Useem has written a major, historical description and analysis of the draft resistance during the Vietnam War. So much has happened since 1968 that it is easy to forget how important the protests of the 1960s were to the politics of the time. And because Abbie Hoffman, the Berrigans, and William Kunstler still occasionally make news today, we assume that no historically valid perspective yet can be gained concerning this period and its explosive events. Useem's book, I think, should overcome both of these impressions, for it is at one and the same time good history and sound social science analysis.

Useem begins with a general review of campus discontent during the mid-1960s. Next, he describes the workings and effects of the conscription system in the Vietnam Era. The heart of the book contains the author's account of the creation of the resistance movement, its relation to other political movements of the time, and finally the gradual demise of anticonscription protest. The treatment of all of these topics is well documented and intellectually sound. Perhaps the most impressive sections of the book are those which analyze the distributive impact of conscription (pages 81–113), the strategy of the movement in its formative years (pages 161–190), and the organizational structure and communications network of the protest groups (Chapters Five and Six).

The book is weakest in the realm of theory. Chapter One provides a number of analytical categories which certainly are useful for looking at protest movements: Social Origins, Structural Deprivation, Political Awareness and Action, Social Organization, Formation, Protest Ideology, Organizational Structure, Recruitment and Socialization, Demise, and Political Impact. However, these hardly constitute a theory of social movements. Useem has provided concepts but little in the way of general linkages to bring the parts together. The book flows well enough from the chronological sequence and the inherent interest in the subject itself. For the most part, unfortunately, theoretical

interpretation is left to the reader. This is not to say that the book makes no contribution. Clearly, the material is presented in such a way as to tie it to other social science studies. Rather, there seems to be no dynamic theory which brings together the author's own theoretical perspectives on his subject. This is a weakness, but not a fatal flaw.

Useem has written a good book. Social scientists and historians will find it useful long into the future.

JOSEPH ZIKMUND II
Albion College
Michigan

R. HAL WILLIAMS. *The Democratic Party and California Politics, 1880–1896.* Pp. vii, 290. Stanford, Calif.: Stanford University Press, 1973. $10.00.

This small volume represents a well-researched and well-written history of the Democratic party in California during a period when that state's rise to national prominence was just beginning. The author strives to place the policies of the California Democratic party within the context of crucial economic and social developments and show the impact of national politics on the fortunes of the local California Democrats. In accomplishing this he does not use quantification techniques nor does he regale the reader with myriad analyses of voting patterns. Instead, he relies on old-fashioned narrative political history to limn the complex interaction among political forces—leaders, issues, and the voters.

Professor Williams opens with a brief consideration of California's main problems at the beginning of the 1880s—the Chinese, the railroads, economic hardship, and labor unrest. At low ebb at that moment, the Democratic party seized upon the Chinese problem and railroad regulation as the primary means to spur membership and effect a return to power. Thereafter, a strong anti-monopolist and nativist element in the party vied with an older more conservative faction for party control. This continuing struggle helped mold

California politics for much of the ensuing decade.

The most traumatic period for the state's Democratic party came during the Cleveland years. California voted for Blain in 1884 and this left the Democratic party more divided than ever. As president, Cleveland found the disunity so serious that he frequently withheld patronage from all factions and sought to rebuild the party from the group up. But such attempts were ineffectual although, in the end, a tenuous compromise was arranged whereby the power of the anti-monopolists was temporarily diminished and the party concentration on the malpractices of the railroads was deemphasized. This compromise, however, did not hold California for Cleveland and the state voted for Harrison in 1888.

Bad times, Republican patronage problems, the advent of Populism, and a resurgence of anti-railroad sentiment combined to shortcircuit the Harrison victory and force the state to Cleveland in 1892. Almost immediately Cleveland's policies toward silver and his handling of the Depression antagonized Californians. In general, they opposed silver repeal, deplored the failure of tariff reform, condemned Cleveland for his Hawaiian anti-annexation attitudes, and were shocked by the Morgan gold deal. By 1894 Cleveland had totally fractionalized and demoralized California Democratic politics.

Meanwhile, local Democratic reform elements were making gains against the railroads and achieving some success in other matters such as the free-harbor fight for Los Angeles. The year 1896 actually brought joy to California Democrats as Cleveland was repudiated by the national party and Bryan was nominated. But the debility of years of antagonism was too much for the Democrats to carry and, despite much pro-silver sentiment, California went for McKinley. Thereafter, California remained a solidly Republican state.

Professor Williams bases this narrative on exhaustive use of Pacific Coast archives. His book fills a gap in the existing coverage of California politics, and he supplies a needed revision by showing that California politics in the 1880s and 1890s was something more than a branch of the Southern Pacific Railroad. In proving this point, he sometimes engages in overkill—his footnotes are often filled with multiple citations and considerable narrative material. But this flaw, if indeed it is a flaw, is about the only one to be found in this book.

Incidentally, the Stanford Press might keep in mind that not everyone has the eyes of an eagle, and that an index printed in type even smaller than the footnotes detracts from its usefulness.

ROBERT K. MURRAY
Pennsylvania State University
University Park

POLITICAL THOUGHT

EDWARD J. BACCIOCCO, JR. *The New Left in America. Reform to Revolution: 1956–1970.* Pp. xvi, 300. Stanford, Calif.: Hoover Institution Press, Stanford University, 1974. $8.95.

PETER CLECAK. *Radical Paradoxes: Dilemmas of the American Left: 1945–1970.* Pp. x, 358. New York: Harper & Row, 1973. $11.95.

Using a metaphrase of Marx and Engels, one could well argue that the history of all hitherto existing leftist movements is the history of myth-and-rhetoric struggles. Such was especially the case with the New Left of the sixties—the subject of the two books under review.

Recently a steady stream of books about the New Left has been pouring from publishers; and the Bacciocco and Clecak books, though flawed, are among the very best of the lot. They neatly complement each other, since each is strong where the other is weak.

Edward Bacciocco, Jr. wrote his book while a Research Fellow at the Hoover Institution, where he had responsibility for the New Left collection. The dustjacket rightly claims, I think, that his book "is the first study of the New Left presenting a comprehensive historical narrative and analysis."

Peter Clecak is Director of the Program in Comparative Culture at the University of California at Irvine. He centers his book around what he calls the "most crucial public question of this century": What is the nature and historical fate of socialism? The bulk of the book is devoted to an analysis of what four intellectual progenitors of the New Left had to say about this question—C. Wright Mills, Paul Baran, Paul Sweezy, and Herbert Marcuse. Though he finds their writings provocative and stimulating, he ultimately concludes that they offer unsatisfactory solutions to the left's "essential paradox of powerlessness."

Bacciocco is strongest on historical description and weakest on interpretive analysis. Thus, he offers a brilliant first chapter describing the "factors contributing to the evolution of the New Left in the United States," and he is likewise a solid guide in recounting how in the mid-1960s the New Left was transformed by the Berkeley Free Speech Movement, the rise of the peace movement, and the popularization of romantic violence. Bacciocco's interpretive analysis is largely confined to his final chapter; and though that is well argued, it is scarcely more than enough to whet the philosophical appetite.

By contrast, Clecak is strongest on interpretive analysis and weakest on historical narrative. But since his main purpose is analytical, this is not a valid criticism of the book. One can quibble, as this reviewer does, with the leftist theoreticians he chose to analyze—especially with Baran and Sweezy—but beyond that, it must be said that Clecak provides a penetrating appraisal of the insights and theoretical failures of the men he calls "plain Marxists." He, of course, raises more questions than he (or the theorists) can answer, and the argument occasionally gets tedious; but by and large, it is a

dramatic presentation of a dramatic subject.

Concluding these excellent critiques of an important contemporary subject, one is led to make the Marxian observation that the New Left first appeared in the early sixties as a kind of tragedy, given the general powerlessness of the American left, and then reappeared in the late sixties as farce in Jerry Rubin, Abbie Hoffman, and the apocalyptic Weathermen. The moral, if there is one, is that those who live by mythic rhetoric shall die by it.

FRANCIS M. WILHOIT
Department of Political Science
Drake University
Des Moines
Iowa

BENJAMIN R. BARBER. *The Death of Communal Liberty: A History of Freedom in a Swiss Mountain Canton.* Pp. ix, 302. Princeton, N.J.: Princeton University Press, 1974. $12.50.

Professor Barber pointedly and correctly insists that, in the Western world generally, liberty has been associated with individualism based on social contract and natural rights. The consequence has been difficulty in developing any effective theory and practice of loyalty to institutionalized community as compatible with freedom. The dominant alternative to individualist theory has been a statist idealism which has been viewed as leading to totalitarianism, destructive of liberty, rather than to the realization of freedom by identification, the position which the doctrine formally espouses. Such statism and totalitarianism have been properly condemned; but no alternative to an atomistic and possessive individualism, unsuited to the modern world, is available, in the absence of a genuinely libertarian local communitarianism, as a viable institutional practice. Professor Barber therefore has studied Switzerland's largest, most sparsely populated, and most locally dominated and geographically divided canton, Graubünden, and the whole development of Raetia from which it originally emerged as a political unit separate from Helvetia.

The story Barber tells is at once interesting and intricate. It involves fascinating analyses of the ambiguous geographical effects of mountain frontiers and limited passes inside the country and to the outer world; significant reflections on the superior support for liberty of living under the harsh conditions of largely barren mountain territories as against the more usual pattern of settled agriculture, along with greater danger of irrationality and violence; pointed emphasis on the values of partial escape from the normal pattern of feudalism against which Western individualism generally developed and on the peculiarly corruptive impact of petty expansionism and empire in the context of local participatory sovereignty; and significantly assessed both the difficulties and dangers in moving to confederation and a federal system, given a passionate localism.

Nevertheless, the dominant impact of the complex Raetian history was the enjoyment of agrarian liberty which yet involved loyalty to, and involvement in, community rather than the Western anarchism of achieved and protected individual rights against authority dominantly central or centralizing. Yet, as the title of the work suggests, the impact of modern industrialism, modern communications, and modern urbanism has been progressive erosion or undermining of communal liberty. Professor Barber raises the issue whether the simpler order of genuine participation and independence, still surviving in Graubünden despite all threats and actual diminutions, may not be preferable to the actual order of selfishness with affluence whose ills we today so conspicuously suffer.

Unfortunately, the cure is, from the point of view of present-day populations and the values potentially present in advanced industrialism, as bad as the disease, which, as we now see in these Nixon years, is manifestly severe and may lead to the decline of the West prophesied by Spengler. The in-

stitutionalizing task is to discover means to combine the values and achievements of an industrial society where individualism, particularly in its revived Social Darwinist form, is nonsensical and unreal, with genuine concern for personality and with workable institutions of community which evoke and express a genuine loyalty and involvement. Graubünden, as Barber indeed makes clear from its own recent trends, is not the answer; not, I think, is the functional community on the bases of calling and craftsmanship. Unfortunately, no really relevant institutional pattern exists; nor does the long overdue synthesis of the two schools of thought whose opposition has been overemphasized, but whose potential interaction to transcend present conflict and crisis remains unformulated in thought, and so unrealized in institutional practice.

THOMAS I. COOK
Department of Political Science
The University of Texas
El Paso

PETER BERGER, BRIGITTE BERGER and HANSFIELD KELLNER. *The Homeless Mind: Modernization and Consciousness.* Pp. 259. New York: Random House, 1973. $6.95.

The authors of the work under review here have attempted to understand, through an investigation of the "intrinsic discontents of modernity," that development of consciousness in contemporary technological society that is commonly but vaguely referred to as "alienation."

While modernity, on the one hand, "has indeed been liberation" in that its technology has opened up to man a broader range of possible developments, it has at the same time specified the avenues by which such realms may be approached. And the personal experience of those avenues has increasingly been that Kafkaesque feeling of anonymity and homelessness that in many quarters is seen as an inevitable result of the ongoing developments in technology.

The authors, however, allow for the possible emergence of a type of de-modernization, as it were, that would retain for mankind a vast part of the fruits of modern technology, as well as restoring those aspects of consciousness essential to man as an individual and communal being. In this regard it is suggested that a link between the American "counterculture" and the Third World movements that it admires is their shared perception of the threats of modernity: homelessness and mean-inglessness.

Incorporating but modifying ele-ments of both the Marxist and the meta-scientific approaches to this ques-tion, the Bergers and Kellner argue that through a sociology of knowledge it is possible to distinguish the primary car-riers of consciousness (the processes and institutions immediately related to technological production) from such secondary carriers as the schools and the media and from the various other fields of consciousness within the world of modernity.

What this analysis above all lacks is an adequate account of how it was that modernity came to be the reality of our present. While the authors do present many interesting particularized de-scriptions, these descriptions are made to serve the purpose of a non-existent general explanation. (Except for a few pages in the last chapter of the book the notion of values is ignored.) In the absence of such a descriptive explana-tion, the authors present in effect only an extrapolation of their initial defini-tions, without providing any philo-sophical, economic, anthropological, or phenomenological grounding. We may hope that the authors will con-front this question in a later work, for it is essential to their project. In the meantime, we are left with a series of important intuitions (in the best sense of intuitions) that are all too unfortu-nately left to dangle in the realm of discourse.

JOSEPH BIEN

Department of Philosophy
University of Missouri
Columbia

ROBBINS BURLING. *The Passage of Power: Studies in Political Succes-sion.* Pp. xiv, 322. New York: Academic Press, 1974. $11.50.

Professor Burling's study of political succession has relevance not only for his own discipline of anthropology but for all of the social sciences. The focus of his inquiry is this: What are the alternative mechanisms by which a new man can be chosen to fill the top position of power in his society? He recognizes that there are, of course, examples of collegial leadership. But he insists that periodic succession struggles are an inevitable feature of all political systems, taking a great variety of forms.

While the emphasis of the study is on succession, it deals with the broader ramifications of political power from a number of perspectives. Much of the study is centered on societies far re-moved in time and space from our own. Consideration is given to a diverse sample of hereditary systems. The col-lapse of hereditary succession as a legitimizing principle in the 19th and 20th centuries was rapid.

The analysis of modern succession systems centers on three main types: (1) The republican regimes—the emergence of which centered in Europe; (2) the regimes based on mili-tary intervention—a widely characteris-tic feature of much of the present day third world. The experience of Latin America provides a rich source of data. Burling sees the politics of much of Africa and parts of Asia falling into patterns disturbingly similar to that of Latin America; and (3) the regimes predicated on Communist political theory. Here attention is directed to the one-party systems in the Soviet Union and Eastern Europe.

With the disappearance of heredity, four techniques are identified as alter-native modes of achieving the top polit-ical office: the strong man; self per-petuation (the top man designating his own successor or some sort of oligar-chical agreement); the coup d'etat; and contested elections.

There is a frank recognition that the

principle of electoral succession has many imperfections and often has been extremely fragile. The relative effectiveness of electoral processes in Europe and America has failed to achieve a comparable stabilizing effect in many parts of the world. Yet whatever inadequacies may attend the process of electoral succession, its superiority to alternative succession systems is manifest. The survival of electoral succession rests on a large measure of faith and a broad popular consensus in this means of resolving conflicts.

Burling recognizes that this writing constitutes a challenge to the cherished cultural relativism of his profession. This is a valuable contribution to the study of political power and how it is attained.

RAYMOND H. GUSTESON
Department of Government
Ohio University
Athens
Ohio

L. P. CARPENTER. *G. D. H. Cole: An Intellectual Biography.* Pp. 271. London: Cambridge University Press, 1973. $14.95.

ROSS TERRILL. *R. H. Tawney and His Times: Socialism as Fellowship.* Pp. v, 373. Cambridge, Mass.: Harvard University Press, 1973. No price.

The British Labour Party has never been a purely working class party; it has always been an alliance of interests. The subjects of these two biographies were amongst those from outside the ranks of the working class who provided inspiration and leadership during much of the twentieth century. Their lives and careers provide both comparisons and contrasts. Tawney, an Anglo-Indian, was born in 1880 while Cole was born in London in 1889. Both were educated at Oxford where Cole had a more distinguished record than Tawney. While Cole got a first, Tawney got a second because his examiners, so it is said, failed to see that though "his mind was chaotic, . . . it was the

chaos of a great mind." Both worked for the WEA (Workers' Educational Association) and taught working-class students, the one in Nottingham and the other in Lancashire. But while, during the 1914–18 war, Tawney enlisted in the army in the ranks and was severely wounded in Flanders, Cole became a conscientious objector and had no war service. Tawney was powered by a special brand of radical Christianity while Cole was characterized as "a bolshevik soul in a Fabian muzzle." Both were particularly active in the 1920s; both then stood for Parliament, unsuccessfully, and both were involved in the General Strike of 1926. Both were journalists as well as academics. As journalists, Tawney wrote often for the *Manchester Guardian* while Cole was actively concerned with the *New Statesman.* As academics, Cole, with his straightforward lucid style, was a better lecturer than Tawney whose convoluted sentences sometimes got entangled in his drooping moustache. But as far as their scholarly works are concerned, it seems that though he had some influence on trade union studies, Cole wrote more with less effect (though *The World of Labour*—1913— is outstanding) than Tawney whose work on the economic history of the period 1540–1640 has led to these years being dubbed as "Tawney's Century." Tawney's other writings on *Equality*, the *Acquisitive Society* and *Life and Labour in China* also wear better than much of Cole's more ephemeral writing. Yet perhaps they were complementary. While Tawney did much to create a climate of social and political thought, Cole more directly provided the intelligent working-man with an armory of facts useful in the conduct of the day-to-day arguments about political and economic affairs. As a Socialist, Tawney was a grand nonconformist. Though he differed from each major strand of British socialism, yet "he is the one twentieth-century British socialist thinker," so Terrill claims, "who can be saluted from every quarter." Cole, on the other hand, was more intimately involved with the practical aspects of the programs of the British labour movement, first in his early days with the campaign for guild socialism and then after 1945 in efforts to rethink socialist economics and the values of democratic socialism "beyond the welfare state." Though both were prominent in the councils of the British Labour Party, they seem to have run on parallel courses and, if these biographies are any indication, their paths rarely crossed. But like the Webbs, what they appear to have in common is a lack of foreign contacts. Indeed while Tawney appears to have traveled little (except to China and the USA), Cole was not even a little Englander, he was a resolute little southern Englander. Alongside the biographies of Labour politicians we now have two substantial biographies of British socialist thinkers to round out our picture of the British Labour Movement in the twentieth century. Both are written by Americans at a time when concern with principle in the technocratic Labour Party of the 1970s is rather low and these books will therefore serve a useful purpose if they direct interest again to the basic presuppositions of British socialism. And one final comment. It may perhaps be of interest that the university press of a poor country can still make life easier for its readers by printing footnotes while its counterpart in a richer country can only manage end-notes. No doubt Tawney would have commented wryly on such a situation.

W. E. MINCHINTON
University of Exeter
England

DAVID W. MARCELL. *Progress and Pragmatism: James, Dewey, Beard and the American Idea of Progress.* Pp. xiv, 402. Westport, Conn.: Greenwood Press, 1974. $13.95.

This book, number nine in Contributions in American Studies (Robert H. Walker, series editor), is well written and will be interesting to the general reader. It provides an introduction to three important American thinkers, relates them to the larger context of the development of different phases and types of the idea of progress in America, and analyzes their individual views on progress, arguing that the pragmatic philosophy is best understood against the backdrop of progress as a problem and that pragmatism with James, Dewey and Beard "became explicitly a philosophy of progress" (p. xi) and, as such, was the inspiration for a generation of American liberals. To Marcell, these thinkers' commitment to "meliorism," "experimentalism," and "civilization" in the end came to the same point: "the conviction that man, by using his intelligence to solve specific problems, could with increasing effectiveness create a future satisfying his developing moral requirements" (p. 324). Structurally, the book is skillfully built around the *fin de siècle* pessimism of Henry Adams, with which it begins and ends, and which is used as a foil for the more robust views of the pragmatists. This book constitutes, then, a useful survey of James, Beard, and Dewey, and by focusing on the interface between their ideas and the whole complex of things involved for them and their generation in the idea of progress, has suggestively illuminated many contours of their thought, although much of what Marcell says does echo such earlier interpreters of pragmatism's era as Morton White and Philip Weiner.

This reviewer's major reservation, however, has to do with the difficult problem of the relationship of ideas to the people and groups who think them. Presumably Marcell is not just dealing with a few thinkers and their ideas but also with a tradition of thought in America and its wider impact; yet sometimes the ideas seem to float in the air unrelated to a social group. For example, opinion in the generation after Darwin is sampled for reactions to evolution—but how representative is this sample and of whom? To what extent did this debate reach into the lives of ordinary people? One way in which this might be assessed, a discussion of the impact of evolution on the churches, is slighted: while H. W. Beecher and a few others are mentioned, little attention is given them; yet clergymen of his type were probably far more important barometers of public opinion than were New England professors. Indicative of this omission is the failure to utilize a book like Paul A. Carter's *The Spiritual Crisis of the Gilded Age* with its discussion of this matter. This is of course not to question the importance of those treated, but to suggest that methodologically an author should make clear to whom and for whom his thinkers speak. It is perhaps this lack of attention to such arenas of popular culture as religion which enables Marcell to conclude that (p. xi) there was not much earlier American influence on the way the pragmatists thought about progress—but then he cited evidence to the contrary: for example, the recurrence in America of the debate over free will and determinism (pp. 9, 50) which he sees as a central issue in the pragmatic and progressivist revolt against formalism, and the use of the analogy of the Puritan spiritual struggle to illuminate the experience of William James (p. 153). Certainly James for one was well versed in the earlier and later varieties of American religious experience and did at least some of his thinking against that background. I would think it possible that the ideas of these three pragmatic progressivists developed importantly not only in relation to problems as defined by intellectuals, but also as they had long been felt in a popular mind largely informed by religious ideals and values—occasionally Marcell does hint at this (p. 260). Such considerations notwithstanding, the book is a valuable complement to the existing literature on its subject.

DEWEY D. WALLACE, JR.
George Washington University
Washington, D.C.

RALPH SANDERS. *The Politics of Defense Analysis.* Pp. xiv, 361. Cambridge, Mass.: Dunellen, 1974. $15.00.

CLARK A. MURDOCK. *Defense Policy Formation: A Comparative Analysis of the McNamara Era.* Pp. viii, 209. Albany: State University of New York Press, 1973. $8.95.

These two books on the formation of defense policy in our federal government cover roughly the same ground, and present similar points of view. The main theme of both books is the growth of systems analysis in the Defense Department after Robert McNamara took over as Secretary in 1961, and while both authors identify weaknesses in systems analysis and note a change of pace after Laird took over, they believe that systems analysis is here to stay. The book by Sanders is the better of the two; its exposition is more ample, it has less technical jargon, it gives more concrete historical examples by way of illustrating the many facets of the discussion, and, on the whole, it is simply more interesting to read. Mr. Sanders, at present Professor of Public Administration at the Industrial College of the Armed Forces, once served on the systems analysis staff of Secretary McNamara. Mr. Murdock is not identified in his book, and is unknown to this reviewer.

During the Eisenhower years, the formation of defense policy was characterized by interservice rivalry and weak central control by the Secretary of Defense. Basic policy decisions were made, not by civilian leaders, but by the Joint Chiefs of Staff. As Murdock points out, the two underlying beliefs of the Eisenhower administration were the primary importance of a healthy economy and stress upon strategic (massive) retaliation. Both had their roots in the desire for a balanced budget.

The Kennedy administration brought in a fundamental change in policy formulation, because it believed in "multiple options"—responses other than massive retaliation—and aggressive management on the part of the civilian leaders of the Defense Department. Policy formation was centralized in the Office of the Secretary of Defense, and McNamara brought in a group of experts in systems analysis—often called the Whiz Kids—and gave that group a prominent role in the formulation of defense policy.

Sanders defines systems analysis as "an art of systematically using logical and, in many cases, quantitative techniques for identifying and illuminating alternative courses of action," and the alternatives are usually evaluated in terms of their cost-effectiveness. Sanders makes the point that systems analysis is more of an art than a science, though it makes great use of the scientific method. Since decision-making has always proceeded upon the basis of logic and evidence, the McNamara managerial revolution was largely one of degree, in that he accelerated pre-existing trends towards centralized control and systematic analysis.

Under Secretary Laird, a great deal of the initiative in policy making was returned to the Service Departments and the Joint Chiefs, and the role of the National Security Council was enhanced. Even so, Sanders believes that systems analysis is here to stay. He points out, for example, that the Services and the Joint Chiefs have developed their own staffs of analysts.

Sanders examines the growth of systems analysis within the context of the total governmental system. Thus he traces the development of what he describes as an emerging profession, and looks into the Congressional response to this development. Both of these learned books point up the weaknesses of system analysis, notably the over-emphasis upon quantification, and the difficulty of coming to grips with social and political matters. Even so, both of these authors regard systems analysis as a great improvement in policy making, and believe that it now has a permanent place in our governmental system. As a non-specialist in public administration, it occurs to this reviewer that if what passes now for systems analysis is all that important, the previous policy making processes must have been rather primitive.

DAVID FELLMAN
Department of Political Science
University of Wisconsin
Madison

COLIN SEYMOUR-URE. *The Political Impact of Mass Media.* Pp. 296. Beverly Hills, Calif.: Sage, 1974. $15.00.

CLAUS MUELLER. *The Politics of Communication.* Pp. 226. New York: Oxford University Press, 1973. $7.95.

Colin Seymour-Ure's thesis is that mass media are very important politically, and that the analysis of their effects is an extraordinarily complex affair. According to the author, to be complete and realistic, the study of political phenomena involving mass media must include the following: elements of the communication process (sender, message, medium, and receiver); the communication context (communication timing, frequency, and intensity); and the political context (relationships among individuals and groups, public opinion, and other things). These ideas are supported by literature discussions and numerous case studies drawn from the United States and Great Britain such as television coverage of the Vietnam War, the rise of Enoch Powell, and the political role of the satirical magazine *Private Eye*.

This volume also includes a brief critique of behaviorally oriented media studies; Seymour-Ure argues that, since they concentrate on "short-run, relatively simple acts of individual behavior," these studies are often highly unrealistic, although, within their limitations and handled thoughtfully, they constitute a sizeable body of useful information.

This work demonstrates the strengths and weaknesses inherent in the case approach: it is realistic, but there is extensive use of anecdotal material, often making generalization from the author's case studies a difficult matter. But this is not his fault. Indeed, it reinforces his thesis—media effects are complex and subtle, often depending on unique situations and personalities for their impact. Recognizing this, Seymour-Ure tries to present hypotheses independent of his cases, but he refrains from extending himself beyond his data and the literature.

Judging from Claus Mueller's misleading title, *The Politics of Communication* would appear to deal with many of the themes covered by Seymour-Ure. Instead, Mueller's topic concerns the sources of instability in the present advanced industrial age in Western

Europe and the United States, and "communication" is no more important to his analysis than a dozen other factors.

Mueller believes that Western advanced industrial societies are in imminent danger of collapse because traditional ideologies which have legitimated political-economic institutions and practices are no longer widely thought about or believed. Traditional legitimating ideologies (such as liberalism, conservatism, and socialism) have been undermined by the rapidly developing technocratic-mass societies of the West. For example, concepts such as freedom of speech, equal political and economic opportunity, and a free marketplace of ideas, all important parts of liberalism, are far removed from the realities of poverty and the domination of society by a small number of people. And even if legitimating ideologies could be revised to fit the new realities, the changes would alienate large segments of society.

As traditional ideologies have faded away, they have been replaced by a legitimating rationale which says that the citizen should support the System because it has created great affluence. But this is an anemic substitute for ideologies of the past which, according to Mueller, offered "transcendent goals that could motivate the population politically." Furthermore, with the disappearance of semi-mystical ideologies which always clouded analytical thinking about politics, people look more critically at the performance of government and the economy. Added to this, the complexities of the industrial age have required progressively greater involvement of government in every aspect of people's lives; thus government calls itself to people's attention more often than ever before.

If, for some reason, the System were to slow its production of consumer luxuries, it would almost surely collapse because it would have no other legitimating features to fall back upon. However, Mueller, writing before the energy crisis, barely considers this pos-sibility. Instead, he focuses on the erosion of support for the System among middle class professionals ("cultural strata"). Most people have accepted our technocratic-mass society on its own terms—working people because their upbringing and education have crippled their analytical capabilities, members of the technically oriented middle class because they helped to design it and benefit from it, and the rich for obvious reasons. But large segments of the cultural strata are withdrawing their support; they are demanding and not receiving greater participation in political decision-making and "life styles incorporating social responsibility, individuality, and autonomy." Their disenchantment is crucial because they are most responsible for transmitting the basic values of society to young people. With their opposition, the system, weak as it is, must fall.

Mueller attempts to apply whatever behavioral studies bear on his theme. Unfortunately, the points on which the greatest empirical work has been done are also the most obvious points in the study. For example, he devotes almost half the book to extensive documentation of the propositions that communication is important in politics, that communication can be distorted in a variety of ways, and that working class people are less able to understand politics than middle class people because of differences in upbringing, education, and other factors related to social class. These points are important, but the average reader would be convinced of their validity well before page 85. Far more critical to his thesis is the notion that ideology has disappeared and been replaced by greed. The conceptual and methodological problems involved in evaluating the political importance of ideologies, their content, and changes in their content are awesome and Mueller owes his readers some notes of caution on this score. The entire book suffers from overkill on obvious points and evasiveness on difficult ones. Despite this, Mueller presents many important power elite themes with unusual clarity and occasional originality.

CARL GRAFTON
University of Houston
Texas

SIDNEY VERBA AND NORMAN H. NIE. *Participation in America: Political Democracy and Social Equality.* Pp. vii, 428. New York: Harper & Row, 1972. $10.00.

Verba and Nie have mined, cut and polished a many-faceted gem for social scientists. Until now we have had to be satisfied with normative appraisals, titillating debates, and scintillas of empirical evidence about the values and consequences of citizen participation in politics. Although the observations and arguments of classical and modern theorists have been of inestimable worth in spurring us to ponder, wonder and opine, the lack of substantial dimensions of hard data had led us sometimes as well, to pander, wander, or fall supine in the face of sweeping generalizations eloquently proclaimed.

The authors have gathered, coded, probed, measured, correlated, scaled, charted and interpreted with precision, candor and fidelity significant realms of data on citizen participation that provide the reader with solid bases from which to indorse, dispute or build upon their methodology and findings.

Not everyone will agree that the procedure and substance of their work are ideal. They limit inquiry and analysis to participation vis à vis the government, thereby appearing to declare irrelevant to politics related instruments for the authoritative allocation of values such as private organizations, families and jobs. The authors also confine their quest to activities "within the system," deliberately excluding activities of protest despite the acknowledged burgeoning of protest as an alternative participative tactic in recent years. Their response to anyone inclined to condemn these omissions is a reiteration of the obvious: to have included them "would be another book, not the one we have written." If

the authors don't merit a special award for exhaustiveness of their research, they still deserve one for combining full disclosure of their priorities with remarkably thorough implementation of them.

With regard to the themes they elect to focus upon, their scholarship is sophisticated and impeccable. In 344 pages of text, seventy pages of appendixes and some 150 charts, graphs and tables, they examine how much participation there is, by whom it is manifested, why people participate in the particular ways they do, the social characteristics and circumstances of participation, relationships to participation of such factors as party affiliation, community structure and the life cycle, and, in the final section of the text, the consequences of participation in terms of policy outcomes, leader responsiveness and problems of equality.

The authors' findings on responsiveness of government leaders to citizen action should bolster the morale of advocates of participation, for, put simply, leaders "respond more to participants than to those who do not participate." A key problem for democratic government continues to be posed, however, by the unequal distribution of motivation, skills and resources for participation. There is "an overrepresentation of upper status groups in the participant population." The current reality of inequality in participation notwithstanding, Verba and Nie convey in the summation of their research an inherent promise of reward if the alienated get involved. Participation is found to be "a powerful social force for increasing or decreasing inequality. It depends on who takes advantage of it."

Any social scientist who fails to take advantage of this pioneering volume runs the risk of becoming a professional wallflower.

VICTOR G. ROSENBLUM
Northwestern University
Chicago
Illinois

LAURENCE VEYSEY. *The Communal Experience: Anarchist and Mystical*

Counter-Cultures in America. Pp. ix, 495. New York: Harper & Row, 1973. $15.00.

Still another book on counter-cultures in America? Haven't we had enough? Given the great proliferation of books and articles on this subject we may justly ask whether there is sufficient intellectual content to warrant the publication and reading of yet another. Although this reviewer must admit mixed feelings, on the whole, this book is worthy of the author and the reading audience.

Veysey, professor of history at the University of California, Santa Cruz, was reared by parents committed to mystical and occult ideas and who lived in retreat from the larger society. Thus it is not surprising that his perception of the contemporary counter-culture scene is informed and empathic.

The focus of the book is on three broad questions: "How much and in what ways is America really changing, how great is the distance between the familiar and the 'far-out' in our society, and how closely do the secular and religious forms of cultural radicalism resemble each other?" (p. 3).

To answer these questions Veysey turns to the study of "cultural radicalism" rather than political or technological or scientific radicalism. It is the ideas which appear to represent new departures in contemporary American counter-cultures rather than the social structures, and psychodynamic processes which draw his primary attention. However, assessment of the strength, vitality, and innovativeness of these ideas requires analysis of the interplay between ideology and social processes. This Veysey attempts to do by digging into two types of communities: anarchistic communities and "communities of discipline."

Within a broad, somewhat superficial, historical framework drawn from nineteenth-century American cultural radicalism, the author describes a relatively tenacious anarchistic settlement which flourished during the early part of this century—the Ferrer Colony and the Modern School of Stelton, New Jersey—and contemporary anarchistic communes in New York, Vermont, and New Mexico. While the former were characterized by greater ideological consciousness of their place in the historical position of anarchism, the latter, although more numerous, displayed little commitment to anarchistic ideology. In fact the contemporary communes, like most of those described by Veysey, tended to avoid theorizing—a position compatible with the anti-intellectual character of most American counter-cultural movements.

With respect to communities of discipline the author analyzes in depth a monastic system, Vedanta, and a New Mexico commune, which he calls the New Age. What characterizes this type is intense adherence to normative patterns under the authoritarian leadership of a charismatic type. In contrast to anarchism, in which personal freedom is central, these communities require rigorous subordination of self to both ideology and guru. This often, in the case of the New Mexico commune—in which the author participated for a number of months—took the form of intense oral aggressive sanctions for real or imagined non-adherence to group prescriptions.

In contrast to the New Age commune in the New Mexico wasteland, the monastic systems were located within short distance of large urban contexts, a characteristic associated with the inwardness of mystical experiences and the capacity to persist without attempting a wholesale reconstruction of society.

The New Age commune emerges as the most interesting because of the author's personal involvement in it and because it is more clearly contemporaneous. Its clear cut differentiation and insulation from the mass society and the clarity of norms and behavior provide a sharp picture of much of what has appeared before in American counter-cultural movements. The final section is devoted to a wide ranging analysis and synthesis of counter-

Political Perspectives

THE EXECUTIVE PRIVILEGE: Presidential Control over Information
By Adam Carlyle Breckenridge

A controversial issue is put in historical perspective in this concise examination of the origins and development of the privilege from Washington's time into the second Nixon administration.   Cl **$7.95**

CONGRESS AGAINST THE COURT
By Adam Carlyle Breckenridge

Covering the decade climaxed by the 1968 Omnibus Crime Act, this study examines factors that influenced Congress to attempt overturning Supreme Court decisions which, it claimed, had upset the balance between the rights of the individual and the needs of society.
                                      Cl **$5.95**

THE RIGHT TO PRIVACY
By Adam Carlyle Breckenridge

"A knowledgeable dissertation on unlawful search and seizure, eavesdropping, First Amendment rights, and police power of the states"—*Library Journal*.
                                      Cl **$5.75**

THE DOCTRINE OF THE SEPARATION OF POWERS AND ITS PRESENT-DAY SIGNIFICANCE
By Arthur T. Vanderbilt

"...a valuable and lasting contribution to a subject vital to the political foundations upon which our government and liberties rest"—*American Bar Association Journal*.
                                      Pa **$1.50**

AFTER SEVEN YEARS: A Political Analysis of the New Deal.
By Raymond Moley

"No student can possibly make a just appraisal of the New Deal without it"— *New York Times*.   Pa **$3.50**

THE TRUMPET SOUNDETH: William Jennings Bryan and His Democracy, 1896-1912
By Paul W. Glad

"An important and persuasive re-assessment"—*History News*. "A significant contribution"—Arthur Schlesinger, Jr.
                                      Pa **$2.25**

A LEGAL HISTORY OF MONEY IN THE UNITED STATES, 1774-1970
By James Willard Hurst

Examines the effects of legal interventions on our money system and pursues themes relevant to the general history of political ideas in the United States.
                                      Cl **$9.50**

FORTHCOMING, SPRING 1975

SEARCH AND SEIZURE: A Dilemma of the Supreme Court.
By Erwin N. Griswold

Focusing on 1972-73 Supreme Court decisions, this important study discusses the dilemma search and seizure cases pose for the Court and suggests possible solutions.

At bookstores or from UNP
Orders from individuals must be prepaid
Minimum shipping charge 50¢; add 3½% tax in Nebraska

University of Nebraska Press
Lincoln 68508

Kindly mention THE ANNALS *when writing to advertisers*

cultural characteristics and their connections with the past.

There *is* continuity, in some ways more than Veysey grasps. The older bohemianisms described by Albert Parry, Carolyn Ware, Harvey Zorbaugh and others were more direct predecessors to today's forms and they never really disappeared. This reviewer's own studies of this phenomenon in Chicago in the late 40s and early 50s and the historical picture described by Grana suggest a persistent subterranean pattern, at least since the French Revolution, with occasional rapid and dramatic expansion in numbers of adherents under predictable conditions in Western societies.

In attempting an almost encyclopaedic review Veysey makes sacrifices (for example, nowhere is there reference to existentialism even though he ends his book with a plea for the desirability of attaining "the magic moment").

We must, nevertheless, judge this to be one of the very best overall studies of the counter-cultural theme to date. This is little short of a fascinating book displaying profound understanding of the communal experience both from the inside and the outside. It deserves to be widely read and it will be frequently cited.

EPHRAIM H. MIZRUCHI
Syracuse University
New York

SOCIOLOGY

RICHARD L. COLE. *Citizen Participation in the Urban Policy Process.* Pp. 178. Lexington, Mass.: D. C. Heath and Company, 1974. $12.00.

STANLEY B. GREENBERG. *Politics and Poverty: Modernization and Response in Five Poor Neighborhoods.* Pp. 282. New York: John Wiley & Sons, 1974. $12.95.

These two volumes are important additions to the literature on the participation of the poor, and each strives, without complete success, to set the topic in the perspective of the 1970s. Cole's book is marred by incredible lapses in proofreading: perhaps he is to be forgiven for misspelling the reviewer's name, but what are we to make of "Robert Nisbert, Eric Fromm, James Vanceko (and Vanecko), and Raymond Wilfinger" as well? Pride of authorship, where art thou fled?

Cole surveys all citizen participation programs in cities over 50,000, and focuses especially on a sample of twenty-six organizations and their members. Studying the characteristics of both groups and individuals, he develops a typology of organizations based on the scope and intensity of participation within them. Then, using "the policy-process model," he searches for dimensions that explain positioning on the citizen participation index, discovering that population size, federal funding, race, mayoral support, and urban violence are most strongly associated with citizen participation.

In what I find his most controversial conclusion, Cole identifies an "optimum zone of program typology" in which participants report most satisfaction with their activity and most trust. Thus, he concludes "that the most rational policy for individual urban areas is one promoting programs avoiding the extreme forms of neighborhood control and large-scale decentralization efforts." Cole takes a position that reasserts the pluralist orthodoxy of the 1960s, except now it is not apathy that is functional, but rather moderate participation. Radical participation is proscribed, because it is frustrating and generates systemic distrust. I would suggest that such participation is only frustrating where political systems prevent access of participants to the making of important decisions. Full participation need not always be frustrating, and the remedy may be systemic and not individual.

Cole's book summarizes a vast literature deftly, and the bibliography will be of great use to scholars.

Greenberg's volume is more historical in its purview, and pays greater attention to the dilemma of urban minorities. Examining political and social patterns in five inner-city neighborhoods—a Mexican-American neighborhood in San Jose; an Appalachian section of Hamilton, Ohio; the East Side of Detroit; Summerhill in Atlanta; and North Central Philadelphia—Greenberg examines political style, lower class culture, alienation, collective consciousness, and concludes with an examination of radical and liberal politics.

The volume is rich in its theoretical and historical range, and seeks as well, though less successfully, to apply biographical data to the understanding of the political beliefs of the poor. It provides a number of empirical advances on the problems treated, such as specifying attitudes congruent with the "culture of poverty" hypothesis to the street-corner men of smaller urban areas, and demonstrating the minimal political impact of the amount of culture of poverty that exists in these limited milieux. Alienation, on the other hand, is found to be more prevalent in the larger urban areas, and its political consequences predispose towards violence and away from a receptivity to conventional politics.

These findings, and the fascinating data presented elsewhere in the book on group consciousness and political predispositions, allow Greenberg to set the participation of the poor in the context of their response to an imposing and threatening reality. Their very allegiance to the system is seen as problematic, in distinction to Cole's view, in which participation is seen as something citizens ought to do, and moderately, to enhance system legitimacy. Ultimately, it is this divergence of perspective that makes Cole the idealist (in the 19th century meaning) and Greenberg the realist, and, in the opinion of this reviewer, Greenberg the more useful as an analyst and policy student of the contemporary politics of the poor.

JON VAN TIL

Rutgers University
Camden
New Jersey

WILLIAM T. COUCH. *The Human Potential: An Essay on its Cultivation.* Pp. x, 410. Durham, N.C.: Duke University Press, 1974. $9.75.

Mr. Couch has been deeply engaged with encyclopedias and has headed both the University of North Carolina Press and the University of Chicago Press. He is much interested in education. He sees our social world as a sad affair, one in which "the human potential" cries for development but is unhappily served, on the educational side, predominantly by specialists who have lost contact with certain very important traditions and have abandoned religious and moral concerns. General education, addressed to a general public, to be sure, and bearing on *theoretical* questions and on knowledge of the good life is very much needed. Mr. Couch thinks that the appropriate standards for such education were stated with some degree of accuracy by Robert M. Hutchins. He would himself revitalize "general education for a free society" and hopes for an institute that may develop an adequate encyclopedia for such education.

In the course of developing his views Mr. Couch covers so much (often somewhat in the manner of free association, but with unmistakable intellectual discipline nevertheless) that it is impossible here to mention even a fair amount of it. He devotes extensive and damaging attention to Marshall McLuhan. He had what to this reviewer appear to be entirely justified strictures on logical positivism. These strictures are connected with some of the strongest features of his polemical bias. For Mr. Couch has a fine eye for the pathetic absurdities of that kind of "cultural relativism" which holds that all cultures represent equally valid "ways" and which of course repeatedly break down for sheer lack of self-consistency. Ruth Benedict inevitably and repeatedly comes in for her share of critical notice since her *Patterns of Culture* presented cultural relativism at its eloquently stated worst.

But with all the profound sympathy that I, for one, can summon for Mr.

Couch's repudiation of this sort of cultural relativism, he can also be somewhat unfair on matters that pertain to it. Early in his book he contrasts the care with which *leading* physical scientists have worked with the looseness of "much of modern sociology and anthropology" (p. 45). Why not match *leading* physical scientists with *leading* social scientists? Ruth Benedict was not in the same class with Alfred Kroeber—and Kroeber clearly displayed skepticism of naive cultural relativism in his *Anthropology* of 1948. (Yet, also in the interest of fairness, I must to some degree qualify my own argument here against Mr. Couch. At least among older social scientists one can find a William Graham Sumner—surely a more considerable figure than Benedict—arguing with a certain rough empirical justification, but also in a fashion that can only be called ethically blind, that "the mores can make anything right.")

Mr. Couch has his crotchets and they are not invariably enchanting (as in his discussion of labor and corporations, pp. 232–233). He can be rather trivial (as in a statement on the basic causes of war that appears on p. 362). But he also has plain strengths and can deliver himself from time to time of highly effective sentences (as when he asserts, on p. 358: "Most of us cannot accept the idea that there is not and cannot be any rightness or wrongness in conduct but do not know enough to appeal to the great tradition that says there is"). He is worth accompanying on his controlled rambles.

LOUIS SCHNEIDER
Department of Sociology
The University of Texas
Austin

RICHARD CRITCHFIELD. *The Golden Bowl Be Broken: Peasant Life in Four Cultures.* Pp. vii, 312. Bloomington: Indiana University Press, 1974. $10.00.

A journalist, Richard Critchfield spent some twenty-one months visiting a number of the world's backwaters. Rather than trace out the economic,

political, social and cultural ramifications of the contemporary population explosion, he seeks to discover its "human" impact on the world's poor. In the face of modern conditions how do they think and feel, and what do they worry about, argue over, anticipate and enjoy? Acknowledging a methodological debt to the late Oscar Lewis and his studies on the "culture of poverty" Critchfield draws on detailed observations of everyday activities, interviews and recorded conversations to let his subjects speak for themselves. He singles out a few characters and events which portray the world's poor as their daily lives intersect with expanding populations and the impact of modern technology.

There is Jacob, a nomadic pastoralist living in the Mesopotamian Plain, surrounded by the ruins of ancient civilizations as he ekes out a subsistence with his flocks. The threats of hyenas and the vagaries of weather and the arbitrary force of Iranian soldiers combine with the problems of overgrazing and the encroachment of other pastoralists competing for the receding grasslands. And, there are Octave, a creole fisherman, and Prem, a poor Hindu student, on the multi-ethnic, post-colonial island of Mauritius in the Indian Ocean. Prem is the most sympathetic character, seeking to escape from the island's overwhelming problems of overpopulation, overfishing and unemployment. His efforts to migrate are frustrated by lack of opportunities abroad and insurmountable bureaucratic hurdles. His life becomes colored with the realization that there are no simple solutions to the island's problems that will work for him, that there is no escape except perhaps in fantasy.

The last two episodes are best developed. One has to do with Charan, a relatively prosperous Sikh farmer, who has, like others in his Punjab village, benefited from the "green revolution" and the use of modern technology. A dispute at harvest time between the *jat* landowners and their traditional *harijan* laborers reveals the perhaps inevitable breakdown of the ancient system of social reciprocities on which village society had once been firmly based. The most intriguing character here is Basant Singh, a thoroughly "modernized" farmer who exemplifies the best and the worst of the post-traditional man. The final story follows Husen, a young Javanese peasant who must periodically work as a *betjak* driver in Djakarta to survive. Caught between the traditional village world and the modern world of the teeming metropolis, Husen is open to both but able to participate fully in neither.

These stories demonstrate the strength of the method employed. Critchfield can flesh out his characters as living, striving and feeling human beings in a way that the technical social scientist rarely can. We can empathize with these characters as human beings, and gain some feeling for how their lives are changing through forces they themselves may only dimly perceive. But, Critchfield relies too heavily on his characters to reveal their own message. The book would have benefited from a summary or concluding chapter in which the author sought to highlight what is common and what is unique in each of these cases, perhaps speculating about what the future holds for them and us as human beings.

A. THOMAS KIRSCH
Department of Anthropology
Cornell University
Ithaca
New York

Encyclopaedia Britannica. 15th ed. Vol. 1–30. Pp. 33,142. Chicago, Ill.: Encyclopaedia Britannica Educational Corp., 1974. $348.00 per set.

Nineteen of the thirty volumes of the fifteenth edition of the *Encyclopaedia Britannica* present 4200 articles on various subjects, arranged alphabetically. These volumes will be referred to by the publishers' term, the *Macropaedia*, and correspond to the conventional encyclopedia. Ten additional volumes with 100,000 short articles are termed the *Micropaedia* and are new to this edition. Among other things, they provide detailed references to the different articles which appear in the *Macropaedia*. Still another innovation is the *Propaedia*, a one-volume introduction and overview of our knowledge of history, technology, religion, man, art, and the like.

The authors of the *Propaedia* are well known scholars. Their task was simply to describe man's knowledge. In practice, this has meant providing an outline of a set of exhaustive subject headings. The publishers say this outline provides a framework into which authors would fit their contributions to the *Macropaedia*, thus minimizing overlaps or gaps in coverage.

The *Propaedia* itself consists mostly of an outline of the broad subjects in the *Macropaedia* with references to their place or places of coverage. Without having used the volumes extensively, it is hard to judge the contribution of the *Propaedia*, though a first impression is that the organization of the *Propaedia* and consequently the articles in the *Macropaedia* are fairly conventional. For example, for subjects like painting, music, and literature, the core of knowledge is treated as Western, although sometimes the Middle East and Japan are included in the core. China and India are usually treated separately. The number of innovations in organization seem few; however, if the *Propaedia* organization has succeeded in eliminating gaps and overlaps, it was worth the effort.

The *Micropaedia* should be a valuable addition for students because it provides more entries then the *Macropaedia*, and gives a brief, but often adequate, discussion of the topic as well as references to where it is treated in the *Macropaedia*. For instance, if the task is to determine the tribes comprising the Iroquois federation, and if—as was the case with the reviewer—one did not know to look it up directly under Eastern Woodland Plains Indians in the *Macropaedia*, then one could look up Iroquois, or Mohican, or any other tribe in the *Micropaedia*, and obtain the necessary information as well as the reference in the *Macropaedia*. Since most encyclopedias, including earlier Britannicas, have had subject indexes with many more entries than their articles, is the *Micropaedia*, which is essentially a fully annotated index, worth it? It will probably be of considerable value to libraries and institutions, but individuals may find it a rather expensive index.

The *Macropaedia* is all new, with mostly new contributors. There are the usual extensive references at the end of each topic, followed by the initials (most annoying) of the author. The text, maps, and illustrations seem to be of excellent quality, and a sampling of the articles suggests that the choice of authors has been carefully done. Articles on things and places seem better than those on concepts, but perhaps that is to be expected. Those who have used and admired past editions of *Britannica* will certainly not be disappointed by the new *Macropaedia*: it is a solid achievement. And it is a pleasure to end by commending the publishers for setting a reasonable price for their product.

ALAN W. HESTON

Department of Economics
University of Pennsylvania
Philadelphia

VINCENT J. FONTANA, M.D. *Somewhere a Child is Crying.* Pp. xii, 268. New York: MacMillan, 1973. $6.95.

JOSEPH GOLDSTEIN, ANNA FREUD, and ALBERT J. SOLNIT. *Beyond the Best Interests of the Child.* Pp. v, 170. New York: Free Press, 1973. $7.95.

These two books have as their common element a primary concern for the rights and welfare of the child and to some extent, in both cases, a corresponding denial of at least the absolute right of the natural parents to determine the child's fate. Together they express the conflict now being publicly waged between two groups equally dedicated to upholding human rights, but from different viewpoints: one group upholds the parent's right to rear his (or more often, it seems, her) children as he or she sees fit, while the other group

upholds the child's right to safety, at least, and to affectionate, wise, and responsible care and guidance during the years when he cannot fend for himor herself. Both books attack the "myth" that parents have always at heart "the best interests of the child," and both call for society's watchfulness and intervention when necessary to protect the child against the parents.

It is the first of these viewpoints, concern for the child's rights, that dominates the book by Dr. Fontana. The title, *Somewhere a Child is Crying,* correctly indicates the tone of the book, which is filled with the author's pity for the helpless child and indignation at the callousness of his supposed protectors and the public apathy which still tolerates it. The author sketches the long history of child maltreatment, permitted by the child's legal status as almost the parent's chattel, and extols the 1869 establishment in New York City by a little band of Catholic nuns of a foundling home where he himself later became medical director. He tells of the increasing rise of conditions which favor this social evil, of its widespread medical recognition as late as 1962, and of his own pathway into concern for its victims.

The book then becomes one long account of the sufferings of the children, their causes, and the barriers against their prevention. He tells in vivid detail of seeing the little ones brought in, seriously injured or even dead, often accompanied by the guilty adult who tells self-protective lies or feigns ignorance of what has occurred. He insists that most of these abusing parents or parent surrogates are not alien monsters but, like ourselves, are subject to frustrations and roused to anger which they sometimes cannot control; and that adults who live in hardship and want are more vulnerable to such failure; and that many who in childhood have been neglected or abused, in adulthood helplessly repeat the pattern. He tells us also that those who have experienced such treatment are responsible for much of the violence so rampant today and endanger our own lives and those of our more fortunate children.

The book contains, however, one element notable in these days of public outcry against any use of punishment and incarceration in dealing with violent offenders and those few of the mentally deranged who are dangerous to themselves or others. Dr. Fontana does not want persons who lose control and harm children to "get away with it" (p. 225) and celebrates the dedication of a young prosecuting attorney who so vividly and irrefutably demonstrates in court the guilt of a common-law husband for the death of his wife's infant that conviction and a prison sentence result.

For the inexpert who may come in contact with children who are being abused, Dr. Fontana provides a list of tell-tale indications. He speaks favorably of a legal doctrine, *res ipsa loquitur* or "the facts speak for themselves," which may at times obviate the need of eyewitness evidence. Like many Catholics, he does not see lowering of the birthrate as a necessary or desirable preventive, but does call for widespread public concern and massive expenditures for the detection of child maltreatment in its earliest stages and for the establishment of a national system of prevention and remedial services. Let us hope that his crusading spirit will prove contagious.

The title of the second book, *Beyond the Best Interests of the Child,* is unfortunately misleading, since it champions what to its authors believe more truly to be the child's best interests, namely his need for the enduring psychological attachments so necessary if he is to develop into a fully socialized adult, trusting others and capable of love and responsibility toward them. Bearing the name of Anna Freud, rightly honored for her sensitivity to the young child's emotional needs and her work in making these known and provided for in Britain, as well as two distinguished legal names, it speaks with authority of an aspect of child maltreatment included but not

extensively dealt with in the Fontana book, psychological neglect or abuse, and speaks also of the law's long-standing tendency to disregard the child's rights and interests in its concern for those of the parents.

The heart of the book is a proposed model law for determining, when legal conflict arises between adults over who shall be awarded custody of a child, which placement will be most likely to benefit the child and ultimately society. The brief model statute, however, is accompanied by a detailed and carefully documented statement of the priority that must be given to the child's rights and an exposition of the relevant characteristics of the child and the limitations of any legal system which must make such decisions. It is set forth that to develop favorably a child must be and feel "wanted,"—that is, cared for and valued by a dependably present parent figure, who may, but need not, be the natural parent; that interruption of such an attachment is intensely painful to the child and imperils his development; that a young child's memory span is short, so that attachment to a lost parent figure is soon—the sooner, the younger the child—supplanted by a favorable current relationship. Stress is laid on the inability of any court to do more than choose for a child that one of the available placements which appears most likely to favor his optimal socialization.

From these principles the conclusions follow that a child early abandoned by his parent or removed from that parent's care must be as expeditiously placed as possible, with the existing emotional attachments being given great weight; that for the sake of the child's security such placement should promptly be made permanent; and that no delayed parental claim should prevail over the child's right to remain with the adult (or adults) who has become in fact the psychological parent. To the present reviewer the implementation of these principles appears much to be desired and the only serious objection is that of impracticality. In view of the current public agitation to protect the rights of the parent, and the recently added concern for the rights of the father even of an illegitimate infant, their hopes of acceptance appear distant. Concern for the child's rights, however, is also rising, and as with the Fontana book, it is possible to hope that the book itself will contribute much to the needed change.

ELIZABETH J. LEVINSON
The Counseling Center
Bangor
Maine

J. DAVID GREENSTONE and PAUL E. PETERSON. *Race and Authority in Urban Politics: Community Participation and the War on Poverty.* Pp. ix, 364. Hartford, Conn.: Printers, Inc., 1973. $12.50.

Reflecting on their own research in the 1960s and on the interpretive constructs of others, Greenstone and Peterson have put together a cogent explanation of the impact of federally sponsored community action programs on the politics of the nation's five largest cities. Above all, in their judgment, the programs, for all of their troubles, demonstrated the importance of black community control and black cultural autonomy in the struggle for racial equality.

Race and Authority in Urban Politics is really three books intertwined: one on the poverty program, another on city politics, and a third on problems of political analysis. Most concretely, the authors describe differing patterns of participation of the poor in policy-making and administration from one city to the next. Their data, not at any point presented in raw form or separately cited, are some three hundred semi-structured interviews with officials, representatives of the poor, reporters, and others in Chicago, Detroit, Los Angeles, New York, and Philadelphia, as well as Washington, D.C., between 1965 and 1968, supplemented by government documents and personal observation of poverty meetings.

At the next level of generality,

Greenstone and Peterson analyze the latent interests of the major participants in urban policy-making and the place of these participants in the urban power structure, as a way of explaining degrees of resistance to black demands, particularly by Democratic politicians. In addition to the more obvious audiences, students of bureaucracy and federalism should find these passages rewarding.

Finally, *Race and Authority in Urban Politics* is a critique of a large body of social science bearing on urban politics. It tests and modifies hypotheses drawn from the works of Robert Agger, Edward Banfield, Robert Dahl, Ralf Dahrendorf, Theodore Lowi, Wallace Sayre, James Q. Wilson, and others. The authors conclude that pluralists, among other social theorists, have overestimated the importance of class and underestimated the importance of race in the politics of the modern American city.

Race and Authority in Urban Politics is not a rousing good book by the likes of Banfield and Moynihan. It is dry scholarship at its best, a careful extension of the urbanologists' discipline. Given the extraordinary confusion among practitioners and theoreticians about the aims and accomplishments of the war on poverty, the detached and methodical tack of this book is apt.

ROBERT J. SICKELS
Department of Political Science
University of New Mexico
Albuquerque

MORTIMER R. and SANFORD H. KADISH. *Discretion to Disobey: A Study of Lawful Departures from Legal Rules.* Pp. viii, 241. Stanford, Calif.: Stanford University Press, 1973. $8.95.

A professor of philosophy and a professor of law have jointly produced a fascinating and useful study of the conditions under which officials and citizens depart from the strict letter of the law, and they have amply demonstrated the conditions under which such departures are both socially necessary and salutary. As they have succinctly epitomized it, "no rule of law can prescribe adequately for every set of circumstances in human life it potentially governs." The thesis may well be stated in another way: all laws and rules must allow for an honest margin of discretion.

It is no secret that juries often nullify the judge's instructions regarding the applicable law, and even disregard some or all of the evidence. Often this means that the jury looks upon a law as too severe or unwise, and the jury takes upon itself the task of rendering a decision based upon its own criteria of fairness and common sense.

Almost all police departments and other law enforcement agencies "exercise a broad power in deciding whether to arrest, even in cases where probable cause is manifest." For a variety of reasons, law enforcement agencies are selective in enforcement of the laws, sometimes to conserve manpower, other times in the interest of justice, and still other times because the law books contain hundreds of obsolete laws.

Prosecutors on all levels at times exercise their own judgments regarding nonenforcement of certain laws, and the legitimacy of this usurped authority has come to be recognized by both the courts and the citizenry.

Judges in the lower courts frequently employ legal fictions in order to hand down a just decision that clashes with the strict construction of the rules. The courts of appeal, and especially the Supreme Courts of both the states and nation, frequently find laws unconstitutional on the basis of the actual wording of the constitution, but also on grounds of social utility and the needs of a dynamic society.

The variety of departures from the strict wording of the law has established some precedents that encourage citizens, under certain conditions, to disobey a law in order to challenge its validity and/or constitutionality in the courts or before a quasi-judicial agency. The authors have dealt with this phase of their study in extenso, and the reader is likely to find some surprises.

They even tell of a case where a defendant was found not guilty despite the admitted fact that he had assisted a friend in escaping from prison.

As a practical matter, officials in other capacities are constrained to depart from or modify the strict provisions of the rules and statutes under which they operate.

Lest the reader derive the impression that the Professors Kadish have written a book which advocates or justifies law-breaking, it is important to point out that the contrary is true. But then the book should be read to really grasp the depth and scope of their research.

This reviewer suspects that some hyper-critical individuals will fault this book for a certain pedestrian quality in some places and for considerable repetition in other places. Whatever the validity of these criticisms, the overall quality of the book makes it worthwhile. Indeed, it is suggested that the book be read twice!

MORRIS KOMINSKY
Lake Elsinore
California

RICHARD G. NIEMI. *How Family Members Perceive Each Other.* Pp. vii, 213. New Haven, Conn.: Yale University Press, 1974. $10.00.

This is a study of the political and social attitudes of high school seniors and their parents. Interviews were held with a national probability sample of 1,669 seniors in 97 high schools. These students were considered representative of all high school seniors in the continental United States attending a school with a senior class of at least ten students. Fathers were selected from a random third of the seniors in the study; mothers from a second one-third of the students; and both parents from the remaining one-third of the young people. A total of 1,992 parents, 56 percent of whom were mothers, were included in the study.

Over one-third of the parents interviewed were unable to identify their sons' and daughters' party loyalties. There appeared to be somewhat fuzzy, even subconscious, limits within which most parents attempt to guide their children. In general, mothers and daughters tended to have the greatest agreement, while sons and mothers revealed the least agreement on the items interviewed.

Husbands' and wives' reports about the family and about each other were compared and evaluated. Spouses tended correctly to describe each other even in areas where some bias might be expected. More husbands underestimated their wives' education (nine percent) than overestimated (five percent). Ten percent of the wives upgraded their husbands' occupational status, while fourteen percent downgraded it. In general, there was a tendency to perceive one's spouse in the direction of one's own feelings. "The actual similarities are overestimated by a low of .24 and by a high of .68. This is far greater bias than we have seen in other reports, even in cases such as parents' political interests, where overall accuracy levels are very low . . . homogeneity with oneself was most often assumed" (p. 172).

The author, who is currently Associate Professor of Political Science at the University of Rochester, concludes, "Although there were some minor variations in agreement rates, even the highest rates revealed substantial discrepancies in the reports of students and parents or husbands and wives from the same families. Moreover, it is not apparent from the suggested causes of the low rates of agreement just how greater family consensus might be achieved" (p. 194). As is usual in methodological research, future studies are seen as adding both directly and indirectly to an understanding of how family members perceive each other.

EVELYN MILLIS DUVALL

Sarasota
Florida

DAVID RODNICK. *Man's Quest for Autonomy: A Background for Modernization.* Pp. xii, 365. Lubbock, Tex.: The Caprock Press, 1974. $9.95.

To bring findings of physical and cultural anthropologists, human geographers, sociologists, and social historians into some sort of coherent relationship is a difficult task. After some decades of reading and teaching, David Rodnick has made this attempt. He is "concerned with trying to determine where we are in the never-ending story of mankind, where we have come from, and where the next possible directions tend to point." Admittedly, this has required "a good deal of speculation to fill some of the many lacunae in the story of man," but in doing so he has made clear what is reasonably verified fact and what he suggests as possible continuities and projections.

Even though the "vast majority of the populations in the developing nations are still made up of inefficient peasants who are marginal participants in the economy," Rodnick is optimistic as to the ability of such peoples to adapt to unfolding opportunities and demands. He sees physical resources as "unlimited even in those countries that are theoretically assumed to be resource-poor. Hydrogen and oxygen in water are plentiful resources, and so are the enormous amounts of energy that come each day from sunshine, the winds, and the still unusable forces of gravitation."

From the vast literature on mankind's past, Rodnick has winnowed crucial changes in human structure and social organization, in technology, the control and manipulation of energy, and in ways of life. He is earthy and realistic, but he is not a pessimist like so many of those who are called earthy and realistic. He does not idealize or romanticize humanity, but he is a humanistic scientist who believes people are actually solving their survival problems and their problems of creative living better than their confused bumbling and wastefulness may make us many times think. "Although many may be pessimistic about the chances of our generation resolving many of the tensions that exist between us, few would deny that in the long run the outlook for such solutions is optimistic." Perhaps over-optimistically, he adds, "We have no other way of going than toward greater freedom, a more sophisticated awareness, a more individual responsibility, more participation by the citizenry, and a stronger forging of the links that tie all of us to one another."

In speaking of greater mass participation in social control, Rodnick does not place his faith in any magical formulas for social renovation. As he notes, "Merely shifting the power base from an authoritarian board of directors to an authoritarian Communist Party does not make a factory more democratic, or for that matter 'socialist.'" He senses a growing "emphasis . . . less upon private-corporate and party-governmental concentrated power and more upon the role of most individuals assuming greater responsibility for the efficient running of their work units within society, and at the same time participating in those decisions which decide the management of the larger segments. The emphasis will also be less upon greater leisure time and more upon the citizen spending his nonworking hours becoming better informed. An educated citizenry is a prerequisite in the smooth functioning of a complex Industrial and Scientific civilization."

For any humanistic scientist, tired of the resurgence of exorcism, of religious ritualism and anti-intellectualism, this is an inspiring, thrilling book. His outlining and interpreting of major human developments provide students with a sweeping perspective on the human lot and human potentialities that they should find to be a tonic alternative to pessimistic and mystical cop-outs.

ALFRED McCLUNG LEE
Brooklyn College and
  The Graduate Center
The City University of New York

EVERETT M. ROGERS. Communication Strategies for Family Planning. Pp. 451. New York: The Free Press, 1973. $12.95.

Like the subject itself, the literature on population continues to proliferate relentlessly. Yet, from time to time there do appear works that demand more than a fleeting attention. Professor Rogers' study is one such book. In it the noted expert on diffusion summarizes a number of useful findings about communications in family planning.

While acknowledging the importance of the availability of contraceptive methods and the suitability of delivery systems in family planning programs, Rogers emphasizes, quite validly, the crucial role that communication strategies could play in changing the reproductive behavior of families throughout this over-populated planet. He questions many prevailing assumptions about family planning, and presents seventy-eight generalizations on programs and strategies of population control.

The book has all the sweep and superficiality one sees in such works of synthesis. Some generalizations are descriptive, others prescriptive. Some, like the following, add little to our knowledge: "Less developed nations with larger total populations are more likely to have a family planning policy and/or program" (pp. 8–9); or "Less developed nations with faster rates of population increase are more likely to have a family planning policy and/or program" (p. 9). Some are quite circular: "Contraceptive clinic services are more readily available in countries with relatively more successful family planning programs" (p. 15); or "Home visiting of clients by full-time field staff is more often found in countries with relatively more successful family planning programs" (p. 15). And what strategic or policy implication can one draw from a proposition such as this: "Countries with relatively more successful family planning programs were relatively early in beginning their programs, are small-sized islands or peninsulas, are rapidly modernizing, and all (except Mauritius) have a 'Chinese-type' culture" (p. 14)? That there is no hope for countries that are not small or which do not have a Chinese-type culture?

Despite such somewhat banal generalizations and other rather questionable if conventional statements on development and modernization, the book is a significant and timely contribution to the field. Its merits are many. It is based on the author's firsthand observations of family planning programs in several African, Asian, and Latin American countries. Its conclusions, thus, are derived from comparative and cross-national data. It carefully reviews and evaluates the immense amount of research in this field. It not only summarizes their findings, but also points out directions for future inquiries. Although, following the contemporary American mood, the author is over-impressed by the supposed success of the Chinese family planning program, he nevertheless places a well-deserved emphasis on institutional and structural changes to promote the small family norm. Policies affecting marriage age, taxation, child health facilities, and retirement benefits are not strictly family planning measures, but such "beyond family-planning" policies are in the long run more effective than any package of clinical or even communication strategies.

Rogers recognizes the role of the mass media, including such traditional means as folk theatres, puppet shows, traveling story tellers and so on, but also stresses the role of interpersonal channels of communications, especially in such a taboo field as family planning. He cautions against the common communication errors in programs of family planning. Chapter 2 is an excellent introduction to the study of human communication. The importance of communication competence for change agents is stressed in Chapter 4. The significance of message symbols and semantic problems in diffusion are recognized throughout the book. Since much of family planning communication so far has been aimed at wives, the author's advice to direct it to the husband—the real decision-maker in many cultures—is sound and sensible.

Behavioral scientists as well as public policy-makers and administrators will benefit from a serious reading of the book. Whether the findings of research or lessons of earlier and existing programs will be incorporated into national policies of family planning remains to be seen, but one can no longer complain that a usable compilation of information about communication strategies in this field is still unavailable.

S. K. KHINDUKA
The George Warren Brown
 School of Social Work
Washington University
Saint Louis
Missouri

LAURA WOOD ROPER. *FLO: A Biography of Frederick Law Olmsted.* Pp. xvii, 555. Baltimore, Md.: The Johns Hopkins University Press, 1973. $15.00.

There is a solid literature on FLO as the father of American landscape architecture. Professor Albert Fein has put together his reports on parks to the Common Council of the City of New York. A national commission to honor the sesquicentennial of his birth organized a superb exhibition in 1973, shown in Washington and New York, reminding us how wide-spread his designs were—from coast to coast, even in Canada. Olmsted looked on Andrew Jackson Downing as the first American landscape designer (under whom FLO's partner, Calvert Vaux, had worked.) But unquestionably it was FLO who gained acceptance among the public and officials for public parks as essential elements of urban life. He was as much concerned with the social meaning as the design.

Mrs. Roper's book is delightfully different. She portrays FLO as a human being—a man with strong family feeling, whose Mayflower ancestors were spread over New England. FLO was so unfocused in his interests that he dropped out of school. He failed as a farmer on Staten Island, as manager of the Mariposa mining estate below the Yosemite. His low-keyed but well reasoned reports from the South on slavery in the 1850s gained little attention in the U.S.A. compared to Harriet Beecher Stowe, but they were well reviewed in the British journals, so that FLO gained acceptance among the literati in New York. His application to be appointed designer and superintendent of Central Park in 1857 had endorsements from Washington Irving, William Cullen Bryant, Albert Bierstadt. Andrew Haswell Green has been hailed as the forgotten civic leader who spent decades on behalf of Central Park and the consolidation of greater New York. Mrs. Rogers reveals why perhaps the only monument to him in the park is a half-hidden cathedra. As treasurer of the Park Board he arrogated to himself a veto power over FLO. Every penny of expenditure must be approved by him. FLO's draftsmen at times had to buy their own pencils.

FLO's crowning achievement was the landscaping of the Chicago World's Fair. He insisted that there not be gardens of flowers, but a landscape for a temporary exposition that would disintegrate and leave a natural park shore. His mind gave way in his old age, but he had trained his son to carry on the profession.

Mrs. Roper is the wife of a partner in a prestigious Washington law firm, with attendant obligations. She has raised a family. She has worked on FLO and published articles in scholarly journals over several decades. She gained the confidence of Olmsted Brothers, who opened FLO's personal papers to her. She persuaded him to put them in the Library of Congress. Perhaps it is her own fresh concern as amateur that has made this so warm and human a book.

CHARLES S. ASCHER

Institute of Public Administration
New York

LEONARD RUCHELMAN. *Police Politics: A Comparative Study of Three Cities.* Pp. xi, 118. Cambridge, Mass.: Ballinger, 1974. $12.50.

STUART PALMER. *The Prevention of Crime.* Pp. 277. New York: Behavioral Publications, 1973. $9.95.

The impact of police officers' organizations as political pressure groups in New York, Philadelphia and Chicago during 1966–69 is traced in this study, which is modeled on Dahl's *Who Governs?* The pluralistic answer to Dahl's question is thereby broadened to include the organized lower-level members of government bureaucracies.

While pluralistic views of municipal politics suggest that government decisions serve the interests of the total citizenry to a greater extent than is implied in elitist interpretations, such as Hunter's *Community Power Structure,* the police organizations in Ruchelman's account worked predominantly to restrict the concern of the city with the interests of its poor ethnic minorities. In all three cities they eliminated or weakened civilian boards to review allegations of police misconduct, they fostered police violation of due process and free speech rights of political and ethnic protesters, they impeded efforts to expand employment of minorities in police forces, and they impaired the relationship of the police with lower status members of minority communities.

Although this 1966–69 account is extended by bits of prior history and by an Epilogue that sketchily stretches it into 1973, the book's main limitation as a contribution to abstract generalizations on evolutionary trends in municipal politics is the short time span on which it is focused. The overall impression it conveys is of triumph for reaction, represented by Mayors Daley in Chicago and Rizzo in Philadelphia, and of doom for those portrayed as heroically fighting for the interests of the broader public, New York's Mayor Lindsay and his short-term police chiefs, Leary and Murphy. Yet if change in police concern for the relatively powerless were traced over a period that began several decades ago, or—I predict—if it could be extended farther forward into the 1970s, a more optimistic impression would be supported. Confirming Talcott Parsons' brilliant analysis of societal evolution in *The System of Modern Societies,* it would show that despite recurrent reactionary backlash the overall trend is one of accelerating inclusion of more and more of the population in those to whose interests local government responds. This, Parsons argues, is an inevitable consequence of the organization and role differentiation, as well as the educational and status upgrading of more of the population, that follow inevitably from technological changes in modern societies.

While this book is fairly well written (despite repeated use of the noun "data" as singular), many may find it too concise and atheoretical.

Stuart Palmer's *The Prevention of Crime* can serve as an introductory text in criminology or as a popular tract on how to cope with crime. It uses a much different organization, style and point of view, as well as many fewer words, than the typical text in this field, yet it touches on most topics dealt with by texts. It also has detailed prescriptions on how to improve community social services, police, courts and corrections. Some of the proposals are highly innovative, but all are consistent with developments already initiated. While they are portrayed in an idealizing manner that glosses over the innumerable pitfalls and setbacks usually accompanying social engineering efforts, the Palmer plans are not excessively Utopian.

"Prevention" is broadly construed in this book, encompassing measures pursued before crime occurs, control of offenders, and rehabilitation. The first part of the book summarizes criminological literature on major categories of offense (including drug abuse and riots in a single brief chapter), crime causation theories, police, courts and correctional agencies. The second part, on prevention, is the most distinctive. It includes detailed proposals for neighborhood service centers to deal with personal problems of all sorts, the retraining of police and judges, and the conversion of prisons to learning centers, supplemented by community employment centers.

This book appears to be intended not so much for scholars as for concerned citizens or beginning students, but it will provide any reader with numerous sound and provocative ideas.

DANIEL GLASER
Department of Sociology
University of Southern California
Los Angeles

JOHN STAPLES SHOCKLEY. *Chicano Revolt in a Texas Town.* Pp. 314. Notre Dame, Ind.: University of Notre Dame Press, 1974. $9.95. Paperbound, $3.95.

This revolt was a nonviolent uprising of Mexican Americans (Chicanos) against the domination of the whites (Anglos) in Crystal City, Texas, "Spinach Capital of the World"; population about 10,000. The Chicanos comprise about eighty percent of the total. They serve as the migrant rural labor force in garden agriculture. Their poverty level of living is too well known for elaboration.

This account is related to a struggle for political rights, although the shadows of poverty are in the background. Young Chicanos with education but no job prospects became the leaders demanding the rights of citizens and the end of abuses. Their demands are elementary: equal education for children, fair labor practices, equal treatment by courts and police, and freedom from humiliating verbal treatment by Anglos.

Shockley speaks of two confrontations, 1963 and 1969. Actually these were major battle dates in a continuous contest which began in 1962 or before. In the first revolt the leadership was provided by outside trade unions and other groups; the poor Chicanos hesitated to follow their own inexperienced leaders. Their confidence grew and local leaders managed very well the 1969 revolt. In the 1963 election Chicanos captured control of the town council but not full control of the board of education, the important goal to them. Total Anglo control of the schools was the sensitive issue Chicano families understood.

Chicano leaders formed themselves into a political party, Raza Unida, free from outside control, an instrument for organized action which apparently stirred the high school Chicanos to articulate their grievances which they did to the discomfort of the Anglo dominated school board. High school students went on a strike of weeks, grammar school Chicanos joining later. This was the acute issue in the 1969 election when Raza Unida gained control of both the town council and the school board. There were ups and downs in the decade of revolt, and there may be setbacks ahead but a return to the pre-1963 order is unlikely.

Shockley's report is well documented, free from name-calling, innuendo, and partisan observations. This appears to be a document other students can accept with confidence.

This bit should be added: Popeye, the Sailor Man, fighter for the poor and downtrodden, is the patron saint of Crystal City because he made spinach popular. This is an aberration. His statue stands in front of the city hall. Anglos have given him the job of selling spinach.

NELS ANDERSON
University of New Brunswick
New Brunswick
Canada

ROBERT S. WEISS. *Loneliness: The Experience of Emotional and Social Isolation.* Pp. x, 236. Cambridge, Mass.: MIT Press, 1974. $8.95.

This book is one of the few where a great deal is to be gained, and it is highly recommended that one reread both the Foreward by David Riesman and the Conclusion by the author. The author sets out to make a comprehensive review of loneliness viewed from the perspective that it is the result of a prevalent condition due to social and emotional isolation, differentiating this condition from the classical depression. In the beginning chapters of the book, an explanation of the forceful dynamics

of a profound sense of loss to this reviewer resembles much which is described in other literature as reactive depression. However, in a most succinct and searching way, Dr. Weiss rather asks the reader to disengage himself from this point of view and view the matter from a pandemic base. This he ably supports from his background of years of practice and teaching and here rests the kernel of new insights, as one is made privy to a distillation of most pertinent material contributed by some of his outstanding Harvard colleagues.

An excellent explanation of attachments is given to make the process more readily understood, especially the need for persons to re-engage themselves with someone they separated from and actually do not want to, nor could they reunite with them again on an intimate level. Nonetheless, there is a need to reestablish and reorient themselves emotionally with a person who previously functioned as a significant attachment. One of many illuminating illustrations is the need of the persons involved to fill the emptiness they feel and in this they make unwise attachments. "The problem of unwise attachments is that they end. One never becomes accustomed to their ending, just as one never becomes accustomed to physical pain or moral humiliation. . . . Yet even though one knows that another abandonment is a possible outcome of every new attachment, it is extremely difficult to give up searching."

A point so often overlooked in the acceptance of our present American premise of what seems to be a complete race for independence on the road to "success," and whatever it means to each and everyone of us, is the author's being able to give visibility to the importance and difference in social and emotional isolation of adults—that is, "Adults need both a social network engagement and an attachment figure to provide security."

The entire work points up the often overlooked premise that loneliness is not so much the individual bringing his own problems into any given situation but is in large part inferred by Weiss as the result of the social pathology of American society. This is due to the nature of its structure, or more precisely, its structurelessness.

This book is certainly recommended reading for those involved in or interested in gerontology, as well as others concerned about specialized groups of people in our society who have been separated from their kinship circle or other meaningful ties; such as one parent family heads, divorcees, military families and the too often overlooked spouse of the successful corporate executive.

In part, some will find this book difficult reading, but it is deserving of the extra effort because the insightful rewards gained are well worth it.

KENNETH G. SUMMERSETT
Administrative Director
Community Psychiatry Program
Newberry State Hospital
Michigan

ECONOMICS

PHILIP S. FONER. *Organized Labor and the Black Worker, 1619–1973.* Pp. ix, 489. New York: Praeger Publishers, 1974. $15.00.

The relationship between black workers and labor unions has been an uneasy and generally hostile one since the emergence of modern labor organizations following the Civil War. With a few exceptions, such as the Knights of Labor and the Industrial Workers of the World and, more recently, the Congress of Industrial Organizations, organized labor has tended to freeze the black worker out or to admit him into its ranks under segregated and inferior conditions demeaning to the black and debilitating to the entire structure of the cause of the working man.

Foner's well researched and avowedly partisan history of this relationship is based on solid and extensive research into both primary and secondary sources, facilitated, it might be assumed, through the author's already gigantic research efforts into the general history of the American worker. The publication of the author's book by this particular publisher is not without its ironies since Foner is an admitted and even outspoken Communist historian and Praeger on the other hand was as recently as the 1950s a conduit for C.I.A. propaganda overseas. Publishing goals evidently make for strange bedfellows and perhaps it might be expected that in the future International Publishers may issue the works of William F. Buckley.

Following an introductory chapter describing the condition and situation of free and black labor before the Civil War, the author discusses the attitudes of infant labor unions in the Reconstruction period toward blacks with an especial emphasis on the important and interesting short history of the Colored National Labor Union which arose not only in response to white restrictions on black labor union membership but more importantly as a manifestation of black culture and the assertion of black self identity. The decline of this organization coupled with the general turning away from black interests by white society in the years following 1876 left black workers adrift until the emergence of the Knights of Labor with a policy of open admissions for blacks unless they were bankers, liquor dealers or gamblers. Blacks played a major role in the Knights wherever they were allowed to do so although the increasing number of racial slights and slurs on the part of the white majority in the labor organization gradually caused many blacks to drop out of the union. Nevertheless, as Foner points out, the disintegration of the Knights in the late 1880s marked not only a serious blow to the general labor movement but especially to black workers who at least in theory were allowed to enter the ranks of the organization.

The attitude of the American Federation of Labor toward blacks was—and to a considerable extent still is—tinged with ambivalence and an overlay of hypocrisy. The emphasis of the AFL on the organization of the skilled worker left most black workers out in the cold since they were members of the un-skilled and semi-skilled segments of the working class. Even where the federa-tion allowed for the creation of indus-trial unions, however, blacks were humiliated and provided with inferior secondary status in segregated locals and powerless federal unions. The overwhelming majority of the white unionists and their leaders was unable to rise above race prejudice and or-ganize the black workers despite the continual employment of the latter as strikebreakers. Here and there, as in the case of the United Mine Workers, blacks did enter unions in large num-bers and even for a time played consid-erable roles in union activity, but by the time of the coming of World War I the doors of union halls had slammed shut against their entry.

The shining exception to the policy of the exclusion of blacks from un-ionism was the Industrial Workers of the World, whose color blind policies resulted in the recruitment of sig-nificant numbers of blacks on an in-dustrial basis in the pre-World War I period. Blacks and whites participated jointly in strikes and various aspects of union activity thus increasing the per-secution by public and private agencies of a union already deeply suspect owing to its revolutionary goals. The collapse of the I.W.W. during and after the war marked another return to the dominance of lily-white unionism on the American scene.

The 1920s in Foner's graphic account was a period of implacable labor union opposition to the mass entry of blacks despite the tremendous growth of the black working class in the Northern industrial cities. A. Philip Randolph's efforts to organize and gain recognition for Pullman sleeping car porters was a decade-long and unrelenting struggle against the hostility not only of the corporation but also of the railroad brotherhoods and the A.F.L. His even-tual victory and the affiliation of the Brotherhood of Sleeping Car Porters with the A.F.L. resulted in an uneasy and never completely accepted position of Randolph as a spokesman for blacks within the ranks of the federation.

The coming of the Congress of In-dustrial Organizations also marked the emergence of black workers as a sig-nificant force in the labor movement for the first time since the demise of the Knights of Labor. Foner states with justifiable pride the important role played by Communists within the C.I.O. and its constituent unions in fighting against "white chauvinism" and he stresses, accurately for the most part, the resultant decline in black influence with the C.I.O. as red-tinged unions were expelled during the post-World War II period.

Although the position of blacks in organized labor today is certainly greatly improved from that of previous years, considerable conflict and stress within the ranks of the labor movement still exist over the matter of race and will probably always continue to exist so long as too many people seek too few meaningful jobs.

Foner's work is an excellent one despite a tendency to overstress and exaggerate the exploits of the extreme left wing of the political spectrum. His book provides considerable illumina-tion of an important and often over-looked aspect of American labor his-tory.

NORMAN LEDERER
Menard Junior College
Merrill
Wisconsin

JOHN W. KENDRICK. *Postwar Productiv-ity Trends in the United States: 1948–1969.* Pp. xx, 369. New York: Columbia University Press for Na-tional Bureau of Economic Research, 1974. $15.00.

In this book Professor Kendrick re-sembles Janus: he looks backward to revise and extend the estimates in his 1961 discussion of productivity trends (*Productivity in the United States*) and, occasionally, forward to give some of the conclusions of a forthcoming work by him on the sources of these trends.

Assisted by Maude R. Pech, Kendrick devotes 245 pages to some eighty basic tables and text describing the sources and methods used to calculate estimates of total factor productivity (output per unit of "total factor input," a weighted average of labor and capital inputs) and partial factor productivity ratios (output per unit of labor or capital input). The rest of the book—143 pages—discusses conceptual issues in productivity measurement and analyzes aggregate and industry-group productivity trends since 1948.

Kendrick finds that the average rate of total factor productivity growth since 1948—between 2.3 to 2.5 percent per year, depending on the measure used—is not significantly different from the rate for earlier periods. (On the other hand, labor productivity growth—3.0 to 3.4 percent—is significantly higher than the rate for earlier periods, principally because the capital-labor ratio has grown more rapidly.) But "productivity advance accounted for almost all of the economic progress [growth in per capita net national product] achieved between 1948 and 1966" (p. 65). He concludes with a very interesting discussion of the interrelationships between trends in industries' productivity, factor prices, output prices and output.

Kendrick's analytical chapters are, while highly suggestive and interesting, not entirely convincing. His discussion of the conceptual issues in productivity measurement might have been more thorough. He apparently assumes (see p. 14) a production function which has a constant elasticity of factor substitution and constant returns to scale—which may not be as valid for individual industries as for the economy as a whole. And while he recognizes that productivity and output trends are interrelated, he specifies that usually the causation runs only from the former to the latter.

But despite these shortcomings, and while some of the book's sources and methodology might be questioned, Kendrick deserves great praise for the conscientious and effective way he has used the sometimes very incomplete and imperfect information available. Deriv-

ing and constructing basic data is perhaps the most demanding and least glamorous job an economist can tackle, and all economists who are interested in economic growth, productivity and structural change in the U.S. economy will be in Kendrick's debt.

MARK R. KILLINGSWORTH
Department of Economics and
  Business Administration
Fisk University
Nashville
Tennessee

JOSEPH A. PECHMAN AND BENJAMIN A. OKNER. *Who Bears the Tax Burden?* Pp. vii, 119. Washington, D.C.: Brookings Institution, 1974. $2.50.

This comprehensive and useful study of tax burden distribution in the United States provides few surprises in its findings. Similar to earlier studies, it demonstrates the neutralizing influence provided by mildly regressive state and local government taxes to the mildly progressive federal tax structure. In fact, it is shown that little difference in the effective rate of taxation occurs over most of the income distribution range when all levels of the public sector are considered. Significant regressivity is found only at the very bottom and significant progressivity only at the very top of the income scale. Moreover, the "very rich" pay substantially higher tax rates than the average family only if it is assumed that capital, not labor, bears the incidence of corporation income and property taxes—a contention very much open to discussion.

The book consists of five chapters and four detailed appendices. The major findings of the study are summarized in Chapter I. This is followed in Chapter II by a discussion of relevant concepts, definitions, and measurement procedures. A review of recent tax incidence literature is presented in Chapter III along with a description of alternative sets of tax incidence assumptions. Also, the economist's "differential tax incidence" approach, which allows a proportional personal income tax to be used as a basis for comparison, is introduced. The overall pattern of tax burden distribution in the United States is described in Chapter IV. In addition, the tax burden distribution of each major type of tax is estimated. In Chapter V, it is observed that when the taxpayer population is disaggregated into various subgroups, the lowest effective tax rates fall upon homeowners, rural farm residents, families with transfers as their major source of income, and large families.

The Pechman-Okner study is extremely useful despite the general similarity of its findings to earlier tax distribution studies. For example, it utilizes some of the most recent and comprehensive data available. It does this by assembling the so-called MERGE file consisting of Office of Economic Opportunity data for (early) 1967 and Internal Revenue Service data for 1966. Furthermore, a broad definition of "adjusted family income" inclusive of such items as transfer payments and annually accrued capital gains, whether realized or not, is applied. In addition, the analysis takes into consideration recent contributions to tax incidence literature. Moreover, the study, though demonstrating once again the considerable need for definitive studies of the incidence of the corporation income and property taxes, circumvents this problem to the fullest extent possible. This is accomplished by means of a methodology which utilizes eight different sets of assumptions concerning the incidence of various taxes. The two limiting assumption sets, the one with the "most progressive" and that with the "least progressive" effects, prove to be the most useful for analytical purposes. Also, a broad range for interpretation is provided by the measurement of effective tax rates as a percentage of both absolute income levels and population percentiles.

In conclusion, it may be said that the Pechman-Okner study gives further proof that taxation in the American public sector fails to yield the type of effective tax rate progressivity that would be required to meet the ability-to-pay principle of equity in the distribution of tax burdens. Yet, one should not reach unwarranted conclusions from this study concerning the overall distributional effects of federal, state, and local government fiscal activities in the United States. Instead, caution is required because Pechman and Okner attempt only to measure the incidence of tax "burdens," *not* the incidence of expenditure "benefits." Yet, the "total" distributional effects of governmental budgetary activities would most certainly encompass both sets of influence.

BERNARD P. HERBER
University of Arizona
Tucson

DAVID B. RUTSTEIN. *Blueprint for Medical Care.* Pp. 284. Cambridge, Mass.: The M.I.T. Press, 1974. $8.95.

Professor Rutstein's blueprint is the outline of a "one best way" to organize medical care under a national health system. The book is written for the layman. As M.I.T. President Wiesner points out in the foreword, many of Rutstein's schema such as emergency care and quality control components can be studied or implemented in whole or in part, however, irrespective of a total national health program.

In a short book, Rutstein has encompassed all aspects of a national medical care system including ambulatory, emergency and inpatient care, communication and transportation systems, medical education, quality control, governmental administration, public accountability and financing. Rather than presenting various alternatives on each aspect, elucidating the pros and cons of each, making recommendations and suggesting opportunities and constraints for implementation, Rutstein simply makes recommendations, often citing successful experience in the United Kingdom as justification. For example, he suggests that the physician be paid a salary supplemented by incentive awards based on contributions to medical knowledge, unusual hazards or hardships and to motivate him to provide better care. Such recommendations are made with no discussion of the advantages of other systems such as fee for service and capitation or of the disadvantages of salary, to include the difficulty in operationalizing the author's incentive system.

More importantly, Rutstein does not discuss in any detail alternative organizational programs to a governmentally administered national health program. Under one possible alternative, for example, the federal government might subsidize the formation of several giant provider organizations similar to the Kaiser plan (which Rutstein praises); a second possible alternative would be to mandate the development of a regional franchising system, similar to that proposed by the American Hospital Association.

For the layman, there is valuable information in the book, especially concerning communication and transportation systems, emergency care and quality control, which is unavailable elsewhere in one source and summarized so briefly. A little learning is, however, a dangerous thing. On the whole, the book is more valuable to the professional for Rutstein does present one approach to all components of a total plan, rather than to the layman unless this is supplemented by alternative perspectives and rationales.

ANTHONY KOVNER
University of Pennsylvania
Philadelphia

CARL DEAN SNYDER. *White-Collar Workers and the UAW*. Pp. ix, 197. Chicago: University of Illinois Press, 1973. $7.95.

Professor Snyder addresses himself to an important problem: the effectiveness of industrial unionism in organizing white-collar workers. Industrial unionism is used in the double sense of being both industrial or factory and of being inclusive. He deals with the problem mainly through an examination of the United Automobile Workers' experience. Snyder writes as a friend of the UAW.

Industrial unionism in Snyder's view has the capability to organize white-collar workers but it is a capability which had not been adequately realized. The reasons are located in imperfections in union methods and resources and in management counterstrategy. Although Professor Snyder cites many detailed union deficiencies for the something-less than optimum union performance, these deficiencies come down to a failure to recognize the white-collar worker's special characteristics which differentiate him from the blue-collar worker.

Industrial unionism for white-collar workers is, in Snyder's view, more socially desirable than is craft unionism. He recommends measures by which the UAW can strengthen its white-collar organizational performance, largely, if I interpret it correctly, by playing down an "obsession with security" and a manualist image that comes on too strongly.

The work can be reviewed on two levels: journalistic—I do not use the term pejoratively—and analytical. Snyder gets a good grade for the first and only a marginal pass at best for the second.

The record of UAW experience in organizing white-collar workers is useful and interesting. I had not seen anything comparable before. Snyder attaches importance to the UAW's willingness "to trade the Union's white-collar organizing future for 'here and now' bargaining gains for blue-collar members" by agreeing with Ford in 1942 not to organize white-collar workers. Snyder's own experience as an auto worker and union activist stand him in good stead in capturing the union ambience which is a very special one in the UAW.

The author's problem with analysis is that he asserts without offering proofs. He alludes to his interviewing materials as the basis for his judgments but we do not get any sense of the data which he relies on. "The white-collar value system" figures importantly in the work but beyond assertion we get no proof of its importance; indeed, some writers, notably George Bain, have discounted its validity. Generalizations about the uniqueness of the white-collar workers and recommendations for improvement of the UAW organizing performance are either vague or are offered with little or no support. Examples: "In view of the difference in white-collar psychology, it is important to emphasize intelligent argument as contrasted with emotion in organizing campaigns." "The single most effective bar to white-collar organization is management's policy of granting tandem benefits." "The establishment of completely new organizations for white-collar workers would be highly wasteful of social resources in the existing industrial union structure."

Most of Snyder's materials stop at the mid-1960s, missing the upsurge of white-collar unionism in the public sector. There are differences between white and blue collar, but how can one explain the eruption of militant teacher unionism in terms of Snyder's polite model of white-collar unionism?

JACK BARBASH
Department of Economics
University of Wisconsin
Madison

J. G. ZIELINSKI. *Poland: Economic Reforms in East European Industry.* Pp. viii, 333. New York: Oxford University Press, 1973. $21.00.

IANCU SPIGLER. *Rumania: Economic Reforms in East European Industry.* Pp. v, 176. New York: Oxford University Press, 1973. $12.50.

These books are part of a series of monographs on economic reforms in East European industry, written under the auspices of the Institute of Soviet and East European Studies of the University of Glasgow under the general editorship of Professors Alec Nove and Janusz G. Zielinksi. Much has been written in the West on these reforms which began almost twenty years ago in some East European countries, yet no systematic study of their evolution along a *uniform detailed outline* encompassing all the countries of the area, has thus far been undertaken.

Zielinski's study of Poland, which opens the series, presents a remarkable picture of the complex interplay between reform *proposals* and *attempts* at actual change of the Polish "economic mechanism" from 1956 to the present.

Having worked for many years at the Central School for Planning and Statistics in Warsaw, Zielinski brings to this study an intimate knowledge of the system and its rationale of the executants and their patterns of behavior, and of the pressures and constraints under which each and all operate. He deepens our understanding of topics covered for instance in the valuable work of George R. Feiwel, *Industrialization and Planning Under Polish Socialism* (Vol. I, II, Praeger Publishers, 1971), while breaking new ground on such topics as planners' preferences and plan construction, information generation and processing and incentive structures.

From the middle of the 1950s, disappointing results with respect to efficiency, growth, technological progress and standard of living prompted the need for reform. Finally under open revolutionary pressures from large strata of the population, and amidst heated discussions among policymakers, planners and economists, the directors of the system started to tinker with the mechanism of management and planning. They tried to change, improve and revise the managers' "success indicators," managerial bonuses and incentives, investment allocation, the financial system of the enterprises and industrial associations, the interconnections between enterprises and these associations, and the methods of plan implementation. Actually, as Zielinski points out, the "turnover" of reforms was unbelievably high: some reforms were applied in rapid succession and discarded as soon as they were found wanting; other reforms, already enacted into law, were never implemented as attention shifted in other directions. Through it all, the directors of the system never gave up their basic conception of the economy as a single-level servo-mechanism with a unique *center of command* formulating the goals and overseeing their implementation, and with all other components (industrial associations, enterprises and their personnel) viewed as *simple executants*.

After nearly twenty years of experimentation the Polish reform appears as a patent failure. The planners' *control* over the employment level, the volume of the wage fund, real wages, and inventories remains as ineffective as ever. Results with respect to efficiency, growth, technological change, standard of living—as documented by Zielinski with official statistics—continue to be disappointing (pp. 300–302). As Zielinski points out, the directors of the system have pursued *simultaneously* conflicting and elusive targets: maintenance of central injunctions while relying on "economic instruments" (faulty and distorted ones on top of it); preservation of the traditional administrative structure while attempting to change managerial behavioral patterns (conditioned by this very structure); continuous manipulation of short-term managerial decisions while attempting to extend the enterprise's investment horizon; and others.

Zielinski illuminates and clarifies a wide variety of problems. He throws new light on: the ways of evaluating planners' preferences (p. 35 ff); the reasons for "tautness" of the plans and of the overstraining of the economy's resources (p. 43 ff); the causes and extent of information distortion (p. 52 ff and 106 ff); the failure of using mathematical planning (p. 79 ff); and on the role of the traditional system in the *first stage* of industrialization (p. 23 ff).

Spigler has a rather thankless task: he has to deal with a far less inspiring subject than that of Zielinski. Indeed, in contrast to the situations prevailing in the 1950s and 1960s in Poland, Hungary and Czechoslovakia, the Rumanian "economic reform" emerged in a period of apparently "normal" economic development. There were no overt economic difficulties, no social unrest, no sophisticated and heated debates about the direction of change. In 1967, the Party ushered in an *administrative-economic* reform, which in fact aimed primarily at further enhancing its controls as such and those of its officials, at all levels.

Rumania, one of the least developed countries of Eastern Europe, has thus far succeeded in maintaining a *high rate of growth in industry*—the touchstone of Communist success in management and planning. The consumer has had to bear the heavy cost of this sustained growth, which has tended to overshadow the familiar problems of all centrally administered socialist economies, namely slow technological change, dispersion of investment over a large number of unfinished projects, under-capacity utilization, low productivity, persistent shortages, output of poor-quality, and of non-marketable goods, disfunctional incentives, and so on. Spigler attributes the continuance of growth to the fact that the country's path of development "is still a predominantly extensive one" (p. 9): in other words, the directors of the system are not yet faced there with an overwhelmingly complex economy, with multiplication of conflicting priorities and with labor shortages. This does not mean that the system effectively implemented the policymakers' own preferences, that the methods used were the best suited for the development of an industrial-agrarian country such as Rumania, or that *higher* rates or growth could not have been achieved with a different system.

As of now, "efficiency, if it contradicts increasing physical production, may be sacrificed, as may be costs, losses, productivity considerations, or sales, though the trend is to regard efficiency as the main criterion which will come before all other considerations" (p. 90). Enterprises, industrial associations, ministries, and the government all continue to strive for output maximization. The reforms have boiled down to the introduction and use of various faulty economic instruments, not as alternatives to, but as props for the traditional injunctions from the center; some devolution to the industrial associations of certain operational decisions with respect to plan *implementation;* a slight opening for supervised contacts between producers and foreign buyers and sellers; and the introduction of secondary changes in the system of bonuses, premia and associated rewards and penalties. Most prices will continue to be administered from the center, but will be reviewed more often than in the past.

In short, the Rumanian economic reform "reflects a desire to avoid risky experimentation and to minimize its scope. The fact that the reform is not called a reform but is called 'improving' the system speaks for itself" (p. 166). Judging from the Polish experience, one may safely bet that this rather nonchalant way of sweeping critical and chronic problems under the rug will eventually call forth a day of reckoning.

NICOLAS SPULBER
Indiana University
Bloomington

OTHER BOOKS

ADAMS, ROBERT M. *The Roman Stamp: Frame and Façade in Some Forms of Neo-Classicism*. Pp. 266. Berkeley, Calif.: University of California, 1974. $12.50.

ALFONSO, OSCAR M. *Theodore Roosevelt and the Philippines, 1897–1909*. Pp. vii, 227. New York: Oriole, 1974. $10.00.

ANAND, RAM PRAKASH. *International Courts and Contemporary Conflicts*. Pp. vii, 479. New York: Asia, 1974. $17.50.

BARBER, JAMES DAVID, ed. *Choosing the President*. Pp. v, 208. Englewood Cliffs, N.J.: Prentice-Hall, 1974. $7.95. Paperbound, $2.95.

BEE, ROBERT L. *Patterns and Processes: An Introduction to Anthropological Strategies for the Study of Sociocultural Change*. Pp. v, 260. New York: The Free Press, 1974. $3.95. Paperbound.

BENDIX, REINHARD et al., eds. *State and Society: A Reader in Comparative Sociology*. Pp. v, 648. Berkeley, Calif.: University of California, 1973. $5.95. Paperbound.

BEREND, IVAN I. and GYORGY RANKI. *Economic Development in East-Central Europe in the 19th and 20th Centuries*. Pp. v, 402. New York: Columbia University Press, 1974. $18.00.

BILLIKOPF, DAVID MARSHALL. *The Exercise of Judicial Power: 1789–1864*. Pp. vii, 438. New York: Vantage Press, 1973. $11.00.

BILLINGTON, RAY ALLEN. *Westward Expansion: A History of the American Frontier*. 4th ed. Pp. vii, 840. New York: Macmillan, 1974. $12.95.

BLACKWELL, WILLIAM L., ed. *Russian Economic Development from Peter the Great to Stalin*. Pp. xiii, 459. New York: New Viewpoints, 1974. $12.50. Paperbound, $5.95.

BLANCK, GERTRUDE and RUBIN BLANCK. *Ego Psychology: Theory and Practice*. Pp. vii, 394. New York: Columbia University, 1974. $17.50.

BLUMBERG, PAUL. *Industrial Democracy: The Sociology of Participation*. Pp. 288. New York: Schocken, 1974. $3.95. Paperbound.

BUEL, RICHARD, JR. *Securing the Revolution: Ideology in American Politics, 1789–1815*. Pp. ix, 391. Ithaca, N.Y.: Cornell University, 1974. $4.95. Paperbound.

BURNS, EDWARD MCNALL and PHILIP LEE RALPH. *World Civilizations*. 5th ed. Vol. I. Pp. v, 615, New York: W. W. Norton, 1974. $10.95. Paperbound, $6.50.

BURNS, EDWARD MCNALL and PHILIP LEE RALPH. *World Civilizations*. 5th ed. Vol. II. Pp. 1319. New York: W. W. Norton, 1974. $10.95. Paperbound, $6.50.

CHANDLER, JOAN M. *America Since Independence*. Pp. 96. New York: Oxford University, 1974. $2.00. Paperbound.

CHAUDHRI, MOHAMMED AHSEN. *United Nations Peace Mechanisms and Rules*. Council for Pakistan Studies. Pp. 93. Karachi, Pakistan: Karachi University, 1973. $3.00.

CHEN, THEODORE HSI-EN. *The Maoist Educational Revolution*. Pp. v, 295. New York: Praeger, 1974. $20.00.

CIVIKLY, JEAN M., ed. *Messages: A Reader in Human Communication*. Pp. v, 393. New York: Random House, 1974. No price.

COCHRANE, JAMES L., SAMUEL GUBINS, and B. F. KIKER. *Macroeconomics: Analysis and Policy*. Pp. 390. Glenview, Ill.: Scott, Foresman, 1974. $11.50.

COMER, JAMES P. *Beyond Black and White*. Pp. v, 272. New York: Quadrangle, 1974. $2.95. Paperbound.

CONNERY, ROBERT H. and ROBERT S. GILMOUR, eds. *The National Energy Problem*. Pp. xii, 194. New York: Academy of Political Science, 1973. No price.

CROMWELL, RICHARD S. *David Friedrich Strauss and His Place in Modern Thought*. Pp. 232. Fair Lawn, N.J.: R. E. Burdick, 1974. $12.50.

DAHL, ROBERT A., ed. *Regimes and Oppositions*. Pp. 411. New Haven, Conn.: Yale University, 1974. $15.00. Paperbound, $3.95.

DALTON, GEORGE. *Economic Systems & Society: Capitalism, Communism and the Third World*. Pp. 250. Baltimore, Md.: Penguin, 1974. $3.95. Paperbound.

DAVIS, HAROLD EUGENE. *Latin American Thought: A Historical Introduction*. Pp. v, 269. New York: Free Press, 1974. $3.95. Paperbound.

DEMAUSE, LLOYD, ed. *The History of Child-*

hood. Pp. 450. New York: Psychohistory Press, 1974. $12.50.

DES FORGES, ROGER V. *Hsi-Liang and the Chinese National Revolution.* Pp. vii, 274. New Haven, Conn.: Yale University, 1973. $12.50.

DEUTSCH, KARL W. *Politics and Government: How People Decide Their Fate.* 2nd ed. Pp. vii, 606. Boston Mass.: Houghton Mifflin, 1974. $9.95.

DOUGLAS, ENSEN X. *A New Deal for Blacks.* Pp. 99. Jericho, N.Y.: Exposition Press, 1974. $4.50.

DOUGLAS, JACK D. *Defining America's Social Problems.* Pp. v, 265. Englewood Cliffs, N.J.: Prentice-Hall, 1974. $6.50. Paperbound.

DRAGNICH, ALEX N. and JORGEN RASMUSSEN. *Major European Governments.* Dorsey Series in Political Science. Pp. vii, 524. Honewood, Ill.: Dorsey Press, 1974. $12.50.

EBBIN, STEVEN and RAPHAEL KASPER. *Citizen Groups and the Nuclear Power Controversy.* Pp. 307. Cambridge, Mass.: MIT, 1974. $6.95. Paperbound.

EFFRAT, MARCIA PELLY, ed. *The Community: Approaches and Applications.* Pp. 323. New York: Free Press, 1974. $4.95. Paperbound.

EIDELBERG, PHILIP GABRIEL. *The Great Rumanian Peasant Revolt of 1907: Origins of a Modern Jacquerie.* Pp. viii, 259. Leiden, The Netherlands: E. J. Brill, 1974. No price.

ELAZAR, DANIEL J., ed. *Publius: The Journal of Federalism.* Vol. 3. The Federal Polity, no. 2. Pp. ii, 299. Philadelphia, Pa.: Temple University, 1974. No price.

EMMERSON, JOHN K. and LEONARD A. HUMPHREYS. *Will Japan Rearm?* Pp. 165. Stanford, Calif.: Stanford University, 1973. $3.00. Paperbound.

ENZENSBERGER, HANS MAGNUS. *The Consciousness Industry: On Literature, Politics and the Media.* Pp. 184. New York: Seabury Press, 1974. $6.95.

FELDSTEIN, STANLEY and LAWRENCE COSTELLO, eds. *The Ordeal of Assimilation: A Documentary History of the White Working Class.* Pp. xii, 500. Garden City, N.Y.: Doubleday, 1974. $4.95. Paperbound.

FITZGIBBON, C. and G. MORRISON. *The Life and Times of Eamon De Valera.* Pp. 150. New York: Macmillan, 1974. $8.95.

FLOUD, RODERICK, ed. *Essays in Quantitative Economic History.* Pp. 250. New York: Oxford University, 1974. $17.75.

FONER, JACK. *Blacks and the Military in American History.* Pp. vii, 278. New York: Praeger, 1974. $10.00. Paperbound, $3.95.

FOOTMAN, DAVID. *The Alexander Conspir-*

acy: A Life of A. I. Zhelyabov. Pp. vi, 354. La Salle, Ill.: Library Press, 1974. $8.95.

FORD, ARTHUR. *Political Economics of Rural Poverty in the South.* Pp. ix, 101. Cambridge, Mass.: Ballinger, 1973. $10.00.

Foreign Relations of the United States, 1948: Eastern Europe and the Soviet Union. Vol. IV. Pp. iii, 1161. Washington, D.C.: U.S. Government Printing Office, 1974. $10.80.

FRANCK, THOMAS M. and EDWARD WEISBAND, eds. *Secrecy and Foreign Policy.* Pp. viii, 453. New York: Oxford University Press, 1974. $15.00.

FRIEDMAN, ISAIAH. *The Question of Palestine, 1914–1918: British-Jewish-Arab Relations.* Pp. 450. New York: Schocken Books, 1973. $12.00.

GEERTZ, CLIFFORD. *The Interpretation of Cultures.* Pp. 480. New York: Basic Books, 1973. $15.00.

GELLNER, ERNEST, ed. *Contemporary Thought and Politics.* Pp. viii, 207. Boston, Mass.: Routledge & Kegan Paul, 1974. $13.25.

GINGER, ANN FAGAN. *The Law, the Supreme Court and the People's Rights.* Pp. vi, 697. Woodbury, N.Y.: Barron's Educational Series, 1974. $10.95. Paperbound, $3.95.

GLASSER, PAUL, ROSEMARY SARRI, and ROBERT VINTER. *Individual Change Through Small Groups.* Pp. vii, 515. New York: Free Press, 1974. $12.95. Paperbound, $7.95.

GLOB, P.V. *The Mound People: Danish Bronze-Age Man Preserved.* Pp. 184. New York: Cornell University, 1974. $12.50.

GOETHEM, LARRY VAN. *The Fifth Horseman is Riding.* Pp. 150. New York: Macmillan, 1974. $4.95.

GOODING, JUDSON. *The Job Revolution.* Pp. v, 212. New York: Collier, 1974. $1.95. Paperbound.

GOODRUM, CHARLES A. *The Library of Congress.* Pp. 288. New York: Praeger, 1974. $10.00.

GORDON, C. WAYNE, ed. *Uses of the Sociology of Education.* Pp. ix, 518. Chicago, Ill.: University of Chicago, 1974. $10.00.

GRATCH, ALAN S. and VIRGINIA H. UBIK. *Ballots for Change: New Suffrage and Amending Articles for Illinois.* Illinois Constitution Making Series. Pp. vii, 117. Urbana, Ill.: University of Illinois, 1974. $3.45. Paperbound.

GREENWAY, JOHN. *Down Among the Wild Men: The Narrative Journal of Fifteen Years Pursuing the Old Stone Age Aborigines of Australia's Western Desert.* Pp. 361. Boston, Mass.: Little, Brown, 1972. $12.50.

GREER, COLIN, ed. *The Divided Society: The*

Ethnic Experience in America. Pp. 416. New York: Basic Books, 1974. $12.50.

GRIFFITH, ERNEST S. *A History of American City Government: The Conspicuous Failure, 1870–1900.* Pp. vii, 308. New York: Praeger, 1974. $10.00.

GRIFFITH, ERNEST S. *A History of American City Government: 1900–1920.* Pp. vii, 352. New York: Praeger, 1974. $10.00.

GROSS, BABETTE. *Willi Münzenberg: A Political Biography.* Pp. 237. East Lansing, Mich.: Michigan State University, 1974. $12.50.

GRUEN, ERICH S. *The Last Generation of the Roman Republic.* Pp. 610. Berkeley, Calif.: University of California, 1974. $18.50.

GUREWITSCH, A. DAVID. *Eleanor Roosevelt: Her Day.* Pp. 160. New York: Quadrangle, 1974. $7.95. Paperbound, $3.95.

HARARI, EHUD. *The Politics of Labor Legislation in Japan: National-International Interaction.* Pp. 233. Berkeley, Calif.: University of California, 1973. $10.00.

HARRIS, JOSE. *Unemployment and Politics: A Study in English Social Policy, 1886–1914.* Pp. x, 411. New York: Oxford University, 1972. $24.00.

HARRIS, MARVIN. *Patterns of Race in the Americas.* Pp. 134. New York: W. W. Norton, 1974. $1.95. Paperbound.

HAVLICK, SPENSER W. *The Urban Organism.* Pp. v, 515. New York: Macmillan, 1974. $12.95.

HAWLEY, WILLIS D. and FREDERICK M. WIRT, eds. *The Search for Community Power.* 2nd ed. Pp. vii, 390. Englewood Cliffs, N.J.: Prentice-Hall, 1974. Paperbound, $6.95.

HAYES, PAUL. *Fascism.* Pp. 260. New York: Free Press, 1973. $7.95.

HAYWARD, JACK. *The One and Indivisible French Republic.* Pp. 306. New York: W. W. Norton, 1974. $10.95. Paperbound, $3.95.

HECKSCHER, AUGUST. *Alive in the City: Memoir of an Ex-Commissioner.* Pp. vii, 294. New York: Charles Scribner's Sons, 1974. $8.95.

HENDEL, SAMUEL, ed. *Bishop and Hendel's Basic Issue of American Democracy.* 7th ed. Pp. v, 658. Englewood Cliffs, N.J.: Prentice-Hall, 1973. $5.95. Paperbound.

HODGES, HAROLD M., JR. *Conflict and Consensus: An Introduction to Sociology.* 2nd ed. Pp. viii, 558. New York: Harper & Row, 1974. $10.95.

HSIAO, GENE T., ed. *Sino-American Detente and Its Policy Implications.* Pp. v, 319. New York: Praeger, 1974. $17.50.

ICHIOKA, YUJI et al. *A Buried Past: An Annotated Bibiliography of the Japanese American Research Project Collection.* Pp.

240. Berkeley, Calif.: University of California, 1974. $10.00.

JABBER, FUAD. *Israel and Nuclear Weapons: Present Option and Future Strategies.* Pp. 163. London: Chatto and Windus, 1971. No price.

JOHNSON, DONALD and JEAN JOHNSON, eds. *Through Indian Eyes.* Pp. 136. New York: Praeger, 1974. $7.50. Paperbound, $2.75.

JOHNSON, DONALD BRUCE and KIRK H. PORTER, eds. *National Party Platforms.* 5th ed. Pp. vi, 889. Urbana, Ill.: University of Illinois, 1974. $20.00.

JOHNSON, NEVIL. *Government in the Federal Republic of Germany: The Executive at Work.* Pp. vii, 218. Elmsford, N.Y.: Pergamon, 1974. $10.50.

JONES, GWYN. *Rural Life: The Social Structure of Modern Britain.* Pp. vii, 129. New York: Longman, 1974. $4.50. Paperbound, $3.00.

JOURARD, SIDNEY M. *Healthy Personality: An Approach from the Viewpoint of Humanistic Psychology.* Pp. v, 370. New York: Macmillan, 1974. $8.95.

KAPLAN, MORTON A., ed. *Great Issues of International Politics.* 2nd. ed. Pp. v, 598. Chicago, Ill.: Aldine, 1974. $17.50. Paperbound, $5.95.

KARTODIRDJO, SARTONO. *Protest Movements in Rural Java: A Study of Agrarian Unrest in the Nineteenth and Early Twentieth Centuries.* Pp. 229. New York: Oxford University, 1973. No price.

KERMAN, CYNTHIA EARL. *Creative Tension: The Life and Thought of Kenneth Boulding.* Pp. v, 380. Ann Arbor, Mich.: University of Michigan, 1974. $12.50.

KIMBALL, SOLON I. *Culture and the Educative Process: An Anthropological Perspective.* Pp. v, 285. New York: Teachers College, 1974. $10.00.

KURLAND, PHILIP B., ed. *The Supreme Court Review, 1973.* Pp. 252. Chicago, Ill.: University of Chicago, 1974. $15.00.

KURTZ, DONALD V. *The Politics of a Poverty Habitat.* Pp. ix, 243. Cambridge, Mass.: Ballinger, 1973. $12.50.

KYTLE, RAY. *Concepts in Context: Aspects of the Writer's Craft.* Pp. 194. New York: John Wiley and Sons, 1974. No price.

LANGDON, F.C. *Japan's Foreign Policy.* Pp. vii, 231. Vancouver, Ca.: University of British Columbia, 1973. $9.00.

LARKIN, JAMES F. and PAUL L. HUGHES, eds. *Stuart Royal Proclamations: Royal Proclamations of King James I, 1603–1625.* Vol. 1. Pp. v, 679. New York: Oxford University Press, 1974. $58.00.

LAW, SYLVIA A. *Blue Cross: What Went*

Wrong? Pp. ix, 246. New Haven, Conn.: Yale University, 1974. $8.95.

LEE, DEY HONG, ed. *Indonesia After the 1971 Elections.* Hull Monographs on South-East Asia, no. 5. New York: Oxford University, 1974. $6.50. Paperbound.

LENSEN, GEORGE ALEXANDER. *The Damned Inheritance: The Soviet Union and the Manchurian Crises, 1924–1935.* Pp. vii, 533. Tallahassee, Fla.: Diplomatic, 1974. $19.80.

LERNER, RALPH. *Averroes on Plato's "Republic."* Pp. v, 175. New York: Cornell University, 1974. $15.00. Paperbound, $2.95.

LEVY, LEONARD W. *Jefferson and Civil Liberties: The Darker Side.* Pp. v, 225. New York: Quadrangle, 1973. $2.95. Paperbound.

LEWIS, RUSSELL. *The New Service Society.* Pp. 179. New York: Longman, 1973. $10.00

LOPREATO, JOSEPH and LIONEL S. LEWIS. *Social Stratification: A Reader.* Pp. viii, 576. New York: Harper & Row, 1974. No price.

LOVELL, JOHN P. and PHILIP S. KRONENBERG. *New Civil-Military Relations: The Agonies of Adjustment to Post-Vietnam Realities.* Pp. vi, 352. New York: E. P. Dutton, 1974. $3.95. Paperbound.

LUBELL, SAMUEL. *The Future while it Happened.* Pp. 162. New York: W. W. Norton, 1973. $5.95. Paperbound, $1.95.

LUGO, JAMES O. and GERALD L. HERSHEY. *Human Development: A Multidisciplinary Approach to the Psychology of Individual Growth.* Pp. 581. New York: Macmillan, 1974. $9.95.

LUKACS, GEORG. *Tactics and Ethics: Political Essays, 1919–1929.* Pp. viii, 257. New York: Harper & Row, 1972. $10.00.

LUTTBEG, NORMAN R., ed. *Public Opinion & Public Policy.* Pp. 477. Homewood, Ill.: Dorsey Press, 1974. $7.50. Paperbound.

MABBUTT, FRED R. and GERALD J. GHELFI. *The Troubled Republic: American Government, Its Principles and Problems.* Pp. vii, 360. New York: John Wiley & Sons, 1974. $10.95.

MACHAN, TIBOR R., ed. *The Libertarian Alternative: Essays in Social and Political Philosophy.* Pp. vii, 553. Chicago, Ill.: Nelson-Hall, 1974. $12.50.

MAJUL, CESAR ADIB. *The Political and Constitutional Ideas of the Philippine Revolution.* Revised edition. Pp. viii, 215. New York: Oriole, 1974. $10.00.

Management Accounting for Multinational Corporations. Vol. I. Pp. iii, 383. New York: National Association of Accountants, 1974. No price.

MCCARTHY, MARY. *The Seventeenth Degree—How it Went: Vietnam, Hanoi, Medina, Sons of the Morning.* Pp. 451. New York: Harcourt Brace Jovanovich, 1974. $7.95.

MCCOY, F. N. *Researching and Writing in History: A Practical Handbook for Students.* Pp. 109. Berkeley, Calif.: University of California, 1974. $7.50. Paperbound, $1.75.

MEIER, GERALD M. *Problems of a World of Monetary Order.* Pp. viii, 305. New York: Oxford University, 1974. $4.95. Paperbound.

MEIER, MATT S. and FELICIANO RIVERA, eds. *Readings on La Raza: The Twentieth Century.* Pp. viii, 277. New York: Hill and Wang, 1974. $8.95.

MEYER, GERALD. *The Memphis Murders.* Pp. 248. New York: Seabury, 1974. $7.95.

MILES, RUFUS E., JR. *The Department of Health, Education, and Welfare.* Pp. v, 326. New York: Praeger, 1974. $10.00.

MILLER, LYNN H. and RONALD W. PRUESSEN, eds. *Reflections on the Cold War: A Quarter Century of American Foreign Policy.* Pp. vii, 206. Philadelphia, Pa.: Temple University, 1974. $10.00.

MILLER, STUART CREIGHTON. *The Unwelcome Immigrant: The American Image of the Chinese, 1785–1882.* Pp. 270. Berkeley, Calif.: University of California, 1974. $3.25. Paperbound.

MILNE, R. S. and K. J. RATNAM. *Malaysian New States in a New Nation: Political Development of Sarawak and Sabah in Malaysia.* Pp. vi, 501. Portland, Ore.: International Scholarly Book Services, 1974. $27.50.

MILTON, DAVID, NANCY MILTON, and FRANZ SCHURMANN. *People's China.* Pp. ix, 673. New York: Random House, 1974. $15.00. Paperbound, $3.95.

MORLEY, JAMES WILLIAM, ed. *Japan's Foreign Policy, 1868–1941: A Research Guide.* Pp. viii, 618. New York: Columbia University, 1974. $25.00.

NAGEL, STUART S., ed. *Law and Social Change.* Sage Contemporary Social Science Issues, no. 3. Pp. 120. Beverly Hills, Calif.: Sage, 1970. $3.95. Paperbound.

NASH, GARY B. *Red, White, and Black: The Peoples of Early America.* Pp. ix, 350. Englewood Cliffs, N.J.: Prentice-Hall, 1974. $9.95. Paperbound, $5.95.

NEUENSCHWANDER, JOHN A. *The Middle Colonies and the Coming of the American Revolution.* Pp. 273. Port Washington, N.Y.: Kennikat Press, 1974. $12.50.

O'CONNELL, MAURICE R., ed. *The Correspondence of Daniel O'Connell, 1792–*

1814. Vol. 1. Pp. vii, 396. New York: Barnes & Noble, 1974. $22.50.

O'CONNELL, MAURICE R., ed. *The Correspondence of Daniel O'Connell, 1815–1823.* Vol. II. Pp. ix, 543. New York: Barnes & Noble, 1974. $23.50.

O'NEILL, JOHN, ed. *Modes of Individualism and Collectivism.* Pp. 358. New York: St. Martin's Press, 1974. $16.95.

OSEN, LYNN M. *Women in Mathematics.* Pp. x, 185. Cambridge, Mass.: MIT Press, 1974. $5.95.

PARENTI, MICHAEL. *Democracy for the Few.* Pp. 307. New York: St. Martin's Press, 1974. $10.95. Paperbound, $3.95.

PAXMAN, JOHN M. and GEORGE T. BOGGS, eds. *The United Nations: A Reassessment—Sanctions, Peacekeeping, and Humanitarian Assistance.* Pp. viii, 153. Charlottesville, Va.: University Press of Virginia, 1973. $10.00.

PHILLIPS, G. A. and R. I. MADDOCK. *The Growth of the British Economy, 1918–1968.* Pp. 188. New York: Barnes & Noble, 1974. $10.50.

PRITCHARD, E. E. EVANS, ed. *Man and Woman Among the Azande.* Pp. 197. New York: The Free Press, 1974. $9.95.

RABINOVITZ, FRANCINE F. and FELICITY M. TRUEBLOOD, eds. *Latin American Urban Research.* Vol. III. Pp. 311. Beverly Hills, Calif.: Sage, 1974. $15.00.

RAINES, JOHN C., ed. *Conspiracy.* Pp. 179. New York: Harper & Row, 1974. $6.95.

RAPOPORT, ANATOL. *Conflict in Man-Made Environment.* Pp. 272. Baltimore, Md.: Penguin, 1974. $2.75. Paperbound.

RENSHON, STANLEY ALLEN. *Psychological Needs and Political Behavior: A Theory of Personality and Political Efficacy.* Pp. ix, 300. New York: Free Press, 1974. $10.95.

RICE, EDWARD. *John Frum He Come: A Polemical Work about a Black Tragedy.* Pp. ix, 262. New York: Doubleday, 1974. $7.95.

RIPLEY, RANDALL B. *American National Government and Public Policy.* Pp. vii, 246. New York: The Free Press, 1974. $4.95. Paperbound.

ROBSON, WILLIAM, ed. *Man and the Social Sciences.* Pp. 284. Beverly Hills, Calif.: Sage, 1974. $12.50. Paperbound, $4.95.

ROCHE, JOHN P. *Sentenced to Life: Reflections on Politics, Education, and Law.* Pp. 359. New York: Macmillan, 1974. $12.95.

ROKKAN, STEIN. *Scandinavian Political Studies.* Vol. 8. Pp. 286. Beverly Hills, Calif.: Sage, 1973. $15.00.

ROSENBERG, PHILIP. *The Seventh Hero: Thomas Carlyle and the Theory of Radical Activism.* Pp. vii, 235. Cambridge, Mass.: Harvard University, 1974. $10.00.

ROSS, A. CLUNIES and J. LANGMORE, eds. *Alternative Strategies for Papua, New Guinea.* Pp. vii, 263. New York: Oxford University, 1974. $14.00.

RUBIN, LESLIE and BRIAN WEINSTEIN. *Introduction to African Politics: A Continental Approach.* Pp. vii, 326. New York: Praeger, 1974. $12.00. Paperbound, $4.95.

SELPEN, MARK, ed. *Remaking Asia: Essays on the American Uses of Power.* Pp. vii, 381. New York: Pantheon, 1973. $12.95. Paperbound, $3.45.

SHEETS, HAL and ROGER MORRIS. *Disaster in the Desert: Failures of International Relief in the West African Drought.* Humanitarian Policy Studies. Pp. i, 167. Washington, D.C.: Carnegie Endowment For International Peace, 1974. No price.

SHILS, EDWARD, ed. *Max Weber on Universities.* Pp. 62. Chicago, Ill.: University of Chicago, 1974. $2.95. Paperbound.

SHIPMAN, M. D. *Social Research: The Limitations of Social Research.* Pp. v, 195. New York: Longman, 1972. $6.50. Paperbound, $3.50.

SHIVELY, W. PHILLIPS. *The Craft of Political Research: A Primer.* Pp. xi, 174. Englewood Cliffs, N.J.: 1974. $7.95. Paperbound, $3.95.

SHORTER, EDWARD, ed. *Work and Community in the West.* Pp. 150. New York: Harper & Row, 1974. $9.00.

SHWADRAN, BENJAMIN. *The Middle East, Oil and the Great Powers.* 3rd ed. Pp. vii, 630. New York: Halsted Press, 1974. $20.00.

SICKELS, ROBERT J. *Presidential Transactions.* Pp. vii, 184. Englewood Cliffs, N.J.: Prentice-Hall, 1974. $6.95. Paperbound, $3.95.

SIEVERS, HARRY J., ed. *Six Presidents from the Empire State.* Pp. vii, 208. Tarrytown, N.Y.: Sleepy Hollow Restorations, 1974. $8.95.

SIMMONS, LUIZ R. S. and MARTIN B. GOLD, eds. *Discrimination and the Addict.* Pp. 334. Beverly Hills, Calif.: Sage, 1974. $15.00.

SKOLNICK, ARLENE and JEROME H. SKOLNICK. *Intimacy, Family and Society.* Pp. v, 598. Boston, Mass.: Little, Brown, 1974. No price.

SLOCUM, WALTER L. *Occupational Careers: A Sociological Perspective.* 2nd ed. Pp. 349. Chicago, Ill.: Aldine, 1974. $12.50.

SMELSER, NEIL J., ed. *Karl Marx on Society and Social Change.* Pp. vii, 206. Chicago, Ill.: University of Chicago Press, 1974. $11.00.

SMITH, GRAHAME J. C., HENRY J. STECK, and GERALD SURETTE. *Our Ecological Crisis: Its Biological, Economic, & Politi-*

cal Dimensions. Pp. vii, 198. New York: Macmillan, 1974. $5.95. Paperbound, $2.95.

SOBEL, ROBERT. Machines and Morality: the 1850s. Pp. 332. New York: Thomas Y. Crowell, 1973. No price.

SPANIER, JOHN and ERIC M. USLANER. How American Foreign Policy is Made. Pp. 180. New York: Praeger, 1974. $8.50. Paperbound, $2.95.

STEINER, JÜRG. Amicable Agreement Versus Majority Rule. Pp. xiii, 312. Chapel Hill, N.C.: University of North Carolina, 1974. $12.95.

STEINER, STAN. The Islands: The Worlds of the Puerto Ricans. Pp. 535. New York: Harper & Row, 1974. $12.50.

STOGDILL, RALPH M. Handbook of Leadership: A Survey of Theory and Research. Pp. vii, 613. New York: The Free Press, 1974. $19.95.

SULZBERGER, C. L. The Coldest War: Russia's Game in China. Pp. 113. New York: Harcourt Brace Jovanovich, 1974. $5.95.

TURNER, FRANCIS J., ed. Social Work Treatment: Interlocking Theoretical Approaches. Pp. vii, 520. New York: Free Press, 1974. $13.95.

VALLIER, IVAN, ed. Comparative Methods in Sociology: Essays on Trends and Applications. Pp. 482. Berkeley, Calif.: University of California, 1974. $4.65. Paperbound.

VANSTONE, JAMES W. Athapaskan Adaptations: Hunters and Fishermen of the Subarctic Forests. Pp. vii, 145. New York: Aldine, 1974. $7.50. Paperbound, $2.95.

WAHLROOS, SVEN. Family Communication. Pp. viii, 319. New York: Macmillan, 1974. $8.95.

WARD, COLIN. Anarchy in Action. Pp. 160. New York: Harper & Row, 1974. $9.50. Paperbound, $3.25.

WATSON, PETER, ed. Psychology and Race. Pp. 491. Chicago, Ill.: Aldine, 1974. $12.50. Paperbound, $4.95.

WILLRICH, MASON and JOHN B. RHINELANDER, eds. SALT: The Moscow Agreements and Beyond. Pp. v, 361. New York: Free Press, 1974. $9.95.

WINTER, RALPH K., JR. Watergate and the Law. Domestic Affairs Studies. Pp. 85. Washington, D.C.: Press Release, 1974. $3.00. Paperbound.

WITTRAM, REINHARD. Russia and Europe. Pp. 180. Levittown, N.Y.: Transatlantic Arts, 1973. $8.75.

ZEA, LEOPOLDO, Positivism in Mexico. Pp. viii, 241. Austin, Tex.: University of Texas, 1974. $8.75.

ZWERLING, STEPHEN. Mass Transit and the Politics of Technology: A Study of Bart and the San Francisco Bay Area. Pp. vi, 159. New York: Praeger, 1974. $14.00.

INDEX

Origin and Purpose. The Academy was organized December 14, 1889, to promote the progress of political and social science, especially through publications and meetings. The Academy does not take sides in controverted questions, but seeks to gather and present reliable information to assist the public in forming an intelligent and accurate judgment.

Meetings. The Academy holds an annual meeting in the spring extending over two days.

Publications. THE ANNALS is the bimonthly publication of The Academy. Each issue contains articles on some prominent social or political problem, written at the invitation of the editors. Also, monographs are published from time to time, numbers of which are distributed to pertinent professional organizations. These volumes constitute important reference works on the topics with which they deal, and they are extensively cited by authorities throughout the United States and abroad. The papers presented at the meetings of The Academy are included in THE ANNALS.

Membership. Each member of The Academy receives THE ANNALS and may attend the meetings of The Academy. Annual dues for individuals are $15.00 (for clothbound copies $20.00 per year). A life membership is $500. All payments are to be made in United States dollars.

Libraries and other institutions may receive THE ANNALS paperbound at a cost of $15.00 per year, or clothbound at $20.00 per year. Add $1.00 to above rates for membership outside U.S.A.

Single copies of THE ANNALS may be obtained by nonmembers of The Academy for $3.00 ($4.00 clothbound) and by members for $2.50 ($3.50 clothbound). A discount of 5 percent is allowed on orders for 10 to 24 copies of any one issue, and of 10 percent on orders for 25 or more copies. These discounts apply only when orders are placed directly with The Academy and not through agencies. The price to all bookstores and to all dealers is $3.00 per copy less 20 percent, with no quantity discount. It is urged that payment be sent with each order. This will save the buyer the shipping charge and save The Academy the cost of carrying accounts and sending statements. Monographs may be purchased for $4.00, with proportionate discounts.

All correspondence concerning The Academy or THE ANNALS should be addressed to the Academy offices, 3937 Chestnut Street, Philadelphia, Pa. 19104.

Kindly mention THE ANNALS *when writing to advertisers*